Contesting Malayness

Malay Identity Across Boundaries

Contesting Malayness

Malay Identity Across Boundaries

Edited by

Timothy P. Barnard

NUS PRESS
SINGAPORE

© Timothy P. Barnard

Published by:
NUS Press
National University of Singapore
AS3-01-02, 3 Arts Link
Singapore 117569

Fax: (65) 6774-0652
E-mail: nusbooks@nus.edu.sg
Website: http://nuspress.nus.edu.sg

ISBN 978-9971-69-845-4 (Paper)

First Edition 2004
Reprint 2006
Reprint 2014
Reprint 2015
Reprint 2016
Reprint 2018
Reprint 2019

Typeset by: Scientifik Graphics (Singapore) Pte Ltd
Printed by: Markono Print Media Pte Ltd

Contents

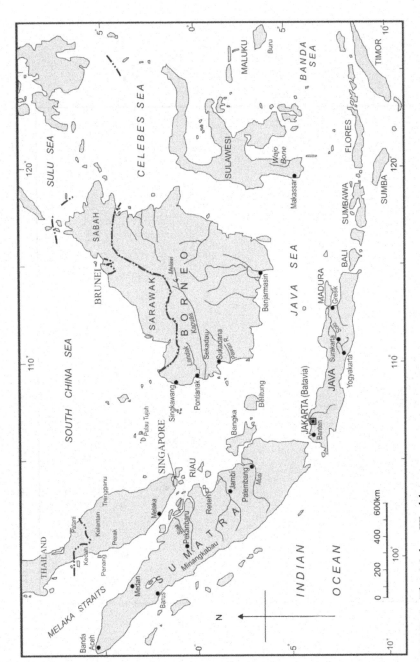

MAP 1: The Malay World.

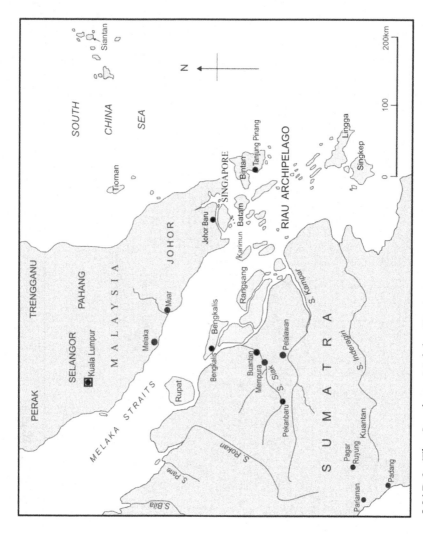

MAP 2: The Southern Melaka Straits.

Melayu, Malay, Maleis: Journeys through the Identity of a Collection

Timothy P. Barnard and Hendrik M. J. Maier*

What is the meaning of 'Malay'? The question seems strange and unnecessary. 'Malays' live in Malaysia, where they are the major population group. 'Malays' are found in Indonesia, in Sumatra and along the coast of Indonesian Borneo. At first glance, it all seems very straightforward, but for centuries definitions, boundaries and origins of this word in the world of Southeast Asia have proved elusive, and it seems unlikely that the word will acquire any greater precision in the future. This question lies at the core of the present collection, and while the reader will emerge knowing a great deal more about the term and the problems it generates, the authors are wise enough not to try to resolve the conundrum.

The word 'Melayu' appears in seventh-century Chinese sources with reference to Sumatra, and as it has been wandering around Southeast Asia ever since, carrying with it notions of a culture, a people and a location. The term may have first been used in Kalimantan, or possibly around the Melayu River on Sumatra. But then, origins are often vague in a world that is constantly undergoing transformation. The words 'Malay' and 'Maleis' begin to appear in British and Dutch writings in the seventeenth century, reflecting both local usage and tales by the Portuguese, Spanish and others who arrived earlier. These three words—Melayu, Malay, Maleis—have been used with reference to a confusing variety of configurations of human beings, locations, languages, customs, states, and objects between Patani and Timor, Manila and Banda Aceh, Makassar and Bangkok, Pagarruyung and Batavia, as well as along the Melaka Straits. Like true manifestations of the *dagang* (foreign, alien), the major figure in Malay tales, the Malays are always on the move and transforming themselves, often very elusively, and theirs is a contested and wandering identity.

In one way or another, 'Melayu', 'Malay' and 'Maleis' refer to a loosely configured world. Official discussions about the meaning of the word have led to definitions that are embedded in various forms of nationalism and regionalism, and have been elaborated into awkward and shaky constructions, throwing uneasy shadows and echoes over Southeast Asia, where 'Malay' can refer to a number of differing groups, ranging from speakers of Austronesian languages to small groups scattered over islands in and around the Melaka Straits.

Both 'Malay' and 'Maleis' are defective translations of 'Melayu'; the three words have a different reach and have been applied to different people, customs and rituals, and to conflicting discursive formations. Pointing in various directions at once, the often careless confusion of the three has led to even more misunderstandings and contests; showing if anything that translations and definitions will never be adequate or satisfactory. Or, that every naming is bound to create new instabilities and movements.

In so far as there are correspondences at all among those three words and the world they evoke, they are based on linguistic considerations: the words are usually connected with a certain language—but then, is everybody who is speaking Malay a 'Malay', a 'Maleier', an *orang Melayu*, and hence part of the 'Malay world', an enigmatic term that corresponds neither with the 'Maleise wereld' nor with 'alam Melayu'? And where is that language to be found but in the mind and the writings of linguists? What is really being discussed? Such questions will only elicit elusive answers. Be that as it may, the primacy of language has been the basis of further explorations into the boundaries of a Malay culture, a Malay nation, a Malay race, a Malay state, or a Malay identity, and each of those concepts has been given an historical depth of which the validity remains highly questionable. The precise meanings of 'Melayu', 'Malay', and 'Maleis', in short, have never been established, and never will be. That very fact makes thinking, writing, and talking about the Malay world a daring endeavour, and the results will continue to be contested.

* * *

With such questions and contradictions in mind, a group of scholars gathered at Leiden University in the Netherlands in April 1998 for a series of discussions. Most of the articles in this volume are elaborations on the papers that were presented. Essential in this endeavour was the exploration of the concept of 'Malay world' (*Alam Melayu*), which was the central term in a research project carried out between Leiden and Pekanbaru in the late 1990s that involved Dutch and Indonesian academics searching for the parameters of this elusive term. A goal of the conference was to better understand how a variety of scholars, across time and disciplines, viewed the Malay world, its boundaries, contradictions, origins and transformations.

The conference's participants were invited to make an effort to circumscribe that unruly configuration of a world—to talk across history and space—and they created unruly conversations. These contestations, however, led to stronger papers that often support and refute the arguments made by participants. As these papers were presented, later re-written, edited and even re-written again, they came to reflect the continuing nebulous character of the Malay world. Each pointed out a key issue in how Malay identity and the Malay world could be understood, whether it be linguistics, trade, colonialism, raiding, literature or the modern nation-state.

While the participants argued for the importance of their own contribution, whether it was Jim Collins and his linguistic research in Borneo or Shamsul A.B. and the role of colonial knowledge, there was a concern that the articles were focused on the trees rather than the forest surrounding them. When the papers were being re-written, the editor noticed that several contributions referred to a paper Anthony Reid had presented at a different conference in 1998 that provided an overview of how theories of the nation and differing understandings of Malayness have been interpreted in various nation-states in island Southeast Asia. Discovering that the piece had yet to be published, the editor contacted Professor Reid who was kind enough to join our disparate group and allow his piece to be the introductory salvo in our various contestations of Malayness. The papers presented at the conference then were gathered together and published as a 'Symposium on Malay Identity' in the October 2001 issue of the *Journal of Southeast Asian Studies*.

The 'Symposium on Malay Identity' also experienced several lucky convergences. One of these was the submission for publication in the journal of an article on Malay traders in the port of Makassar in the eighteenth century by Heather Sutherland. The piece appeared in the same issue as the 'Symposium', and Sutherland's work on trade in the VOC archives allows another dimension to be added to the debate, bringing in the Malay traders, *dagang*, who lived outside of the world that most of the participants in this volume had considered. Her piece has thus voyaged across the artificial divide in the original journal, where the piece was published as part of another symposium, on Makassar, to join our collection.

The publication of the special issue on Malay identity was quite a success. The issue quickly sold out, and the editor began to realise that the collection could be stronger with the addition of a few pieces that had been left out at that time. At the original conference in Leiden, Virginia Hooker had presented a paper on the influence of Islam in the development of Malay politics and understandings of Malay identity.

This paper was published in the *Review of Modern Indonesian and Malaysian Affairs* (*RIMA*) in 2000.[1] After contacting Professor Hooker and the editor of *RIMA*, the piece returns to be among the papers with which it originally was presented.

In another strange coincidence, Adrian Vickers, the editor of *RIMA*, was visiting Leiden at the time of the conference. Vickers had just published a paper entitled '"Malay Identity": Modernity, Invented Tradition, and Forms of Knowledge', and it became a major talking point for participants. While it was never part of the original conference, it influenced many of the contributions, and with the agreement of the author and of the journal, it too is being reprinted as part of the present collection.

Circling around many of the discussions in Leiden was the role of literature in creating and perpetuating understandings of Malay identity. In one of the papers included in this collection, Will Derks discusses how literature in the Malay world remains a living tradition, even though it often does not fulfil many of the criteria that are emphasised in the print-oriented literature of the West. While discussing the performance of traditional forms of Malay literature that have recently been written down, Derks mentions a performance he witnessed of an epic poem titled *Syair Nasib Melayu* (An Epic Poem of the Malay's Fate). The composer of this *syair*, a long chain of quatrains with a rhymed pattern of words and phrases, is Tenas Effendy, a well-known cultural figure in eastern Sumatra who takes great pride in collecting 'pearls of wisdom' (*butir-butir budaya*) about Malay culture.[2] A translation of this epic poem is included in the present collection. It allows for the voice of a modern Malay to express his understandings of how history, local politics, the modern nation-state and globalisation have influenced Malay identity today. In other words, it provides an eloquent overview of many of the issues contained in this collection.

In many edited volumes, the introductory essay attempts to guide the reader through each chapter, explaining its importance to the larger whole. This preface is simply an invitation to the reader to enjoy the collection. With this in mind, and also realising that most journeys end where they began, a special mention is needed for the final essay in this collection. Anthony Milner attended the original conference in Leiden, both as an observer and as a commentator. He contributes the last essay in this collection as a conclusion, but also as an assessment of the issues raised and a statement of the direction where his own notions of Malay identity are moving.

In the end, the essays collected here only manage to sketch some additional lines and patterns in the Malay world. Their conclusions are disjunctive and divergent. They emphasise the fact that it is still not possible to define, or even to describe, 'Melayu', 'Malay' and 'Maleis' in satisfactory ways, that is, in terms that are not riven with gaps and contradictions. Somehow, the three words remain elusive, open to multiple interpretations, no matter how hard scholars might try to confine them within distinct boundaries, or around unequivocal cores, to produce concrete and conclusive meanings. The process makes it clear that the way certain groups have co-opted 'Malayness' as an identity or nationality in order to justify their actions is something that should be subverted and questioned. The nature or essence of 'Malayness' remains problematic—one of the most challenging and confusing terms in the world of Southeast Asia.

* * *

Although writing or editing a book involves much personal labour, it is never possible without the help of others. The editor wishes to acknowledge the assistance of those who helped with the original conference as well as the editing and writing of the papers since then. There were numerous people who helped in the organisation of the Leiden conference, while many of the participants were unable to appear in this volume, particularly Amin Sweeney, Noriah Taslim, Suryadi, Al Azhar, Taufik Ikram Jamil and Sirtjo Koolhof. They helped contribute to the discussion and hone the arguments that are present in the various chapters of this book. Without their assistance, the time in Leiden would not have been as enjoyable, or as intellectually challenging, and their help is greatly appreciated. In particular, special thanks should go to Will Derks, who was instrumental in arranging for the conference to take place, and helped guide the papers through the early stages of submission once it was over.

In Singapore, Paul Kratoska and Bruce Lockhart provided their own editorial insight into the collection when some of the papers were published in the *Journal of Southeast Asian Studies*, as well as support for this present publication. Tony Milner, Shamsul A.B., Parouche Coldstream and Jan van der Putten also provided input into how the volume should be presented, and their help is much appreciated. Adrian Vickers, as editor of *RIMA*, graciously made arrangements for the reprint of Virginia Hooker's article, and his own. Without the help of all of these friends and colleagues, and we apologise to those left unmentioned, this volume would not have been the rewarding experience it has turned out to be. To all, we would like to express our thanks for their support.

Understanding *Melayu* (Malay) as a Source of Diverse Modern Identities

ANTHONY REID*

A s the world stumbles hesitantly towards post-nationalist ways of understanding identity, it has at last become possible to discern what nationalism is, and the roles it has played in dominating the last century of our common history.[1] It no longer seems as 'natural' and uncontroversial as it did at its height before 1945. Yet the plethora of fine analyses which began to appear in the 1980s has barely begun to be integrated into the study of Southeast or indeed East Asia, where nationalism is still new enough to arouse more excitement and sympathy than concern or serious analysis.

The work of Benedict Anderson,[2] global in reach but drawing more heavily than most on anti-colonial examples in the New World, is the most influential of these theoretical models among writers on Southeast Asia. I wish to draw attention here however to a different strain of analysis well established in the European-focused writing—the distinction between civic and ethnic nationalisms.

Hans Kohn, writing at the depth of Germany's disastrous experiment with extreme nationalism, was the first to point out how differently nationalism developed east of the Rhine. "French nationalism was born (as English and American had [been] before it) in a wave of generous enthusiasm for the cause of mankind; the opposing nationalisms ... were directed to laudable but narrower goals, self-centred but antagonistic."[3] He showed how territorial nationalism developed earlier, gradually admitting more and more groups within the borders in question into citizenship in the nation, which was always territorially defined. Anthony Smith makes this distinction crucial to his discussion in *The Ethnic Origins of Nations*.[4] Where in the older territorial model the geographically bounded state eventually created the culturally coherent nation, the ethnic model was the other way around: an ethnic group with unclear borders attempted to acquire appropriate borders and political status.

Liah Greenfeld's *Nationalism* is so far the most careful historical analysis of the relationship between these two models in the context of European history. She sees the concept of nation developing in sixteenth-century England in the sense of a sovereign people, entitled to representation in the body politic. It was thus a concept closely wedded to the emergence of democracy in early modern Europe. As it spread eastwards through Europe in the eighteenth century, however, the unique quality of the nation became more marked than its sovereign or democratic character. The sovereignty of this type of nation was held to lie in its distinctiveness, not its participatory civic character. While in the civic variant "nationality is at least in principle open and voluntaristic", in the ethnic variant "it is believed to be inherent—one can neither acquire it if one does not have it, nor change it if one does".[5] Although the distinction on the ground cannot be as sharp as the one in abstract analysis, her study of 'five roads' shows Germany and Russia more influenced by this ethnic path, while England and the United States (in common with most anti-colonial New World nationalisms) can be characterised more by the civic path, and France by an ambivalent path eventually veering towards the civic.

Southeast Asian nationalisms sit interestingly within this dichotomy. Since all the anti-colonial nationalisms espoused a territorial definition of the nation—in every case accepting the arbitrary colonial boundaries rather than some ethno-cultural unit—they must lean towards the civic idea that all within their borders are equally members of the nation. Island states like Indonesia, the Philippines and Singapore are particularly congenial to this type of territorial nationalism by reason of having boundaries seemingly demarcated by nature, not by the ambivalent destiny of a people. It is significant that the strongest challenge to colonial boundaries (before Indonesia's 1975 annexation of East Timor) came from Thai nationalism, the only one for which anti-colonial sentiment was not the driving force, when Japanese hegemony provided the opportunity in 1941–43. But anti-colonial movements in Southeast Asia tended to gain more popular support in opposing foreign control than in seeking broader democratic rights, and always contained a populist edge that was opposed to the ethnic 'outsider', whether that target was European, Chinese, Vietnamese (in Cambodia and Laos) or Indian (in Burma).

Crucial also are the ways these movements have dealt with the set of central symbols (name, language, historical myths, 'national' dress and style) around which they seek to mobilise the population. Anthony Smith argues, with a certainty that seems no longer justified in a new century, "Nations require ethnic cores if they are to survive. If they lack one, they must 'reinvent' one."[6] Looking at the Southeast Asian evidence in particular, I prefer to speak of a core culture. There must be some way of defining what constitutes the nation-state. The question is whether that definition is explicitly ethnic, thereby encouraging ethno-nationalism and marginalising those outside the core ethnie, or whether it is defined in relation to shared, neutral symbols (territory, biota, constitution, shared history). All the nationalisms of mainland Southeast Asia experience this dilemma, in that they have tried to build from a core ethnie and culture to a civic one, with much ambivalence. Malaysia expresses the dilemma most acutely, for example in Dr Mahathir's expressed desire to negotiate the shoals between *Bangsa Melayu* (Malay Race/nation) and *Bangsa Malaysia* (Malaysian Race/nation) by 2020.

If Malaysia, Indonesia and Brunei today each have a 'core culture', as I think they do, its historical basis in all three cases seems to be Malayness, a cultural complex centred in the language called Melayu. This at least is the language all chose as their national language (though developed in different standards, with different patterns of modern borrowings from English, Dutch, Javanese, Sanskrit and Arabic). Eventually the three modern states have made their respective versions of Malay almost the sole medium of education, and thereby the social cement intended to hold their respective societies together.

It may be helpful therefore to trace the term and content of Malayness historically, to attempt to establish what this core culture represents.

Origins of Malayness

The term 'Melayu' is very ancient, in a sense which appears to apply to a place in Sumatra or possibly the Straits of Melaka region more generally.[7] Ptolemy, the second-century (CE) Egyptian geographer, inserted the toponym 'Melayu Kulon' (west Melayu, in Javanese) on the west coast of his Golden Khersonese, thus somewhere near the southern border of Burma today. The twelfth-century Arab geographer Edrisi also reported 'Malai' as a large island off southern Asia full of gold, spices, elephants and rhinoceros.[8] In Chinese records, beginning with Yijing in the seventh century, 'Malayu' appears as a more specific kingdom to the north of Srivijaya, absorbed into the latter in the 680s. The Tanjore inscription of 1030 and Marco Polo around 1290 also identify 'Malayur' as one of Sumatra's ancient kingdoms. Most specific are the references of the fourteenth-century Javanese texts, *Pararaton* and *Nagarakertagama*, to the *Pamalayu*, or the expedition to conquer the great Sumatran kingdom of Malayu decreed in 1275 by King Kertanegara of Singasari, though perhaps not undertaken until some decades later.[9] By this time, 'Malayu', probably centred primarily in the Jambi area, had definitely taken over the mantle of Srivijaya, even if Chinese imperial records in their conservative way went on using the term Srivijaya after it had disappeared on the ground.

Malayu thus appears to be an old toponym associated with Srivijaya, and indeed better represented in the non-Chinese sources than Srivijaya itself. While the scholarly reconstructions usually identify Malayu with Jambi and Srivijaya with Palembang, the reality is much less clear cut, with Malayu frequently representing the larger area. Nevertheless, Malayu did not establish itself as the name for a people at that time. The most common term used by foreigners to designate the Archipelago or its people was 'Jawa' or 'Yava'. Ancient Indian sources used terms such as 'Yava-dvipa', and Arabs and Europeans followed by using 'Jawa' as an island or collections of islands, and 'Jawi' as a people. For Chinese of the seventeenth and early eighteenth centuries, as for Vietnamese and Cambodian sources of this period, the most general term for seafaring people of the Archipelago was 'Jawa'. Thus Chinese junk captains reporting to the Japanese harbourmaster in Nagasaki around 1700 declared that both Melaka and Patani "belonged to Jawa".[10] The first Chinese source to use 'Melayu' (*wu lai yu*) rather than 'Jawa' to refer to the same broad culture area (including the Philippines), as Wang Gungwu has pointed out, was a text of 1730.[11]

Malay-language sources themselves are surprisingly obscure about the heritage of Srivijaya or Malayu. They do not use these terms, but cite Bukit Siguntang as the place of origin of their kings. There is a small sacred hill by this name in the modern city of Palembang. Although today graced only with Islamic graves of much later date (and some bizarre contemporary fantasy structures), this is presumed to be the sacred site of Srivijaya/Malayu. The *Sejarah Melayu* gives Malayu only as the name of a small river said to originate near this hill and flowing into the Musi (though it is in Jambi, not Palembang, that modern maps show a Sungei Malayu flowing into the Batang Hari at precisely the point of the ancient ruins). Other than this, the *Sejarah Melayu* uses the term Melayu sparingly, in most cases as an adjective for kings (*raja-raja Melayu*) or for custom (*adat Melayu*), or to indicate the line of royal descent from Bukit Siguntang.[12]

When Melaka is shown in conflict with Siam, Majapahit and other states, their opponents are *orang Siam* (Siam people) and *orang Jawa*, but the home team is usually *orang Melaka*. Once Melaka is firmly established as a Muslim kingdom, however, the term *orang Melayu* begins to appear as interchangeable with Melakans, especially in describing the cultural preferences of the Melakans as against these foreigners.[13]

When describing the defence of Melaka, the *Sejarah Melayu* refers as usual to the struggle of the *orang Melaka*, but when the king is wounded in the hand he strikingly holds up his wound and says, "Hai, anak Melayu, lihat-lah" (Hey, Malays, look at this).[14] This seems to reinforce the idea that what Brown translates as 'Malays' are seen in the text as the clients (*anak*) of the *raja Melayu*. By the end of the Melaka sultanate, it appears, Melayu had become a way of referring to the minority of the Melaka population who had lived there long enough to speak Malay as a first language and to identify with the sultan as his loyal people. This group traced its origins, or the origins of its ruling dynasty, to Srivijaya, which they recognised through their literature as Malayu or Bukit Siguntang.

The *Hikayat Hang Tuah* is still more emotive about Melayu as a people supporting a line of Malay kings, but the long period over which it was compiled (sixteenth to nineteenth centuries) makes it hard to specify when this characteristic came to be central. The great Malay folk-hero Hang Tuah was pre-eminently a man of the sea, a naval commander always going on long sea voyages for the sultan of (fifteenth-century) Melaka, to distant places like India, Java, Turkey and China. As an exemplar of modern-style 'Malayness' he is, however, at best ambivalent. When the people of Kampar seem ashamed of their poor dancing because they were not real Malays from the Melaka metropolis, he reassured them that he was no better: "the Melaka people seem to be bastardised Malays [*Melayu kacokan*], mixed with Javanese from Majapahit".[15] This passage seems among those likely to have been written in the sixteenth century, evoking as it does the world of the *Sejarah Melayu*, whose readers were presumed to understand Javanese, and of the earliest European reports, which suggest Javanese as the most numerous inhabitants of Melaka.[16]

When the Portuguese arrived in the region after 1500, they initially adopted the same view, that *Malayos* were essentially the pro-sultan ruling people of Melaka, one kind of people among many in the city. Tomé Pires explained how the Melaka sultanate itself classified visitors to Melaka in four groups, according to which *syahbandar* (the harbourmaster) they reported to:

1. Gujeratis
2. South Indians, Pegu, Pasai
3. Javanese, Malukans, Banda, Palembang, Tanjungpura (W. Borneo), Luzon
4. Chinese, Ryukyu, Chancheo and Champa[17]

Malayos do not appear in this list, suggesting they were not then regarded as a category outside Melaka itself. The city appears to have categorised traders in terms of the direction they came from and the intermediate ports they visited rather than any sense of common ethnicity or language. Far from being regarded as a coherent group, Austronesian-speakers are spread among all the *syahbandar* except the first and most explicitly Muslim one. The Portuguese did, however, describe Malayos as traders in other places such as China and Maluku, and it appears that initially they meant traders from the ruling group in Melaka.

João Barros, somewhat inclined to attribute Chinese ancestry to all the maritime elites of the Archipelago whom the Portuguese encountered, has an interesting description of the coastal people of Sumatra—generally described as Malay in recent times. For Barros, they were not Malay but Jawi (*Iauijs*), the same term used by Arabic-speakers and by Hamzah Fansuri in describing himself.[18] Barros says that these Jawi "are not natives of the land which they inhabit, but people who come from areas of China, because they imitate the Chinese in their appearance, their political system and their ingenuity in all mechanical work".[19]

Although this seems a strange claim, there are other indications of a strong Chinese presence on Sumatra's east coast, notably at the only well-excavated eleventh- to fourteenth-century site of the area—Kota Cina near Medan.[20] There are also Chinese connections at Palembang or Bukit Siguntang around the time its heritage was being claimed by the dynasty that founded Melaka. Some upheaval occurred in Palembang between 1377, when the last king of Srivijaya sanctioned by the Chinese court was reported to have died and his son asked for Chinese approval in his turn, and 1397, when Palembang appears in Chinese sources to be in rebellion. A few years later, in 1405, the Zheng He missions visiting the region reported that Palembang was dominated by a Cantonese defector named Liang Dao-ming, who had been there for many years along with "several thousand military personnel and civilians from Guangdong who followed him there".[21]

The Chinese intervened to impose an imperial commissioner, but this did not work and Palembang remained for the next 20 years out of imperial favour but active in trade and seemingly still dominated by the Cantonese renegade group. Since this is about the period when Palembang appears to have played a role in the founding of Melaka on the one hand, and the Islamic dynasties of Java, through Raden Patah, on the other, we can only surmise that people of part-Chinese descent played some part in creating new mercantile elites, including those known to Barros as Jawi but to later observers as Melayu.

The heritage of Melaka went in two directions after the city fell to the Portuguese in 1511. A number of lines of kingship sought to continue the royal lineage and court style of Melaka, of which the most successful for two centuries was the Riau-Johor line centred in the region of modern Singapore. On the other hand, the merchants who had given Melaka its life spread almost throughout Southeast Asia in their quest for entrepôts sympathetic to their trade. Their diaspora helped give new life to a range of port-states like Aceh, Patani, Palembang, Banten, Brunei, Makassar and Banjarmasin, and even Cambodia and Siam. This was a community of wonderfully mixed ethnic origins: many of the numerous Javanese of Melaka, as well as the 'Luzons' who were also prominent traders there, appear themselves to have been partly descended from the Chinese who came en masse to Southeast Asian ports at the time of the Zheng He fleets.[22] In addition, there were large Gujerati, South Indian, Chinese and Ryukyuan communities in Melaka, many of whom were assimilating to the extent of speaking Malay and practising Islam. When dispersed around the Archipelago this diaspora (or at least its Muslim majority) became simply Malays. A decade after the fall of Melaka the Magellan expedition, which visited only the eastern part of the Archipelago—Brunei, Maluku and Central Philippines—produced a Malay word-list which defined *cara Melayu* (lit. Malay ways) as "the ways of Melaka".[23]

The farther away from the heartland of Sumatra and the Peninsula one travelled, the more likely it was that the trading community of Muslims would be known collectively as Melayu, whatever their ethnic or geographical origin. The Malay entrepreneurs recorded in Makassar chronicles as entitled to the kind of autonomy and guarantees of property that traders everywhere require, were reported to originate from "Johor, Patani, Pahang, Minangkabau and Champa", while Indian Muslims later also played a prominent role in the community.[24] As if prophetically aware of the stereotype into which British colonialism would caste Malays two centuries later, the Melayu community who had helped spread Islam in the island of Sumbawa refused to be rewarded with rice-fields, for "we are sailors and traders, not peasants", and asked instead for exemption from port duties.[25]

In the sixteenth and seventeenth centuries Malayness in maritime Southeast Asia retained these two associations—a line of kingship acknowledging descent from Srivijaya and Melaka or Pagarruyung (Minangkabau), and a commercial diaspora that retained some of the customs, language and trade practices developed in the emporium of Melaka. The kingship role was more prominent in the Straits of Melaka area, the diaspora one elsewhere. Although this second sense was exceptionally open to new recruits from any ethnic background, it can be seen to have evolved towards the idea of *orang Melayu* as a distinct ethnie. Ence Amin, for example, writer for the Makassar court and author of the *Syair Perang Mengkasar*, declared himself to be "a Malay of Makassar descent" (*nisab Mengkasar anak Melayu*) and took pride in his fellow Malays' heroism in defending Makassar against the Dutch.[26]

Beyond these two uses of Malayness, there was a broader community of Muslims of a variety of ethnic backgrounds who wrote in Malay (whatever their mother tongue), dressed in a similar Jawi style (distinguishing themselves thereby from the less orthodox Bugis or Javanese) and took part in the widespread Malay-language 'civilisation' of Islam. Such people might be referred to as 'Malays' by Europeans, but there seems little evidence that they saw themselves in this light.

The Malay Category in Seventeenth/Eighteenth-Century Dutch Records

In the Dutch ports, there were almost from the beginning a variety of ethnic labels for the seafaring population who settled for shorter or longer periods. Apart from the Europeans, the key ones were Chinese, Malay, Bugis, Javanese, and in early days *Mardika*, or freed and Christianised slaves. In both Batavia (from 1644) and Makassar (from the Dutch conquest, c. 1670), the leaders of the Malay maritime community were large traders from Patani—thus the second-generation of those who participated in the diaspora after the initial dispersal from Melaka. These were highly valued merchants and intermediaries. The first *Kapitan Melayu* of Batavia, Encik Amat, was sent as a Dutch envoy to Mataram four times, and often arranged the protocol for the reception of Asian dignitaries in Batavia. When the fourth generation of this distinguished family to be *Kapitan Melayu* was caught swindling his fellow-Malays in 1732, and exiled to Ceylon, he was found to have 329,000 *rixdaalders* in property and hundreds of slaves.[27] He must have been one of the richest men in not only Batavia but all Southeast Asia.

This Malay community of Batavia was wealthy but not particularly large—between 2,000 and 4,000 in the period 1680–1730, dropping to below 2,000 in the mid-1700s (mainly due to malaria) but rising sharply to 12,000 at the end of the eighteenth century.[28] By then the category had expanded in meaning to embrace all the Malay-speaking Muslims who came to Batavia from Sumatra, Borneo and the Peninsula. This group of traders expanded as trade itself expanded in the late eighteenth century.[29]

The Chinese and South Sulawesi communities were always more numerous in Batavia and Semarang.

Dutch harbourmasters were required to record numerous things about the vessels which called at their ports, and recent work by Heather Sutherland, Lee Kam Hing, Raden Fernando and Gerrit Knaap on their shipping registers enables us to see more clearly what Malay and other categories may have meant at this time. In Java they appear to have declined as a category in the eighteenth century, representing 24 per cent of the captains among the hundreds of vessels that took east Java salt to Dutch Melaka in the 1680s, but only 7 per cent in 1735.[30] The reason may have been a more careful set of distinctions by Dutch harbourmasters in the later period, but these figures may also suggest that ethnic labelling was changing in other ways, with shippers resident in the salt-exporting east Java ports more likely to consider themselves as 'Javanese' and 'Chinese' (the two main maritime categories at that stage) who belonged there, rather than first-generation 'Malays' and 'Bugis', who didn't.

Gerrit Knaap's more detailed study of shipping records from Java ports in the 1770s shows that Malay skippers had in fact held up very well in the overall trade between Java and the Melaka Straits, still representing 35 per cent of these ship movements. In his total of 20,000 ship movements in and out of Java ports in all directions, Malay captains scored 8.6 per cent, compared with 40 per cent Javanese, 30 per cent Chinese, and a great variety of smaller labels like Bugis-Makassar, Balinese, Madurese, European and Arab. Malay captains were most strongly concentrated in Batavia and on the Java-Malaya and Java-Borneo routes. They had some interesting similarities with Chinese skippers. Both used the title *Encik* and a similar range of boat types, while the average boat size for both was well above the average, at about 26 tons (13.9 last for Chinese and 13.2 for Malay). Javanese boats averaged only half this size, while the other Indonesian ethnic labels were somewhere in between. Since ownership of ships is often also given, we know that Javanese aristocrats often employed Malay captains, whereas most other owners used captains of the same ethnicity as themselves.[31]

In Dutch Melaka in the period 1760–85, Malay captains showed an extraordinarily rapid rise, from 54 ship calls in 1761 to 242 in 1785. From having been a category with relatively large ships until 1775, the Malays start to approach a modern stereotype of many small boats on local sectors in the 1780s. The reason may be that Dutch Melaka was becoming more attractive as a local entrepôt at that period, especially after the Dutch conquered its busy rival Riau in 1784 and created such enmity with local Bugis that 'Malay' became a more acceptable label for small boats in general.[32]

Within Melaka itself the 'Malay' category of resident *nakhoda* (captain) was large and growing. Of all Melaka-based captains, Malays were responsible for 30 per cent of the ship movements (20 arrivals) in 1761, and 43 per cent (86 arrivals) in 1785.[33]

English Understandings of 'Malay'

There is no doubt that Thomas Stamford Raffles' view of the Malays had a great effect on the imagining of English-speakers. He should probably be regarded as the most important voice in projecting the idea of a 'Malay' race or nation, not limited to the traditional Malay sultans or even their supporters, but embracing a large if unspecified part of the Archipelago. Raffles, like the other influential English writers of the period, William Marsden and John Crawfurd, was imbued with an Enlightenment view that peoples should be scientifically classified, much as Carolus Linnaeus and Charles Darwin classified the natural world. Marsden explicitly set out "to distinguish the several species or classes" of inhabitants of Sumatra.[34] Marsden's scientific method led him to deplore the tendency of his countrymen little experienced in the East "to call the inhabitants of the islands indiscriminately as Malays". He attempted to formulate a clear definition based on what he understood as their own usage: "every Mussulman speaking the Malayan as his proper language, and either belonging to, or claiming descent from, the ancient kingdom of Minangkabau".[35] Elsewhere he conceded that in the developed Malay-language letter-writing tradition "the term 'malayu' as applied to themselves or other eastern people, very rarely occurs", the phrase "people below the winds" being preferred as a way to distinguish islanders from Europeans and others.[36]

Stamford Raffles was at the romantic edge of this Enlightenment quest, seeking in the rustic Javanese or highland Sumatran the noble vestige of once-great civilisations. Soon after arriving in Penang in 1805 as assistant secretary and commencing his study of the Malay language, Raffles became intimate with Dr John Leyden, a learned Scottish surgeon of almost his own youthfulness and romantic disposition, who had been a collaborator of Sir Walter Scott before leaving Edinburgh. Together they formed their vision of the Malays as one of the language-based 'nations' that Johann Gottfried Herder and his counterparts in the English Romantic movement, such as Scott, had seen the world divided into. Influenced by Leyden's slightly earlier essay on "The Indo-Chinese nations", Raffles' first literary essay, sent to the Asiatic Society in Bengal from Penang in 1809, insisted on a similar vision for Malays: "I cannot but consider the Malayu nation as one people, speaking one language, though spread over so wide a space, and preserving their character and customs, in all the maritime states lying between the Sulu Seas and the Southern Oceans".[37] Having been forced to abandon his dream of an English vocation to uplift and extend the once-great Javanese people,[38] Raffles transferred this romantic vision to the Malays. From his new post at Bengkulu, he mounted an expedition to the old Minangkabau capital of Pagarruyung, which he declared "the source of that power, the origin of that nation, so extensively scattered over the Eastern Archipelago". Eagerly he explained to his patron how "Sumatra, under British influence, [would] again rise into great political importance" by reviving the prestige of the ancient kingdom.[39]

But still more influential for Malays was his renaming of the major Malay text as *Sejarah Melayu* in Malay and *Malay Annals* in English. The Malay concept of this text was as a description of a line of kings and their ceremonial, so that its author explicitly called it "the rules of all the rajas" (*peraturan segala raja-raja* or, in Arabic, *Sulalat Us-Salatin*).[40] But when Raffles for the first time had printed, in 1821, the translation of the text by his late friend John Leyden, he inserted these titles as if to show it was the story of a people. In his introduction to the translation, Raffles moved the Malays on from a nation to a race, and sought to convey the enthusiasm of Leyden to find in the Malay stories "a glimmering of light, which might, perhaps, serve to illustrate an earlier period."[41]

The idea that the Peninsula was particularly 'Malay' appears also to have been an English one. In his late eighteenth-century work, *The History of Sumatra*, William Marsden thought that the idea of the Peninsula as 'Malayan' or 'Malay' was of exclusively European origin, which had thereby confused many into thinking of the Peninsula as the place of Malay origins.[42] In fact this was an almost exclusively English perception since other Europeans usually called the Peninsula 'Malacca', after its most famous city. The term 'Malaya' goes back at least as far as Alexander Hamilton in the early eighteenth century, especially in the phrase "Coast of Malaya" to indicate the ports of Kedah and Perak.[43] English maps, like French and Dutch ones, more often called the Peninsula by the name of Melaka until around 1800, however. As the British became more concerned with the Peninsula after the founding of Georgetown at Pulau Pinang in 1786, they appear to have generally adopted the usages 'Malay' or 'Malayan' for the Peninsula; Raffles and Crawfurd frequently did so. Once the London Treaty of 1824 restricted British activity to this Peninsula, they were much more disposed to see it as a coherent unit under one of these labels. The first book explicitly on the subject, that of P. J. Begbie in 1834, used 'Malayan' in the title but 'Malay Peninsula' in the accompanying map.[44]

Dating the Malay term *tanah Melayu*—the land of the Malays—for the Peninsula is more difficult, though it seems possible that it was influenced by this English evolution. The *Hikayat Hang Tuah* is the only pre-modern Malay text to use this term, sometimes applying it to Melaka and sometimes to a broader area where there are Malay kings.[45] Marsden's 1811 edition and Crawfurd's first (1820) publication both indicate that this Malay usage had already taken hold.[46] Both found this appellation puzzling since they wanted to see a single origin-place for 'the Malay race', and were equally convinced that it was to be found not in the Peninsula but in Minangkabau. Crawfurd resolves this conundrum by concluding: "It was from the [Peninsula] colony, and not the parent stock, that the Malayan name and nation were so widely disseminated."[47]

Three Nineteenth-Century Understandings of Malayness

(1)   Melayu as the vestige of concern with royal lineage

This sense continued in a host of courts around the Straits of Melaka, from Deli and Langkat in northeast Sumatra to Pontianak and Brunei in Borneo by way of the mini-states of the Peninsula and eastern Sumatra. Much of the 'classical' Malay court literature that has survived in modern collections was composed or copied in the nineteenth century, preserving the preoccupation of an earlier time to assert the legitimacy and sacred *daulat* (sovereignty) of Malay kings. But by the mid-nineteenth century, especially as represented in the work of the greatest of these court writers, Raja Ali Haji of Riau, there was a growing concern to establish principles of Malayness which were bigger than the frequently unworthy individual king. Malay kings must behave justly; Malay subjects must be loyal; if either rulers or subjects submit to lust and passion (*nafsu*), the judgement of God will bring the kingdom down, as was already happening to one ancient court after another. For the Bugis-descended Raja Ali Haji, there was no Malay ethnie in the positive sense, but rather a negative, anti-Bugis, parochial Malay faction (*kaum Melayu*) on the one hand, and a glorious tradition of kingship (*raja Melayu*) on the other, no longer dependent on any one lineage.[48]

(2)   Melayu as an emerging notion of modern nationality or race

In the urban world of the nineteenth-century Straits Settlements, which from 1824 comprised Penang, Melaka and Singapore, modern European ideas of nationality (and later race) carried much weight. In the person of Munshi Abdullah, in particular, the prolific Malay writer and teacher for a succession of Europeans in the Straits, it is possible to observe the evolution of a new sense of Malay identity in close proximity to Europeans and Chinese. Despite the mixed descent he shared with many residents of the Straits, Abdullah considered himself a Malay. Malay was his preferred language, and he was accepted as an authority on Malay culture and language. But he had no time for the lineage of Malay *rajas* that had hitherto been the key definition of Malayness. In his urban perspective, much influenced by the progress and sense of community of other groups in Singapore, the Malay kings were the greatest threat to the well being of what he called *bangsa Melayu*—the Malay race or people. Writing in the 1840s he was perhaps the first Malay writer for whom, as Anthony Milner puts it, "the race was the primary community"—although in the view of many later Malay nationalists, he was not properly part of it.[49]

This developing idea of Malayness in the Straits as an essentially racial category, with its own ethnic origin and genealogy, its own language, its own relatively broad boundaries against other ethnicities, was the newest of the three versions of Malay in the nineteenth century. In the Straits Settlements, there were undoubtedly many *Abdullahs*, for whom Malayness was a new identity acquired in the ethnically competitive world of these port-states. Austronesian-Muslims seemed to be outnumbered and outcompeted by Chinese, Europeans and Indians in these ports. Although of various origins, they were too small a minority to carry much weight separately as Bugis, Aceh, Java or Mandailing, and in any case they intermarried with each other in the ports. The English rulers of the Straits used 'Malay' as the collective term to refer to them, and to a considerable extent it became internalised. When the first Malay-language daily newspaper appeared in the Straits Settlements, in 1907, it was named not after a place but after a language and potential ethnie—*Utusan Melayu*.[50]

The tenuousness of this concept until the 1930s should be emphasised, however. It had to compete not only against specific diaspora ethnicities (Mandailing, Bugis, Aceh, Banjar, Rawas, Jawi Pekan, etc.), but among Malay-speakers with loyalties to particular rulers, and among English-speakers with the continuing idea that all speakers of Austronesian languages were in some sense 'Malay'.

(3)   Malayness as urban superculture

In the cities of the Netherlands Indies, a Malay-speaking urban population of mixed origins took root in the nineteenth century, for whom Malay was predominately a *lingua franca* and a language for popular written expression.

It had little to do with ethnicity, and was less used as a label for a particular commercial diaspora than in the previous century. In fact, the majority of those who first turned modern Malay in Romanised script into a vehicle of print journalism were of mixed Chinese-Indonesian descent and generally labelled 'Chinese'. Dutch had never taken the path of the English, referring to all who spoke Malay as 'Malays'. Malay had been the *lingua franca* of the Dutch empire in the Archipelago since the mid-seventeenth century, and it was the principal language of the new Christianised minorities in Ambon and Minahasa. In the western Archipelago *"masuk Melayu"* meant to become a Muslim, but in parts of eastern Indonesia the phrase meant becoming Christian.[51] As a vague collective term for the inhabitants of the Archipelago, 'Malay' did not recommend itself to the Dutch. They used the term 'native' (inlander) in everyday disparagement of the people now known as Indonesians, an option not available to the English in the Straits, who used the loose and pejorative 'native' for all the Asians under their authority. When they sought to be neutral, the Dutch called their non-Chinese subjects Indians (Indiers), and the Spanish did the same in the Philippines. When in the early years of this century the novel idea began to spread among the people of the Dutch-ruled Archipelago that they were a collective unity, they initially used the Malay version of this term—*orang Hindia*—to describe themselves.

Malay as Race—Bangsa Melayu

As Britain took ever greater responsibility for the whole of the southern Peninsula, a plural society was created in which Europeans and Chinese were encouraged to develop Malaya's resources, produce the exports and pay the taxes which made Malaya one of the wealthiest economies in Asia by the 1920s. Malay rulers provided the legitimation of this lucrative development, and a colonial discourse quickly developed about 'protecting' them and their people. Colonial statesmen had a clear idea of what sort of Malay they should protect. Many distrusted the Straits Malays as cultural exemplars, and even dismissed them as *mestizos*. The 'real Malay' of colonial discourse was rural, loyal to his ruler, conservative and relaxed to the point of laziness. One Malayan governor, Sir Hugh Clifford, devoted one of his novels to showing the catastrophic results of Malays becoming infected with Western ideas.[52]

The most influential Malayan administrators professed great liking for this gentlemanly but non-competitive Malay stereotype. By contrast, the negative elements of a rampant capitalist order tended to be attributed to another stereotype, that of 'the Chinese' inherently dedicated to making money by any means possible. The dominant element of the Malayan Civil Service took the view that its role was to protect the stereotyped Malay identity, not to change it. Clifford, the most sentimentally paternal of the governors, insisted as late as 1927, when effective power was wholly in British hands, that there must be no change in the Islamic monarchies which Britain was sworn to protect. "No mandate has ever been extended to us by Rajas, Chiefs, or people to vary the system of government which has existed in these territories from time immemorial."[53] In this view Malays should have the kind of education "to breed a vigorous and self-respecting agricultural peasantry such as must form the backbone of every nation".[54] Malay reservations were created in 1913, in which agricultural land could only be alienated to people defined as racially Malay, irrespective of their place of birth. In 1917–18 regulations were passed to oblige rice-growing land to continue to be used for that purpose, in the hope of discouraging Malays from becoming commercially oriented rubber-growers rather than sturdy self-sufficient peasants.[55]

Despite its greater wealth, Malaya spent a smaller proportion of public money on education than did other Southeast Asian colonies. In 1920, only 12 per cent of the Malay population aged 5–15 was in school, and virtually all of these were in the vernacular Malay-language schools the government believed best equipped to keep the Malays in their stereotyped place: "It will not only be a disaster to, but a violation of the whole spirit and tradition of, the Malay race if the result of our vernacular education is to lure the whole of the youth from the kampung to the town."[56]

The education provided was particularly well designed to rediscover the first of the nineteenth-century meanings of Malayness mentioned above— a tradition of Malay kingship descended from Melaka—and impose it on the varied Muslim immigrants to the Peninsula. R. J. Wilkinson, the learned patron of the Malay school system,[57] was convinced that the forgotten classics should be introduced to Malay reading to rescue it from the modernising urban literati—"the Anglomaniac with his piebald diction and the pan-Islamic pundit with his long Arabic words".[58] As Henk Maier puts it, this most idealistic of the British scholar-officials still held that "the gap between East and West should be confirmed rather than bridged. And the seeds of the necessary regeneration of the Malay people should be sought primarily in the past, when everything had been so much better."[59] The 'classic' court texts introduced to schools stressed unswerving loyalty to the ruler as the key element of Malay identity. Wilkinson's successor, R.O. Winstedt, also had a large hand in producing the first modern 'Malay history' (*Kitab Tawarikh Melayu*) in 1918 to give Malay schoolchildren a sense of their historical identity. This encouraged the modern Malay nationalist understanding of Malayness. It was no longer the product of an Archipelago diaspora, nor a civilisation into which all could assimilate, but a racial sense of lost grandeur set within the geographic boundaries established in 1909. The greatness of the Melaka sultanate had been succeeded by Portuguese, Dutch and now British rule.[60]

For racially-conscious Englishmen sent to administer Malaya in the early years of the twentieth century, the protection of a 'Malay race' was a more attractive justification for colonial rule than the protection of 'Malay rulers' that had been the original pretext. Charles Hirschman points out that while the early colonial censuses, in 1871 and 1881, listed Malays, Boyanese, Achinese, Javanese, Bugis, Manilamen, Siamese, and so on as separate groups, the 1891 Census demarcated the three racial categories of modern Malaysia— Chinese, 'Tamils and other natives of India', and 'Malays and other Natives of the Archipelago', each elaborately sub-divided. The report on the 1901 Census advised "the word 'nationality' should be changed for that of 'race' whenever it occurs. It is a wider and more exhaustive expression than 'nationality' and gives rise to no such ambiguous questions in classifying people."[61] Race was of course believed by many Europeans in the early part of this century to be a scientific category, capable of being determined on biological grounds regardless of how people defined themselves. The director of the 1931 census pointed out this was a purely European fantasy. "The difficulty of achieving anything like a scientific or logically consistent classification is enhanced by the fact that most Oriental peoples have themselves no clear conception of race, and commonly regard religion as the most important, if not the determinant, element."[62]

Two generations of being referred to and educated as if they were a distinct race, however, had a predictable impact. Identity took shape around *bangsa Melayu*, a term which goes back at least to Munshi Abdullah but was more widely internalised from the 1920s as the equivalent of 'Malay race' in English. Like 'race', *bangsa* derived from common descent, but its Sanskrit origins refer to lineage or even caste. In the old texts someone who has no *bangsa* is of low birth. For the young graduates of the Malay teachers' colleges who wrote in the growing Malay press of the 1930s, *bangsa Melayu* became the primary locus of political passion. It was defined by what they perceived as two overwhelming facts—they were the 'natives' with primary claim on the country, and they were the weakest group in it. They concluded that *bangsa* required unity and solidarity to make stronger demands of the British.

Malay nationalism developed explicitly as an ethnic or racial variant of nationalism in the 1930s and 1940s, responding to a similar kind of ethnic nationalism among English and Chinese. Ibrahim Yaacob complained in 1941 that there were still too many who thought of themselves as Minangkabau or Boyanese, or as subjects of a particular *raja* instead of as members of the Malay *bangsa* pure and simple.[63] One of the new Malay newspapers responded to the demands of Malayan-born Chinese for political rights in Malaya with the words: "The Malays have rights not because they were born here but because they belong to the Malay *bangsa* and are the first *bangsa* that owns the land."[64] As with all such definitions, of course, the problem of how to measure racial identity became the greatest irritant. Like earlier British administrators, the Malay radicals wanted to find the 'real Malay'—*Melayu jati*—excluding both Anglophile aristocrats and the part-Indian or part-Arab Muslims of Singapore and Penang.[65]

During the Malayan Union controversy of 1945–46, what had been a minority view became politically dominant as the voice of United Malays National Organisation (UMNO), the Malay party formed around the ethno-nationalist idea. Malay loyalties should be given to the *bangsa Melayu* rather than to the separate Malay rulers or to the British. *Hidup Melayu* (Long live the Malays) replaced the deferential *Daulat Tuanku* of salutation to royalty as the slogan of the *bangsa*.[66]

The British were obliged to back down from their Malayan Union project and replace it with a Federation of Malaya in which the centrality of Malayness was explicitly expressed. In effect the 'Malayan' civic nationalism the British belatedly sought to encourage after 1945 was rejected in favour of an almost equally recent ethnic nationalism. The Malay press throughout the controversy denounced *bangsa Malayan* as foreigners. Federation of Malaya might be acceptable in English, but only so long as it was understood as a translation from the real (Malay) name of the country, *Persekutuan Tanah Melayu*—Federation of the Malay Lands. The Anglo-Malay committee that recommended the name noted that "the Malays took the strongest exception to being called or referred to as Malayans".[67] Citizenship, the British stipulated, was to be extended to those who regarded Malaya as their real home and had lived there for 15 years, but this was distinguished sharply from nationality (*bangsa*). The constitutional report insisted that citizenship:

> was not a nationality, nor could it be developed into a nationality... It is an addition to, and not a subtraction from, nationality, and could be a qualification for electoral rights ... and for employment in government service ...[But] oaths of allegiance would be out of place.[68]

The Federation of Malaya was emphatically designed to be a state constructed around not simply a core culture, but a core ethnie. The defining identity, or nationality, was to be *bangsa Melayu*. On the eve of Malayan independence in 1957, the conflict between ethnic and civic nationalisms had to be skirted around again, in a formula which finally granted a single Malayan nationality, but only after hard bargaining for concessions which would acknowledge the definitive position of *bangsa Melayu* at the core—chiefly in symbolic forms and the 'Malay privileges' in education and government service.

One of the most important effects of the formation of Malaysia in 1963 was that it created a neutral name for the country distinct from that of its core ethnie—a major advance on Thailand and Vietnam, or for that matter Russia, Japan, and most other countries of the old, Eurasian world. But there were still profound tensions between the concepts of core ethnie and of neutral citizenship. Lee Kuan Yew's Singapore was expelled from the new country after less than two years because his vigorous campaign for a civic or territorial nationalism—'Malaysian Malaysia' and the assertion that "We are here as of right"—was considered by Alliance leaders as certain to lead to violent conflict with Malay ethno-nationalism.[69]

The most forceful case for a core ethnie within Malaysia is that of Malaysia's present and longest-serving prime minister. Dr Mahathir's 1970 book, *The Malay Dilemma*, written in the aftermath of the traumatic 1969 riots, argues the ethno-nationalist case in terms of both the need for protection and prior rights to the land. Leaning heavily on the example of Australia and the USA, he argues that every country has a 'definitive people' who were the first to set up states in the territory in question. Since the aborigines did not do this, it was the Malays in Malaya, and the English-speaking Christians in Australia, who defined the core culture and set the conditions by which subsequent migrants were admitted.[70]

Because Dr Mahathir had strong credentials with ethno-nationalists, he was well-placed as prime minister to move Malaysia towards some long-term resolution of the tensions between ethnic and civic nationalism. In opening up UMNO to non-Malay *bumiputra* in 1994 (a particularly important issue for the peoples of Borneo), and still more by declaring the future goal of a *bangsa Malaysia* as part of his Vision 2020, he raised the possibility in the mid-1990s of movement towards a genuinely civic nationalism.

Malayness as Inclusive Culture—*Bangsa Indonesia*

The relationship between state and ethnie was profoundly different in Indonesia. The colonial cities of Netherlands India, like those of Malaya, represented a sort of melting-pot where people from diverse origins came to see a common adherence to Islam as the most important thing that separated them from Europeans, Chinese and stateless unbelievers like the Balinese, Bataks and so on. Unless quickly assimilated into the Chinese or European communities through marriage (an option only available to women), the people brought to Batavia, Makassar, Palembang or Medan by slavery (before 1800), or by the attraction of commerce, quickly became Muslim as an indication that they were civilised and urban. This new identity was generally called 'Islam', though in some of the cities and coastal areas of Sumatra, Borneo and the Peninsula it might also be called 'Malay', while in Semarang and other cities of Java, the loose ethnic marker associated with Islam was 'Javanese', even if Malay was the principal language spoken in the city. Thus a Chinese writer of the 1780s complained that Chinese who stayed too long in the cities of Java forgot "the instruction of the sages" and "do not scruple to become Javanese, when they call themselves Islam".[71] In the early twentieth century, 'Javanese' became a self-conscious label for those who spoke the Javanese language as their mother tongue, and the Malay-speaking people of Batavia, of very mixed Balinese, Chinese, Makassarese and other origins, adopted the name 'Betawi', and were so recorded in colonial censuses.

Though Islam remained the key marker of common identity, and served as such in the first modern mass movement, *Sarekat Islam*, this religious affiliation did not present itself as a nationalism in the sense of defining the boundary of the core ethnie. Among the first to feel the stirring of an Indies-wide anti-colonial secular nationalism expressed in the Malay language were Indonesia-born non-Muslims classified as Peranakan Chinese and Indo-Europeans. As this nationalism became more popular in the 1920s, these pioneering figures were marginalised, but educated Christian Ambonese, Minahasans and Bataks continued to play prominent roles in defining the nation. After 1914, Marxism made a heavy emphasis on race and religion seem old-fashioned.

The first newspapers serving the polyglot majority population of the colonial cities were Malay-language publications set up by Eurasians and Europeans in the mid-nineteenth century. The literary standard of printed Malay that began to form the basis of creating a new urbanised ethnie during this period was in Roman script and characterised by straightforward expression, somewhat influenced by Dutch and Chinese.[72] It became in the 1920s the only serious candidate for the language of anti-colonial nationalism, Dutch and Javanese both having fatal flaws for that role.

The name for this national language and cultural identity was more problematic. Neither Melayu nor Jawa, the two indigenous labels with claims to both antiquity and comprehensiveness, was ever seriously considered. Both had been clearly established in Dutch and later in educated Indonesian discourse as particular ethnie, separate 'races and tribes', according to the English rendering of the *landaarden* of the colonial census. Until the 1920s, the only way to describe the new pan-colony identity was 'Indian' (Dutch *Indier*, Malay *orang Hindia*). The esoteric term 'Indonesian', used in some European linguistic and anthropological circles since the nineteenth century and popularised to some degree in the weighty *Encyclopaedia van Nederlandsch-Indië* (1918) as the term for Malayo-Polynesian, was therefore readily embraced by students in Holland as a new all-encompassing identity. In 1924, they changed the name of their students' association to "Perhimpunan Indonesia", and its journal to the rousing *Indonesia Merdeka*. Young Minangkabau intellectuals such as Muhammad Yamin and Dr Mohammad Amir, who had championed a unified Sumatran identity with the Malay language as its special glory, quickly became champions of a broader Indonesian identity. Yamin had published a patriotic poem extolling his Sumatran identity in 1920 (*Tanah Airku*), but in 1928, he was keynote speaker at the Indonesian Youth Congress, making a strong case that Malay had already become the national language—Bahasa Indonesia.[73] Within four years of being launched in Holland, the concepts of an Indonesian nation and language spread through the political organisations in the colony.

The privileged students at colleges and senior high schools in the main colonial cities, very far removed from their birthplaces and mother tongues, had begun in the 1920s to form youth associations deriving from their ethnie or their islands—Jong Java, Jong Minahassa, Jong Sumatra (primarily Minangkabau, and therefore challenged by Jong Batak). In 1928, guided by the growing enthusiasm for broader solidarities, most of these groups came together for an Indonesian Youth Congress. They subscribed to a stirring oath of imagined unity—"one fatherland, Indonesia; one bangsa, bangsa Indonesia; one language, bahasa Indonesia". The larger language groups had already been in process of reimagining themselves as mobilised ethnie— *bangsa Jawa, bangsa Bugis*, and so on. But here, earlier than in Malaysia, the social Darwinian idea of competition between races, and the logic of being educated together in Dutch schools, had worked towards a broader definition. Its core was an agreed compromise, a *lingua franca* dissociated from any particular group. There was a core culture, in the sense that Minangkabaus and coastal Sumatrans spoke Malay as their mother tongue, and for decades they would dominate the nascent literature in modern Indonesian. But because Ambonese, Minahasan and Kupang Christians,

Peranakan Chinese and various other urban minorities had spoken the same language for centuries, it was not perceived as belonging to any ethnie. The nationalists proposed, in effect, the radical and difficult path of building a bounded state without a core ethnie.

The Indonesian federalists of 1946–48, who sought with the poisoned chalice of Dutch help to build space in Indonesia for the autonomy of various ethnies and regions, fought a losing battle against the emotional pull of *bangsa Indonesia*. Several of the federal states, notably the one in East Sumatra that had contained the wealthiest Malay *rajas*, attempted to build an enthusiasm for *bangsa Melayu* or even for the hybrid *bangsa Sumatra Timur*. But when Sukarno passed through the capital of this doomed state in 1949 he proclaimed to cheering crowds at the airport:

> There is no *bangsa* Kalimantan, there is no *bangsa* Minangkabau, there is no bangsa Java, Bali, Lombok, Sulawesi or any such. We are all bangsa Indonesia. There is no *bangsa* Sumatera Timur. We are part of a single bangsa with a single fate.[74]

The destiny of every ethnie within the former colony was to be no more than a *suku*, a tribe.

Indonesia's anti-colonial nationalism, then, has been more territorial than ethnic. To this extent it may seem to have a stronger basis for developing in a civic direction, like some of those in Western Europe and the New World. At moments, in 1945–54 and again in 1998–2000, there did indeed appear to be strong forces trying to push it in that direction. On the positive side, the core culture defined by nationalism seemed to be inherently plural in religion, culture and ethnicity, in a way analogous to that of India, if not Western Europe. As one lays out these broad comparative options, however, the need seems inescapable for a third type which we might call revolutionary or post-revolutionary nationalism, inviting comparisons with the Soviet Union, Yugoslavia and China rather than India. Like the revolutions in those systems, Indonesia's revolution of 1945–50 sought to consolidate its national project through a mixture of force, a heroic revolutionary myth which invalidated the distinct pre-revolutionary histories of ethnies and regions, and a heavy central direction of education.

This type of revolutionary nationalism seems at least as likely to develop or unravel in the direction of ethnic, as of civic, nationalism. Although some of the founding fathers of Indonesia did talk as if the collectivity was about citizenship, democracy and a constitution, the emphasis on uniqueness was more popular, notably with Sukarno. Many Indonesians, in practice, had difficulty acknowledging that *bangsa Indonesia* could include the Chinese, and still more those of European descent (though citizenship was widely offered to such people in the 1950s). A half-century after its revolution, Indonesia offers a bewildering variety of both ethnic and civic forces which have surfaced since the demise of Suharto's imposed post-revolutionary order.

Melayu as Ideology

Since Brunei's declaration of independence in 1984 as "forever a Malay Islamic monarchy", Malayness has been a more prominent feature of that country than is true for either of its neighbours, despite appearing to have relatively shallow roots there. In the literature of the sixteenth century, Brunei people were described by their place of origin or as Luzons, because of their reputed closeness to the people with whom they traded in Manila Bay. With Islam, Brunei undoubtedly became part of the high culture of Malay letters, though not playing as large a part in it as Aceh, Palembang, Johor, Patani or Makassar. Although the tradition of Brunei rulers includes early contact with Johor, sometimes involving marriage to a Johor princess, Brunei did not seek to play a role in the conflicts among rulers who claimed descent from Melaka. Brunei seemed distinctive enough to be the centre of its own world, through its pluralistic Borneo populations, its unique and in some respects archaic form of spoken Malay, and its links with China and the Philippines as well as the Malay world.

It is not clear when the Islamic elite of Brunei began to see themselves as 'Melayu', but the nineteenth-century English habit of wanting to classify peoples by race or nation rather than place seems likely to have had something to do with it. English writers such as Hugh Low, Henry Keppel and James Brooke use the phrase "Brunei Malays", to distinguish the Muslim population of the capital and the court from other peoples of the interior. Once the British Residency was established in 1906, British habits of counting and classifying enjoyed greater influence. 'Malays' were counted as 54 per cent of the population at the 1921 Census, 49 per cent in 1931, 41 per cent in 1947, 54 per cent in 1960 and 66 per cent in 1971.[75] The reasons for this variation were in part the rapid rise in the Chinese population by immigration in the period 1921–60, and some immigration of Malay population thereafter. The biggest factor, however, seems to have been changes in classification.

While the early censuses under British control found ever more ethnic groups distinct from Malays in the strict sense, the 1959 Constitution that returned self-government to the sultan insisted that the major groups held to be indigenous (Malay, Kedayan, Bisayah, Dusun, and so on) were all 'Malay' in a legal sense. Subsequent censuses took this declaration literally.

The report of the 1971 Census appears to have had different authors for its English and Malay sections, at least as regards ethnic divisions. In English, the report states that the Malay group in the census "consisted of the Malays, Kedayans Bisayah, Dusuns and Muruts. Also included were those who called themselves *orang Brunei*, Belait, Tutong." It goes on to explain that this was "to standardise the term 'Malay' as applied here with the term 'of the Malay race' as applied in the Brunei nationality Enactment 1961". The former ease of classifying people according to their place of origin, the English report noted, had tended to break down with urbanisation, population movement and intermarriage, so that "there are now little differences between the various groups".[76] The Malay text, while briefer on these matters, added that:

> Melayu means the grouping of indigenous groups of the Melayu race. It contains Malays, Bruneis, Totong, Belait, Kedayan, Dusun, Bisayah and Murut. This division of communities is to avoid the mistakes found in the 1960 census, since many indigenous communities acknowledged themselves Malay because they follow the Islamic religion.[77]

A *titah* (order) of His Majesty in 1984 already referred to the concept of *Melayu Islam Beraja* (MIB: Malay, Muslim, Royal Subject), and it has been particularly emphasised since 1990. In that year, the Academy of Brunei Studies (*Akademi Pengajian Brunei*) was established at the University, and undertook responsibility for teaching the obligatory undergraduate course in MIB. MIB has subsequently been repeatedly enunciated as part of the official philosophy of the state, around which a national identity in the fashion of Anderson's 'official nationalism' might be built.

Of the three elements in this trinity, 'Melayu' is the most interesting, since it emphasises not Brunei's national uniqueness or its Bornean heritage, but its membership in a supranational culture whose centre might appear to be elsewhere. In practice, the limited formulations of Malayness suggest that it is seen as consolidating existing traditions rather than seeking some external standard. "Melayu in MIB means the consolidation of inherited Malay values, customs and culture as the dominant cultural heritage in national culture."[78] It does however establish as normative a standard Malay essentially the same as that in Malaysia, and some aspects of Malay high culture at the expense of local tradition. More notably it seeks either to marginalise or incorporate minorities. "Clearly, this state is not a multi-racial or multi-religious state. This fact does not arise from any spirit of anti-non-Malay or anti-non-Muslim, but what has to be stressed is that this state is the property of Malay Muslims."[79]

Brunei's experiment with Malayness as a core identity is the youngest of the three examples discussed, and it is much too early to assess what effects this move may have on popular consciousness and the sense of identity in the state in the long term. Despite some of the rhetoric of its apologists, MIB seems not intended as the basis of a future ethnic nationalism. It is not sufficiently distinctive from its neighbours for that purpose. As long as the monarchy remains the central political fact of Brunei, nationalism of any but a contrived 'official' sort will be viewed with suspicion.

'Malay Identity': Modernity, Invented Tradition and Forms of Knowledge

ADRIAN VICKERS*

In 1858, the police were established in Iskandar Puteri, i.e. the present Johor; that was on 3rd October, 1858, and I was sent to work as a clerk in Iskandar Puteri. At that time the Hon. Raja Kecik Ahmad was administering there. Not only was I the clerk handling all the correspondence and answering letters to the government in Teluk Belanga; all the work connected with the court and the police was my responsibility alone: writing out all the plaints, and writing down what was said by the persons who brought suits before the court, in the place where legal proceedings were held. I was also charged with supervising the farmers of the opium and arrack revenues, and with issuing summons, warrants and river passes ....[1]

Summarising his life, Mohammed Saleh bin Perang describes the way Malay rulers took on the forms of British bureaucratic structure. He then goes on to discuss a war in which he was sent on behalf of the Sultan to put down rebels in the Ulu Muar area who supported the traditional claimant to the local throne, against the moves by the British and sympathetic officials who were attempting to merge the area with Johor. The Johor forces were successful, and the merger was effected.

On 24th May, 1885, His Highness set off for London, accompanied by the Hon. Engku Mohammed Khalid, Encik Abdul Rahman bin Andak ... Encik Abdullah bin Tahir, an attendant named Firus, a maidservant and a cook. During His Highness's absence in London, I continued my surveying work without a break. In 1886, His Highness returned from London, having obtained the title 'Sultan of Johor', and news of this title was proclaimed in Johor Baru on 13th February....[2]

No longer, as in the days of Sultan Agung of Mataram, did one send an emissary to the Caliph of Baghdad to receive the Islamic title of Sultan. Rule came through the British, and this archetypical new Malay Sultan was a man of Bugis descent who did not have the genealogical credentials emphasised by other rulers of the Malay Peninsula. British hegemony, in this case, was partly constituted through a recognition of mutual interests, a recognition which could be used to short-circuit previously existing modes of legitimacy. But did that leave anything of the 'Malay' in the new version of tradition?

Such glimpses of a constructed 'Malayness', set against the ethnic diversity of the Malaysian states, establish tradition as the basis of a mode of modernity. Does this mean necessarily that 'Malayness' is essentially colonial? What can we know of its genealogy? Can that genealogy provide alternative models or representations of nations and states?

I survey here some of the recent discussions of colonial constructions of identity, and suggest how the study of literary texts allows us to view a more complex and ambiguous 'Malay' identity. Such an identity has been defined in different ways with reference to literature, geography and language, and was always interacting with the European presence in the region, but at the same time it was formed in conjunction with other indigenous categories that we might term 'ethnic'. This is not a matter of a colonial 'invented tradition', but a local construction onto which colonial forms of hegemony were imposed.

Despite the way recent analyses have drawn attention to local or 'native' agency in the formation of colonial discourse, the geographic separations and entities created in the processes of colonisation are still accepted as the basic terms for analysis. I seek to show how those separations occurred in terms of forms of knowledge, concentrating on the separation of 'Malay' and 'Javanese' revealed in recent studies. The isolation of those terms for analysis runs against the grain of indigenous discursive fields. That is to say, the colonial reconstitution of 'Malay' as a field of knowledge and a point of identity cannot be separated from the reconstitution of the term 'Java'. Both may be part of invented traditions in Malaysia and Indonesia, but they were not invented from nothing.

I examine older forms of discursive practice through the term 'Pasisir' or 'Coastal'. Such a term can be understood with reference to the concept of 'scale of forms', which comes from Ronald Inden's use of Collingwood's phenomenology. As Inden notes, the concept is similar to Foucault's 'discursive formation', but involves a notion of complex agency that is not directly presented in Foucault's studies.[3] It is preferable to use the notion of a 'scale of forms' rather than talking about Southeast Asian versions of 'civilisation' or 'culture', not least because these latter terms are inseparable from colonising discourses.[4] The *Pasisir* scale of forms has been constitutive of the 'Malay' in terms of language, literature and space. In the processes of colonisation, such a scale of forms is displaced by localisations of the European terms 'traditional' and 'modern'. Displaced but not quite erased, since much of the *Pasisir* coexists with the later discourses. To discuss the terms that come out of a colonial context in a way that assumes the extinction of all other forms is to deny the possibilities of difference. My explication of the '*Pasisir*' opens up the possibilities for examining different modes of knowledge and forms of history.

Colonial and Post-colonial Malay Identity

Is Malay identity 'Malay'? Could it be colonial, or even Javanese? The ruling class of the nation state of Malaysia maintains a hegemonic Malay identity based on the difference between supposedly indigenous Islamic Malays and 'outsiders', namely Chinese and Indians. This identity is regarded as a natural ethnic base of the state.

'Malay' in practise is a fraught term. Many of these core 'Malays' are descended either from Malays from outside the Malay peninsula, or from Bugis and Minangkabau who came from what is now Indonesia. In addition, some of those categorised as 'Malays' belong to non-Muslim groups who do not see themselves in the same ethnic terms. Malay is meant to be coterminous with *bumiputera*, which in its literal meaning of 'sons of the soil' denotes the indigenous status of the Malays, making others non-indigenous. In colonial times, the term was 'native'.

Kessler has dealt extensively with the processes of inventing this Malay identity, particularly in relation to Islam, with which it is meant to be synonymous, just as 'Thai' and 'Buddhist' are in Siam.[5] As Loh Kok Wah shows, this process is particularly problematic for the indigenous peoples of Sarawak and Sabah who fit into the broad anthropological grouping 'Dayak', many of whom practice Christianity or indigenous religions.[6] A similar problem exists for the Aboriginal peoples of the Malay Peninsula, whose designation *orang asli* or 'Original Peoples' makes the Malay non-autochthonous. Legally the Malaysian state has had to balance an absolute term, 'race', against a contingent type of definition, for one might be 'Malay/*bumiputera*' in opposition to 'Chinese', but 'Dayak' in relation to the 'Malay' in Sabah politics.

In what must be the supreme irony of Prime Minister Mahathir's long anti-Western stance in international affairs, the Malaysian constitution is based on the ultimate colonial discursive device, 'race'. It was 'race' that organised populations and reasserted the hegemonic position of Westerners, and was elided into notions of 'civilisation' and 'culture' in the process. In

Malaysia, the categories of 'Malay', 'Chinese', 'Indian' and 'Eurasian' are used in censuses and in legislation as the taken-for-granted basis of the nation state. The difference between 'inside' Malays and 'outside' Chinese and Indians has its origins in colonial attitudes and policies. The colonial invention of Malay tradition served an important legitimating function in the classic divide-and-rule scheme of British expansion, and post-colonial elaborations likewise serve important legitimating functions for political leaders of the so-called Malay community. It is one of many colonial 'invented traditions' passed on to and elaborated by the post-colonial world. Yet the colonial and pre-colonial cultural interactions between Malays and British, particularly outside the the Johor-Riau zone, the central region of Malay culture, should not simply be seen as active British interventions in the invention of a passive Malay culture.

As the opening quotation shows, the colonial regime worked with specific definitions of what it meant to be Malay in relation to a tradition that the colonial authorities claimed to know. It was the Malay elite who fitted this tradition, and who worked out their own position in relation to the British. Students of Harry Benda such as Heather Sutherland[7] and Onghokham[8] have shown this to be a problem of colonialism and collaboration: a dialectical relation of traditional elites to colonial administrators.

It is significant that only now has the 'new man' of the Malaysian state, Dr Mahathir, overturned the constitutional guarantees that maintained this image of the rulers as all that is traditionally Malay. Significant too is the way the Malay peasantry still labours under the obverse of this image of tradition. As Donald Nonini notes in his study of peasantry and resistance, if you were 'Malay' and not an aristocrat, you were consigned to the rice fields, and not allowed to venture from there to become involved in any kinds of enterprise.[9] Nonini demonstrates that this policy particularly served the interests of British capitalists in times of crisis. But more importantly, he elaborates on the work of Malcolm Caldwell, James C. Scott and others to show that the peasants did not take this lying down. There is now a considerable body of literature on subaltern resistance to colonial power, to which Nonini contributes, but this literature depends on a dichotomous idea of power: colonial rulers versus indigenous ruled. The dichotomy is only slightly modified by including the indigenous ruling class amongst the oppressors of the peasantry. But what happens if you take Foucault's micro-politics and apply it to colonial relations? What of subaltern collaboration, for example? Where might that fit a more nuanced picture of class and gender power relations?

Subaltern power relations belong to questions of hegemony. The colonial invention of Malay identity was negotiated between a native ruling group and a European group, but it involved the co-option and consent of people on various levels, from the village heads who became agents of imperial rule to the ethnic groups like the Ambonese and Menadonese in the Dutch Indies who became the backbone of colonial armies.

Post-colonial Critiques and Colonial Invented Traditions

Invented traditions have to be considered as achieving forms of consent because they entrench groups in power and naturalise or dehistoricise sets of historical relations, something they can accomplish because they are inaugurated alongside discourses of the modern. Hobsbawm and Ranger's study of 'Invented Traditions', which provided the starting point for studies of colonial traditions, makes this clear.[10] The study coincided with the reconsideration of another discourse of the modern, Benedict Anderson's now classic study of nationalism, *Imagined Communities*.[11] However, the studies of Southeast Asia that have followed on from these leads have accepted the nation as the unit of study. The nation is seen as describing the limits of the cultures of modernity. The Andersonian view reinforces such parameters because it is built around the idea of colonialism forming a radical break which introduces modernity to a hitherto un-modern Southeast Asia.

In the Anderson mode is John Pemberton's study of constructions of 'Java' in and around Solo.[12] A crude statement of his argument might be that the constructed (Solonese) Javanese tradition that legitimates the New Order government of President Suharto is a hegemonic colonial construct, that is, a cultural form that subsumes or appropriates alternative cultural modes of action. The similarities with Kessler's arguments about Malaysia are obvious, and many elements of Pemberton's argument are found in earlier studies of Java. For example, Jennifer Lindsay's 1985 dissertation had long before developed the arguments about the colonial construction of Javanese culture and its transference into the New Order regime,[13] just as Supomo had examined the politics of reconstructing ancient Majapahit.[14]

Because Pemberton has under-theorised his notion of New Order hegemony, he falls back on 'New Order' as an essentialised explanatory key to different kinds of changes in ceremonial action and representation. The major agents of his account are the Dutch and the New Order leadership. Pemberton passes over without examination forms of modernity that could have provided alternatives to the New Order. The Communist Party of

Indonesia (PKI) had, prior to 1965, made Solo a site of a radical socialist modernity, but in Pemberton's narrative, this is passed over to emphasise the continuity between Dutch and New Order constructions of culture. Forms of Islamic modernity, or the 1990s clashes between Ikatan Cendekiawan Muslim Indonesia (ICMI) technocratic modernities and Suhartoist mystical invented traditions do not intrude into the elegant narrative. We catch glimpses of resistance in the refusals of modernity by rural mystics, but such forms of agency are denied to urbanised Javanese, who are judged as passive acceptors of the New Order, for example in their enthusiasm for the kitschy *Taman Mini* theme park.[15]

Pemberton's interpretations of the inception of the process of recreating 'Java' trace it back to the founding of Kartasura. M. C. Ricklefs shows in his book on Kartasura between 1677–1726 just how a mutual dependence based on warfare, economic appropriation and cultural opposition grew up between the VOC and the Central Javanese courts. This mutual dependence relegated the coastal courts to the cultural periphery, particularly as those such as Cirebon were directly placed under Dutch 'protection' and others were completely wiped out. As Ricklefs notes, the period of interaction was one in which, "Cultural identities appear to have drawn even further apart...there may have been a growing sense of Javaneseness as a consequence of the foreign interventions in Java in this period". The sense of the Dutch as Java's cultural defining 'Other' comes at a number of key points, particularly where one of the major *babad* texts describes Amangkurat II as dressing up to resemble the Dutch Governor General. Ricklefs' evidence shows mutable identities changing in relation to other points of reference, of which 'Dutch' (or *Kompeni*) was one.[16] This Javanese 'Othering' of the Dutch, a kind of Occidentalism, is a dimension that is played down by Pemberton.

An alternative to the state-centred or regime-centred projects of Anderson and Pemberton can be found in constructions of identity that either cut across present-day national boundaries, or instances where Europeans colonisers are not the principal agents of such construction. The studies of French fantasies of 'Indo-china' by Norindr and of the mapping of Thailand by Thongchai respectively demonstrate this.[17] Norindr elucidates the nature of continuing French attempts to impose a geographical orientalist fantasy over Cambodia, Laos and Vietnam, from the Colonial Exhibition of 1931 to the film *Indochine*. The continuation of the fantasy into post-colonial times helps to explain why the current French regime's manipulations of cultural and economic aid in the region have been accepted at home, even if the recipients of that aid strongly resist being cast as

'Francophone'. It is only unfortunate that Norindr does not refer to the earlier actions of mainland Southeast Asians in resisting or reconstituting these French fantasies, actions documented by writers such as Geoffrey Gunn, David Chandler and David Marr.

Thongchai's deconstruction of nationalist representations of Thailand as a geographic entity implicates British and French imperial ambitions, but he shows that the reconstitution of earlier modes of representation represents a radical discontinuity that the use of 'colonialism' as a heuristic device cannot explain. The violence, physical and epistemological, of colonialism is undeniable, but was it a homogenous process that explains all aspects of present-day Southeast Asian nations? What is at stake in Thailand is the replacement of a form of geographical knowledge based on Buddhist principles with modern forms of mapping that are distinctively nationalist. Buddhism did not disappear in the process, it was transformed in particular ways. In the complex transformation, Westerners were often used by the Thai ruling class: these Westerners, like the photographers and advisors who worked under independent Indian rulers or Chinese warlords, or the artists and musicians who worked in Bali, were instruments of local power. To understand the version of Thai modernity created out of this process, and why it was effective in hegemonic terms, we have to know something of the earlier knowledge it transformed.

The Andersonian approach presents such transformations as complete discontinuities, with colonialism the causal factor even when colonials are not the principals. A number of writers from the Subaltern Studies Group have raised other suspicions which can be applied to this fundamentally Weberian approach. Chakrabarty, for example, cites discourses of the modern in Bengal.[18] Participants in nationalist movements base their claims to authority on their command of this modernity, which explains the emergence of post-colonial movements of the 1940s to 1960s that in the Indonesian case were much more radically 'modern' in their claims than the later New Order regime owing to their emphasis on the secular as the basis of a nation. Both Mahathir and Suharto took their own paths away from this form of secular nationalism. While inferring that there is only one 'nationalist' project of modernity, Chakrabarty quite rightly notes that it cannot 'contain' difference.[19]

Refusing to use the word 'ideology', Chakrabarty instead says "the modern, no doubt, is a myth in that it naturalizes history. This is 'ideology' in the sense Gramsci uses when talking about hegemony as a kind of achieved consent."[20] In most colonial contexts, consent is achieved through forms of coercion that include what Gayatri Spivak has called 'epistemic violence'.

But just as there is no essence of the modern, there is no essence of colonialism. It is a series of related practices of domination, related not only through economic connections but also because the personnel of different forms of colonial rule moved between colonies. These colonial personnel and the policy makers and planners of the European and American metropolises were constantly comparing and learning from each other.[21]

Chakrabarty's project "to attempt to write difference into the history of our modernity" does not deny that there may be something other than the 'modern' or 'the traditional'.[22] There may be categories that disturb the dichotomy, making modernity something other than nationalist, and tradition something other than co-opted rituals.

So what kinds of historical rupture are we talking about in the Southeast Asian case? 'Rupture' should not be a taken-for-granted category, as if all traces of local knowledge have been killed off, as if power were bipolar rulers oppressing the ruled. Foucault's uses of rupture, for example in *The Order of Things*, do not assume such totalising effects. Nor do his ideas of power, explicated in the first volume of his *History of Sexuality* assume dichotomies in operation. Stoler's nuanced readings of the Dutch in the Indies illustrate the complexities.[23]

With this in mind we can return to Thongchai's position, which is in turn comparable to Sumarsam's study of gamelan. Sumarsarn contextualises the Javanese localisation of Western modes of understanding music against earlier Javanese modes of localisation. Nineteenth-century transformations of gamelan, he argues, are multi-agentive, not just the product of Dutch colonial officials dominating Javanese aristocrats.[24] Recent works on the reconstitution of the 'Malay' further illuminate this multi-agentive approach, demonstrating the manipulation of cultural categories and the operation of hybrid forms of culture which provide alternatives to colonial and national constructions of identity.

Milner's study of the 'invention' of Malay politics is more than a study of 'invented tradition',[25] and he is thus more prepared to cast Malays as agents manipulating British forms of education and knowledge than is Pemberton writing of the Javanese *vis-à-vis* the Dutch. The literary and linguistic studies produced by British colonial administrators created circumstances in which a new 'Malay' political discourse could be constituted. Milner documents the way in which this political discourse constituted the particular kinds of Malay 'modernity'—liberal, aristocratic and Islamic—that have constituted post-colonial Malaysian politics.

Up until the late nineteenth century 'Malay' was a fluid category both for those who became 'Malays' and for Europeans. It was a category frequently combined with or used alternately with 'Javanese'. These two identities were terms in a complex of elements used to define the *Pasisir* or coastal world of Southeast Asia. Their valencies as meanings, however, depended as much on their usage by Europeans as on their relationships with each other. I wish to argue that 'Malay', like 'Javanese', has no essence, and particularly no national essence. 'Malay' is a hybrid identity formed by combinations of antipathies and interchanges predating the one-way street view of late nineteenth-century colonialism.

Using Literature to Question Colonial Authority

Two important studies of Malay texts from the so-called periphery of the Malay world demand that the interactions between Malays, Europeans and non-Malays be looked at again in terms of incorporating European and other 'outside' elements into the genealogy of Malay writing and space and language. Henk Maier's *In the Center of Authority*[26] and Jane Drakard's *A Malay Frontier*, with its companion volume, an edition of two texts under the tide *Sejarah Raja-Raja Barus*,[27] have completed a move in Malay studies signalled by Amin Sweeney in his *A Full Hearing*.[28] This is a move away from the kind of nineteenth-century literary history that upbraided Malay literature for not fitting into the schema used to evaluate European literatures, social sciences and sciences, and towards an understanding of literature as a series of texts implicated in a complex set of historical and social processes. In this re-examination of texts, important questions are raised about the 'indigenous' in the map of the Malay, and the problematic nature of a Malaysian nationalism that overlaps with some of the bases of Indonesian nationalism.

As Maier argues, the genealogy of the 'Malay' has had to be retrospectively redrawn, working back from the present-day needs of Malaysia via the colonial formation of the modern nation-state of Malaysia. Modern Malay culture in this sense has to be seen through the colonial authorisation of Malay literature, that is through the British and Dutch, and even Portuguese and Spanish, roles in the shaping of the Malay world. Maier's and Drakard's examples from the edges of what is now regarded as the 'core' Malay zone display this process of ongoing historical formation of the 'Malay' at work from two sides, Maier from the colonial side through an examination of the processes of text selection and treatment, Drakard from the Malay side through interrogations of the texts of the once important pepper state of Barus. Their work links up with a plethora of new translations, analyses and editions of texts that are changing the picture of Malay literature and its relationship to culture, showing them to have existed more outside what is now Malaysia than inside.

The different levels of the hybrid nature of the Malayness displayed by Saleh bin Perang and Sultan Abu Bakar are carefully surveyed by Maier. Part of his intention, signalled in the title of the book, is to move attention to 'the centre of authority' in Malay literature. He shows that this 'centre' is not the literary area of Riau-Lingga-Johor as it is presented in European accounts, but the colonial processes by which the British decided what was properly 'Malay', and what was peripheral. These British (and Dutch) processes elevated that area to its present status, just as Dutch colonial scholarship made the language of the central Javanese courts paradigmatically Javanese. Maier's book has its own layers of irony, being produced by a Leiden professor and published by Cornell University, a movement between centres of authority in the study of the cultures of Indonesia and Malaysia.

Maier looks at how one Malay text, *Hikayat Merong Mahawangsa*— the so-called history of Kedah, has been read at different times and in different places. This is a study of 'fragments of reading', as he termed it in the original Leiden dissertation (1985) on which the book is based. But readings are not innocent, they are implicated in processes of power, as Maier shows. Kedah itself was an early stake in the power struggle between the British and the rulers of Siam for control of the region that now forms the north of Malaysia and the south of Thailand. Following Foucault, Maier looks not just at the grand plays of power, the movements of colonial ideology by which Kedah was originally claimed, but at the micropolitics of power. Discourses on this text established not only which Malay voices were heard in defining the Malay culture of this British colony, but which British voices were authorised to speak in the processes. Low, the Resident of Penang who had translated the *Hikayat*, was not a successful figure. One of the things he was unsuccessful at was translating the text into the discourse of the Scottish Enlightenment that shaped British colonial thought in the first half of the nineteenth century.

Compared to 'core' works such as the *Sejarah Melayu,* the text itself had a certain recalcitrant quality in it, which made it 'difficult' to present as a work of 'reality'. Equally important to the processes of textual edition Maier describes were the processes by which other colonial figures, notably Anderson, were able to establish more dominant voices of authority in their 'factual' descriptions of the Malay world.

In constructing their own narratives of Malay history, Maier shows, the British scholar-conquerors constructed their power, and it was left to the late nineteenth- and early twentieth-century scholar-administrators such as Winstedt and Wilkinson to turn the text into a piece of printed 'literature', of no value for knowledge of the world, and only existing as a piece of fable, or at best "an assemblage of popular recollections of historical events".[29] So the 'evolutionary positivist' quest for a provable reality was brought to bear on the text, and it was found wanting in terms of its 'reliability'. It is no coincidence that this same problem of 'reliability' still persists in what Maier calls 'Malayistics'. His colleague and sometime collaborator Gijs Koster, for example, was involved in a debate with the late Cyril Skinner, who wanted to argue for historical reality in another Kedah text, the *Syair Sultan Maulana,* against what he called the "'literary' analyses of the Dutch structuralist Koster".[30] The maintenance of the dichotomy of 'literature' and 'history' remains one of the most potent of the positivist legacies, dominating the majority of works in the field. The work of Maier, Drakard and others who dispute the dichotomy, is part of a radically different view of the relationship of formal and historical processes.

Since Maier's book began its life as a dissertation, the number of studies on what is generally called traditional Malay literature has increased enormously. It is these studies that open up the problematic sites of the 'Malay'. Many of the key texts of the Malay tradition are now available in printed transcription, largely through the work of the Dewan Bahasa dan Pustaka, one of the latest examples being A. Samad Ahmad's edition of the important *Hikayat Amir Hamzah.*[31] Either alongside such editions, or as separate works, have come analyses that identify themselves either as generally literary or explicitly structuralist, for example Rattiya Saleh's and Abdul Rahman Kaeh's studies of Malay Panji texts in relation to Thai and Javanese narratives respectively.[32] Significantly, the latter of these two studies was carried out as a Ph.D. thesis at the Institut Keguruan dan Pendidikan Malang in Indonesia, and acknowledges the importance of Indonesian scholars such as Achadiati Ikram as well as Western scholars such as Teeuw and Robson, in the development of Malayistics. Likewise the important study by Siti Chamamah Soeratno, who looks at the *Hikayat Iskandar Zulkarnain* in terms of its structure and reception, acknowledges the importance of the work of her supervisor, Teeuw, but also of two of the other key Indonesian figures in the study of traditional Malay literature, Sid Baroroh Baried and Sulastin Sutrisno.[33]

The issue of what is 'Malay' in literature becomes more complex in relationship to attempts to find what is 'modern' in Malay literature. Monique Zaini-Lajoubert, in a study of the early nineteenth-century author Abdullah bin Muhammad al-Misri, author of *Hikayat Mareskalek, Cerita*

Siam and *Hikayat Tanah Bali,* shows that the descent of modern Malay literature from Abdullah bin Abdul Kadir Munsyi in Singapore, a protagonist in Milner's study, did not follow a single line.[34] The Dutch East Indies had its own ambiguous characters contemporary with Abdullah, among them al-Misri, a Malay of Arab origins, born in Palembang, with family in Kedah and Pontianak, whose sometime employer was the Arab trader Sayyid Hassan bin Umar al-Habsyi, an intermediary for the Dutch in their contacts with independent parts of Southeast Asia.

Al-Misri's travel texts, describing his journeys to Siam and Bali, belong within the genre of travel writing that is a recognised part of Islamic historiography. In Islamic terms they were old, but they were new to the Southeast Asian world when he and Munsyi Abdullah produced them in Malay. Al-Misri's various versions of *Hikayat Mareskalek* are particularly important, for it provides a new form of commentary on the colonial world. It is a history of the rule of that agent of modernity, Marshal Daendals, the product of the Enlightenment and the Napoleonic era, but a history heavily laced with quotations from the Qur'an, full of marvellous contestations between the Marshall's and the kings of Java and illustrations of Daendals' own grand claims to Javanese-style kingship.

'Malayness' seems almost peripheral to these texts. Its hybrid nature is revealed by the double concerns of *Hikayat Mareskalek* with the European presence and with Java. The Malay discourse is displayed as being formed by Javanese spiritualism, Islam with an Arabic reference, and a range of positions that could be adopted with reference to the Dutch and British. 'Malayness' is here shown to be the product of all that is outside what is now regarded as 'Malay'; that is, the writer continually shows the impossibility of an autochthonous Malay identity, or of a 'Malayness' indigenous to the Malay Peninsula.

As if to illustrate the pervasiveness of the Orientalism criticised by Maier, the institution where Maier worked published a study of Malay literature by V. I. Braginsky.[35] His comparisons of *syair* and *hikayat* draw on the Russian tradition of Structuralist analysis, but this study, like the demonstration of the intertwining of Sufi mysticism and ideas of beauty in the second half of the book, is written as if the works were produced in a historical vacuum. Braginsky does this by passing off Malay literature as 'medieval', produced before the Portuguese, Dutch and British intrusions into the region, thus ignoring the ongoing production and performance of such literature in the Malay world.

The Malay 'traditional' literature and language taught in the British school system was a literature that had been appropriated by the British scholar administrators. As a reaction, modernising Malays turned against their own traditions in these boring and frozen forms that the British presented, and attempted to contest the British on their own terms.

Questions of Agency

As with British discourse on India, or Dutch discourse on Java, Malaya was constructed by the agents of colonialism in terms of essences and traditions that were by definition inferior to those of Europe. Discursive similarities are no coincidence, since British colonial policy and administration were two aspects of what Inden calls a "complex agent".[36] This is not a unified or unitary body, but a discursively constituted set of overlapping entities with common relationships that are constantly changing. Thus within a complex agent one can find opposing tendencies and differences in kind. Sets of complex agents, such as those found in colonial administrations and European colonial societies, do not constitute a machine-like system so much as what Collingwood calls a 'scale of forms', where overlapping entities are involved in a dialectic interaction tending towards a form of agreement.[37] Only by this complex method of definition, Inden argues, can one talk about historical processes without falling back on notions of a constitutive essence, a concept that is implied in the unitary metaphors by which 'systems' are described. In using Collingwood's terms, Inden's language is consistent with that of Deleuze and Guattari, whose *Mille Plateaux* maps ways of talking about processes of difference, differentiation and multiplicity that may be opposed to totalising discourses.[38]

The difficulties with using these concepts are legion. Inden's brilliant deconstruction of discourses on India and caste finishes with a more positive project: to restore agency to pre-colonial Indian 'scales of forms' by reconstructing their discourses. The danger here is that this could be read as a 'true' Indian discourse opposed to the 'false' discourse of the West. Inden does not talk about Indian roles in colonial discourse to the same degree as Maier. He gives examples of a few Indians who are part of the essentialising process that he criticises, but without displaying the mechanisms through which they became caught up in the process. Further, his book contains no mention of the school of Indian and Western scholars that has most heavily attacked Orientalist and colonialist discourse, the Subaltern Studies group. By not engaging with them, he leaves his espousal of pre-colonial discourse as an opposite to the essentialising discourses of the West, with no inherent relationship, dialectical or otherwise, with present-day critical discourses.

Maier does something different. He too ends with the positive: a set of rhetorical possibilities for 'reading' the *Hikayat Merong Mahawangsa*. But to reach these readings he works through the ways in which Malay readers have had the nature of their reading processes changed. He explores what he calls "the tradition of text production, a 'tradition' broken by modernity in the form of English education".[39] The distinction is too simple, but what he is talking about is the way the text moved from being a rhetorical performance to being an object to be discarded. It was made into an object by being printed, but the physical fact of printing was done on the initiative of "tuan R. J. Wilkinson, Esquire, Acting Inspector of Schools".[40] It was a part of education, part of the making of modern Malays.

Maier begins his own reading of the *Hikayat* on the other side of the colonial divide. Before he posits his possibilities for understanding the text, he finishes his chapter on the printing with a discussion of the analysis of the *Hikayat* by Ali Ahmad. This is a point at which Malay readers have returned to texts such as the *Hikayat* with a new understanding of the old, one based on the multiple positions established towards "Westernisation of 'culture'" that Milner discusses.[41]

In the terms of Maier's critique of the British genealogy of the study of Malay literature, the rejection of Westernisation is a redemption of the Malay. Maier constructs a kind of historical movement from tradition to Western disruption to a modernity that began poorly but has been redeemed by a return to a Malay understanding of Malay culture. The redemption is achieved through Maier's kind of Western self-doubt represented in the shattering of confident authority. He finishes with open questions, not answers. Yet is this narrative complete? If it were simply a matter of the printed versions of texts now entering a revitalised national culture, primarily (as some of the Malaysian intellectuals cited by Maier argue) as the basis for a modern literature, this would be unproblematic. However, at several steps the path becomes rather muddy or overgrown: not all those engaged in the analysis of Malay literature are Malaysians; the politics of being Malay are never straightforward, modernity and modernism in the Malay world are older than Maier's narrative would allow, and the more 'Malayness' is defined the more elusive it becomes. In the remainder of this chapter, I want to demonstrate these points with particular reference to the problem of an endlessly receding origin of Malay 'culture'.

Rather than going forward into the late nineteenth and early twentieth centuries, as Milner has, I wish to turn back to earlier moments in the genealogy of the term 'Malay' in order to scrutinise its wider regional base.

The literary examples cited above cut across Malaysia and Indonesia, making them problematic as natural geographical entities to define the 'Malay' world. But attempts to find a space for 'Malay' as an ethnic concept mean that other sites of constitution need to be examined.

Defining the Malay World in Space

'Malaya' for the British was a geographical region, and studies of 'the Malay world' assume some kind of spatial contiguity. An example of nineteenth century constitution of Malay identity outside of the peninsula, in Sri Lanka, illustrates the negotiations of ethnic definition that went on in the colonial context. The Sri Lankan 'Malays' have been the subject of a number of studies by B. A. Hussainmiya, including his *Orang Rejimen,* the name given to the 'Malays of the Ceylon Rifle Regiment'.[42]

Hussainmiya is principally concerned with the designation of the 'Malay' community as soldiers and police for the British. Having been at the receiving end of the Malays' weapons, he argues, the British decided to make use of their bravery and skills. However, he shows other motives also came into the decision, principally anxieties that the Malays were a displaced community, prone to criminality (the recurrent image of a tendency to run amok coming into play here), and that therefore giving them a military role would give them purpose. The colonial tactic of assigning one or two discrete ethnic groups to serve as a military force is a familiar one, although it is somewhat ironic that in order to do this the British then had to increase the number of 'Malays' by bringing others from India and possibly St. Helena, and made them more 'Malay' in the process by inducing others to come from Penang and Melaka. Interestingly Ambonese, the colonial troops of the Dutch, could not be induced to come. Even after the consolidation of the group as a militarised ethnic unit at the end of the eighteenth century, they still took some time to come to terms with the British concept of 'loyalty'. Their existence as a regiment lasted less than a century.[43]

What Hussainmiya offers is a picture of a community in which the formation of the regiment was a central event, leaving a distinct 'before' and 'after'. The 'after' is an image of a very Malay community, terribly impoverished, but proud of its military past. With an eye to using high culture as an indicator of culture in general, he places great emphasis on the literature of the community. Intriguingly this makes him pass over other aspects of the community's arts. He simply reproduces, for example, a tantalising photograph of 'A modern Malay musical group' with two violinists and a tambourine player.

The community produced their own literature in Malay, but also copied and maintained some of the standard 'classics' of Malay literature: *Hikayat Sri Rama, Hikayat Amir Hamzah, Hikayat Muhammad Hanafiyyah, Hikayat Inderaputera, Hikayat Si Miskin* and the Panji tale *Syair Ken Tambuhan* among them. The one note that disturbs this picture of pure 'Malayness' outside the area usually designated as the Malay world is the popularity in the community of a text in Malay called *Hikayat Raden Bagus Gusti,* which is a unique version of the life of Sunan Giri, one of the Wali *Sanga* or founders of Islam on Java.

The *Hikayat Raden Bagus Gusti* draws attention to the problematic nature of the 'before' side of the equation. When the British took over Ceylon, as it was then known, they called the community 'Malays'. To the previous overlords, the Dutch, they were 'Javanese'. One of the main communities of 'Malays' in Colombo lived in the area traditionally known as 'Slave Island', an obvious indicator of the origins of at least some of the community. The Dutch, and the Portuguese before them, brought slaves from what is now Indonesia, and sent others to Ceylon as well, notably political exiles. One list of such exiles, compiled in 1788, reads like a Who's Who of Indonesian aristocracy—the Sultans of Gowa and Tidore, the kings of Kupang and Padang, queens, princes, princesses and nobles from Banten, Tidore, the Mataram kingdoms, Madura, Palembang and Bacan. The Javanese roll-call is an impressive one: Pangeran Adipati (Susuhunan) Amangkurat III (Sunan Mas), Pangeran Purbaya, Arya Mangkunegara, brother of Pakubuwana, and Raden Adipati Natakusuma, key figures in the kingdom of Kartasura. Even Indonesia's great slave-king, Surapati, had two sons there. Some of these were later allowed to return to Java, most were not. Ambonese, Balinese, Bugis and Javanese troops (mostly from Batavia, and most likely all followers of Islam) were the backbone of the Dutch garrison on the island, and they and the exiled aristocrats interacted on various levels with the community of 'Moors' already present on Sri Lanka. Originally the 'Javanese' community was under the Moors, but later a Javanese prince was appointed as its 'captain', while the sons of Batara Gowa Amas Madina II became military leaders.

This 'outside' example of a 'Malay' community whose 'Malayness' resulted from colonial intervention should be kept in mind when re-examining 'Malayness' in Southeast Asia. The Malaysian constitution, as quoted by Hussainmiya, defines a Malay in article 160 (2) as follows: "a Malay is a person who professes the Muslim religion, habitually speaks the Malay language, conforms to Malay (*adat*) custom and is a Malaysian citizen."[44] Once you remove the last element, Malaysian citizenship, the rest becomes problematic. Profession of Islam includes cultural elements that are 'Javanese'; the Malay language used by the Sri Lankan 'Malays'—from Hussainmiya's comments quite different from present-day Malay; and Malay *adat*, which is nebulous in this case. From various photographs, the costumes, *kris* and music of the community seem to be a mixture of Malay and Javanese styles, while there is little available information on what else may constitute the practices of 'custom'.

The geographical and temporal problematics of the 'Malay' are described in different ways in a collection of essays produced in the Leiden SEMAIAN series of studies on Indonesian culture, *Looking in Odd Mirrors*, which features Maier as editor and as the author of a key article.[45] The collection is concerned with 'The Java Sea', or more specifically a Braudellian mentality of the Java Sea region. The book is a conceptual follow up to *Indonesiana*, an introduction to Indonesian culture oriented towards undergraduate teaching and published as the first book of the series.[46] The idea of the 'Java Sea' has a number of alternative dimensions, from weak or loose nationalism to stronger historical concepts. The weak concept can be loosely associated with the Indonesian use of the term *nusantara* as a term for the archipelago, but more specifically to the earlier form of what is now the Indonesian nation-state.

J. J. Ras restates the *nusantara* concept in his paper in the *Odd Mirrors* volume. Taking as his starting point the Round Table Agreement of 1949 that defined the present Indonesian state, he argues that *Nusantara* corresponds historically to Javanese and Malay sphere of influence. These, he argues, were defined by the Javanese and Malay cultural practices that existed prior to the coming of Europeans, and were disturbed by the establishment of the Dutch in particular, who in their port of Batavia took over the role of the Malays.[47] Ras's article is a return to the dual image of the archipelago's glorious ancient past produced by Dutch scholarship and elevated by essentialising Indonesian nationalists into the images of the kingdoms of Srivijaya (and its successor Melaka) and Majapahit. He blurs the distinction between the historical kingdoms of the area and their later images, which were the passive ideas of 'Jawa' and 'Melayu'. Ras to some degree remains within the positivist paradigm deconstructed by Maier.

Ras, like the rest of the contributors to the volume, ignored Supomo's path-breaking essay on the image of Majapahit in Javanese, Malay, and Indonesian writing.[48] Supomo, unlike Ras, is quite clear on the distinction between the nature of the kingdoms, particularly Majapahit, and the image of them created by later historiography. In the context of the present-day Indonesian state, the image of Majapahit is that of the centralised Javanese state militarily holding power over the whole of the archipelago, something which has more to do with the nature of the present regime than the loose forms of alliance, prestige and tribute which allowed the historical Majapahit to maintain contact with a variety of islands. The image of the centralised absolute state was one developed through Dutch contact with the later kingdom of Mataram. It coalesced in a policy by which a Javanese aristocracy claiming Matararn descent was the instrument of colonial rule.

Ras's arguments are contradicted by his own work and by the evidence of the other articles in the book. This is where the strong concept of a historically formed identity comes in. Other essays in the Java Sea book deal with elements of the equation: A. Reid with the economic dimensions, through the example of Sino-Javanese shipping; V. J. H. Houben with the relationship between trade and Java's cultural contact with the rest of the archipelago in the fifteenth, sixteenth and seventeenth centuries; S. O. Robson and W. van der Molen with studies on Malay views of Java and Javanese views of foreignness respectively. Time and time again, as in these two essays, the Panji stories which are common throughout the 'Java Sea' and 'Malay Sea' regions (as Houben and others call them) come up as sources of data or as parts of the process of cultural contact and interaction.

The essay that does most to undermine Ras's 'weak' concept is by Maier, who deals with Malay literature's idea of the *dagang* as trader, traveller, and mystic traveller. Maier describes two aspects of the images of Majapahit and Melaka that are important: first, "Majapahit is a mysterious never-never land ... and not a military power that tries to stretch its tentacles along the coast of the Java sea, across the Java sea, like a demon hidden in the sea"; and second, in the *Hikayat Hang Tuah*, "Malay glory is founded by Java, Malay well-being is dependent on Java, and both are constantly undermined by Java as well".[49] Attempts to identify geographically '*Jawa*' and '*Melayu*' as discrete entities (or even 'the Java Sea' and 'the Melaka Straits') are bound to failure—the two constantly overlap, they need to be seen one or more 'scale of forms'—overlapping and dialectical historical processes of continually defining and redefining collectivities through acts of representation. Likewise, Maier overstates his case by elaborating on the image of Majapahit in Malay literature: Majapahit too can be considered as a 'scale of forms'.

Other dimensions of the Malay side of the equation are presented in an essay that begins with the chauvinism of Malay nationalism expressed during the period of *Konfrontasi* in the early 1960s and works back through the creation of a specific Malaysian Malay identity. This essay, "'Malayness': Confrontation, Innovation and Discourse" by A. C. Milner, forms an important complement to Clive Kessler's study of the uses of Malay tradition in the contemporary Malaysian state in Kahn and Loh's edited collection.[50] Here Milner shows just how 'Malayness' was constructed in the different forms that the concept of a Greater Malay identity, *Melayu Raya*, took in the first half of this century.

As Milner notes, citing an earlier essay by Virginia Matheson,[51] the meaning of 'Melayu', originally referring to kingdoms based in East Sumatra and then Melaka, was transformed into its present form of 'Malay' around the eighteenth or nineteenth century. It was, Milner notes, transformed in reaction to different waves of migration to the Malay Peninsula, and the transformation was influenced by the perceptions of 'outsiders', namely Chinese and Europeans.[52] Milner identifies the specific points at which Malay became more narrowly Malaysian, but glosses over two of the steps along the way to this. The first of these is the specific form of the interaction with European perceptions that provided impetus to the defining of 'Malay'. The second is the nature of the overlapping and hybridising reference to Java (or more precisely, '*Jawa*') in the processes of being Malay. This reference to Java may have existed when Melaka and Majapahit were contemporary kingdoms, and it certainly continued into the nineteenth century. Milner's essay identifies the point at which the 'Malay' breaks from the earlier hybridised Javanese-Malay reference, the time of independence when Ibrahim Yaacob's *Melayu Raya* was superseded by Tunku Abdul Rahman's 'Malaysia'.

'Malay' and 'Java': Examples from Borneo and Sumatra

The way that 'Melayu' is written into 'Jawa', and vice versa, can be construed in relationship to a hybrid scale of forms. In discourse the heartlands of the 'Malay' and the 'Javanese' are Johor-Riau and central Java, but the presence of 'Malay' kingdoms in Borneo and Sumatra is usually explained by their being coastal kingdoms created through trade with other Malay kingdoms and therefore taking on Malay language as the language of commerce, and from the language came cultural influence. These Malay coastal kingdoms exist in contrast to interior spaces defined as 'primitive' or 'tribal' in colonial discourse, and also in such endogenous terms as 'Batak' and 'Dayak'.

J. J. Ras was professor of Javanese at Leiden, but his most influential work concerned a set of Malay texts written on or about Kalimantan, generally known under the title of *Hikayat Banjar*. In this, his 1992 article "Java and the Nusantara",[53] and his various articles, collected under the poetic title *The Shadow of the Ivory Tree*,[54] Ras has demonstrated the close relationship between the *Hikayat Banjar*, the court culture of the coastal

Islamic kingdom of Banjarmasin, and Javanese culture. This collection of essays is full of insights into the links and parallels between the cultures of the archipelago: for example, similarities between Malay and Javanese Panji narratives and Ngaju (Dayak) myths; the formal nature and intentions of major works of Javanese literature; and a revealing structural comparison between the already-mentioned *Hikayat Banjar* and the *Pararaton*, a text written on Bali in 1600. The latter essay reveals the importance of what Ras has achieved, but also shows him to be to some degree limited by his sense of a need to work within existing academic traditions, traditions that his essays dealing with Rassers, Brandes and Djajadiningrat show to be mainly reconstitutive of Leiden as a centre of authority.

As Ras says, the texts with which he deals, "give an insight into the political ideology prevailing at the time of their latest reception".[55] However, Ras's essays are not predominantly concerned with these 'latest receptions'. Even as he provides a wealth of material for such studies, Ras keeps looking back to the times to which the texts refer, rather than their times of writing. Thus the *Pararaton is* consistently called 'Javanese', despite the lack of evidence that the text that we now know through Brandes' edition of Balinese manuscripts ever existed in that form on Java. The Balinese scribes may indeed have employed various Javanese sources in their writing, but they were writing for a newly-created court at Gèlgèl that wanted to establish its continuity with ancient Java. Thus time and time again Ras looks back with the ghost of 'historical reliability' dogging his footsteps. How much more productive to treat these texts and comparisons as part of a set of historical interactions and cultural overlaps, a 'scale of forms' carried out from the seventeenth to the nineteenth century. The Ngaju myths could be seen in terms of the representations Ras uses in his essay on Rassers, one of which includes a 'soul boat' with Dutch and Malay passengers alongside the Ngaju shaman figure.

The main resistance to this approach is found amongst those who, like Ras, want to see a 'pure' Javanese or Malay world prior to the coming of Europeans. Instead, why not see Europeans such as Marshal Daendals as part of the processes by which manifestations of Malay and Javanese culture come into being? This may not suit the priorities of the present Malaysian and Indonesian governments, which proclaim that influences from the outside are inherently negative, staining pure nationalisms that have direct continuities to an ancient past, but those national constructions of the past cannot account for the rise of modern states.

Ras's Ngaju example is important for a number of reasons. The contrast between the inland peoples of Borneo (usually designated as Dayak, although they do not like the term) and the coastal peoples of the island is typical of a contrast found throughout most of Southeast Asia. In Indonesian and Malaysian terms, it is a contrast of inland or *darat* peoples, frequently animist, although now often Christian, and coastal or *pasisir* peoples, most often Islamic and usually designated by the term 'Malay'. There are several aspects of this relationship that deserve closer scrutiny: 'Malay' is a term that covers a multitude of possible identities; the two types were never separate but were constantly interacting; and in some areas the differences between the two were not differences in essential nature, but differences designated by certain signs.

Separating 'inland' and 'coastal' is something Europeans have actively encouraged from the time of their first visits to Southeast Asia. The Spanish and Portuguese separated those with 'chiefs', later to be called 'tribal', from those with kings. The Dutch and English followed, with different classifications and divisions. The eighteenth-century scientific ethnography contains a range of taxonomies, only some of which survived into the hierarchical racial orderings of nineteenth-century Darwinism and colonial regulations. An interesting example of one of these eighteenth century attempts at classification is William Marsden's views of the Rejang people (as analysed by James Boon).[56] Early eighteenth-century Dutch (and German) descriptions of the East Indies, such as those of Rumphius and Valentijn, were part of an encyclopaedic project of sorting out peoples and things through a new kind of scientific gaze, one that left its most enduring legacy in natural science and in the technological advances at which the Dutch excelled.[57] The Encyclopaedias of the French Enlightenment owe a debt to this effort to catalogue and depict the objects and peoples of the New and Old Worlds. Their direct descendants are the British (Irish, Scottish and English) 'Dictionaries' and 'Histories' of the late eighteenth and early nineteenth centuries. In these the science of the Scottish Enlightenment finds its most direct link with the development of a new type of colonialism. From the copious descriptions of Valentijn and the more contemporary accounts of Marsden, that great policy maker and field worker Joseph Banks married science to colonial interests.[58]

For Marsden, writing in 1783, the Rejang represented a prime example of the essentially Sumatran. Other ethnic groups, such as the Batak, were too contradictory to fit into existing scheme. They were both 'civilised' and 'cannibals', like the Maori, a disturbance to the Enlightenment order of historical development in which European civilisation stands as the end point. Sumatran Malays were, in Marsden's view, not proper representatives of anything because they were 'Mahometan', whereas the Rejang were more authentically a type of (noble) 'savage' that could stand opposed to 'civilisation'; they demonstrated the efficacy for European self-understanding of the idea of an opposite society.[59] In Marsden we can see the earlier European categories of 'savage' and 'bestial' peoples become the modern notion of the 'primitive'. And the 'primitive' was a category that nineteenth-century imperialists thought it their duty to safeguard from the deleterious effects of modern Western society. It was the fate of a number of Indonesian societies to be relegated in Dutch policy to the museum-like 'primitive', a category from which many are still trying to escape.

The problematic nature of the 'primitive' label, as well as the links between 'inland' and 'coastal', have been examined recently in different ways, most interestingly through the exhibition "Beyond the Java Sea", which presents the "Malay court cultures of the outer islands of Indonesia alongside those of the inland peoples, and thus breaks down the distinctions between them."[60] The Ngaju example is one of the most direct. If there are similarities between the Panji narratives known and performed in the Banjar court (and which heavily influenced the *Hikayat Banjar*) and Ngaju legends, why does this have to be the result of some ancient process of diffusion of pan-*Nusantara* themes? The hinterland Ngaju were constantly trading with the coastal Banjarese. Coastal shells, beads, gongs and Chinese pottery all went into the interior. Such goods, readily used in interior art, were part of a set of exchanges that involved a relationship of mutual dependence. The trade goods from the interior were the mainstay of coastal wealth, and in order to obtain them interior peoples had to be fashioned into forms of subjecthood by being shown court rituals and dances. In this process objects of trade took on symbolic meanings. By the giving of such 'outside' signs of prestige as the interior peoples found need of, coastal kingdoms entered into dialogues with peoples of the interior. Such goods could include the un-Islamic pigs from Bali given by Muslim Sultans to interior peoples,[61] or rifles that could be used in conflicts, and were readily incorporated into sacred representations such as Ras reproduces in his article on Rassers.[62]

Ras treats Banjar as belonging to the 'Javanese' sphere of influence, based on the testimony of Banjar texts that talk about adopting Javanese styles, as well as the reinforcement of this view implicit in the cultivation of Javanese artistic styles and dances in the arts of Banjar (and, it should be added, its neighbour Kutai). If it were a simple case of either being 'Javanese' or 'Malay' in culture, why then were the texts written in Malay, and not in Javanese? If 'Javanese' and 'Malay' describe geographical areas of influence, then what is the situation of the 'Malay' courts of Eastern Indonesia—especially the courts of South Sulawesi, Ternate and Tidore—or even the courts of Sumatra?

In Palembang and Jambi, for example, the courts produced literature in both Malay and Javanese, with textile styles that can be related to both those of Java and the Malay Peninsula. Likewise in South Sulawesi literature not in the Makassar or Bugis languages was produced in Malay. The architectural styles of the palaces are close to Malay styles, and have influenced the palace styles of Sumbawa. However, the crown of the Sultanate of Gowa-Makassar shows amazing similarities to that of the Sultanate of Banten, and the elaborate *kris* hilts of South Sulawesi could be variant forms of the coastal Javanese style, although the sheath ornamentation is often closer to the styles of Sumatra.[63] In the islands of Southeast Indonesia, myths of origin of people or of important cultural objects and styles indicate a wide variety of sources: amongst others, Makassar, Ternate, 'Jawa', Bali, Melaka, 'Malayu', China and Portugal.

The situation is not one of demarcated physical spaces of influence but rather of patterns of cultural overlap. These patterns go along with patterns of physical movement, movement of texts from one area to another, movements of wandering princes throughout the areas of the Malay Peninsula, Sumatra, Kalimantan and further afield, movements of Bugis and Makassarese throughout Southeast Asia, particularly after the fall of Gowa-Makassar to the Dutch and Arung Palaka, movements of 'pirates' and 'mercenaries' (who were often the same people as princes), marriages across the waters, movements of the nomadic *bajau* or 'sea gypsies', and the numerous exchanges involved in the slave trade.[64]

Being Malay in Barus

Closer to the heartland of 'Melayu' the definitions remain equally difficult. Jane Drakard's study of Barus shows how elusive the category of 'Malay' may be when referring to the courts of West Sumatra. Barus is the area once known as Pansur, from whence came the great mystic poet of the late sixteenth century, Hamzah Fansuri.[65] Barus may be marginal to the Malay world in some senses, but its most famous product, before pepper, is considered a central authority in Malay literature. Drakard's two texts are much later, from around the middle of the nineteenth century the heyday of the *Rejimen* in Sri Lanka, a time prior to the British takeover of the whole of the Malay Peninsula, but one when the Dutch consolidation of power over Java, and the resulting division of the Javanese entity of Mataram-Kartasura was well and truly history, and the Cultivation System was in full swing.

Drakard has done a fine job in editing and presenting two alternative accounts of the policy of Barus, one from the 'Hulu' or 'Upriver' rulers, the other from the 'Hilir' or 'Downriver' rulers. The texts exist in a number of variants, each carefully described by Drakard, which describe rival claims to rule in a situation where the two types of rule coexisted. And despite their geographical designations, they actually shared the same 'space' of rule. One way of looking at these two courts, 'Malay' in style and court language, is as 'Malayised' Batak or Minangkabau courts. The Hulu text begins with the origins in Batak lands of the rajas it describes; the Hilir text begins with the Minang origins of the Hilir rulers in Pagaruyung, but then goes on to ascribe to their ancestor Sultan Ibrahim the origins of the Batak ruler Singa Maharaja (as he is called in the text).

Dual kingship is a common feature of Southeast Asian politics. Drakard, in her text editions and particularly in the companion volume of analysis, draws attention to the importance of the Barus case for understanding the coexistence of differentiated models and forms of status, authority and power within one polity. Although she herself is cautious about unduly extrapolating her case outside western Indonesia, the comparisons with other parts of Indonesia and Southeast Asia are highly suggestive, particularly because her work brings discussions of differentiated forms of rule out of the province of anthropological analyses of clans and tribes (particularly in eastern Indonesia) and into the area of kingship.

The comparison with the anthropological work of John R. Bowen in the nearby Gayo area of Aceh is significant.[66] Bowen's accounts of the Gayo are based on oral sources, particularly a comparison between songs he collected and those assembled by Snouck Hurgronje at the turn of the century, so chronologically his work is more limited than Drakard's. What he shows is an older differentiation of Gayo power and authority into clans, or 'blocs' (in the eastern Indonesian manner) being converted by Dutch colonial structures into a more straightforward and singular hierarchy. Stories of clan origins and ancestors structure this organisation, and the transformation of these stories is part of the transformations involved in the movement from pre-colonial to colonial and post-colonial politics. The colonial impulse to construct single 'heads' or 'kings' out of more complex systems is found virtually throughout the world, and corresponds to general juridical and ideological imperatives of colonial rule.

The case of Barus is one in which such colonial imperatives came up against the wall of a strongly differentiated formation that could not be united without destroying the formation itself. The limits of textual studies are demonstrated by a lack of information on how the models of kingship presented in the texts correspond to 'clans' or 'blocs' to which larger numbers of people belong or belonged, but comparison with Bowen's study would suggest that a situation similar to that of the Gayo existed in Barus. Nevertheless, the texts demonstrate that the social entities designated by each of the types of coexisting kingship were meant to include the whole of Barus society.

The textual materials with which Drakard deals, like the poems and ethnographic information presented by Bowen, further indicate the limits of discussing such means of social differentiation as 'dualism'. The preference for seeing dualities is a product of structuralism, particularly in the Dutch structuralism so important in Indonesian ethnography, and ultimately of Western epistemologies. Indigenous models are not so much 'dual' as multiple. Instead of reductions of complex patterns into ones and twos, most indigenous models expand in an open fashion towards talking about, for example, three-fold, five-fold, nine-fold, even thirteen-fold, differentiations. The figure in Bowen's book that attempts a schematic representation of the operations of the various levels of Gayo differentiation shows complex patterns of interaction.[67] These cannot be reduced to a duality, which was always the schematic equation in the Dutch Structuralist tradition of Rassers and his followers, but are better seen as interactions of patterns of five-fold models. So too Drakard's texts talk about a difference between 'upstream' and 'downstream', but only in terms of a larger differentiation between the categories of 'Malay', 'Aceh', 'Minangkabau' and 'Batak'. The category 'Batak' is further multiply divided, and each of these segments forms an overlapping set of 'inside' and 'outside' denominators of the formation 'Barus'. To these terms are added lists of Sumatran kingdoms, and references to Java. Both of the major texts discussed further make clear that there is one more relevant and determining 'outside' category that organises the differentiation of the 'inside' of Barus: the Dutch (*Kompeni*). Such coexisting 'outside' categories are hierarchically organised. The texts recognise that such hierarchies are relative, and thus constantly shifting. At one point, the relationship to or conflict with the rulers of Minangkabau may be crucial to determining the relationships of authority and power in Barus; at an earlier point 'Batak' was a key determinate. But both texts, produced in the colonial context, eventually have 'Dutch' as the major determinate, as does the historical formation analysed by Bowen.

Foreigners and the Malay language

Various studies of 'Malay' literature indicate that it was formed in relation to other local categories by those who wrote in the language, but that European groups came to be part of these local categories. Language, as

the examples of Marsden, Valentijn and some of the other European
commentators discussed above show, was a primary concern in locating
ethnicity in schemes of knowledge and power.

Post-colonial readers of such texts tend to construe any references to
Europeans as 'outside' penetrations, signs of colonial violence. Such a view
ignores the fact that European imperialism and colonialism are heterogeneous:
different styles and modes evolved out of the trading companies and successive
national governments of the Dutch, French and English, and the practices
and modes of colonisation, social life and economic exploitation practised
by the trading companies ("Rival Empires of Trade", to use Holden Furber's
term) were quite different from early nineteenth century colonial practices
and politics, which were different again from those of the post-1870 age of
high imperialism, or anxious post-1918 reconstituted imperialism.

Maier's critique of the knowledge of Malay literature involves questions
of language, which he has explored in greater depth in relation to the Dutch
study of Malay.[68] His concern is similar to Johannes Fabian's discussion of
the processes by which Swahili was appropriated by Belgian colonialism.[69]
Like Swahili, Malay was not just a way into societies to be dominated, it was
something constructed anew in the processes of domination. Both languages
were integral to the processes of knowledge and education by which 'native'
instruments of colonial power were formed. In the case of varieties of Swahili
in the Belgian Congo, language took on forms that were appropriate to the
constitution of a controllable labour force. Malay language and the study of
texts under the British was an intimate part of the formation of an 'educated'
class of Malays who would be instruments of rule.

Milner's citation of Matheson's work draws attention to the almost
simultaneous process in Malay, Chinese and European accounts of defining
a number of different areas and groups as 'Malay or 'Maleyu' from the late
eighteenth century.[70] These different categorisations converged around
language. In the light of Fabian's study, this process of definition has to be
seen in terms of the way the Malay language and Malay literature has been
described by Europeans. As Amin Sweeney notes, many of the Malay
manuscripts preserved in libraries and museums were commissioned by
Europeans. European attention to the Malay language in the seventeenth
and eighteenth centuries produced a number of descriptions of its nature
and extent, descriptions analysed by Sweeney.[71] In these descriptions, 'Malay'
exists on a number of levels, and is a language known throughout Asia,
as far away as Persia.

Malay's existence as a *lingua franca* and the possible uses of it as
such, were what first attracted European attention. Old Malay inscriptions

exist but the first European evidence of the language was the wordlist of 426 items compiled by Pigafetta, the chronicler of Magellan's voyages, at the beginning of the sixteenth century.[72] Pigafetta's listing, as Boon points out, follows a rhetoric that is emblematic, with 'words for the natural', 'words about words', 'words for the sociopolitical realm', and, primarily, 'words for the supernatural', meaning specifically Islam in this case.[73]

Following Fabian, we should treat such word lists not simply as the evidence of a thing/culture called 'Malay', but as part of a process that is constitutive of its object, 'the Malay'. Sweeney describes this process as beginning with the coming of the Portuguese (although it may have already been underway thanks to Persian- and Arabic-speaking traders), and reaches its high point in the first part of the eighteenth century with the descriptions of Malay by the Dutch and German commentators Valentijn and Werndly. The 'Malay' presented by Pigafetta is indeterminate: a product of voyages to Maluku and the Southern Philippines, with a Sumatran slave on board.[74] A century later Europeans are still trying to make 'Malay language, and with it Malay culture, identifiable and definable. Sweeney traces the various steps involved: sorting out subtypes of 'Malay' ('book', court, aristocratic, mountain/peasant, market), identifying a specific 'motherland' (either the entire peninsula, or Melaka/Johor), identifying Malay with Islam, and showing that the language has a 'literature'.

Involved in this was identification of levels of Malay language. Valentijn and Werndly's identifications of 'high' and 'low' Malay were refined into a list of five different levels: *Bahasa Dalem* or court language, *Bahasa Bangsawan* or aristocratic language, *Bahasa Gunung* or 'mountain/peasant' language, *Bahasa Kacukan* (*Pasar/Bazar*, or 'market Malay'), and 'book Malay' or *Bahasa Jawi*. The local terms already cited, which we call part of ethnic identity, appear here in different forms, and Sweeney notes the conundrum that while for peoples of Southeast Asia the term "*masuk Melayu*" meant 'to convert to Islam', in the wider Islamic world things Malay were called '*Jawi*'.[75]

Later scholarship had trouble coming to terms with this complex of identity, language and literature. H. N. van der Tuuk, one of the greatest linguists of the nineteenth century, disputed the centrality of Riau as a linguistic zone. He distinguished between 'centralising' or 'standard' Malay (spoken and written by educated Malays), 'local' Malay (the forms of Malay in various parts of Southeast Asia, such as Batavia), and 'conventional' Malay, which he equates with the *lingua franca* and dismisses as 'gibberish'. These categories cut across other scholars' ideas of 'high' and 'low', 'literary' and 'non-literary'.[76] His was one of many Dutch attempts to create a standardised Malay, attempts viewed with ironic distaste by those engaged in the process.[77]

The complicated nature of the attempts to define and explain each of these means of demarcating the language draws attention to just how far the act of description has to go in helping to form that which is being described. Each criterion used shows a set of problems: the levels and types of language make it impossible to distinguish which is the 'real' or 'core' language, which the lesser forms; the 'motherland' cannot be precisely described, or at least its locus is a shifting one; Malay exists as an Islamic language alongside Arabic and Persian, but not all Muslims in Southeast Asia were necessarily culturally 'Melayu', nor all speakers of Malay necessarily Islamic in any twentieth-century orthodox sense; and even the examples of 'Malay' literature contain points of confusion.[78]

One of the crucially indeterminate points in the eighteenth-century map of the Malay is the term *Jawi*. As Sweeney restates, this term is the Arabic adjectival form of *Jawa* (Java).[79] It was used in some sources to indicate an area from Siam to New Guinea, and in most instances was used almost interchangeably, or at least synonymously, with *Melayu* in ethnic or in more technical senses. The shift from 'Javanese' to 'Malay' that occurred when the British took over from the Dutch in Ceylon may be seen as the resolution, some hundred years later, of what the nascent colonial powers felt to be a general problem of terminology. The terminology, however, had consequences for identity beyond the semantic.

When considering the problematic nature of 'Malay', one needs to keep in mind that 'Javanese' is also a shifting and indeterminate category, as Pemberton, Sumarsam and others have shown. But why not see inland Mataram culture as *darat* to the *pasisir*, in the way that Batak is to Malay Barus? Peter Carey has done as much by showing that the Central Javanese courts sustained themselves by feeding off the arts of the coastal kingdoms and Madura.[80] Carey draws on the earlier work of Pigeaud on theatre, as well as musicological analyses by Amrit Gomperts, to show that almost all the 'core' elements of Java's 'core' culture are in fact from the so-called 'periphery'. *Jawa* became a much more fixed term as the eighteenth century wore on, just as 'Malay' did.

The problem of colonial powers determining an identity for the Malay language should be seen as particularly related to the perceived connections between 'Melayu' and Islam. Pigafetta's wordlist, as Boon observed, does start with 'Allah'. For both the Dutch and the British, as for the Iberians before them, separating the Islamic world from other parts of what is now Southeast Asia was important. In the early nineteenth century, this was done in various negative ways by the British: particularly by finding 'pure' examples of groups which represented the pre-Islamic and thus indigenous nature of the Indies (the Rejang), or by paying attention to those who 'preserved' the Hinduism that preceded Islam (the Balinese).[81] These are but a small part of a long history of antipathy to Islam now generally subsumed under the category of 'Orientalism'.

There is also another way to look at the relationship between Islam and Malay (either as a language or as an ethnic category). As recent studies have emphasised, Islam came into island Southeast Asia not just as a competitor with Hinduism (to saying nothing of the various 'animist' religions), but principally, for the missionaries on both sides, and for the various local rulers involved, as a competitor with Christianity. The brand of Christianity was particularly Catholic, and mostly Portuguese and/or Jesuit. The coexistence of Islamic and non-Islamic in the one area, and, as Pelras remarks, in the one person, should be seen in terms of a long historical shift that is still occurring for many peoples of the region.[82]

The irony of paying attention to Pigafetta's wordlist only for what it says about the Malay language was that just as Catholicism and Islam were in competition, so Portuguese and Malay became competitors. From the sixteenth century until at least the eighteenth, both were potential *lingua franca* for the 'East Indies', not only in places such as Batavia but also in other regions where slavery, trade and colonisation involved the creation of hybrid communities and hybrid power relations. Islam won, as did Malay, partly, I suspect, as a result of Dutch antipathy to Catholicism and to using an Iberian language for communication. The role of the Dutch in promoting Malay, particularly in areas where they had entered into convenient relationships with particular ethnic groups (the Ambonese and the Rotinese spring to mind), is too well documented to need further explication here. The Dutch did not cause Malay to come into existence, nor did they determine its spread, but the VOC constituted one locus of power in the complex formation of Malay as a multi-layered language used throughout Southeast Asia in statecraft, religion and trade. With the formation of the language came the formation of the ethnic identity.

Complexities of Identity

Is there any centre to the 'Malay'? Only in the sense that first the role of the Portuguese, then British and Dutch, policies, practices and sciences, provided one from the 'outside'. Working backwards chronologically, as

I have, it is impossible to separate the 'authentic' Malay from colonial Malay identity, and in attempting to do so the 'colonial' becomes just as problematic a category. The texts, as representations of social formations, require the categories of Portuguese, Dutch or British (and these are not exhaustive) to achieve identity. The most interesting point, and the hardest to track, is the one at which European attempts to identify or describe become indigenous discourse.

The process is a multiple one, by which I mean that it is more than two-way. It is not just a matter of 'colonial' versus 'indigenous' views, perceptions and roles, but of Malay/Javanese, British/Dutch, Dutch/Portuguese, coastal/inland, and of multiple formed ethnic identities (Barus Malay/Batak/Minangkabau/Acehnese). These points of identity were created and shifted in resonance with and in relation to the other terms from at least the sixteenth until the nineteenth century, when the formations of high imperialism froze or ossified them into strict and exclusive categories. Throughout the earlier period the key indigenous terms that dominated the formations of identity were *Melayu* and *Jawa*. These were not exclusive or separable terms. They were foci of what might be called a civilisation of the region, which I have elsewhere referred to as *Pasisir* civilisation, although Inden's term 'scale of forms' is a better expression, since it avoids the imperial baggage that 'civilisation' infers.

The historical and political implications of discussing this *Pasisir* scale of forms are many. Historians have tended to take one of two views of the period prior to about the eighteenth century in Southeast Asia. On the one hand an older, Europe-centred type of history holds that from the sixteenth century onwards Europeans formed the dynamic and dominant powers of the regions, they were the engines of change. On the other is the reaction to this view, begun by Van Leur and implicit in the writings of Anthony Reid, rejects European causality in regional change. In this view, up until the eighteenth century, Southeast Asian politics may have been affected by the establishment of the different empires of trade, but the fundamental aspects of society and culture were uninfluenced by Europe. Ricklefs' study of Kartasura in the seventeenth century shows that direct influence was not necessarily occurring, but that the two changing formations, VOC and central Javanese, changed in relation to each other. They may have existed in states of mutual ignorance and hostility only occasionally modified by political symbiosis, but this symbiosis was part of a much more indirect type of change.

A *pasisir* scale of forms explains why 'Javanese' was becoming a stricter category as the *darat* of Central Java was forced apart from the coast, and it also explains why the formation of a new type of 'Javaneseness' occurred not just as VOC/Javanese interactions, but within the complex and overlapping interaction of VOC, Kartasura, Madura, Bugis, Banten, Bali and other groups (with the English and Portuguese somewhere on the margins as well). The resulting Central Javanese court identity was no less authentically and autonomously 'Javanese' in cultural and social terms, but closer scrutiny renders these ways of looking at it almost meaningless.

This is the second major historical implication of the notion of *pasisir* civilisation. The idea may, on first appearances, resemble the way the notion of *nusantara* or similar kinds of trans-archipelagic terms have been used to argue for a proto-nationalism. But looking at *pasisir* in terms of shifting identities undermines nationalist agendas. A Malaysian nationalism reliant on a set 'Malay' identity looks very shaky in this light. So too for an Indonesian nationalism which holds up ancient kingdoms as geographically based military imperium as the prior basis of the state. Take away the idea of Majapahit (or Sailendra, or even Mataram) as a European-style holy Javanese empire, take away the centrality of Central Javanese culture as the continuous, dominant and paradigmatic basis of Javanese identity, and give the peripheral inland cultures of the Batak, Nias or Toraja areas equal status in the hierarchy of ethnic identity with 'Malay' and 'Javanese', and you have undermined some of the major tenets of Indonesian state ideology.

Pasisir histories are one variety of counter history, alternative to the European/anti-European histories of colonialism and nationalism. They demonstrate interactions and types of identity that provide alternative models of ethnicity and alternatives to nationalism. Without the idea of a fixed, essential and immutable national culture, it becomes difficult to mount the kinds of culturalist arguments used to justify everything from abuse of human rights to the creation of trade zones to be inhabited by those who are essentially 'Asian'. But '*pasisir*' is just one term, one scale of forms in Southeast Asia, with its own categories and exclusions. Other counter-hegemonic potentials await.

3

The Search for the 'Origins' of Melayu

LEONARD Y. ANDAYA*

In recent years a number of writings have examined the meaning of Malayness.[1] While most scholars would agree that ethnic identity is constantly being reconstructed in the face of changing circumstances, there is less support for the idea of an 'essential' core that defines a group.[2] Yet popular belief in a primordial core persists and often is the primary stimulus for group action. The shifting elements that constitute the core reveal important concerns of a certain ethnicity at a particular point in time, and illuminate the impact of a specific historical situation. A group is always aware of its past, and examines it periodically to identify elements that emphasise its uniqueness in response to pressing circumstances.[3]

An excellent example of this process was the ancient rivalry between polities on both sides of the Straits of Melaka seeking to become the leading centre of the Malay world. The outcome was not determined until the establishment of British colonial rule on the 'Malay' Peninsula in the late nineteenth century. Eager to justify their presence on the peninsula and forestall conflicts with the Dutch across the Straits, the British created an entire colonial intellectual enterprise termed by one scholar, 'Malayistics'.[4] The enterprise reinforced ideas that the homeland, and hence the centre, of the Malays was on the peninsula, and that the fifteenth-century kingdom of Melaka was the cradle of Malay civilisation. Proper behaviour, customary laws and standards of government, language and literature derived from the oral and written traditions of Melaka became 'primordial' values associated with being Malay. The independent Federation of Malaysia retained this view of Malay history. Historical evidence of Malay antecedents outside the peninsula was rarely discussed, and few identified the ancient kingdom of Srivijaya as a Malay state because it was located on the Indonesian side of the Straits.[5] Much greater interest was shown instead in the recent archaeological finds in the Bujang Valley in Kedah because, unlike the story of Srivijaya, they provide greater depth to the history of a Malay presence in the peninsula. This is an example of how the so-called primordial essence of a group may change or be reinforced through reference to a specific past that is identified and interpreted, or reinterpreted, for current ethnic needs.[6] Moreover, as in the case of the Malays, attention to the past may reveal linkages that have been obscured by modern nation-state boundaries and shifts in ways of defining ethnicities.

In this paper I will hereafter use the term 'Melayu' in preference to its English translation 'Malay' for two reasons. First of all, the term is mentioned in the earliest documents and continues to be the appellation for particular places and peoples throughout history. Second, 'Melayu' is less political, and is suitable for discussing a region that in the past crossed present-day international borders. By tracing the use of this term historically, it is possible to suggest that a Melayu ethnicity was being developed along the Straits of Melaka beginning perhaps as early as the seventh century. Only much later did the culture of the Melayu begin to spread beyond these shores.[7]

In asking where and how Melayu ethnicity may have evolved, the issue is not to pinpoint the exact time and place of the origins of the group, but to reveal the process of ethnic formation. Throughout history various events and aspects of society have been selected, rearranged and reinterpreted to create the 'core' of an ethnic identity. As new research extends knowledge of the Melayu, fresh components become available for inclusion in what people see as 'primordial', and so the dialectic continues to the present day. In this essay the search for origins of the Melayu is intended not to provide definitive answers but to sketch the historical environment which produced the conditions for a specifically Melayu ethnic awareness.

Appearance of the 'Melayu'

The story should perhaps begin in Taiwan, the homeland of the Proto-Austronesian speakers. Based on archaeological and linguistic evidence, it is believed that these people were in Taiwan between 4000 and 3000 BCE. They then migrated outward between 2500 and 1500 BCE through the Philippines, the northern half of Borneo, Sulawesi, central Java and eastern Indonesia. From about 1500 to 500 BCE, there was a further movement southward in Borneo, then out to the western half of Java and westward to Sumatra, the Malay Peninsula and the central part of Vietnam.[8]

Archaeological records for island Southeast Asia indicate that during this migration of Proto-Austronesian speakers, only after good coastal sites were occupied were there any major attempts to colonise the interior areas.

Founder-rank enhancement played an important part in this process. Because founders of new settlements and their line were elevated to almost god-like status, there was strong motivation for members of a junior branch to seek an empty area to become, with their followers, a new senior line with priority over resources.[9] Early Proto-Austronesian speakers were principally subtropical coastal and riverine peoples with a Neolithic economy based on cereal and tuber cultivation and domesticated animals. Within island Southeast Asia, descendants of these early Proto-Austronesian speakers introduced a wide range of subsistence economies. These included rainforest foraging and collection for trade; sea nomadism; differing types of irrigated and rain-fed rice cultivation; shifting cultivation of cereals, fruits and tubers; and palm exploitation.[10]

Proto-Malayo-Polynesian, derived from Proto-Austronesian, began to break up by at least 2000 BCE as a result probably of the expansion southward into the southern Philippines, Borneo, Sulawesi and Maluku.[11] Proto-Malay was spoken in western Borneo at least by 1000 BCE and was, it has been argued, the ancestral language of all subsequent Malay dialects. Linguists generally agree that the homeland of the Malayic-Dayak language is in Borneo—based on its geographic spread in the interior, its variations that are not due to contact-induced change, and its sometimes conservative character.[12] James T. Collins has even proposed a location for the ancestral area of these speakers some 100 kilometres into the interior along three parallel river systems: the Sambas, Kapuas and Pawan. K. A. Adelaar, however, has urged caution in identifying a precise area since there is still much linguistic investigation to be done in Borneo.[13]

More controversial among comparative linguists and historians is the question of the homeland of Melayu culture. Collins cites archaeological discoveries in western Borneo of Indian carnelian beads and Dongson drums of the fourth century CE, and silver and gold Buddha images from the eighth century CE, as strong evidence of links between India and "the watery homeland of the Malays".[14] The implication is that a Melayu culture influenced by Indian ideas would have begun here before the development of a similar culture in southeast Sumatra at Srivijaya/Malayu between the seventh and eleventh centuries CE. While R. A. Blust and Adelaar agree that the homeland of the Malayic speakers was in Borneo, they believe that the culture generally identified with the Melayu most likely developed in southeast Sumatra.[15] The contact between southeast Sumatra and particularly coastal Borneo would have been established at the time of the expansion of Srivijaya trade networks, which extended as far as the northern Philippines.

Peter Bellwood has added an archaeological dimension to the linguistic debate by noting that the southward expansion of the Proto-Malayo-Polynesians at about 2000 BCE was characterised by adaptation to the new environment. While rice, foxtail millet and other cereals of Southeast Asian origin continued to be grown on a small scale, there was increasing foraging mobility. The discovery in 1987 of the Bukit Tengkorak assemblage near the town of Semporna in Sabah revealed a community of skilled seafarers and possibly traders who may have had ties as far away as northern New Britain.[16] The presence of a mobile trading community expanding to the coasts and later the interior of the island world is a likely scenario of the Malayic speakers. It is possible that an Indianised Melayu culture did develop in the riverine environment in interior west Borneo as suggested by Collins, but too little evidence is available at present to support this idea. By contrast, as will be demonstrated below, the historical and linguistic evidence for a Melayu cultural homeland in southeast Sumatra is overwhelming.

Bernd Nothofer and Collins have suggested that around 100 CE Malayic speakers left their riverine and swamp environment in west Borneo and sailed outward through the Tambelan and Riau Islands to Sumatra and then to the Malay Peninsula. They also posit later migrations from western Borneo northward along the west coast of Borneo, and then south and westward. From eastern Borneo, a further move carried these people to southwest Luzon, especially the Manila Bay area, and then eastward to Maluku. Another migration from western Borneo went directly southward to the Karimata Straits to Belitung, Bangka, south Sumatra and the west coast of Java. While there is agreement among scholars that the homeland of Malayic speakers was somewhere in western Borneo, there is not yet universal acceptance of Nothofer's and Collins' proposed waves of migrations.[17]

When the Malayic speakers moved into the Malay Peninsula, they came into contact with the ancestors of the *Orang Asli* (indigenous people) who descended from two major races: the Australoid and the Southern Mongoloid.[18] It is believed that the Negrito population stemmed from the former, while the Senoi were descendants of the later Southern Mongoloid migration. The archaeological record becomes more detailed on the Peninsula with assemblages found in Hoabinhian sites dated between 16000–8000 BC. It is believed that the hunting and gathering Hoabinhians were ancestral to the Negritos and to a lesser extent to the Senoi. The latter's biological affinity is more with the Neolithic Southern Mongoloid population which migrated into the Peninsula about 2000 BC. There appears to have been a rather sharp transition from the Hoabinhian to the Neolithic, with the change marked by the introduction of agriculture and Austroasiatic languages.[19] The Negritos adopted Austroasiatic languages, and so today both the Negritos and the Senoi speak Austroasiatic languages in the subgroup Aslian, which has distant relationships with Mon and Khmer. The Negritos, however, continued to maintain their hunting and foraging lifestyle and did not adopt the agricultural developments of the Neolithic. In this regard they were much more descendants of the Hoabinhians than the Neolithic Southern Mongoloids associated with the Senoi.[20]

Geoffrey Benjamin believes that when Malayic-speakers came up the west coast, they encountered an Austroasiatic Mon-speaking population in the Kedah area, which did not become culturally or linguistically incorporated into a Melayu culture until the twelfth century.[21] The presence of a number of Mon-Khmer loan words in northern Malay dialects, including terms for wet rice fields (*bendang*) and irrigation canals (*glong*), may indicate that the Melayu on the Peninsula learned wet rice cultivation techniques from the early Mon population in the area.[22] Nevertheless, there is still a strong case for an early Melayu link to Srivijaya prior to the twelfth century. Earthenwork pottery found at Pangkalan Bujang in the Lembah Valley of Kedah is very similar to that found in Kota Cina, an old port in north Sumatra associated with Srivijaya.[23]

In southeast Sumatra the Malayic speakers spread along the Musi and the Batang Hari and their tributaries, and into the interior highlands.[24] The name 'Melayu' appears for the first time in literary sources as a settlement in southeast Sumatra that sent a mission to China in 644. The earliest detailed account is by the Chinese Buddhist pilgrim Yijing, who spent time in Palembang and Jambi on two separate occasions in 671, and was there again from 689–95. He spent six months learning Sanskrit grammar in a place whose name for both the country and the capital was transcribed as (*Shili*) *Foshi*. He was then sent by the ruler to the country of Melayu, where he stayed for another two months. On his second visit, Yijing again went to 'Melayu', which he says had now become (*Shili*) *Foshi* [Srivijaya], meaning either that it had supplanted Srivijaya, or more likely that it had become a part of Srivijaya. He noted that there were many 'states' under this kingdom, and that in the fortified city there were more than a thousand Buddhist priests who had come to study religion. He even suggested that Chinese Buddhist priests should study religion in *Foshi* for a year or two before seeking further wisdom in Central India.[25]

Yijing's presence in southeast Sumatra coincided with the earliest inscriptions written in Old Melayu at Kedukan Bukit (Palembang, 683

CE), Sabokingking (near Telaga Batu in Palembang, undated), Talang Tuwo (Palembang, 684 CE), Karang Brahi (upper Batang Hari in Jambi, undated) Kota Kapur (Bangka, 686 CE), Palas Pasemah (Lampung, undated), and at Boom Baru (Palembang, undated).[26] All of these inscriptions, plus another written in Sanskrit found in Ligor on the Malay Peninsula and dated 775 CE, mention a polity known as Srivijaya and use the Pallava script in a style associated with south India and Sri Lanka in the same period. According to J. G. de Casparis, the absence of any clear local differentiation in the Sumatran inscriptions may indicate a recent borrowing of the script.[27]

Even more important is the location of these inscriptions. The presence of four in the vicinity of Palembang, especially the oldest found at Kedukan Bukit, suggests that this was the centre of a major polity. The Kedukan Bukit inscription is unlike the others in providing chronological detail about a victorious expedition that resulted in power and wealth for Srivijaya.[28] Coedès suggests that the true significance of this particular inscription is that it commemorates the founding of a dynasty. In Indianised Indochina and Indonesia, the establishment of a kingdom or a dynasty was often accompanied by magical practices. Coedès argues that the founder of the dynasty underwent a ceremony known as *siddhiyatra*, which is a voyage or a pilgrimage from which one returns endowed with magical powers. To support his view, he cites the following phrases from the Kedukan Bukit inscription as an indication that a new dynasty was being founded: "His Majesty boarded a ship to go in search of magic powers"; and "Srivijaya, endowed with magic powers...". The discovery of the inscription at the foot of Bukit Siguntang, the sacred mountain of the Srivijaya rulers, reinforces his belief that the dynasty was following the well-documented practice of 'kings of the mountain' in Southeast Asia. One of the other two inscriptions found in the vicinity of Palembang, the Talang Tuwo stone (684 CE), proclaims the ruler's Bodhisattva status and his concern for the salvation of all beings, emphasising the importance of the ruler and his realm as a centre of a form of Tantric Buddhism. The inscription at Sabokingking (Telaga Batu) contains an imprecation against those who may wish to challenge the authority of an expanding kingdom. The list of officials and other occupations included in the oath of allegiance seems to imply a well-differentiated society, with a number of officials associated with the new dynasty.[29] The Boom Baru inscription may be a fragment of a similar oath.

The other inscriptions are found outside the vicinity of Palembang and indicate the extent of Srivijaya's pretensions. Inscriptions at Karang Brahi in the upper Batang Hari, at Kota Kapur in the southwest corner of

Bangka, at Palas Pasemah in the Lampungs, and at Ligor on the east coast of the Malay Peninsula are all in strategic positions. The upper Batang Hari was one of the major interior entrepôts where goods from the Minangkabau highlands could be traded for external goods going upriver. The headlands of the Musi, the major river in Palembang, do not link up with the Minangkabau highlands, unlike the upper Batang Hari River in Jambi. It is for this reason that Jambi came to play an important role as the alternate capital of Srivijaya. The archaeologist Soekmono was the first to suggest that Karang Brahi may have been essential for the protection of the land route between Palembang-Jambi and the Minangkabau highlands. For a similar reason, according to Soekmono, Kota Kapur was ideally located to safeguard trading vessels plying the Bangka Straits from Palembang to the Lampungs and West Java.[30] Palas Pasemah was a collecting and redistribution centre for products from both the Lampungs and West Java. Finally, Ligor, also known by the toponym Tambralinga, was for centuries an important east coast port in the isthmian trade route.

The limited number of inscriptions emanating from Srivijaya restricts any detailed examination of the functioning of this polity. Nevertheless, the placing and the nature of the inscriptions reveal the character of an ambitious new polity that quickly sought to control all the major nodes of a trade network in the late seventh century. Yijing was present at the time of Srivijaya's establishment and expansion, and noted the importance of Srivijaya as a centre of Buddhist learning, which is reaffirmed in the Talang Tuwo inscription. This observation is further testimony to the self-confidence and wealth of a court able to host more than a thousand Buddhist priests in the capital city itself. The Sabokingking (Telaga Batu) inscription confirms this view in the listing of a number of functionaries and occupations associated with Srivijaya.

Though the inscriptions were in the Melayu language, in the seventh century the land called 'Melayu' was in the vicinity of present-day Jambi. O. W. Wolters argues that Jambi was never called Srivijaya, and his assertion appears to be supported by the Chola Tanjore inscription of 1030–31 CE, which clearly distinguishes between 'Srivijaya' and 'Malaiyur'. G. P. Rouffaer believes that 'Malaiyur' referred to the city of Jambi. Equally fascinating is Rouffaer's assertion that the Melayu and the Tamils regarded Jambi as the "motherland of the Melayu".[31] Between 1079 and 1082, the capital of Srivijaya moved from Palembang to Jambi, and tributary missions to China in 1079 and 1088 were now sent from *Zhanbei* (Jambi). Zhou Qufei (1178) and Zhao Rugua (1225) both comment on the fact that *Sanfoqi* (the Chinese name given to Melayu-Jambi) compelled ships to enter its harbour to trade. In the thirteenth and fourteenth centuries, Melayu is the name of a kingdom ruling over the Jambi area.[32]

The extent of Srivijaya's influence in the western half of the archipelago is attested to by evidence of seven Old Melayu inscriptions in Java and one in the Philippines. Those on Java date between the seventh and the ninth centuries, and, with the exception of one found at Candi Sewu in the south, originate from north central Java. From an examination of the language of the inscriptions, de Casparis concluded "the use of Old Malay in Java reflects direct or indirect influence from Srivijaya".[33] Another Old Melayu inscription written in Pallava script and dated 942 CE was found near Bogor, Java. Although it refers to the restoration of a ruler of Sunda by the order of a Javanese lord, a Rakryan Juru Pangambat, it is written in Old Melayu and again suggests influence from Srivijaya.[34]

Laguna in Bulakan province in southern Luzon in the Philippines is the furthest location where any inscription written in Old Melayu has been found. It is a copperplate inscription dated 900 CE and is related, but not identical, to those on Java and Sumatra. It records the clearing of an individual's debt and demonstrates an awareness of debt, slavery and class distinction. There is a mix of languages used in the inscription. While the main language is clearly Old Melayu, it is not identical to that found in Sumatra or Java. Old Javanese words are used to express ceremonial forms of address, while Sanskrit words, in simplified spelling and supplied with local affixes, are used for technical terms. The place-names in the inscription are all located on rivers with access to the South China Sea, which strongly suggests that Melayu language and ideas most likely accompanied trade. The Laguna inscription is the first indication that Old Melayu had developed a vocabulary to deal with matters of debt and class distinction.[35] Of course, such a development would have been expected from a society of the sophistication implied by the occupations listed in the seventh-century Sabokingking inscription from Palembang.

While the Philippines remained at the edge of Melayu influence, Java at the very outset was central to the idea of Melayu. The desire to emulate Srivijaya is evident in the manner in which ambitious rulers in Central Java used Old Melayu documents to consolidate their positions. On the north coast of Central Java, the inscriptions invoke the gods of different regions, while that found in the Kedu Plains to the south simply calls on the spirit of Tandrum Luah, the Protector Spirit of Srivijaya.[36] An Old Melayu inscription found at Sojomerto on Java mentions Dapunta Selendra, an 'ardent Saivite', whom Boechari believes to have been the founder (*vamsakara*) of the Sailendras, one of the powerful families that governed central Java from the second half of the eighth to the first half of the ninth centuries.[37] Mahayana Buddhism flourished with the establishment of the dynasty, possibly because the Sailendra overlord was from Srivijaya, a Mahayana centre since the seventh century. In 856, Balaputra, a son of a Srivijayan princess and a Sailendra ruler, was defeated in battle and fled to Srivijaya. After this time, Sailendra power flourished in Sumatra and waned in Java.[38] The struggle between the former and the new centres of Sailendra power for control of international trade is recorded in both Chinese records and inscriptions.

Arab and Persian sources reinforce epigraphic evidence indicating the presence of an important polity somewhere in Sumatra or Java. About 916 CE, Abu Said, a Persian amateur geographer, compiled an account based on his own readings and on interviews with people who had sailed to the east. He writes of the king of Zabag, called 'Maharaja', whose possessions are principally on the island of Srivijaya.[39] In a story repeated in later Arab and Persian sources, he describes a daily ritual in which the Maharaja throws a gold ingot into a pool of water. Only at low tide could one see the vast accumulation of gold ingots in the pool. At the death of the Maharaja, the gold was recovered and distributed to the princes and the royal family, among men, women and children equally; and to the officers and eunuchs according to their rank and prerogatives of their offices. What remained was given to the poor and unfortunate.[40]

Masudi, an Arab writing in 943, repeats this story and adds that in the empire of the Maharaja is the 'island' of Srivijaya, as well as the 'islands' of Zabag (which Gabriel Ferrand believes to be a general reference to Java and Sumatra), Rami (Aceh?) and Kalah. He then offers a formulaic description of wealth and power by reporting from 'a reliable source' that, when a cock in that country crows at sunrise, others answer in a wave through contiguous villages extending outward to over 600 kilometres.[41] An account by Edrisi in 1158 explains that when there was turmoil in China, the Chinese merchants transferred their commerce to Zabag and to the islands subject to it. This decision was taken because of the latter's reputation for fairness, good conduct, amenable customs and facility in trade. For these reasons, continues Edrisi, the island of Zabag was highly populated and well frequented by foreigners.[42]

In the Persian and Arab accounts, the Maharaja is said to be the ruler of Zabag, with possessions in Srivijaya, Rami and Kalah. The reference to 'islands' does not refer literally to islands but to regions, polities and even settlements. Being ruler of Zabag, that is, of Sumatra and Java, and having the polity of Srivijaya and the settlements of Rami and Kalah as possessions, accord with the evidence from Old Melayu inscriptions of this and earlier periods. All of the sources indicate that the area including southeast Sumatra and parts of Java was at one time subject to the influence of one ruler.

In 1024–25 the situation changed dramatically when the Chola invaded Srivijaya's territories on both sides of the Straits. Jambi appears to have been little affected by the Chola invasion, or else made a rapid recovery, for it was able to dispatch tributary missions to China in 1079 and 1088 under the name *Zhanbei* (Jambi).[43] But the name 'Melayu' may have still been used for the areas formerly known as Srivijaya, for in 1275, Kertanagara, the ruler of Singosari in Java, launched the Pamalayu expedition against southeast Sumatra. Although there is little in the sources about the expedition, subsequent events indicate that as a result of this campaign there may have been a retreat from the coast to the interior of Jambi. An inscription dated 1286 found in the upper reaches of the Batang Hari commemorates the arrival of religious statues from Java and their establishment at Dharmasraya at the orders of Kertanagara. It states further that all the inhabitants of Melayu—*brahmans*, *ksatriyas*, *vaisas* and *sudras* and especially the king, Srimat Tribhuwanaraja Mauliwarmadewa, rejoiced at the presentation of the gifts. In a period of about a decade, Javanese forces had penetrated as far as the upper Batang Hari, which was still regarded as part of Melayu. Based on archaeological evidence, F. M. Schnitger suggests that Melayu consisted of two centres: one on the coast and another in the interior.[44] This view seems substantiated by a Melayu mission to China in 1281 led by two envoys with Muslim names, who were most likely foreign traders based on the coast.[45] The existence of upstream and downstream kingdoms continued on the Musi in Palembang and the Batang Hari in Jambi into the seventeenth and eighteenth centuries.[46]

The placement of religious images at Dharmasraya continued an earlier Srivijaya tradition of distributing sacred inscribed documents on stone at crucial locations. For non-literate communities, these were visible signs of the power of the ruler and his supernatural sanction. Dharmasraya was located in the transition zone between the downriver centre and a new interior one which was beginning to develop in the highlands of Minangkabau. The first evidence of this new centre came in the form of an inscription dated 1347 made on the back of a religious image originally brought in 1286 from Java. The image was taken to Melayupura by Adityavarman,[47] who bore a title which one scholar believes is an attempt at a synthesis of the royal titles traditionally employed in Srivijaya and

Melayu.[48] Other inscriptions associated with Adityavarman were found in the vicinity of Pagar Ruyong in 1347 and in the highlands of Minangkabau.[49] These inscriptions dating from Adityavarman's reign which lasted till 1375 suggest that the 'upriver' Melayu centre had moved even further inland to the Minangkabau highlands.

Wolters contends that Adityavarman was most likely the same person as the Melayu-Jambi ruler known as Maharaja Prabhu. He reaffirms an earlier view that there were two parts of Melayu, but believes that the Melayu-Jambi ruler moved inland to become the ruler of Melayu in the Minangkabau highlands, while coastal Melayu came to be associated with Palembang.[50] If this reconstruction is correct, it would explain the close cultural relationship between the Minangkabaus and the Melayu. It may even explain why the Melayu in subsequent centuries continued to speak with awe of Minangkabau and to describe it as 'the cradle of their race'.[51] When Mpu Prapanca, a Majapahit court poet, wrote the *Desawarnana* (more generally known as the *Nagarakrtagama*) in 1365, he listed the Melayu lands as including not only Jambi and Palembang, but also Dharmasraya and Minangkabau. All the polities in east Sumatra from Lampung in the south to the northern tip and around to Barus were regarded as part of the Melayu lands.[52] At one time or another these areas had come under the influence of Srivijaya/Melayu and were therefore placed together as being part of Melayu. Writing in the early fifteenth century, Tomé Pires identifies a very precise location of 'Tanah Melayu' (Land of the Melayu) at the southeastern end of the province of Palembang, where he believes the founder of Melaka originated.[53]

To summarise, linguists have identified a Proto-Melayu language dating to at least 2,000 years ago. Speakers of this language spread from west Borneo to southeast Sumatra and the Malay Peninsula. The first evidence of a written Melayu language was in the seventh-century inscriptions found in Palembang, and the first mention of the name 'Melayu' is from a seventh century Chinese document referring to the area of Palembang and Jambi. In the eleventh century, the Srivijaya centre moved from Palembang to Jambi, and the Chinese began to use the name *Sanfoqi* for both Melayu and Jambi, which may refer to the same place. In the thirteenth century, a new centre of Melayu was established close to the Minangkabau highlands on the upper Batang Hari River. From about the mid-fourteenth century, Melayu could be said to incorporate the coastal areas of present-day Palembang and Jambi; the settlements along the major Batang Hari and Musi river systems and their numerous tributaries; the lands which formed crucial links between the two rivers; and finally the interior headlands of these great rivers. The *Desawarnana* lists the entire east coast of Sumatra around to Barus on the west coast as belonging to the 'land of Melayu'. Settlements on the Malay Peninsula, on the other hand, appear as 'Pahang' rather than Melayu.[54] Finally, there is a Portuguese comment in the early fifteenth century locating a very precise homeland of the Melayu in southeastern Palembang. Conventional practice of naming people by a settled area would suggest that those inhabitants occupying lands identified as Melayu, wherever and however it was defined, would be known as *orang Melayu*, or 'the people of Melayu'.

Melayu Antecedents on the Peninsula

Prior to the foundation of Melaka in the early years of the fifteenth century, 'Melayu' referred solely to Sumatra. While there is ample evidence of the existence of earlier entrepôts on both the northwest and the northeast coasts of the Malay Peninsula and the isthmian region to the north, the sources make no mention of the name Melayu.[55] Recent excavations in the area have been the basis of a reconstruction of early 'Malaysian' history, though one scholar believes that they were most likely Mon speaking and linked to the Mon civilisations to the north. Nevertheless, he believes that the people eventually adopted Islam and became Melayu.[56] The presence and antiquity of these settlements on the peninsula and the isthmus may have had an important bearing on the development of Melayu identity.

A number of inscriptions dating from the fifth century CE have been found on the northwest coast of the peninsula and the isthmus. The writing is similar to that found in contemporary southern India and employs various 'deliberate deviations' which demonstrate long familiarity with the literary system. One of the inscriptions found south of the Muda River in Kedah, in an area known today as Seberang Perai, mentions a sea captain known as Buddhagupta who was a resident of "Raktamrttika". The latter name is not used in India, and its meaning of 'Red Earth', or *Tanah Merah* in Malay, is a common place name on the peninsula. It may be a reference to *Chitu* ('Red Earth' in Chinese), a kingdom on the east coast of the peninsula, which was also an area of significance during this period. The texts of these inscriptions found in an area between Gunung Jerai and the Muda River indicate that this area was already intellectually and commercially linked to the outside world by the fifth century CE.[57]

Between the fifth and the early eleventh century, Sungai Mas in the Bujang Valley was the centre of Kedah. Buddhist inscriptions found in the Valley are evidence of Indian contact from the fifth to the sixth centuries.

In the seventh century, it became a collecting point of local products for an expanded trade in the Straits. At a time when mariners could not calculate longitude but could determine their latitude through stars, Southeast Asian ships could sail due west from Kedah to reach southern India or Sri Lanka, while Indian ships went due east to Kedah. Sometime in the fifth century, Buddhagupta of 'Red Earth' inscribed a prayer on stone at Bujang Valley before setting sail for India, and the Chinese pilgrim Yijing stopped in Kedah in 671 on his way to study Buddhism in India. Indian traders obviously found Kedah an important landfall, and even after Srivijaya became the overlord of Kedah (by 685), Indian sources continued to regard Kedah, not Palembang, as the centre of Srivijaya.[58] Archaeological discoveries of large shell midden sites in Kedah and directly across the way in east Sumatra are indications that these were areas of substantial populations. There is no evidence, however, that the Sumatran site was ever a trade port,[59] which suggests that it may have provided the forest products that were then brought to the trading port of Kedah. The pattern of collection centres of local products serving major trade emporiums became well established in the history of the Straits of Melaka.

The Bujang Valley continued to be important, but from the end of the tenth century the centre in Kedah gradually shifted from Sungai Mas to Pangkalan Bujang, which maintained its dominance until the end of the fourteenth century.[60] Pangkalan Bujang is located on the first firm ground after the mangroves of the Merbok estuary. The concentration of wares and the large amounts of porcelain imply, according to Alastair Lamb, that this was a site for the loading and off-loading of ships. Goods may have been carried through the overland river route to the east coast of the peninsula, and would have reached local populations engaged principally in fishing and rice cultivation. In the nearby Kuala Selingsing site in Perak, identified as a 'feeder point' most likely supplying an entrepôt in the Bujang Valley,[61] locally made beads, some from recycled foreign glass, as well as clay, bronze and iron items were found. Similarity of pottery designs on the Malay Peninsula, southeastern Sumatra and southwestern Borneo, and the discovery through metallurgical analysis that the gold used in ritual deposits in a tenth to eleventh-century CE temple in Kedah originated from western Borneo, are evidence of trade between these areas.[62] Perhaps these links, dating back to the period of migrations of the Melayu from their homeland in western Borneo to the new areas of settlement in southeast Sumatra and the Malay Peninsula, were never severed. By about 1300 CE, the sites of southern Kedah and Kuala Selinsing were abandoned.[63]

Some archaeologists have suggested that a major trading centre referred to as Kataha (Skt.)/Kadaram, Kidaram or Kalagam (Tamil)/Kalah (Arabic) was located in Takuapa, believed to be somewhere in the Tenasserim/Tavoy area, from the seventh to the tenth centuries, and in the Merbok estuary in Kedah from the eleventh to the fourteenth centuries.[64] From here, traders could sail inland along the rivers, transfer to land portage, and then reload on boats on rivers flowing to the east coast. Alastair Lamb places Takuapa some 100 kilometres north of Phuket Island and about 500 kilometres north of Pangkalan Bujang on the Merbok estuary in Kedah. At this location, at the end point of the crossing at the Isthmus of Kra, Kakao Island protects the river mouth from breakers from the Bay of Bengal. There is evidence of habitation on the site between the seventh and the tenth centuries, and excavations have produced a mixture of glass, beads and ceramics from the Middle and Far East. A ninth-century Tamil inscription *in situ* mentions the Manikkiram, a powerful Tamil mercantile corporation. In the early eleventh century, Takuapa fell victim to the Chola invasion of the Srivijayan lands.[65]

A second significant area of settlement on the peninsula in the proto-historic period was along the northeast coast. While the Indian connection was particularly strong in the northwestern part of the peninsula, the Chinese were involved with the settlements in the northeast. Between the third and the seventh centuries some of the names mentioned by the Chinese are *Dunsun, Chitu, Panpan, Dandan,* and *Luoyue.* The third-century BCE settlement of *Dunsun,* according to the Chinese, had 500 Indian families and 1,000 Brahmans. An early seventh-century Chinese source describes *Chitu* (possibly in the upper reaches of the Kelantan River) as a wealthy city-state with control over other city-kingdoms and a developed administration. Although a former king had abdicated to preach Buddhism, there were several hundred Brahmans serving the court. The same source describes *Panpan* (Kelantan or Terengganu?) as Buddhist in orientation, and *Dandan* as having 20,000 families and eight state officials who were Brahmans. In Tang sources, *Luoyue* is the only settlement in the southern part of the peninsula mentioned, and it is only remembered as a collecting point for forest products.[66]

Although it is Chinese sources that describe these settlements in the northeast of the peninsula, the societies reflect Indian rather than Chinese influence. It was therefore much more likely in these early centuries for Indian traders to have taken the less dangerous though difficult passage across the isthmus or the peninsula by boat and land portage into the Gulf of Siam. In addition to the well-known trans-peninsular route at the

Isthmus of Kra, the Tembiling Valley played an important role as a highway between the two coasts. From the Straits, one could go up the Muar River, then overland a short distance at the Penarikan ('Portage') to enter the Serting River, which flowed on to join the Pahang, Jelai and Tembiling Rivers. Sailing down these rivers to the east, one would reach the Lebir Valley in southeast Kelantan and then proceed onward to Patani.[67] Archaeological sites along these interlocking river systems indicate that these waterways, linked by short land passages, were actively used in the past and may account for a greater amount of commercial traffic than previously believed.[68] Paul Wheatley identified five major trans-peninsular routes linking the Bay of Bengal with the Gulf of Siam.[69] Written sources mention that goods from the ports on the northwest coast were transported to the east coast to Ligor (Nakhon Si Thammarat) and Langkasuka, which scholars locate in the vicinity of Patani. Langkasuka was ideally located for ships coming from China, being almost due west from the southern tip of the Mekong Delta. Moreover, like Kedah, it was a stopover for Buddhist pilgrims on their way to India. A further attraction was the ability of Langkasuka to provide very high quality camphor, which was highly prized in China. Langkasuka's importance is attested by the frequency of its embassies to the Chinese court in the sixth century.[70]

The significance of these entrepôts for international trade made them vulnerable to ambitious and aggressive kingdoms such as Srivijaya. The eighth-century Ligor inscription provides evidence of Srivijaya's pretensions over the peninsula and the isthmus, but it does not mean that these settlements had become Melayu. Archaeological finds in the Bujang Valley do not link its inhabitants with a specific ethnic community. Given the strong presence of Mon-Khmer settlements immediately to the north, particularly at the Satingpra complex to the south of Ligor, it is likely that these Kedah sites would have been subject more to Mon-Khmer than to Melayu influences. By incorporating archaeological studies with his own linguistic and ethnological research, Benjamin has proposed that the ancient communities on the peninsula experienced influences from two different directions. Inhabitants in the north, influenced by nearby Mon-Khmer-speaking civilisations, may have been Mahayana Buddhists and Mon-speakers, even though there would have been many residual Austronesian (though non-Melayu) loan words present in the language dating from an early migration. Only later did the northern inhabitants switch to the Melayu language and adopt Islam. In the south, on the other hand, the people were Austronesian speakers, including early speakers of a Melayu language.[71]

With the demise of Srivijaya as the most prestigious Melayu centre, there would have been a jockeying for dominance among groups formerly regarded as part of the Melayu lands on Sumatra. Sometime perhaps in the fourteenth century, according to the *Sejarah Melayu*, a refugee Palembang prince from the lands associated with Melayu went with his followers to the peninsula. The traditional association of the name 'Melayu' with Sumatra made it doubly important for any group on the peninsula to assert its right to be regarded as the heirs of Srivijaya. For the migrant group from Palembang seeking to recreate the glory of Srivijaya on the peninsula, it was necessary not only to re-establish the conditions for favourable trade, but also to promote itself actively as the new centre of the Melayu.

An interesting contest thus ensued not on the battlefield but in the creation of rival texts. It would have begun in the fifteenth century when the Melaka court asserted its centrality in the Melayu world through a court document entitled *Sulalat al-Salatin* (Genealogy/Descent of Kings). Better known as the *Sejarah Melayu* (The History/Story of the Melayu), it is a document that makes Melaka the ultimate measure of all things Melayu. The first known recension dates from 1610 when Johor, which viewed itself as the direct heir of Melaka, was greatly weakened by frequent invasions from both the Portuguese and the Acehnese.[72] The writing of the *Sejarah Melayu* was intended as a reaffirmation of its central position in Melayu. At about the same time the *Hikayat Hang Tuah* (The Story of Hang Tuah) is believed to have been first set down on paper. It is a well known and popular work that began as oral tales associated with the legendary heroes of the Melaka kingdom, particularly the exploits of Hang Tuah, the ideal Melayu subject. Scattered throughout this *hikayat* the phrase "tanah Melayu" (Land of Melayu) is frequently and consistently employed to refer to the peninsula, not Sumatra. It is no coincidence that both these two texts were first committed to paper in seventeenth-century Johor, at a time when that kingdom was being challenged by Aceh in north Sumatra for dominance in the Melayu world.

Despite the appropriation by Melaka and later Johor of Melayu identity for the peninsula, the Sumatran contenders continued to dispute this claim. In the sixteenth and seventeenth centuries, Aceh demonstrated its political, economic, religious, and literary leadership of the Melayu world and offered its own claims to Melayu leadership through its court text, the *Hikayat Aceh* (The Story of Aceh).[73] Not to be outdone the Minangkabaus in central Sumatra reasserted their claims to Melayu in a later and different recension of the *Sejarah Melayu*, which gave prominence to the eldest of three brothers who became the progenitor of the Minangkabau monarchy in Pagar Ruyong.[74] The

Hikayat Siak (The Story of Siak), an extended version of the *Sejarah Melayu*, emphasises the significance of the founder of the kingdom of Siak, Raja Kecik, who is legitimised through his connections to both the Palembang and Minangkabau lines of Melayu.[75]

In summary, the pre-Melakan inhabitants of the peninsula were never considered to be part of the Melayu lands. There was, moreover, a distinct divide between the Mon-Khmer-influenced northern populations from the people of the southern part of the peninsula, who were more influenced by Austronesian culture. Only with the foundation of Melaka in the fifteenth century by Melayu immigrants from Palembang did the peninsula become part of Melayu. Melaka then sought to make it the centre of the Melayu world, a pretension that did not go unchallenged by those along the eastern coast of Sumatra.

The 'Primordial' Melayu

The search for origins of any ethnic group can be controversial, particularly if it is motivated by nationalist or colonialist concerns. In many countries archaeology has had to endure unrelenting political pressure by governments to 'uncover' ancient roots of a dominant group for nationalist or racist purposes. Archaeology has even been used at times to undermine or colonise certain groups by denying their indigenous past.[76] Geoffrey Benjamin is one scholar who has dared to suggest that some of the archaeological sites located in the Bujang Valley may not have begun as 'Melayu' settlements, and that some of the present-day Melayu of the peninsula were descended from *Orang Asli* through a long process of adaptation. Because of the lower status of the *Orang Asli* and the current controversy over what constitutes indigenous in Malaysian society, there has not been much support for such views.

As these comments reveal, the historical reconstruction of the 'origins' of the Melayu is not a straightforward task. It involves an interaction between political concerns and historical evidence. Historians seek to uncover as much of the past as is possible given the limitations of the sources themselves, and then suggest the significance of their findings. Yet, governments can manipulate these conclusions for their own purposes, such as elevating a particular historical incident to a national symbol, or identifying a period in history as the cradle of that group's culture and civilisation. The Melaka kingdom has become for the present-day dominant ethnic group in Malaysia the essence of what it means to be Melayu. Through the mainly inadvertent but at times overt collaboration of academic scholarship and governmental directives, there has been an imaginative historical reconstruction of the dress, the customs, and the values of the Melaka Melayu based principally on the *Sejarah Melayu*. This reconstruction of Melayu culture, reinterpreted at various times to accord with changing times, has been made the basis of a new Malaysian cultural identity, and Melayu 'values' have come to be primordially associated with the beginnings of Melayu civilisation.

One should not confuse the 'use' to which governments may put historical conclusions with the evidence itself. While it may still be too early to make bold statements about the prior lifestyle of a group that eventually came to settle Melaka in the fifteenth century, it is possible to make some supportable generalisations. New research suggests that the ancestors of the Melaka 'Melayu' may have originated in western Borneo and developed in southeastern Sumatra. They practiced a mixed economy of swidden agriculture and foraging along the rivers, the tributaries, and the coastal regions. When international trade began to flourish from about the sixth century, there was greater specialisation of tasks. Foraging on land and on the seas became the dominant occupation for some. Requests by foreign traders for supplies of aromatic woods, resins, and rattans created groups who specialised in acquiring the knowledge and expertise to fulfil this demand. Similarly, those who scoured the seas and shores for edible seaweeds, sea tortoises, and pearls began to intensify the search in response to international trade. The presence in the society of officials, lawmakers, law enforcers, food producers, shippers and so on, as part of the organisation of the labour resources for trade, is mentioned in the seventh-century Old Melayu inscriptions from Srivijaya.[77]

The greater organisation of Melayu society and specialisation of functions did not, however, lead to a massive bureaucracy and greater control from the centre. Instead, the society continued to revolve around personal relationships established between the ruler and his subjects.[78] Recent archaeological studies have located multiple 'hubs of activity' along some 12 kilometres of the northern bank of the Musi River in Palembang.[79] In a riverine polity linked by multiple hubs, there was little need for an extended bureaucracy for the efficient functioning of government. Rivers and tributaries were linked by short land passages, and *pangkalan* (collection and redistribution ports) dotted the interior. These *pangkalan* were strategically located at sites easily accessible to those bringing goods from the interior forests or highlands.[80]

The great distances between the coasts and the interior areas, and the difficult and sometimes dangerous rivers, which all traffic had to traverse, made control irregular. The nature of the polity based on a principally riverine environment limited the options available to the government to enforce its decrees throughout the realm. Military expeditions were fruitless because a recalcitrant lord and his followers could easily move further upriver or inland to await the inevitable departure of the invading armies. Instead of physical force, persuasion was employed to convince people of the benefits of cooperation in return for titles, status and access to external goods. But the most effective appeal was the reputation of the ruler. He was the source of the highest status in the land through the distribution of rank and wealth, and his attributes included supernatural powers that could be invoked against those who failed to uphold his laws. Solemn oaths of allegiance were administered, culminating in the drinking of water in which a royal *keris* had been placed. The water thus impregnated with the magic force of majesty became the instrument of supernatural punishment if the subject did not adhere to the oath.[81] Inscriptions on stone were also placed at strategic locations, at *pangkalan* or along well-travelled routes, to remind the inhabitants of the long reach of the ruler's sacred powers. Even in the twentieth century, local inhabitants viewed with considerable awe certain stones bearing markings because of the heritage of an earlier time when stones inscribed with indecipherable letters represented the supernatural potency of the ruler.[82]

It is this heritage from southeastern Sumatra and western Borneo that inspired the Melayu of Melaka. The new settlement adopted its lifestyle and methods of governance, including the use of sacred oaths, from these sources. From the middle of the fifteenth century, Islam and a rise in court literary production helped to reinforce and export Melaka values to other parts of Southeast Asia. Melaka's success as a centre of commerce, religion, and literary output made it synonymous with Melayu civilisation in the fifteenth and early sixteenth centuries. Melayu identity was therefore wrenched away from Sumatra and became a major source of conflict in the later sixteenth and seventeenth centuries with the principal Melayu contender in Sumatra: the kingdom of Aceh.[83]

Despite efforts by Aceh and other areas on Sumatra to reclaim the right to be regarded as the heart of the Melayu lands, the identification of Melayu with the peninsula became increasingly entrenched. With the division of the Melayu world into Dutch and British spheres by the Anglo-Dutch treaty of 1824 and the subsequent creation of independent nation-states in the mid-twentieth century, Melayu finally became identified politically and in the popular mind with the peninsula. Although to this day Melayu groups elsewhere, particularly in the Indonesian provinces of Jambi and

Riau, claim to be the original and pure Melayu, their story is rarely heard. The political struggle for the right to claim to be the centre of the Melayu has been won by Malaysia. It continues to monopolise the study of Melayuness, with the kingdom of Melaka made to represent the 'core values' of the Melayu.[84]

4

The Makassar Malays: Adaptation and Identity, c.1660–1790

HEATHER SUTHERLAND*

Ethnic classification was central to both the description and the administration of Asian port-cities. Local rulers and, later, colonial officials catalogued their subjects, delegating authority over them to the dominant men within each community. But reality was less categorical. Intercommunal commercial, sexual and social relationships were inevitable and often advantageous, so sorting out goats from sheep was far from easy. Flocks were mixed, hybrids abounded. Theoretically ascribed status was, as everywhere else, undermined by human ingenuity. Relationships were pliable, and they determined social identity. Trans-ethnic family ties could be created by adoption, concubinage or marriage, while switching allegiance between patrons entailed, by definition, changing sets of duties, rights and privileges.

Skills were highly sought after, and kings might recruit Turkish gunners, Chinese miners, Portuguese interpreters or Gujerati harbourmasters to strengthen their realms. Slaves from all over Asia were incorporated into households. Preference, opportunism and strategic considerations also encouraged people to exploit whatever flexibility there was in less hierarchical communal ties. For the officials of the Dutch East India Company (VOC), which gradually extended its influence over much of maritime Asia in the seventeenth and eighteenth centuries, such protean local politics were far too unpredictable. They struggled to manage the unruly native inhabitants of their settlements by imposing a fixed grid, and people were expected to stay in their assigned ethnic boxes.

The history of the Makassar Malays in the eighteenth century offers an excellent example of how the apparent continuity of an 'ethnic community' could mask fundamental shifts. The Malays of Southeast Asia, heirs to the renowned maritime tradition of Srivijaya and Melaka, enjoyed considerable prestige.[1] Their ancestral territory fringed one of

76

the world's main trading arteries, the Straits of Melaka, and their consequent expertise underpinned their extraordinary influence. Islamic since the early fifteenth century, Melaka was not just a magnet for traders from China, India, Europe and Southeast Asia; it also provided the archetype of the ideal Malayo-Muslim polity. Its capture first by the Portuguese in 1511, and then by the Dutch in 1641, caused the torch of Malay pride to pass to sultanates such as Aceh and Johor, while traders fled to independent ports.[2]

The resulting Malay refugee communities, including that at Makassar, could draw upon collective commercial know-how and Islamic credentials. These enhanced their ability to access protection, products and markets in palaces and coasts from the Straits of Melaka and Cambodia to the Philippines and West Papua. The Malay language was a recognised *lingua franca* of trade and diplomacy (alongside Portuguese), and was also central to burgeoning Islamic court cultures.

Makassar, on the southwest peninsula of Sulawesi (Celebes), was home-port and political centre of the Goa-Tallo' polity. Since the early sixteenth century it had developed as a multi-ethnic port, sheltering a cosmopolitan court, floating populations of seafarers and various diaspora communities. Both Makassar's rapid rise to success in the sixteenth century and its subsequent subjugation (in the 1660s) by the Dutch East India Company (VOC) were driven by its crucial role in the spice trade. Commercial revenues strengthened the court, and in return elite patronage and protection sustained commerce.

This virtuous circle was broken with the coming of the VOC. Makassarese kings were replaced by Company officials, and access to spices was denied, disrupting the entire system. New constellations of power and wealth gradually emerged, with Buginese Bone replacing Makassar as the paramount regional kingdom. Economic reorientation was a painful process, and only towards the mid-eighteenth century did a strong new commercial thrust emerge with the export of sea-products to China. Role redefinition was particularly acute in the case of the Malays, as they made the transition from fierce opponents of Dutch encroachment to trusted allies of the Company. Nonetheless, they managed to maintain a strong economic position, where others fell back in the face of Chinese competition. These realignments were accompanied by the rise to dominance of one particular extended family.

The following account of the Makassar Malays locates them in two arenas: trade and the town itself. We will begin by considering the character of Makassar's commerce and the early history of the Malay community before turning to the Dutch conquest. We will then trace their further history in sections entitled 'Society and Settlement' and 'Authority and Identity', before concluding with an assessment of Malay adaptation to Company rule, and of the ambiguities inherent in discussing ethnic communities.

Trade and Early History

Makassar's development into an essential link in Southeast Asia's seventeenth-century trading system has been well described.[3] As Anthony Reid has observed:

> It had a better environment to offer than other ports for the exchange of Moluccan spices, Indian cloth, Chinese metalwork and silks, Spanish-American silver, and Sumatran or Bornean pepper. What the traders who brought these goods required was security of life and property, on the one hand, and freedom of commercial and personal exchange on the other.[4]

Within limits, this is what the state known as 'Makassar' provided.

In Makassar terms, anyone from the west, including Javanese, was known as 'Malay'; even the stricter definition of Malay-speaking Muslims included Minangkabau from west Sumatera, and people from Patani, the Straits and coastal Sumatera and Kalimantan (Borneo).[5] Makassar's Malay traders were key handlers of Southwest Sulawesi's main exports (rice and slaves), and of the spices shipped from Maluku to the Straits of Melaka. They are also credited with inviting to Makassar the *ulama* (religious scholars) responsible for the decisive phase of Islamisation. Consequently, they were crucial to early seventeenth-century commercial expansion and conversion, and hence to the making of Makassar. The Malays' commercial acumen, seafaring skills, and frequent commitment to Islam frustrated and angered the monopolistic Protestant Dutch based in Batavia.

On 24 September 1638, the VOC chief merchant, Henrick Kerckerinck, sent his superiors a detailed account of Makassar. He described how European merchants were protected by the King, and noted that the local community of Malays was held "in high esteem, having their houses in the settlements scattered among the houses of the Makassarese". He described how the Malay fleet of around 25 to 40 ships, *tingans* and other large *perahu* built up into junks, used to leave Makassar for Buton in December, January and February loaded with textiles, rice, porcelain and especially *rijksdaalder* (rixdollar) coins. There they exchanged cloth for slaves before proceeding to Ambon, where they would stay for about three months, trading for cloves until September. He estimated that they would bring as much as 1,000 *bahar* (c.182,000 kilogrammes) of spices back to Makassar, of which the English might buy 400 and the Danes 150–200. The rest (about 300 *bahar* in 1638) was traded by the Malays as far away as Aceh and Melaka in the west, or sold to the Portuguese and then taken to Indian Goa, and to Manila. According to Kerckerinck the amount remaining in Makassar itself was not more than about 11 *bahar*, while the year before (1637) it had been about 450.[6] The traditional spice trade between West and East Indonesia, in which Makassar played a crucial role, was already feeling the cold wind of Dutch intervention.

Dutch East India Company agents like Kerckerinck reported regularly on the Malay traders in Makassar, who linked Melaka, Cambodia, Aceh, Johor, Batavia, Banjarmasin, Nusa Tenggara, Maluku, Manila and Sulu.[7] However, the impressive extent of trading networks should not blind us to their limitations. In the 1650s, only three Asian merchants were deemed able to outfit ships in Makassar; one of them was Ince Assam, a Malay; the other two were Indian Muslims.[8] A listing of captains involved in the trade to Maluku and Nusa Tenggara in 1658 showed that while Bandanese and Makassarese had more shipping on those routes than did the Malays, their vessels were mere "coast-hugging creepers". It was only Ince Assam's *perahu* of 15 last (7.5 tonnes) and 30 crew members which could remotely approach the volume of the two 15-tonne galleys belonging to the Portuguese Francisco Viera or the large *tingan* of the Moor (Indian Muslim) Mapulle—the two most famous merchants of seventeenth-century Makassar.[9]

The first official settlement of the Malays in Makassar had been established in 1561, when the Malay skipper Anakoda Bonang (Datuk Maharaja Bonang) brought gifts of textiles and weapons to the ruler of Goa, *Karaeng* Tunipalangga. In exchange, the Malays were granted land on which to settle and limited self-government. The *Karaeng* asked only who was to be included among the Malays. Anakoda Bonang replied that the term 'Malay' covered all those who wore a *sarong* sash, such as men from Pahang, Patani, Champa, Minangkabau and Johor.[10]

Datuk Maharaja Bonang's chief line of descent could be traced back to a *Sayid* (descendant of the Prophet) from Mekka, whose lineage ran down through the Malay centres of Aceh, Johor, Singapore and Patani, to a Wan Umar, who married a princess from Banjarmasin. Their descendants spread to Sumbawa, Bima and throughout South Sulawesi. According to tradition it was also Anakado Bonang who invited a Minangkabau *ulama* to Makassar, this revered Dato' ri Bandang was responsible for the court's Islamisation.[11] This must have enormously strengthened the prestige and influence of the Malays.

The Malays' position was further consolidated with the arrival in 1632 of a nobleman from Patani, Datuk Maharaja Lela; he was chosen as chief of the Makassar Malays.[12] By the mid-seventeenth century Malays were prominent in the life of the court. Ince Amin, a 'Malay of Makassarese descent', was secretary to the ruler of Goa, and wrote a rhymed chronicle of the war between Goa and the VOC. This *Sya'ir Perang Mengkasar* gives many examples of the diplomatic and military activities of the Makassar Malays, and confirms VOC accounts of their mediating role. The *Sya'ir* also reveals Ince Amin's familiarity with Islamic mysticism and Malay literature. As his editor C. Skinner observes, as royal secretary—a kind of resident intellectual—Ince Amin would have been expected to contribute to court culture.[13] In his *Sya'ir*, Ince Amin celebrates the heroism of Datuk Maharaja Lela, as the Malays' political and military leader. The Datuk's descendants were to dominate the community for over 200 years, or, to adopt a slightly different perspective, those who later rose to power sought legitimation by establishing their connections to his lineage.

Conquest and Trade

It was Datuk Maharaja Lela who led the Malay community through the traumatic period of the mid-seventeenth century. He pledged his support to the Goa ruler in the 1666–69 wars, which culminated in Makassar's defeat by a Dutch-Bugis alliance, led by the VOC's Admiral Speelman and the exiled Bone prince Arung Palakka. Ince Amin's *Sya'ir* describes the fierce opposition of the local Malay community (*segala Melayu anak peranakan*); the well-armed Malay contingent was a significant force in Goa's struggle against the accursed Hollanders (*Welanda saitan*).[14]

Ince Amin's account of the important role of the Malays in battle is substantiated by other sources. Speelman himself told Batavia that dislodging the Malays with their firearms was a prerequisite for victory, remarking that they "were even more virulent enemies of the Company than the Makassar people themselves".[15] Leonard Andaya also notes the commitment and courage of the Malays fighting for Goa.[16] Malay ties with the implacably anti-Dutch chancellor of Goa, *Karaeng* Karunrung, and other royal clans such as that of Soppeng, also strengthened their opposition. Speelman described the Soppeng king as a "bitter Mohammedan very close to the Malays", whose Malay wife "with all her retinue, at least a hundred strong, and piles of baggage" took refuge from the fighting in the mosque within Goa's fort.[17] Among those prominent Malays who later refused to return to a Dutch-ruled Makassar after the defeat of Goa were the Johorese

Ince Jabar, who was married to a Malay ex-wife of the Soppeng ruler, and Ince Amar, a Makassar-born Malay of Minangkabau descent, who was a close relative of the Malay wife of Kaicili' Kalimata, one of the main Makassarese war leaders.[18] No doubt there were many more.

Once defeat was inevitable, in 1667, the Malays scattered throughout the straits between Kalimantan and Sulawesi, to Mandar and Pasir, to Nusa Tenggara,[19] and also to more local havens such as the forest near Maros and islands such as Masalambo and Sabutung.[20] After the Treaty of Bungaya had been signed, another wave of South Sulawesians and Malays fled, to continue their careers elsewhere. For the Malays, this meant commerce; for the Buginese, it often meant politics and war.[21]

A weak and humiliated Goa ruler remained in South Sulawesi. The victorious Arung Palakka established his court at Bontoalaq, the ancestral home of the Makassarese leaders, to the east of the now VOC-dominated port settlement.[22] The Dutch priority was to restore some normality to the town, and Speelman inventoried the remaining inhabitants, assessing the various communities' potential contribution to rebuilding. His list included the Malays in Makassar, some 33 men. The largest group, 11, came from West Sumatra, 6 being identified generally as Minangkabau and 5 others specifically as coming from Pariaman. The second most numerous category comprised 9 Makassar-born men. For 5 of these descent was still considered relevant, as 3 were described as being of Johor lineage, and 2 as descendants of Minangkabau. Four other Malays came from Johor itself, and 3 from Kalimantan; the rest were individuals from South Sulawesi, Java and Sumbawa. As a group, the Malays exceeded the Chinese, but were far less numerous than the *Moors*, or Indian Muslims.[23]

We cannot assume that this remaining group was in any way typical of the pre-conquest period. Although Speelman characterised some of those who had remained in Makassar as having been relatively neutral during the war, others, despite their role in the fighting, had nonetheless chosen to stay or to return. These included the Malays connected to the Buginese elite of anti-Dutch Soppeng. It is worth looking at these men in more detail, as their affiliations can provide us with valuable insights into the background and relationships of the Malay community.

The ruler of Soppeng had married a Malay woman, a daughter of one Datuk Tuan, a Jepara-born Malay who was described by Speelman as being primarily of 'Moorish' descent. Speelman notes that despite being a '*Santery*'(*santri* or devout Muslim), Datuk Tuan had not been very involved in the war. Other daughters of his married Daeng Malaba, son of the ruler of Soppeng, and Ince Ahmad, the Makassar-born son of a Johorese father, whose brother Abdul was also reckoned as part of the Soppeng group. Datuk Tuan's nephew Ince Tengah, son of his full brother Ince Mahmud, married a Malay daughter of the Radja of Soppeng. The father of Datuk Tuan and Ince Mahmud, Ince Sambas from Pariaman, died during the fighting—at the age of 150, according to Speelman. The geographic reach of Ince Sambas's family is typical. He himself came from West Sumatra, but his name could imply connections with Kalimantan. His son Datuk Tuan was born in Jepara of partly Indian descent, and his daughters married Buginese and men with Johor backgrounds.

Of this closely related if diverse group, two were regarded as not being very committed to the anti-Dutch struggle (Ince Ahmad and Datuk Tuan), while three (Ince Abdul, Ince Tengah and Daeng Malaba) were seen as strongly pro-Makassar. Another pair of Makassar-born Malay brothers (also of part Indian descent) was similarly divided. Of the two sons of the Moor Pattan, who had been *Anakoda* or ship's captain for the Soppeng king, Datuk Gommo was regarded as acceptable by Speelman, but his brother Ince Said had been a bitter fighter on the Makassarese side; he left Makassar for Jepara. All the others chose to stay on in the town.

Speelman and his successor, Jan van Oppijnen, reported to Batavia that there was little trade in Makassar immediately after the conquest, because of the destruction of the Makassarese and the expulsion of "that untrustworthy Malay rabble".[24] The majority of Malays were poor, earning their living as sailors, and only about eight were regarded by Speelman as being of any consequence. However, this handful of significant traders constituted an economic factor of real importance. Anti-Dutch or not, the Malays were needed, and so Speelman invited the refugees to return. His overtures were not always successful. He identified a group of "hostile creatures, mostly devotees of Karunrung", and listed the most prominent. Heading them all was Datuk Maharaja Lela himself, "upper chief of the whole nation". Earlier, in between the two major campaigns necessary to defeat the Makassarese, Speelman had tried to co-opt Datuk Maharaja Lela. He wrote, "I in person have sought out Radja Lella in the English lodge twice, thrice, more often, wanting to talk to him", pointing out the needs and benefits of stabilising trade—to no avail. The Malay leader, a *hulubalang yang betul* or 'true warrior',[25] followed *Karaeng* Karunrung's advice and fled to avoid the repercussions of the fall of Goa. He died at Balanipa in Mandar. Another notable Malay who turned his back on Makassar was Ince Assam. This most prominent trader of the pre-war period had retired to Jepara, where he was said to be old and sick, and indifferent to Speelman's invitation.[26]

Other Malays took advantage of the Dutch welcome and returned in 1670, with—the Malay account is careful to stress—the agreement of the ruler of Goa. Some Buginese who had fought alongside the Makassarese also returned, notably the skilled traders from Wajo', whose communal history paralleled that of the Malays in many ways.[27] Some Malays also saw real possibilities in the new regime. One prominent figure, Ince Abdul, was regarded as a friend to the Dutch, although he was also suspected of having been in touch with Datuk Maharaja Lela before the last round of fighting. Born in Makassar about 1620, the son of a Minangkabau father and a Buginese mother, Ince Abdul had obviously been a major trader before the war. His outstanding debts after the conquest included 1,270 rds (*rijksdaalders*) owed to him by *Karaeng* Karunrung, while the ruler of the Borneo trading state of Pasir was in his debt for 1,200 rds, being payment due for three metal cannon Ince Abdul had brought him from Patani. Ince Abdul later became a translator for the VOC; his wife was maintained by the Dutch, and lived in their settlement. Another prominent and relatively wealthy Malay, Ince Allaudin, was married to a Buginese woman, and linked to Arung Palakka, the ally of the VOC. He was closely involved in Speelman's post-conquest attempts to induce the Malay refugees to return to Makassar.[28]

Gradually the VOC forced Makassar's trade into a straitjacket, reserving the most profitable commodities and routes for itself and only allowing free trade where there was no threat to Company profits. During the 1670s, elements of the old patterns persisted, with Malays from Melaka and Aceh frequenting ports traditionally within Makassar's sphere of influence, such as Pasir and Buton, Bima and Kaili. Textiles and slaves were important commodities. Ince Patani, a Malay captain operating out of Aceh (a typical fusion of place-based identifications) came every year to the eastern archipelago, and is recorded in Dutch sources from at least 1679.[29] He visited Buton annually, bringing textiles from the Melaka Straits, Chinese goods and weapons to exchange for slaves. In September 1683, the four big, three-masted ships of Ince Patani, his son Ince Abdul Rahman and Ince Ranta took 1,400 slaves from Buton to Aceh.[30] In 1686 Ince Patani was back in Buton (at the same time that another prominent Malay trader, Sri Lela Wangsa, from Johor, was shipwrecked there), and in 1687 he and his son are again recorded exchanging textiles for slaves, but now in Bima.[31] In the same year Sri Lela Wangsa was also noted, this time buying up rattan in Pasir.[32]

But already a new regime was being established. The Dutch deployed both diplomacy and force to control Malay trade. Individual Malay communities such as that in Makassar were subjected to increasing restriction, as wider networks came under pressure and as local VOC authorities imposed regional limitations. Some requests to the Company in Makassar were granted on strict conditions, as when Makassarese Malays sought permission to trade in Banjarmasin, while others were refused, as in the case of the Mandar-based Minangkabau 'pirate' Datuk Jelany.[33] Definitions of piracy and smuggling were of course very subjective: a Malay trader going about his traditional business might find himself labelled "the well-known smuggler Ince Kasim" and have his ship and cargo seized.[34]

By about 1706 trade between Makassar and Johor was greatly reduced, and by 1709 commercial links had been broken because of the turmoil in the Johor sultanate, where 'Bugis' adventurers exacerbated internal crises.[35] The Makassar Malays' trade suffered, and they petitioned the VOC to allow them to sail to Jambi, Palembang and even Melaka. But this was forbidden.[36] Cut off from their traditional wide-ranging networks, denied access to commodities and markets west of Batavia, and with Manila out of bounds, the Malays became increasingly dependent on the Batavia, Maluku and Nusa Tenggara traffic. By the early decades of the eighteenth century, accounts of Malay activity in the VOC archives of Makassar are already shifting in tone. In the early and mid-seventeenth century, the emphasis had been upon how the Malays, with the Portuguese and English, were 'ruining the market' for the Dutch. Then, from the conquest up to about 1720, reports focus on efforts to force Malays, including those in Makassar, to accept Company restrictions and monopolies. By the 1730s or 1740s the Malays seem to have become more domesticated. They remain important, particularly in the slave trade, but seem to have been operating more in Dutch-approved circuits.[37]

There are several possible explanations for this apparent shift. The Malay trading networks of Southeast Asia had weakened, part of a wider process the Andayas have characterised as the eighteenth-century 'demise of the Malay entrepôt state'. This was a result of strains in the pre-eminent Malay state of Johor; the expansion of Bugis, and to a lesser extent Minangkabau, influence in the Straits; and growing Dutch and English involvement.[38] Another, simple, reason for the decline in Malay commerce as reflected in the Dutch sources could be decreasing registration or changes in descriptive categorisation. Old commercial networks may have continued, or new routes developed, beyond Company supervision, and often in competition with VOC-approved channels. This seems to have been the case with those Bugis traders *par excellence*, the Wajorese. After Wajo's wars with the Company in the 1730s, their role in Makassar's trade becomes invisible in the sources, although they continued to live in the town.[39]

No doubt some Malays, for political, religious and/or commercial reasons, preferred to sail outside Company-controlled circuits. Those who chose to return to Makassar gradually, albeit reluctantly, accepted the new limitations on their trade, though they probably evaded them when possible. The extent of this is difficult to ascertain, as continuing links with wider, perhaps anti-Dutch networks are by their nature unrecorded in the VOC archives. Questions concerning the ways in which Asian communities, under Dutch control and living in Company-controlled settlements, accommodated to the new regime are equally intriguing; the answers almost as elusive. There are, however, indications that the Malays of Makassar adapted successfully and, by the 1730s, had consolidated their position within the VOC-dominated port town.

Society and Settlement

The focus of power in post-conquest Makassar was Fort Rotterdam, built upon the remnants of Goa's northern fort of Ujung Pandang. Just north of the castle was the new, palisaded settlement of Vlaardingen, where the growing community of 'Europeans' (*mestizos* and *burgers*, non-Company personnel) lived, as did many Chinese and other Asians. Still further north, along the beach and, later, south of the fort, new mixed and 'native' settlements proliferated. At first the Malays lived dispersed among the rest of the population: in Vlaardingen, along the coast to the north and east of Fort Rotterdam, and up as far as Ujungtana, close to Tallo'. This was a time of disorder, as the victorious Bugis asserted themselves through violence and plundering. The Malay leaders complained that their rights, as established in 1561, were being ignored. They were then given permission by the Company (and, contemporary tradition makes clear, by the Raja Goa) to clear secondary forest from the land just north of Vlaardingen.[40] This new settlement of Kampung Melayu was to be the focus of Makassar's Malay life for some 300 years, while its physical location between *mestizo* European, Chinese and Bugis quarters epitomised the role of the community in both trade and politics.

In the oldest surviving census for the Dutch enclave of Vlaardingen, from 1676, Malays are not distinguished as a category, which suggests that they lived outside the stockade.[41] Chinese, *Mardijkers* (Asian Christians, often ex-slaves) and *Moors* (Indian Muslims) were allowed inside, but the recently-defeated Makassarese, like the Malays, were in principle excluded. The Buginese had their own settlements: Arung Palakka's court at Bontoalaq, east of the Fort, and a growing Kampung Bugis about half an hour's walk

north of the Dutch castle, past the Kampung Melayu. However, as subjects
of native rulers, the Bugis were not counted.

The Malays first appear in the 1680 Vlaardingen Census, as a small
group of 18 comprising four men, nine women and five children, all living
between the beach and the Chinese street. Other groups were much more
numerous. There were 97 *Mardijkers* and 87 Chinese, and even the 20
Moors and Javanese outnumbered the Malays. The total population of the
enclosed settlement was 1,135.[42] As usual, the census did not cover VOC
employees, and women, children and slaves were all subsumed into the
same category as the heads of households. The inhabitants of unregulated
settlements beyond the walls were not counted in 1680.

The census for 1685 was more complete. For the first time,
communities outside Vlaardingen are listed, the *kampung* quarters or
informal semi-rural clusters of compounds, often named after ethnic
groups.[43] The free Malay community of 279 showed a balanced
demographic picture: 103 men, 110 women and 66 children. They owned
209 slaves, and controlled 23 debtors, so their number was reckoned at
511.[44] The Malays tended to own, per head, more slaves than the indigenous
East Indonesian groups, but fewer than the Chinese or the *Mardijkers*, and
nothing near the concentrations held by the *Moors* or Europeans.
Nonetheless, the members of Malay households in 1685 outnumbered
those of all other groups, except the Chinese. The total population of
Makassar (excluding Company personnel) had grown to 2,751.

Twelve years later, in 1697, the non-VOC population had grown to
3,238. If in 1685 Malays (counting slaves) had formed about 19 per cent
of the population, by 1697 the 764 Malays comprised roughly 24 per cent
of the whole. '*Mardijker*' no longer existed as a category, but '*Moors* and
Kodjas' had increased to 531.[45] No breakdown is available by age, sex or
place of residence. Malays had become the most numerous group in the
city. However, by 1722 they were again surpassed by the Chinese (917),
and by the non-VOC inhabitants of European status, the *burgers* (899),
although with their 881 they far outstripped the 371 Indians.[46] In subsequent
population counts all non-Europeans were subsumed in one category. By
1770 the 'native' population numbered over 3,750: a generally modest
increase compared with the rapid growth between 1685 and 1697. While
this early census material provides us with rudimentary information, we
need more if we are to have some image of Malay neighbourhoods. Such
information is only sporadically available.

Fires were one of the most devastating events in Makassar's urban
life, and descriptions give us some insight into settlement patterns. In 1679,

a great fire, fanned by a strong sea wind, destroyed 80 houses in Vlaardingen, including the living quarters of two Moor-Malays, Ince Buang and Ince Tengah, sons of the famous merchant, Mapulle. Their compound consisted of four large houses, and assorted small dwellings where their people lived.[47] The many slaves and debt-bondsmen were expected to earn their own living; some occupations—cooking coconut oil, baking sweets for sale in the market—were high fire-risk activities. After the Vlaardingen compound was burnt out, this 'great rabble' moved into the Moorish quarter between the beach and the Kampung Bugis. Here, in August 1680, their enterprises triggered a new fire which destroyed 150 houses, including their whole compound, much of the Wajorese area and part of the *kampung* for Moors and Bugis.[48]

Over a hundred years later, on 6 August 1791, another fire swept through the Kampung Melayu, destroying it completely. The Dutch authorities saw this as an opportunity to improve town security, and contemplated resettling all Malays in Kampung Baru, south of the castle. This would involve the removal of 38 *kampung* (used here in the sense of compounds belonging to individual extended families), of which just more than half were actually Malay-owned.[49] It was reckoned that these 38 compounds comprised at least 300 houses, and accommodated 2,300 or 2,400 people.[50]

Since the total non-European population of Makassar in that year (1791) was 4,934,[51] about half the town would have had to be re-housed. The densely settled Chinese street was not involved in this plan, nor were the more peripheral *kampung*. It is, therefore, likely that a very high proportion of the 'Malay' population lived in the 20 Malay-owned compounds considered for removal. Since they probably varied in size from poor clusters of a few huts to large complexes, it is not possible to be precise, but many compounds could have consisted of more than ten houses, with dozens of inhabitants. If this was so, then it illustrates probable patterns of dependency, with dominant patrons sheltering many clients. However, the ethnic mix of compound ownership (not to mention their undoubtedly even more heterogeneous inhabitants) warns us against any assumed congruence between formal classification and social reality. The relocation plan was submitted to the VOC High Government in Batavia, which rejected it as impossible, given the scale of resettlement required.[52]

The Dutch regarded the integration of the Malays and Chinese into town life as important, for both economic and security reasons. In 1728, for example, Governor Gobius noted that the Malays could muster 265 armed men, capable of turning out in "good order, under the command of their Captain and lesser officers". This Malay contingent was an effective armed force, outnumbering the combined manpower of the 70 *burgers*, the 60 Chinese (including *Peranakan*) and 60 *Mardijkers*.[53] Half a century earlier, Ince Amin and Speelman had both noted the important role of Goa's well-armed and cohesive Malay company.[54] The Malay *kampung* itself was also seen as a reliable barrier between the volatile Bugis settlement and the castle.

Authority and Identity

The VOC always worked together with local leaders, giving them military titles, symbols of power and privileges in exchange for their cooperation in governing the various communities.[55] Loyalty to the Company was rewarded by Dutch support, a major political asset. It is usually said that the first Malay *Kapitan*, or Dutch-appointed headman, was Ince Cukka, Abdul Razak, who took office in May 1705. The sources are somewhat contradictory on this point. A Wajorese manuscript records an agreement between the leader of Makassar's Wajorese, the *matoa*, and the two *Kapitans* (Chinese and Malay) in February 1698, in which Ince Cukka is described as the *Kapitan Melayu*.[56] But Makassar's VOC archives for 29 May 1705 note that prominent Malays reported the death of their *Kapitan* Abdul Nazul, and requested that a new *Kapitan* be appointed from their midst, suggesting Ince Cukka. Their petition was passed to Batavia for approval. Pending confirmation, Ince Cukka was given the symbols of office: a silver ornamented cane (which Ince Abdul Nazul's widow had returned to the governor) and a new ceremonial umbrella.[57] Malay sources record that Ince Cukka was given the right to build a mosque, and construction began on 22 Radjab 1117 AH (1706).[58] The Company allowed him an income from the fish market he built, and from fees derived from registering his subjects' property. These *Kapitan*'s perquisites were again confirmed by Governor Mossel in 1752.[59]

Ince Maulud, the second *Kapitan Melayu* (or third, if we include Abdul Nazul), was appointed in January 1724. He was born in Banjarmasin, but had been brought up in Makassar, and was about 38 years old when he became *Kapitan*. He soon came into conflict with the VOC authorities, and his case has interesting implications. The immediate cause of Dutch dissatisfaction seemed simple: in 1726 some Buginese attacked two Europeans in the market, and a riot ensued. Ince Maulud was informed that two Dutchmen were being murdered, but he simply closed his door. When the Company legal official tried to call upon the *Kapitan* to mobilise

Malay resistance to the Buginese, some 20 Malays blocked his entry to the house, and no help was forthcoming. The Malays simply stayed inside until the Buginese had left, avoiding any confrontation. The VOC authorities felt that Ince Maulud had failed in his duty to maintain order and support the Dutch. At the same time, they were also investigating his finances, as he was heavily in debt and one of his creditors—"a Batavian native woman"—wanted to seize his assets, but these were proving difficult to locate. The Company authorities suggested he had defrauded his creditors, by giving at least 11 slaves away to the King of Bone. But Ince Maulud responded with simple answers to such accusations of bad faith. He claimed there had been no people in his house who could have helped the beleaguered Dutchmen, and that the slaves had not been given away, but had fled.[60]

Subsequent questioning, however, indicated that Ince Maulud found himself in a delicate political situation. Although he had been told that the ruler of Bone was planning an incident in the market to humiliate the Dutch, he had neglected to warn the authorities. When asked why, he replied that his information came from a mixed Malay-Moor, a follower of a Buginese nobleman, who was also in the service of the translator Gerrit Brugman. Consequently, Ince Maulud had presumed the Dutch were aware of the plot. 'Translators' such as Brugman were, after all, the main links between the VOC and local states or communities.[61] Ince Maulud was also asked why, when Brugman had given him the use of Company rice fields (no doubt as a perquisite of office), did he then give the produce to the King of Bone? He explained that the Buginese had come and taken the harvest. Finally, the Dutch inquired why he failed to pay his respects to the VOC authorities on the customary feast days. Because he was ashamed, he replied, as he had lost all his possessions.[62]

It is of course possible that Ince Maulud's excuses were genuine. But the pattern suggests another interpretation: that either willingly or unwillingly, Ince Maulud was acknowledging the authority of the Bugis ruler of Bone. Since the conquest the King of Bone had maintained a house close to Makassar, at Bontoalaq, and spent months there every year; this gave him every opportunity to expand his influence in the port-town's *kampung*. For example, Bone's rulers were able to demand services from the Wajorese in Makassar, undermining the authority of the head of that community, the *matoa*. The fact that, coincidentally, the Bone kings also bore by right a high title from the Bugis state of Wajo reinforced their claims, heightening tensions between *matoa* and court.[63] The temptation must have been great for them to seek similar influence over that other prominent Muslim commercial group, the Malays. It is clear from the line of questioning that this was the suspicion of Makassar's Dutch authorities. Ince Maulud did not survive long as *Kapitan*, being replaced in 1728.[64]

Ince Maulud's successor, Ince Samba, hardly did any better. He was appointed in 1728 but dismissed by Governor Arrewijne in December 1733 on the grounds that he was addicted to opium. His replacement was the 'free Malay' Ince Bendak,[65] a descendant of Datuk Maharaja Lela, and hence of the highest birth. His daughter's marriage to the wealthy trader Ince Ali Asdullah was to have dramatic consequences (see below); it also secured his descendants' grip on the Malay community for over a century and a half.

The position of *Kapitan Melayu* had its privileges and obligations, as did those of the other community headmen.[66] Ince Cukka had received the right to collect fees for registering property, and one of his successors as *Kapitan*, Abdul Kadir (see below) complained in 1768 that a proposal to remove this right to levy fees on house sales would further reduce his 'sober income'. The percentage on the sale of the simple bamboo dwellings in Kampung Melayu did not amount to much, and money was needed, he said, to repair the mosque. The Company agreed to leave him this privilege.[67] Abdul Kadir was probably being disingenuous. The right to levy such fees was a minor aspect of his ability to profit from his position, as his responsibility for law and order and his access to men of influence made him a force in community life and commerce. There is no doubt that the officers enjoyed many perquisites (such as Ince Maulud's rice fields), and probably many semi-illicit fruits of power. The Wajorese *matoa*, in a similar role, benefited from considerable advantages in trade.[68]

If responsibility sometimes weighed heavily on the *Kapitan*, apparently being subject to his authority could also be onerous. In 1769, Ince Mursidin, requesting permission to retire after 20 years' service as lieutenant of the Malays, petitioned the VOC to free him and his family from the authority of the *Kapitan Melayu*, and to take him under direct Company rule. The authorities granted his request, seeing this as a due reward, so like the people of 'other free *kampung*', he then fell under VOC jurisdiction, as exercised by the translator Brugman. But this did not mean that Ince Mursidin could ignore his communal obligations. He had still to contribute to the maintenance of the mosque, and the guard, and he was sternly admonished to continue to show respect to the *Kapitan* and his officers, just as the *Kapitan* would now respect his new status, and renounce all claims on him.[69] Ince Mursidin was one of the few Malay officers who did not come from Abdul Kadir's own family, which might have been a reason for his request.

One of the problems facing the *Kapitans* and other community headmen was the need to maintain the integrity of their group. Each leader strove to maximise his following. In the mid-eighteenth century, for example, the Wajorese *matoa* was continually struggling to prevent his followers from drifting out of Makassar's Kampung Wajo' into other *kampung*, such as Bandang, Buton, and Melayu.[70] The Malays' main competitor in communal boundary disputes seems to have been the Muslim Chinese community. No doubt there were other on-going processes of blending and crystallisation (witness, for example, the gradual disappearance of *Mardijkers* and *Moors*, or the tug-of-war over the Wajorese), but perhaps because both Chinese and Malay communities were living under direct Company protection, their tensions are the best documented. The theoretical rigidity of ethnic classifications, especially those imposed by the bureaucratic VOC, was at odds with the pragmatic opportunism and cultural flexibility typical of the settlement's social life.[71]

Many Chinese in seventeenth- and eighteenth-century Makassar were very much part of the town; a majority may well have been Muslim. Even many of the so-called 'junk' Chinese, who came from Amoy (Xiamen) to trade and stayed for six months in most years after 1746, had their own local families, and some of these merchants were Muslim. As Makassar's dominant trading communities (excluding the VOC), the Chinese and Malays were often locked in competition, but their activities were also in many ways complementary, so long-term partnerships developed. There were close ties—personal and commercial—between the two communities. This can be seen in genealogies.

The forefather of many prominent Malay families was Datuk Maharaja Lela, whose central role in seventeenth-century Makassar has been outlined above. He had two children: a son, Megat Kasim, forefather of inhabitants of Kampung Butung, and a daughter, Puteri Johor Manikam, whose descendants lived in Kampung Melayu. Puteri Johor Manikam married Ince Subuh, who was of Chinese-Makassarese descent. His family story relates how two Chinese trader brothers left Melaka and went to Cirebon in West Java. One source specifies that these men were Muslim.[72] The younger, Layti (Lai I Tjio), settled there after marrying a daughter of one Tumenggung Batang, while the elder brother, Failantia (Pao Lau Tia) took his share of the trade goods and went to Sanrabone, south of Makassar, where he was given permission to settle. In accordance with the ruler's request, he married a well-born local woman. Their son, Ince Abdul, also married well, and his son Ince Subuh, alias Ince DaEng, became the son-in-law of Paduka Raja Maharaja Lela. Their children married further into

Chinese Muslim families. One grandson, Ince Bungsu, the seventh Makassar *Kapitan Melayu* (1750–52), was married to a *Peranakan* Chinese, and their grandson, Ince Taman, was an imam of the Kampung Butung mosque, as were several cousins.[73] This '*mesjid peranakan*', now officially the Mesjid Mubarrak, lies directly opposite the modern Butung market. The imams there seem to have been *Peranakan* Chinese until 1973 or 1975.[74]

Although intermarriage between Malays and Chinese Muslims was common, it is often invisible in genealogies because of the use of Muslim names. However, it is clear that some branches of Malay families were closer to the Chinese community than others. For example, Ince Muhammed Saleh , a son of the famous Datuk Pabean (or Ince Ali Asdullah, see below) married I Na'na, whose father Ince Abdul Gaffar Datuk Gaddong, was the son of the Chinese Muslim Ong King Cong and his wife Ong Nio, who probably lived in Makassar in the early eighteenth century. Their descendants mainly have Muslim names, though some bear the prefix 'Baba' or 'Nyai', and a few had Chinese names. Some spouses are identified as *Peranakan* Chinese. Like many groups in Indonesia, the Malay association today runs several rotating credit associations, or *arisan*, and in 2000 one was still specifically for wives of Chinese Muslim descent.[75]

The closeness between the two communities, with the concomitant blurring of boundaries, could also be problematic. The Makassar Chinese had their own version of their relationship with the Malays immediately after Speelman's victory. They claimed that at that time the *Kapitan* of the Chinese community, Ong Watko, had been given authority over all the *Peranakan* Chinese and Malays. But the Malays had a powerful ally. The wife of Arung Palakka—the Company's Buginese partner and ruler of the dominant kingdom of Bone (1672–96)—interceded with the Dutch on their behalf. She argued that the Malays should have their own headman, and so Ince Cukka was appointed.[76] But it was specified that Chinese Muslims were to remain under the *Kapitan China*. This was later to be a source of conflict.

In 1750, the *Kapitan China* complained that, in violation of established rights and custom, the contentious *Kapitan Melayu* 'Ince Banjar' was claiming authority over 'Chinese', and emotions ran so high that a 'bloody fight' was narrowly avoided. The Malay *Kapitan*, Abdul Kadir (perhaps his nickname was Ince Banjar?), counter-attacked with the statement that the Chinese were asserting rights over *Peranakan* Malays married to Chinese. This was regarded as very unfair, as the Malays felt they had much heavier obligations to the Company than did the Chinese. The Malay community had to provide men and ships whenever required, which they did willingly. Ince Abdul Kadir appended a list of Malay men and women married to *Peranakan* Chinese to illustrate the scope of the problem: 13 Malay *Peranakan* women married to *Peranakan* Chinese men, and 6 Malay men with *Peranakan* Chinese wives. The Dutch authorities finally decided for the principle of territoriality over genealogy, and so all who lived in *Kampung Melayu* or areas under the *Kapitan Melayu* had to accept his jurisdiction or move out.[77]

The *Kapitan*'s control over people was necessary to generate income and preserve status, and the importance attached to these 19 households reminds us again of how small these communities were. The Wajorese drifted out of their Kampung Wajo' to live in other areas of the town, and resisted attempts to force them to return. As inhabitants of Kampung Melayu, they were exempt from services and enjoyed more freedom than they would have if they returned to their own kampung and the authority of their *matoa*.[78] There is a hint in the documents that there was a comparable financial element involved in Chinese resistance to Malay authority. The Chinese *Kapitan*, when referring to the rights of the *Peranakan* Chinese, only specifically mentioned one: that when a *Peranakan* died intestate and without relatives, his estate, according to Batavia practice, was to be taken over and administered by the Dutch orphan chamber (*weeskamer*).[79] The chamber would then be responsible for investing the capital, and the orphans would receive their inheritance, including any profits, on reaching their majority. This was probably more advantageous than alternatives which might be applied should the *Peranakan* Chinese fall under the *Kapitan Melayu*, and recalls the Malays' emphasis on their own exemption from Makassarese customary law in their agreement of 1561. Residence, allegiance and ethnic classification determined legal status, and that could have significant economic as well as social consequences.

As always, there were some who seized the opportunities offered by a new regime, and one particular family arose to dominate the Malay community from the mid-eighteenth to the mid-nineteenth century. The decisive figure was Ince Ali Asdullah, whose title of Datuk Pabean reflects the source of the family's sustained wealth: his ability to purchase from the Dutch the monopoly right to levy import and export duties. His control of the lucrative customs farm during the 1770s and 1780s laid the foundations for his family's success. Ince Ali Asdullah's descendants provided the *Kapitan Melayu* from the 1730s till the 1880s. His own Arab-Malay origin, reinforced by eighteenth-century marriages into families of *Sayids* (descendants of the Prophet), helped reinforce his family's hold on the prestigious position of Imam of the Malay mosque built and endowed by Ince Ali Asdullah and his brother (see table at the end of this chapter).

Ince Ali Asdullah's forebears were characteristically peripatetic. His grandfather, Datuk Abdul Mannan Amir, went from Bima to Sinjai on south Sulawesi, where he married a daughter of the Arung Bulo-Bulo. He took his wife to live in the Kampung Melayu in Makassar. There he had a son, called Ince Abdul Rachman, who was adopted by a Sayid, Achmad Bochari. When Datuk Abdul Mannan Amir returned to Bima (where he died), Sayid Achmad Bochari gave Ince Abdul Rachman into the hands of the Raja of Tallo', Sultan Syafiuddin, who married him to his granddaughter. The sultan also gave him the lordship over all of the small islands from the Spermonde Archipelago opposite Makassar which belonged to Tallo' and began with Sa- (Sabutung, Satando, Sanga-sanga, Salemo, Sagara, Sabangka, Sarappo etc.). Ince Abdul Rachman became known as Datuk Sabutung. This island of Sabutung had been a Malay place of refuge in the final phase of the war against the Dutch-Bugis alliance.

Ince Abdul Rachman had five sons, including Abdul Kadir and the younger Ali Asdullah, who were brought up in simple circumstances, but studied the Koran and learnt to read, write and calculate. Their livelihood came from their islands—they were traders, or sailors, or *perahu*-builders, or they took sea products such as tortoiseshell, *agar-agar* (seaweed) or *trepang* (sea-cucumbers) to the town of Makassar, where they sold them to Chinese traders. It is probable that they also maintained commercial relationships with the Bajo, as the Spermonde Archipelago was also frequented by these 'sea-nomads', who were experts in the exploitation of marine resources. This period, the 1730s, was a profitable time for Makassar, when the trade in sea products with China was transforming the economy.[80] This growing source of wealth must have strengthened those groups who were able to capitalise on the new opportunities. The resulting social mobility is reflected in the eventual admission of Datuk Sabutung's descendants into Makassar's Malay elite.

The *Kapitan Melayu* of the time, Ince Bendak, as we have seen, was descended from Datuk Maharaja Lela, and a man of high status and wealth. He was acquainted with a Chinese Muslim merchant called Musalaf, who was also Datuk Sabutung's friend. All three were no doubt engaged in commerce. While visiting Datuk Sabutung, Musalaf's eye fell on Ali Asdullah, who was by then trading regularly with Kalimantan (Pegatan/ Pasir and Kutei) and Java (Batavia). Musalaf asked why the young man was unmarried, and suggested that a suitable candidate would be the *Kapitan*'s daughter. Datuk Sabutung replied that the difference in rank between his family and that of Ince Bendak was like that between the earth and the sky, and Musalaf said no more, but prayed that God would unite the pair. Two months later, one of the authorities from Makassar, a Dutch *Tuan Besar* (probably the governor) stayed on Sabutung for a couple of days, at the same time that Musalaf was also visiting. When the *Tuan* asked why Ali Asdullah was unmarried, Musalaf said that only Puteri Ratna Kasian, the daughter of the *Kapitan*, would be a suitable match. The *Tuan Besar* asked Datuk Sabutung if this was so. Once again, Datuk Sabutung emphasised the difference in rank and wealth, stating that he himself was poor and of low birth. The *Tuan Besar* stood up, thumped the table with his hand, and said he personally would arrange the marriage; Datuk Sabutung need only wait, and before the next east monsoon he would be called to Makassar.

The *Tuan Besar* was as good as his word. Datuk Sabutung was summoned to Makassar, met by the *Kapitan* Ince Bendak, and taken to the palace of the *Tuan Besar*, where the leaders of the Malay community and other nations waited. The *Tuan Besar* told Ince Bendak that he wished to see a marriage between the *Kapitan*'s daughter and Ince Ali Asdullah to which the *Kapitan* replied, "Whatever my lord wants, I will accept willingly". The *Tuan Besar* produced paper and pen, and the elders of Kampung Melayu all witnessed the engagement.

In fact, *Kapitan* Ince Bendak was far from happy, but on attempting to withdraw from the arrangement, he was reminded by the Malay leaders of his commitment, so he had to let the wedding proceed. However, he was tormented by regrets. On the day that Ince Ali Asdullah arrived to claim his bride, with full customary pomp, her father was nowhere to be seen. A search revealed his body hanging from the rafters. This must have been in 1739, as a new *Kapitan* was appointed in August of that year.[81] The wedding feast became a funeral, and the family of the groom, instead of sitting facing their new relatives, was set apart, and a fight followed. When Ince Ali Asdullah realised that Puteri Ratna Kasian's entire family opposed the match, he withdrew to Sabutung, and then left again on his trading voyages to Kalimantan, Java and beyond. After two years wandering he returned with rich profits and jewels, but thinking only of his unclaimed wife at Makassar. Some time later, his bride's family realised that they should not keep the two apart, and sent someone to tell Ince Ali Asdullah to collect Puteri Ratna Kasian and take her to Sabutung. This he did, and she came, bringing with her only the clothes she was wearing.

Ince Ali Asdullah became a man of great wealth, and gradually his family-in-law became reconciled; one by one they came to Sabutung, and he was accepted. His reputation grew further, until the Malay community asked him to follow in the footsteps of his father-in-law as *Kapitan*, replacing Ince Jamaluddin, who had succeeded Ince Bendak. But Ince Ali Asdullah refused, as he preferred to sail and trade throughout the archipelago. Also, he had his eye on a more lucrative proposition: the monopoly on in- and outgoing duties of the port of Makassar. He succeeded in holding this office for years, and so was known as Datuk Pabean, or Datuk Syahbandar.[82]

Just as the *Kapitan*s were the political link between the VOC and the Asian communities, of which the Dutch had very limited knowledge, so were the *pachters* or tax-farmers the instrument for tapping profits from those sectors of the local economy claimed by the Company.[83] The Dutch wished to take advantage of any possibility of making money, but it was often more practical for them to sell exploitation rights, rather than attempt to penetrate and manage local networks. The oldest recorded farm in Makassar, dating from 1685, was the monopoly on the sale of alcohol (which included gambling, opium and the keeping of taverns); this was usually held by a retired Company soldier.[84] But Batavia was dissatisfied with the low level of income generated; after a scandal the system of farms was extended, and from 1745 the right to collect duties on incoming and outgoing vessels and their cargoes was auctioned. Previously, this had probably been controlled by the harbourmaster, a VOC official.[85] A few years later, a tax-farm was also introduced for markets.

Initially, farms were usually controlled by the *Kapitan China*, and it is highly probable that they were a formalisation of existing rights and a compensation for investment, as well as an attempt to increase town revenue. Later, in the mid-1750s, more farms were added. The farmers' identities reflect relative access to economic resources. The alcohol monopoly was in European hands until the 1770s, when they were replaced by Chinese; the gambling, slaughter and Chinese head-tax collecting rights were all Chinese-controlled (except for one year when a *mestizo* was collecting the tax). The monopoly on running the town's markets was much more open, falling to Chinese, Malays and *mestizos*. But far and away the most valuable farm was that of the customs duties. For a quarter of a century, this was a bone of contention in the fierce struggle waged by Ince Ali Asdullah and his elder brother, Abdul Kadir, the *Kapitan Melayu*, against Makassar's Chinese elite.

During this period, the annual amount paid for the farm rose from around 12,000 to over 20,000 rds, considerable sums when one considers that a bamboo house and block of land sold for about 50 rds and a good slave for 30. The real value of the farms—their profitability—is hard to ascertain, given the tendency of aspiring farmers to form cartels, fix the bidding and undervalue, on the one hand, as opposed to the desire to win and gain social prestige on the other. Trade is always a risky business, and wars or policy changes—in the region, Batavia or China—could reduce commerce to such a degree that the farmer lost heavily.[86] But Ince Ali Asdullah's grip on the customs monopoly was impressive. His first sally, in 1766, gained him the farm for one year only, at a cost of 8,244 rds, considerably less than the previous Chinese had paid (12,000). But the trade between Makassar and China was both crucial and complex, and in his calculations as to the profitability of the farm he had banked on collecting duty on imports from China. But that year no junk came directly to Makassar from Amoy, so commodities from China arrived via Batavia.

Ince Ali Asdullah had not realised—he said—that Chinese tobacco imported from Batavia was exempt from duty, and tried to collect his percentage. He appealed to the harbourmaster but was told he could levy no claims on the cargo. Makassar's *Peranakan* Chinese were also up in arms, claiming that the marginal existence of their small community would be further undermined if double taxation was allowed, with duties paid first in Batavia and then again in Makassar. The VOC refused Ince Ali Asdullah's request for restitution of part of his payment.[87] It could be that he was able to take the farm for such a relatively low amount because his Chinese competitors had inside information on the junk's non-arrival in Makassar. But their lack of interest in 1766 may have backfired, as Ince Ali Asdullah was now committed to gaining control of the farm.

He lost the customs monopoly the following year, to a Chinese prepared to pay 13,000, but then his older brother, *Kapitan Melayu* Abdul Kadir took over, for 14,376. The farm then passed to Ince Ali Asdullah for three years, before a Chinese recaptured it for over 17,000 rds. Ince Ali Asdullah retook the monopoly and subsequently held it for 14 years, from 1776 to 1789, on a fixed annual tariff of 18,000 rds. In 1781, Ince Ali Asdullah had further problems with Chinese complaints; he was accused of overcharging, and he himself had noted that differences of opinion on the prices of opium, Chinese tobacco and cotton led to conflict. However, inspection of his books (to the accuracy of which he swore every year on the Koran), and the support of the previous Chinese farmer, showed that he was keeping to the farm conditions, and he retained his position.[88]

This continuity was ensured by a contract with the Company, removing the custom's farm allocation from competitive bidding. Batavia was not happy with this, fearing lost income, but the Makassar authorities defended it on the grounds that stability and peace was ensured because of Ince Ali Asdullah's close connections to the native courts. This reversed the opinion expressed earlier, in 1766, that Chinese were preferable to Malays as *pachters*.[89] Then the issue had been the need to maintain a smooth relationship with the Chinese traders handling imports from China, but by 1784 the emphasis had switched to avoiding problems with the Sulawesian rulers, particularly expansionist Bone.

This shift probably reflected an awareness on the Dutch side of their vulnerability, as the Fourth Anglo-Dutch War (1780–84) had caused a visible collapse in VOC shipping and prestige.[90] The governor of Makassar explained that in principle he would prefer to auction the farm, but "the present farmer (HS Ince Ali Asdullah) is now accustomed to dealing with all the native kings and other important men, particularly with the king of Bone, and if a Chinese or someone else should come in, then daily squabbles could be expected".[91] A successful customs farmer had to have considerable commercial and political acumen, excellent connections and enough capital to ride the inevitable fluctuations of trade. The fact that Ince Ali Asdullah was able to hold this position for so long is a tribute to his skills and influence.

While he was by the far the most important, Ince Ali Asdullah was not the only tax-farmer from the Malay community, although it is striking that most of the other farmers were also from his family. In 1766, the same year that Ince Ali Asdullah obtained the customs farm, his older brother Ince Abdul Kadir purchased the market farm for 197 rds, but it reverted to Chinese control the following year. However, in 1769 Ince Ali Asdullah's son, the Letnan Melayu Ince Suleiman, paid 475 rds to obtain the farm, and held it for that year and also for 1776, 1782, 1784, 1785, 1788–90. While his main competitors were Chinese, a couple of other Malays did run the markets for a year at a time. A tendency towards family continuity in holding high community office could also be observed among Makassar's Wajorese *matoa*.[92]

This financial pre-eminence of Ince Ali Asdullah's family brought with it attendant obligations. Around 1756 (AH 1117) he and his brother Abdul Kadir built a new mosque for the community, close to the old one which had been built by 'Datuk Punggawa' in the late sixteenth century, soon after the agreement between the Malays and the ruler *Karaeng* Tunapilangga.[93] As we have seen, the earlier *Kapitan* Ince Cukka had also built a mosque, in 1705 (1117 AH).[94] The mid-eighteenth-century mosque, later known as the Mesjid Makmur, was supported by a number of charitable endowments (*wakaf*). Ince Ali Asdullah entrusted this mosque to his posterity, the future *Kapitans*, Letnans and Imams of the Makassar Malays. Only they could wield legitimate authority over it. Access to leadership of the community was further restricted to those descendants who were *anak kosomah*, having Malays as both mother and father. *Anak gundik*, men with a non-Malay parent, were disqualified.[95] This last stipulation seems to have proved impracticable.[96] Such arrangements translated the wealth gained through the Dutch monopolies into legitimate social pre-eminence, and ensured the family's status.

The importance of tax-farming in the history of the Southeast Asian Chinese has received considerable and well-deserved attention. The most famous and lucrative, the opium farms, not only provided an important means of investing and accumulating capital, but were also closely linked to the consolidation of political and economic networks. Wealthy tax-farmers had access to colonial officials; close ties and influence with indigenous elites and networks of subordinate traders and agents were also essential.[97] While a customs farm did not require the same elaborate distribution network, it did need authority, knowledge and sound judgement. In the case of Ince Ali Asdullah, it seems to have offered comparable opportunities for commercial consolidation and social mobility. The customs farm was undoubtedly only one source of Ince Ali Asdulah's wealth. The foundations of his fortune lay in his trading; it was the money earned on his journeys to Kalimantan and Java which enabled him to pay for the farm—and to win the support of powerful Dutch and Chinese allies for his ambitious wedding.

Although Dutch descriptions of Malay trade are few and far between in the later eighteenth century, some general trends can be identified through analysis of the harbourmaster's registers.[98] The mid-century, including the 1770s, showed little development, although Malay skippers probably remained strong in their traditional commodities of rice and slaves. Their main imports into Makassar were sea products, coconut oil and rice, while marine produce and cloth dominated exports. They were probably also bringing (unregistered) slaves into South Sulawesi. By the 1780s they had consolidated their decades-long domination of coconut oil imports, most of which came in from Ende on Flores, which was a centre of Sulawesian settlement and one of the archipelago's main slave markets. The Malays were shipping in almost 400 slaves a year, mainly from Ende. They were still importing rice, raw cotton and Indian textiles. Their main exports were coins (*rijksdaalders*), Chinese earthenware, Chinese linen and Indian cloth. As was to be expected, given their commodities, Nusa Tenggara (the Lesser Sundas) was the favoured trading partner of Makassar's Malays.

It is estimated that while the share of trade held by other Indonesian groups and locally born Europeans was declining in the face of the growing Chinese role in commerce, the Malays not only managed to hold their own, but showed a slight strengthening.[99] Their share in the volume of shipping grew from 2 per cent in the 1720s through 11 per cent in the 1760s, to 15 per cent in the 1780s.[100]

The VOC archives also provide intermittent information on ship-owners. As is to be expected, the *Kapitans* and the farmers seem to be among the wealthiest. In 1715, the Malays owned the most vessels in Makassar, a total of 30: 28 local *gonting* and 2 smaller *pancallang*. There were 13 ships (mainly the larger *chialoup*) possessed by Europeans or *mestizos*, 28 in Chinese or *Peranakan* Chinese hands (2 *chialoup*, 25 *gonting*, and one much smaller *pancallang*). Forty-four other ships, almost all *gonting*, were held by Moor *Mardijkers* (11) and Buginese (9) while the mercantile Wajorese owned 24. Among the Malays, the *Kapitan* Ince Cukka owned a *gonting* and a *pancallang*, one Ince Jemal, Bumi Parisi, possessed 3 *gonting*, while Ince Kamar and Ince Japara had 2 each.[101]

By the 1730s and 1740s, the number of registered ships had shrunk dramatically, probably for tax reasons. Only four to six Malays were listed, all *gonting* owners, and the numbers of Chinese- and European-owned vessels had also sharply declined, if not to the same degree—it seems registration had little to do with actual shipping.[102] Few owners are recorded for 1775: five Europeans, three Chinese, and a lone Malay. This was Ince Ali Asdullah, who is listed as owning a *chialoup* of 30 last (15 tonnes); the ship was 29 years old, so had been built in 1745/46.[103] In 1784 he was still sailing the same vessel, and this was probably taken over later by his son, Ince Suleiman (*Kapitan Melayu* since 1789), who is listed in 1790 as owning a 43-year-old *chialoup*. However, his father appeared as owner again in 1795.[104]

Another Company source, the lists of merchants who bought textiles from the VOC shop, offers information through negation. While *mestizo* traders predominated, and Chinese were strongly represented among the purchasers—and there was even the occasional Makassarese—the absence of Malays shows that they obtained their trade textiles through other sources.[105] The Malays were similarly peripheral in other VOC institutions. In contrast to the Chinese and even—though to a lesser extent—the Buginese and the Makassarese, they very seldom, if ever, borrowed money from the orphan chamber or deaconate, Dutch charitable institutions which were an important source of credit. They were, however, prominent borrowers from a private *mestizo* money-lender who offered smaller loans, so it could be that Malays were just not involved in the more substantial European credit market.[106]

Malays are also absent from another source of social information; the urban tax rolls. While VOC officials, *mestizos*, *burgers*, Chinese and 'free natives' had to pay their 5 per cent on house and ship sales, no Malays were subject to these taxes. Even when incidental information, such as the 1742 extra levy on Vlaardingen residents to pay for lamp-oil, shows five 'Ince' residents,[107] we cannot be sure that these were Malay: they could well be *Peranakan* Chinese. This apparent marginalisation of the Malays is, however, a product of community-based taxation practice. They paid their dues to the *Kapitan Melayu*, who obviously had greater fiscal power over his subjects than the *Kapitan China* did over his. There was one arena, however, where the Malays were subject to the Company, and that was the law. If arbitration and judgement within their community proved impossible or unacceptable, plaintiffs could apply to Makassar's Council of Justice. Many Malays were involved in disputes over trade or loans; Ince Ali Asdullah himself applied to the court in 1787 to recover a debt of 90 rds from the Chinese Andiko.[108] In significant criminal cases, such as murder, the Council would also act.[109]

Conclusion

Our account of the Makassar Malays requires us to consider two linked historiographical issues. The first is primarily a question of assessing their changing role in town and trade, given the dramatic transformation of the region after the Dutch conquest. The second, more recalcitrant, need is to consider the implications of ethnic categorisation, both for the social and political processes of the society itself and for our perceptions and analyses.

When writing of Speelman's invitation to the Malays to return to Makassar after the conquest, a contemporary Malay source, rather uncharacteristically, offers a commentary: "*Dalam hal ini ada kemungkinan besar orang₂ Melayu dianggap dapat menjadi perantara yang netral antara VOC dan Raja Goa dan dapat menstabilkan keadaan*" (In this case it is very probable that the Malays were considered as neutral mediators between the VOC and the King of Goa, and that they could stabilise the situation).[110]

The very language is revealing, and not just because of the Anglicisms. 'Neutrality' and 'stability' would probably have fallen far short of the aims of victorious Bone, bent upon further expansion of its influence, and offered very cold comfort to the shattered Makassarese trying to recover from the devastation visited upon them. But these terms do reflect the priorities of the Dutch in 1670, who wanted an end to war, and clear political and commercial hegemony. Pragmatic traders of all communities no doubt also looked forward to peace, although few would have welcomed the crushing economic restrictions which accompanied it.

In retrospect, the role of neutral mediator seems to have served the Makassar Malays well, and the comment quoted above reflects that perception. This is rooted not only in the trends of the 1700s, but also in those of the subsequent nineteenth and twentieth centuries, when the Makassar Malays were prominent in (post-) colonial administration, education and law. But this perception also resonates with images from earlier times, when the Malays were brokers between the wider Islamic world and the kingdoms of South Sulawesi. A similar cosmopolitan breadth of vision might be detected in their openness to all members of the *ummat*, the brotherhood of Islam. Arab *sayid* and Chinese imams appear in their genealogies, as do Buginese and Makassarese.

Writing of the founders of Melaka, Oliver Wolters praised their greatness. They were "masters of political intelligence, quick to exploit changes in their environment", shrewd in their choice of alliances, and effective in their mobilisation of "folk identity, shaped by memories of the past".[111] The same could be said of the Makassarese Malays, *mutatis mutandis*. Being Malay was to possess a cultural and social passport, providing potential access to the commerce of the diaspora networks and the political advantages of a respected lineage. The combination of Malayness with more locally grounded identities offered the opportunity to capitalise upon these wider linkages, without abandoning more narrowly focused solidarities.

Although the VOC's repressive policies dismantled the extended trading system in which the Malays had played so central a role, within a few decades they had re-oriented themselves. Traders successfully re-deployed to new routes, and the economic and social institutions of the VOC town—the farms and the *Kapitan* system—were effectively manipulated. The Malay community became a mainstay of Dutch rule, and a central element in Makassar's (re)emerging urban society. In that sense, they were indeed 'neutral mediators' who helped 'stabilise' the situation. But this stability was maintained by constant negotiation. Ethnic boundaries and relative status in the colonial hierarchy were contested, and involvement with the Dutch did not necessarily mean rejection of local rulers. Malay resilience can not be read as simple continuity. Tunipalangga, Speelman and the Malay *Kapitans* Ince Maulud and Abdul Kadir all confronted the political dilemmas raised by the ambiguity of 'the Malay'. Malays might be Minangkabau or Moor, from Johor, Patani or Banjarmasin. These specific origins could be subsumed into Malayness, the very essence of which was its supra-local character.

Ethnic labels reify. This tendency is reinforced when we couple them to the word 'community', with connotations of solidarity and harmony. It is then all too easy to presuppose the existence of an enduring group, characterised by a common culture and a cohesive social structure. In Makassar, the various *kampong*—Ternate, Banda, Butung, China, Melayu, Belanda—and the 'nations' under their headmen, *Mayor Melayu, Kapitan China, Matoa Wajo*, seem to form a stable system. But, as we have seen, category boundaries are problematic. The Wajorese tended to dissolve into their neighbours, *Peranakan* flexibility blurred boundaries, few Butonese lived in Kampung Buton, and even the thriving Malay 'community' could be deconstructed into clusters of heterogeneous compounds. Assumptions of uniformity deny the protean character of constituent elements—factions, families or even specific men or women. The presumed whole overrides the agency of the part. The reverse can also happen, when personal or specific actions are seen as exemplifying a communal reality.

Seventeenth- and eighteenth-century Dutchmen write of 'Malays' or 'the Buginese' as being competitive traders. But failure to differentiate within the ethnic category can mean that the activities of the few are seen as typical of the whole. No-one can fail to be impressed by the number of slaves Ince Patani took from Buton in 1683. But we do not know if this voyage, recorded by chance, was a random example of a wider Malay slave trade, transferring thousands of victims from the eastern to the western archipelago. Or was this transaction recorded precisely because it was noteworthy? These three or four ships might have taken the bulk of the year's exports, the slaves having been gradually accumulated at a central market, awaiting the exceptional Ince Patani.

It is very difficult to pin down the social reality behind the labels. Anyone from the west was 'Javanese' in sixteenth-century Makassar, just as later refugees from South Sulawesi tended to become 'Buginese', whatever their origins. In 1561, King Tunapilangga was uncertain who was Malay. '*Moors*' and '*Mardijkers*', once so numerous, disappeared from the Makassar census in the early eighteenth century,[112] while Speelman's notes underline the persisting diversity, and importance, of local origins and family blood-lines within the Malay category. Ince Amin, himself a 'Malay of Makassarese descent', generally uses the term

Peranakan to identify the Malays fighting alongside Goa, and his translator, Skinner, glosses *Peranakan* as 'the Malay community', but the category is ambiguous.[113] The inhabitants of eighteenth-century Makassar also had problems in reconciling the unruly realities of their social life with an increasingly rigid classification.[114]

If we are to do justice to both the 'essential' and 'constructed' dimensions of ethnicity, we need to acknowledge the interaction between the social capital (trust, norms, networks) that is transmitted and adapted from generation to generation, and the institutions and rules which channel access to resources. Being 'Malay' was an important element in both self-definition and ascribed status, associated with a supra-local or transcendent identity rooted in the cultural and commercial traditions of Melaka and Islam. This was true in Goan Makassar, and also under the Dutch. In the pre-conquest polity, where commerce was central and Islam flush with noble patronage and military success, Melaka refugees and Malay merchants were welcomed, and wealthy newcomers married into leading local families. The VOC, however, was hostile to the Malay heritage of open seas and Muslim knowledge, and so it closed doors. Trade routes were blocked, Islam relegated to the darker fringes of native society, and a more inflexible administrative grid imposed.

The result, for the Malays, was a process of localisation. Their role was more restricted, and their attention increasingly focused on Makassar itself. They had lost those previous essential advantages in trade and religion which had both sustained, and been supported by, their transcendent identity. The Dutch East India Company based social control and access to resources on ethnic categories, and the Malays mobilised effectively, using the new institutions to defend and expand their turf. This sharpened boundaries between groups, raising the profile of ethnicity for VOC administrators. The modern researcher, using Company sources, can share their perceptions. But at the same time, like the other inhabitants of Makassar, the Malays ignored Dutch-imposed barriers which impeded the search for profits, advantageous alliances, or attractive marriage partners. Ethnicity was a very real force in Makassar, but it was adjustable. The meaning of being Malay in Makassar also fluctuated. Malayness resonated with the power of a glorious past, shared by cultural kin throughout the region. But it was also contingent, driven by personal strategies and constraining contexts. The resulting tensions created a complex social environment, the negotiation of which demanded considerable navigational skills from the Malays themselves, their fellow townsfolk and Dutch officials.

Table of Makassar Kapitan and Letnan Melayu

	?–1706	Ince Abdul Nazul (not included in established lists, including that in KKIKM)
(1)	28/5/1706	Ince Cukka, alias Abdul Razak
(2)	27/1/1724	Ince Maulud
(3)	27/5/1728	Ince Samba
(4)	24/12/1733	Ince Bendak
(5)	27/8/1739	Ince Jamaluddin
(6)	29/10/1747	Ince Abdul Kadir
(7)	4/5/1750	Ince Bungsu
	17/6/1751	Ince Mursidin, Letnan.
(8)	17/4/1752	Ince Abdul Kadir
	5/6/1781	Ince Sulaiman, Letnan
(9)	9/3/1789	Ince Sulaiman
	9/3/1789	Ince Muhammad Hasan, Letnan
	9/3/1789	Ince Abdul Kadir, Mayoor
(10)	14/8/1813	Ince Muhd. Hasan
		Ince Abdul Gani, cousin of above, appointed by British
(11)	18/4/1827	Ince Abdul Gani
	30/5/1825	Ince Abdullah Husain, Letnan
(12)	27/7/1839	Ince Abdullah Husain
	16/5/1840	Ince Tajuddun, Letnan
	31/7/1862	Ince Ince Abdul Rachman, Letnan, replaces father
		Kampung Melayu divided into two: Kampung Melayu and Kampung Endeh
	24/10/1873	Nuraddin Daeng Nombong, *Kapitan* Endeh
(13)	28/6/1880	Ince Abdul Rachman
(14)	31/5/1888	Ince Lele Ali Asdullah
(15)	26/5/1906	Ince Abdul Wahab Daeng Massikki
(16)	1910	Mas Nuralim (non-Malay)
		Muh. Amin Daeng Masarro, *Kapitan* Endeh
(17)	1912	Haji Wan Abdullah Bau' Sandi
(18)	1918	Kamaruddin Daeng Parani

Partial List of Pre-1800 Imam of the Kampung Melayu Mosque

1740–47	Ince Budiman
1752–70	Ince Ibrahim bin Haji Abu Bakar
1800	Sayid Muh. Machdar b. Sayid Alwi

These two lists are based on KKIKM, *Sejarah*; see also 'De Kapitein Melajoe'.

Texts, Raja Ismail and Violence: Siak and the Transformation of Malay Identity in the Eighteenth Century

TIMOTHY P. BARNARD*

What makes a person 'Malay'? Today, Malays would be likely to answer that a 'Malay' is someone who speaks the Malay language, follows Malay customs and is a Muslim. Such a relatively simple answer, however, masks more complex issues. Identity is a continually evolving aspect of every individual and group, and to identify with an ethnic group involves negotiating a maze of religious, linguistic and social issues. While scholars such as A. C. Milner, Shamsul A. B. and William Roff have examined questions surrounding Malay identity during the colonial era and following independence in Peninsular Malaysia,[1] the few studies that have dealt with this issue in a pre-colonial context have focused on how certain Malay texts glorify the role of the Melaka polity.[2] Although communities in Sumatra and Borneo shared a common culture of trade, language and religion with Melaka, the latter controlled the Melaka Straits in the fifteenth century and set the standard for Malayness. Under these circumstances, Malay identity evolved into an association with the Melaka ruler, who provided protection, ceremonial splendour and economic stability. Oral tales and traditional texts, often commissioned and maintained by these same rulers, reinforced the central position of the ruler in this identity.[3] Using Malay texts, however, Virginia Matheson has shown that Malay identity began to change in the eighteenth century as new residents entered the region and formed polities that challenged Melaka's successor state, Johor. Part of this changing political, social and economic transformation involved shifts in the identity of other local societies, such as Trengganu, Pahang and Siak, to the point that they became identified as Malay.

Although it can be established that Melaka provided the standard for Malayness over several centuries, the meaning and context of this

Malay identity remained obscure. Henk Maier has pointed out that traditional literature often addresses Malayness playfully, apparently because of the uncertain nature of the subject. For example, the hero of the epic *Hikayat Hang Tuah* responds to a description of the 'purity' of Melakan Malayness by saying, "We are Malays, but also '*kacukan*'", using a word whose root, *kacu*, means mixed or not pure.[4] The remark implies that Malay identity was a complex issue in the Melaka Straits, even during the height of Melaka's power. When Melaka's rulers fled to Johor in the sixteenth century they attempted to maintain their position in the region, in part through their association with Malayness itself. By the early eighteenth century, however, Malay identity was no longer clearly linked to Melaka, but involved a range of cultural, political and economic issues.

An important turning point in the transformation of Malay identity occurred with the murder of Sultan Mahmud of Johor in 1699, an event that shattered the position of Melaka-Johor society in the region. Sultan Mahmud was the last ruler who could trace his ancestry through a mythically powerful line of rulers, and his death severed the link between Johor and the greatness of Melaka. Even traditional accounts that would benefit from downplaying the importance of the event, such as the *Peringatan Sejarah Negeri Johor*,[5] consider that the death of Sultan Mahmud terminated the powerful Melaka *daulat*, or sovereign authority, which was vital to its identity as the Malay state. Although Leonard Andaya has looked at this event in political and economic terms, his comment that followers of the ruler were "cast adrift" is equally applicable to the interlinked issue of identity.[6] Johor could no longer claim exclusive rights to determine Malay identity. A century of upheaval followed the death of Sultan Mahmud, as competing groups strove for economic and political dominance, and the right to assume the Malay identity associated with power in the region.

As Johor's grip on Malay identity weakened, some of the groups that had migrated to the Melaka Straits and South China Sea in the sixteenth and seventeenth centuries grew in importance. Although they had been present as traders, settlers and warriors for some time, these groups had been continuously identified as either Minangkabau or Bugis and treated very poorly by Johor. The haughtiness connected with this Malay polity, and its influence on these migrants, was evident in letters written to the VOC (United East India Company) in which leaders of these groups complained Johor rulers treated them as 'slaves'.[7] The murder of Sultan Mahmud created opportunities for these outsiders to achieve positions of authority in the region by the early eighteenth century. Once in power, some of these groups began the slow and complex process of developing a Malay identity.

One of the first attempts to co-opt the power of Johor, and its status as the centre of Malay identity, occurred in eastern Sumatra along the Siak River during the eighteenth century when a leader named Raja Kecik, possibly of Minangkabau origin, arose and claimed to be the son of Sultan Mahmud, and thus the rightful heir to the Johor-Melaka mantle.[8] Although this attempt to circumvent the position of Melaka-Johor as the sole fount of Malayness was subsequently derided in many non-Siak texts,[9] the Minangkabau migrants living in eastern Sumatra were beginning to negotiate their identity, in what amounted to a creative process in which they became Malay. It was a fluid identity, in which anyone living in the region could become Malay while remaining outside the control of the powerful Melaka polity. This Malayness was not associated with Islam, although religion did play a part; it was based instead on a common trading culture along the Melaka Straits and South China Sea. While connections to Melaka remained important, they were no longer the sole requirement for claiming a Malay identity.

As the Siak polity moved from the periphery of Malay consciousness to the core, the early attempts of Raja Kecik to 'become Malay' by associating himself with the ruling family of Melaka/Johor were not emphasised in subsequent generations of the ruling family of Siak. The descendants of Raja Kecik began to construct their own Malay identity, one that was not necessarily dependent on connections to Johor. Central to the development of a Malay identity for Siak were the numerous coups that occurred among the descendants of Raja Kecik after 1740, resulting in power being rotated between two lineages, with transitions often marked by a period of conflict or open warfare. As these two factions competed for the throne, the temporary victor would oversee a system of trade networks among the villages and eco-niches of central eastern Sumatra that funnelled goods to and from the Melaka Straits. The leader who had fallen out of power would flee to the Melaka Straits and South China Sea, where he searched for support (material and spiritual) to allow for his restoration to the Siak throne. The leader of the Siak polity ruled an increasingly prosperous state, and the exiled princes, living among the various groups residing in the numerous competing states and groups of the Straits, learned tropes of Malayness that subsequently began to permeate the expanding Siak society.

The *Hikayat Siak* and Changing Malay Identity

The transformation of Siak into a Malay polity during the eighteenth century is emphasised in traditional texts that were one of the most common forms of 'teaching manuals' in the region.[10] Siak had several texts that clearly centred the polity as a burgeoning Malay state. One of the best known is the *Hikayat Siak*. Written with the support of factions of the Siak ruling family living in exile, this epic tale shows how a group slowly shifted its identity away from its central Sumatran origin to that of a more broad-based Malay identity. Their Minangkabau origin, however, was never completely denied, and residents of Siak became one of the more complex examples of *kacu*. The acceptance of a wider definition of Malayness was also supported by a growing uniformity of Malay culture and identity that stretched across the region, particularly by the nineteenth century.[11]

The change from a Melaka-centred Malay identity to one that includes much of the Straits region can be traced in the structure of the *Hikayat Siak*, which can be divided into two sections. The first half is a copy of the text better known as the *Sejarah Melayu*, a point that is easy to overlook since the published transliteration of the Siak text omits this section.[12] *The Sejarah Melayu* is one of the main texts that depicts Malayness as inexorably linked to Melaka. Within the *Sejarah Melayu* the ties between Melaka and Siak are based on the subjugation of Siak, whose leaders were "descendants of the rulers of Pagar Ruyung [the Minangkabau capital]" attempting to act independently of Melaka. The method of controlling the rulers of Siak, who lacked the Malay heritage promoted in the *Sejarah Melayu*, was through marriage into the Melaka royal family and the granting of royal titles. When this did not achieve the desired effect, Siak was attacked. This relationship culminates in an episode in which a Melaka official berates the Siak ruler, calling him a 'jungleman', for executing a man without permission from Melaka: "Are you going to be a law unto yourselves here in Siak?"[13] The actions of Siak rulers are thus held up as contrary to exemplary Malayness.

The inclusion of the *Sejarah Melayu* as the first section of the *Hikayat Siak* reinforces the idea of Melaka as the fount for Malayness, and conveys the notion that residents of Siak must be taught to act like proper Malays, particularly with regard to respect for centralised authority. Such respect for the ruler remained important, especially after the fall of Melaka to the Portuguese. Since the circumstances of the Melaka rulers' flight brought their sovereignty into question, they needed to emphasise that neighbouring territories, including Siak, should continue to honour their status in the region.[14] Malayness would remain linked to the Johor-Melaka ruler. Once Johor fell into decline in the early eighteenth century, however, regions like Siak began to assert their own position as possible claimants to pre-eminence and its association with Malayness. The rise of former dependencies of

Johor and the diversity of their populations are addressed in the second section of the *Hikayat Siak*, which unsurprisingly includes little detail concerning the period of Malay rulers in Johor. The story only begins again with the death of Sultan Mahmud, once more emphasising the importance of this event in Malay identity.

The second section of the *Hikayat Siak*, the part published as the *Hikayat Siak*, allows for a closer reading of how new understandings of Malay identity were being created. One of the clearest ways of perceiving this is through the ways residents of Siak are described throughout the text. As Raja Kecik founds the state, the residents are referred to as '*orang Minangkabau-Melayu*' (Minangkabau-Malay people). The term 'Minangkabau' is used to describe Siak troops in the next few pages of the text, but then is dropped abruptly in favour of '*orang Siak*', an expression that then appears frequently, reminding the listener (for the text records an oral tradition) about the creation of a new identity. The text distances this identity from Minangkabau when the term '*anak* Minangkabau' is clearly used to describe Siak opponents living on the coast of Cambodia.[15]

While the *Hikayat Siak* reflects a change in identity for these residents of eastern Sumatra from Minangkabau to people of Siak, the text clearly places this new identity within the borders of Malayness. '*Orang* Siak' are attached to the newly founded polity, which is part of a larger Malay world. This is designated not only by the use of the expression 'people of Siak' (*orang* Siak) but also by the descriptions of all other peoples in the region as people of other places. Such labels signify that all of these groups existed within the same cultural parameters, and the only difference between them was the polity to which they were beholden.[16] '*Orang* Siak' has become one sub-group within the larger identification of *bangsa Melayu* (the Malay race).[17]

This same transition for Siak residents, from Minangkabau to Malay, is also present in other eighteenth- and nineteenth-century texts from the region. The *Peringatan Sejarah Negeri Johor*, a court-based diary from Johor that was used to compile the more literary court records, initially refers to the Siak leadership in various ways as 'Minangkabau', but the meaning changes over time. In 1727, the people from Siak are referred to as '*anak* Minangkabau'.[18] While the term '*anak*' may signify that they are followers of the Minangkabau ruler, its presence in the diary of the Johor court is significant, for it implies a growing dissociation between the Siak leadership and the Minangkabau ruler. This is supported in a citation recorded in the 1740s, in which Raja Kecik's son, Raja Mahmud, who had become the Siak ruler, requested an alliance with the sultan of Johor so that '*anak cucu* Minangkabau' (descendants of the Minangkabau) and '*segala Melayu*' (all Malays) would not destroy themselves.[19] The use of the term '*anak cucu*' (descendants) reflects the increasing distance of Siak residents from a Minangkabau identity, but one that is not yet quite Malay. Even Raja Ali Haji, the nineteenth-century author of the celebrated *Tuhfat al-Nafis*, described Siak (along with many other states) as Malay by the end of the eighteenth century, despite misgivings about eastern Sumatra, thus accepting an extension of who could be classified as Malay.[20]

Summing up, between the 1740s and the 1790s Siak identity had been transformed from Minangkabau migrants to something clearly in the 'Malay world'. By the 1790s the period of rotating rulers in Siak came to an end when Said Ali, a great-grandson of Raja Kecik, gained the throne through force and manipulation. The losers in this context went into permanent exile and eventually became the rulers of Sukadana, in Borneo. These exiled members of the Siak royal family maintained the *Hikayat Siak*, and in this text the phrase '*orang* Siak' comes to mean the followers of Said Ali.[21] Once the exiled faction left Siak, they were no longer able to claim the designation '*orang* Siak'. More importantly, they had entered a sphere where they could claim a Malay identity despite, or perhaps because of, the variation within it. The groups that traced their descent from Raja Kecik and the founding of Siak now took pride in their Malay heritage while distancing themselves from Minangkabau. This is clearly apparent in the *Hikayat Siak* when a group of these exiled princes receives a request to join an alliance with a ruler of a migrant Minangkabau community in Palembang. One of the princes rejects the invitation by replying, "we are descendants of the rulers of Siak, not the ruler of Palembang. We are comfortable riding the waves, children of the sea, not like those from upstream."[22] This final placement of Siak identity within the confines of the oceans and trade routes of the Malay world occurs in the last 30 folio pages of a 600-folio page text. Malay identity has expanded beyond the polity of Johor-Melaka.

Raja Ismail and the Basics of a Siak-Malay Identity

What characteristics were expected of an eighteenth-century Siak-Malay beyond 'riding the waves'?[23] The *Hikayat Siak* provides a manual for this new Malay identity as it follows the exploits of the Siak rulers while they negotiate their place in the Melaka Straits and the South China Sea, and as they move from a Minangkabau to a Malay identity. One of the most important figures in this transformation is Raja Ismail, a grandson of Raja

Kecik, who ruled Siak for several months in 1761. Following a defeat at the hands of a VOC-led force, Raja Ismail roamed the region for 18 years before returning to Siak as its sultan.

The tales in the *Hikayat Siak* about Raja Ismail, who probably commissioned the writing and maintenance of this text, provide lessons for the listener/reader on how to become an eighteenth-century Malay. As is true in most Malay texts, the tales are not told in a straightforward fashion. The heroes, Raja Ismail and his followers, are placed in situations where they must negotiate their status, place and role in society. As might be anticipated, the *Hikayat Siak* places particular emphasis on the maintenance of *adat* (customs, customary law), but also stresses how the sea and raiding allow Raja Ismail and his followers to fulfil their destiny as Malays. Much of this begins when Raja Ismail fled Siak in 1761. He and his followers sailed to the Pulau Tujuh area of the South China Sea, a region of scattered islands spread between the Malay Peninsula and Borneo that was an important source of manpower for many of the warring states in the region during the eighteenth century. Traditionally the area had been under the control of Melaka-Johor, and the sultan of Johor was able to call upon its leaders to support him, but the ability of Johor to control the area had come into question following the upheaval that swept the region in the early eighteenth century and the influx of migrants who may have had no ties to a distant Malay ruler. The manner in which Raja Ismail presented himself would determine the fate of these exiles. Although Raja Ismail was from the ruling family of Siak, he was an exile roaming the Melaka Straits and South China Sea, looking for followers who might allow him to return to the throne. If he could develop and reinforce his Malay identity, as well as that of his followers, they might be able to return to Siak in triumph.

In the course of his early wanderings in the South China Sea, Raja Ismail had many experiences that allow the authors to place his actions in the context of a Malay identity. Under trying conditions during the initial phase of his flight, according to the *Hikayat Siak*, Raja Ismail nevertheless received numerous honours and tributes, while also upholding *adat*, reflecting his role in a wider Malay society. These stories convey the message that Malay leadership should be honoured and acknowledged. When Raja Ismail and his brothers arrived in Pulau Tujuh, local inhabitants presented him with gifts in the form of Spanish *reals*.[24] Another sign of his acceptance is the willingness of the ruler of Trengganu to marry his daughter to Raja Ismail. Such links could be critically important not merely for a leader, but also for his followers.[25] The marriage provided the exiled Siak leader with a residence in Trengganu and a *kampung*. The *Hikayat Siak* also emphasises

that the wedding followed traditional Malay *adat* at the insistence of the
Siak elite. Although they were in familiar territory, Trengganu was
negotiating its own Malay identity, and the maintenance of a Siak-Malay
authority received precedence.[26]

A Malay leader also dispensed justice. In the *Hikayat Siak* this
aspect of leadership is exemplified in an episode that occurred shortly after
Raja Ismail's wedding. Raja Daud, who shared the same mother and father
with Raja Ismail, was accused of an incestuous relationship with their half-
sister, Tengku Saliah, and she was sentenced to death. Although this
judgement was acceptable under *adat*, the execution upset the hotheaded
Tengku Abdullah, another of Raja Ismail's brothers, who asked permission
to execute Raja Daud. Raja Ismail attempted to cover up the affair by
claiming that Tengku Saliah died from a gastric illness, and refused to
allow Tengku Abdullah to take further action. An infuriated Tengku
Abdullah questioned Raja Ismail's ability to rule. A proposal to exile Raja
Daud 'to the Bugis' failed to satisfy Tengku Abdullah, who declared that
he could no longer follow Raja Ismail. In the midst of this challenge a calm
voice reminds those present that they had all agreed Raja Ismail was their
leader (*dia kita rajakan*) and that opposition to his wishes would be a sign
of treason.[27] Thus, the importance of maintaining and respecting *adat*,
leadership and consensus is emphasised for those present in Trengganu,
and for those who listen to the story in the future, as a key factor in
assuming a Malay identity.

While the maintenance of *adat* is stressed throughout the *Hikayat
Siak*, the controversy over the execution of Tengku Saliah also points to
important aspects of Malay leadership during the period. Although Raja
Kecik associated himself with some of the founding myths of the Melaka-
Johor dynasty, most eighteenth-century leaders in the Straits could not do
so. Their leadership could no longer be based in descent from Melaka but
depended on the innate ability (charisma) to gain support and attract
followers. A Malay leader was one who could negotiate the multifaceted
societies of VOC outposts, sojourners, ships, eco-niches and fluctuating
local states. That Raja Ismail had been chosen (*rajakan*) as the leader
reflects more immediate factors determining who would become the leader
of these emerging Malay communities, and some of the determining factors
in how Malayness was formed at the time.

In addition to the emphasis on *adat* and charismatic leadership in
the formation of a Malay identity, there is a continual focus on violence
in Siak society during this period. Tales of raids and battles preoccupy the
author(s) of the *Hikayat Siak*, and these raids were not only to gain economic

and manpower advantages. Violence itself seemed to occupy a primary position in Siak-Malay identity, as it did in states throughout the region in the eighteenth century.[28] The rapid fluctuations in Johor power, and the presence of new trading systems and technology, allowed autonomous states to rise, mostly led by immigrants. After a period of conflict during which they carved out their niche in the region, one that was not under the subjugation of Johor, these new states became important centres of trade and power. Much of the violence was directed at other states within the wider Straits community as each tried to establish its position and role within the region. This situation allowed for the creation of separate Malay identities, not solely linked to the Melaka-Johor polity but associated with any of the states in a region in which minor variations existed. Malays roamed the sea, 'riding the waves', which connected all of the scattered states that shared the same identity. The glorious past of Melaka, celebrated in tales and poems, was only a guide. Residents were now able to negotiate, or even violently seize, Malay identity, within what was becoming a larger Malay designation that was an umbrella covering the numerous states of the Malay Peninsula, Borneo and eastern Sumatra.

One example of the use of violence to achieve status and respect within this Malay community occurred in the 1760s when, after a failed attack against Kelantan, the Trengganu leader appealed to the Siak princes for help. After two unsuccessful assaults, a Siak prince volunteered to lead his warriors in a daring frontal attack. Firing their muskets, hacking with their swords, stabbing with their spears, and using *pencak silat* (a Malay form of martial arts), these warriors penetrated the Kelantan defences. Afterwards the Siak troops looted the forts, and the booty enabled Raja Ismail to attract more followers. The ferocity of the Siak warriors was such that opponents supposedly proclaimed that, "the men of Siak fight as if they are possessed, they are not like ordinary men".[29]

While such statements in the *Hikayat Siak* can be seen as a celebration of the prowess of the Siak warriors, and perhaps a bit of hyperbole, the followers of Raja Ismail were famous throughout the Malay world for their often brutal raids, which led Dutch observers to categorise them as notorious pirates.[30] Such were the martial skills of Raja Ismail's followers that rulers sometimes offered them refuge to forestall attacks on their own states.[31] From the perspective of the *Hikayat Siak*, these raids illustrate the adventures of youthful and impetuous princes as they asserted their will and upheld their *adat*, represented in the text as an ideal of Malay courage and masculinity. In addition, raids and warfare were a common feature of polities during the period, and flew in the face of Dutch assertions that they had created a stable and secure trading environment in the region. It was precisely these unsettled conditions that allowed a princely raider such as Raja Ismail to use violence to carve out an identity on the sea and in a Malay world that was quite distant from a Minangkabau heritage.

The main opposition to Raja Ismail and others creating nascent Malay identities, and to the states they developed, not surprisingly, came from Johor. This point is addressed in the *Hikayat Siak* and is also reflected in archival accounts of battles between Raja Ismail and representatives of Johor. One of the most famous of these episodes occurred when Raja Ismail and his followers sailed to the Riau-Lingga archipelago to attack Javanese vessels and raid Riau ports in 1767.[32] This direct threat to Johor led to a confrontation in the Singapore Straits and along the Singapore River between the followers of the Johor ruler and Raja Ismail. The latter suffered a defeat in the fighting that ensued, but the battle at Singapore in 1767 was symbolically important for his new Malay identity since he was attacking the remnants of Melaka, the state that had previously dominated the concept of Malayness that the new residents then were adopting.[33]

The battle cost Raja Ismail access to the sea-lanes in the Riau Archipelago but did not dampen his bid to assert a Malay identity. By October he and his followers were in the Bengkalis Straits, opposite the Siak River, and trying to carve out a Malay state in the coastal stretches of Siak. To further these efforts, he formed alliances with other burgeoning Malay states that bordered the seas from which he gained much of his power. By November 1767, the VOC reported that Raja Ismail had approached and received, albeit reluctantly, the support of the rulers of Jambi, Palembang, Trengganu and Batu Bahara.[34]

During this period, many of the tropes of Malayness were beginning to fuse for Raja Ismail and his followers. For example, upon arrival in Palembang Raja Ismail informed the sultan that rival raiders were planning an attack, and was rewarded with three baskets filled with 1,000 *ringgits* each.[35] In the meantime, other Siak princes were establishing themselves semi-permanently on the tin-rich islands of Bangka and Belitung, near the mouth of the Musi River, the home of many former residents of Pulau Tujuh.[36] From their new bases in southern Sumatra, Raja Ismail and his followers continued to harass shipping throughout the South China Sea in an attempt to exert their authority. Residents of Siak were no longer limited to the rivers of eastern Sumatra, the interior and home of Minangkabau influence, but could now dominate the seas, trade and even other regional rulers. In 1769 Raja Ismail took his fleet to Mempawah, a small state on the western Borneo coast, and defeated a rebellious Muslim cleric at the request of the Sultan of Palembang.[37] After this battle, Raja Ismail raided communities in the southern Thai Peninsula. The *Hikayat Siak* summarises the splendour of such royal leadership over the seas in its account of a reception Raja Ismail and his fleet received upon return to Palembang. As they advanced up the Musi River, the ships were greeted with cascades of *duku* fruit, and Palembang dignitaries presented the expeditionary force with new titles and robes. Raja Ismail was further honoured with the grant of a permanent residence in Palembang along with numerous gifts.[38]

Although Raja Ismail's close ties with various Malay leaders, especially the ruler of Palembang, allow the audience of the *Hikayat Siak* to comprehend his power and the ease with which he moved within his Malay identity, in VOC sources he is depicted as a threat to the authority of all Malay states. This sometimes also comes through in the *Hikayat Siak*. When the Palembang ruler presented Raja Ismail with the 3,000 *reals* in 1767, the *Hikayat Siak* describes it as a reward for not joining in a proposed raid upon Palembang. The money was hidden in baskets of sugar, and, upon receiving it, Raja Ismail claimed that he was being "treated like a Dayak".[39] The incident passed with some mild joking, but the tension between the two sides was palpable. In courts such as Palembang, Raja Ismail's credentials as a Malay leader remained suspect, although little could be done to curtail his power. Raja Ismail had gained a position within the wider Malay community through violence and raiding. One solution for other Malay rulers was to try and set parameters for his activities. A sign of these boundaries was when the Palembang sultan allowed a Siak prince to live at Bangka, a tin-producing region and the home of *Orang Laut* raiders. Although the prince drained *Orang Laut* manpower from the Palembang ruler, Raja Ismail and his followers were allowed access to his coastal frontiers in order to appease them. The ambivalence with which Malay rulers regarded Raja Ismail is reiterated in the *Hikayat Siak* when the Palembang sultan presents Raja Ismail with 1,000 *pikuls* of tin to finance his return to central eastern Sumatra, a move that would give Raja Ismail a sphere of influence that was relatively distant from Palembang.[40]

Raja Ismail did not immediately return to Siak, despite the support he received from other Malay rulers. For six years he settled in Rokan, also in eastern Sumatra, where he worked fitfully alongside the Siak sultan, Raja Muhammad Ali, who ruled much of eastern Sumatra. Raja Ismail finally returned to Siak as its sultan in 1779. According to the *Hikayat Siak*, Raja Ismail prepared 16 ships from his base on the Rokan River, and proceeded to the Siak River, accompanied by his brothers. As this force went up the Siak, they stopped at Buantan to pray at the grave of Raja Kecik, the founder of the Siak state and original claimant to a Siak-Malay identity. Upon learning about the approaching fleet, Raja Muhammad Ali sent an official named Encik Hasan to lead the defensive forces, and he quickly forced all of the Javanese trading ships in Mempura, the Siak capital, to form a barricade across the river. As Raja Ismail and his vessels approached the defensive blockade, they saw Encik Hasan standing on the deck of a vessel adorned with royal insignia. One of Raja Ismail's followers shot and killed him. The death of their commander created chaos in the defensive forces, and the invaders quickly breached the blockade of ships and entered Mempura. Learning of these events, Raja Muhammad Ali fled upstream. The Siak capital and the entire river had fallen to Raja Ismail.[41] The violence that had helped Raja Ismail become Malay had also helped him return to the Malay throne of Siak.

While Siak leaders evinced pride in their newly developed Malay identity and their enhanced role in the region, they never forgot their origins. This point is clearly illustrated by a tale from the *Hikayat Siak* about a journey that Raja Ismail's son, Raja Yahya, made in 1786 to Trengganu following his father's death. During the voyage heavy winds damaged the sails of the main royal vessel, and the fleet had to stop at Pahang for repairs. During the interval, the commander of the fleet carried out raids in the vicinity. When he came upon two Batu Bahara *perahu* coming from Java, he requested rice for the Siak fleet, claiming this was the *adat anak Minangkabau*. The captains of the two vessels refused, arguing that this was not proper. One of the captains was killed and both vessels were seized.[42] While the request for rice may not have necessarily been in accordance with the *adat* of Minangkabau migrants to the region, the use of this phrase and the violence so late in the text is a wink towards the reader concerning the forceful nature by which a Siak-Malay identity was achieved in the eighteenth century. Their origins had been in Minangkabau, but through violence, and the mastery of the sea that it allowed, Siak residents had moved into the complex world of Malay identity as immigrants from central Sumatra.

Conclusion

Malay identity in Siak during the eighteenth century was continually contested. Malayness was equated with the political and economic power of the trading states of the Melaka Straits and South China Sea, and attempts to wrest it from the traditional control of Johor were met with not only the sword but also the pen, as traditional literature often derided the Minangkabau migrants from Siak as usurpers of a Malay heritage stretching back over centuries. This is apparent in the *Tuhfat al-Nafis*, a nineteenth-century literary account of these conflicts, in which Siak claims to a Malay identity are frequently mocked. However, even this text portrays Siak residents as Malay by the end of the eighteenth century. One of the factors in this transformation was the formidable rise of Siak as a power in the region. Another was the *Hikayat Siak*, a text that made a concerted attempt to tie the Siak elite into the Malay system of identity.

Siak understandings of Malayness placed great emphasis on the maintenance of *adat*, consensus and the position of the ruler in society. These common attributes of Malay identity during the period were also reinforced with violence. Previously, as celebrated in texts such as the *Sejarah Melayu*, Melaka subjugated many non-Malay states and forced them into a Malay trading system, which provided benefits such as trade goods and honorifics. In contrast, the eighteenth century was a period when states such as Siak had to fight for their Malay identity. It would no longer be handed out under the supervision of Melaka or Johor. To 'ride the waves' of this region, Siak leaders had to adopt local attitudes and cultures that had been associated with Malayness, and this included raiding. These actions were not simply piracy, an accepted practice in the region,[43] but vicious attacks on those who questioned their place in the region and identification as Malay. That violence is held up as a vital component exposes an important aspect of Malayness during the period. Eighteenth-century Malays were not docile farmers or fishermen, but identified with the vibrant trade, politics and cultures of the Melaka Straits. Once Siak had the opportunity to form its own state, it took such attributes to new heights. Violence, *adat* and trade had become interlinked in the formation of a Siak-Malay identity.

The rise of the Siak state in the eighteenth century caused much consternation among neighbouring polities. Siak was centred far up a river in the heart of Sumatra, led by Minangkabau migrants, and threatened trading patterns that had been established for centuries. The violence that allowed this marginal state to rise up as a power is one reason Siak is often placed outside the parameters, or at least on the frontiers, of Malayness in most literature. It was a place where 'junglemen' ruled. The denigration of Siak government, society and even its basic texts also was mirrored in European reports. Throughout the eighteenth century, Siak was described in VOC records with vivid adjectives such as 'piratical' or 'chaotic'. Siak identity and rule had become a puzzle for the Europeans as well as other

Malay states. The nature of Siak authority appeared to be beyond understandings of how polities in the Melaka Straits functioned and how Malayness should be represented.

The uncertainty over how to categorise and depict states like Siak in traditional texts, which often revert to discussions of the possibility of identifying a 'pure' (*sungguh*) Malay culture and society,[44] overlooks the changes that had occurred in the eighteenth century. All states in the region had become successor states to Melaka's heritage; it was no longer solely the prerogative of Johor. The region had become a cultural, economic and geographic frontier that was home to various groups inhabiting its numerous islands, straits, forests and ports, all influencing the development of its societies. Under such circumstances the mantle of Malayness was broadened to encompass not only Melaka and Johor but also all of these relatively new migrants. The descendants of Minangkabau, Bugis, Javanese, as well as other migrants to the area could now accept a Malay identity that went beyond a simple loyalty to Melaka. This process was complicated, and often violent, but the rulers of Siak and the tales of their adventures in the *Hikayat Siak* provide a glimpse into some of the earlier aspects of the contestation of Malay identity that would continue well into the colonial era and beyond.

6

A Malay of Bugis Ancestry:
Haji Ibrahim's Strategies of Survival

JAN VAN DER PUTTEN*

S tudies of pre-twentieth-century Riau history often point out the clear separation of power between the sultan and his family on Lingga and the viceroy (*Yang Dipertuan Muda*) residing with his family on Penyengat, and note that the divide coincided with a clear ethnic division between Malays at Lingga and Bugis at Penyengat. Ethnic distinction thus is presented as extremely significant, at least since the time when five Bugis brothers provided assistance to the struggling Johor Malays in the early eighteenth century. These mercenaries helped the Malay sultan deal with 'Minangkabau' intruders who claimed to be the rightful successors to the throne. Reading historical sources, we are told that the Bugis in the nineteenth century associated very much with the colonial government and helped to get rid of the troublesome Malay Sultan Mahmud in 1857. At the turn of the century, however, the same group of 'Bugis radicals' was the main reason for the troubles between the Dutch government and the Malay/ Bugis sultan, a conflict that led to the expulsion of the ringleaders and the abolition of the sultanate.[1]

In indigenous historical sources the division is also obvious. Legitimising the presence of the Bugis faction in the kingdom seems to have been the key motivation for the compilation of two of Raja Ali Haji's most famous works: the *Tuhfat al-Nafis* and *Salasilah Melayu dan Bugis*.[2] However, there seems to be little proof of any open conflict between the two factions based on ethnic differences. Obviously there were tensions between them, most clearly reflected when the Malay Sultan Mahmud was deposed with the support of the Bugis in 1857. But it seems that the tensions were much more politico-economic than they were inspired by ethnic differences. Malay society in general, and local communities in particular, seem to have been much more accommodating towards other ethnic groups than common views on identity would allow.

It would be strange if the 'intrusion' of a certain group into a society that was dominated by another entity did not cause tensions ascribable to differences in language, culture, traditions and religion, and ultimately to different ethnic backgrounds. And indeed the arrival of the Bugis in Riau and their acquisition of high positions in the power structure of the state did cause problems and tensions. However, these tensions do not seem to have been caused by ethnic distinctions between the two groups, but rather by the 'political incorrectness' of the Bugis pedigree, for they could not trace their ancestors back to Bukit Siguntang, a prerequisite to holding a high position in a Malay polity. The distinction between the Malays at Lingga and the Bugis at Penyengat became visible and grew in importance after the Dutch developed a post in Tanjung Pinang from 1819 onwards. This is not to say that the division into separate ethnic groups was merely a colonial construct, but the demarcation between the groups seems to have become sharper and better defined as time went on, to the colonial policy-makers as well as to the members of the groups themselves.

Considering the disparity of the two groups as 'just' a matter of lineage, because the Bugis Raja-family at Penyengat could not claim descent through the Melaka sultanate,[3] would imply that the Bugis were the inferior element. However, in the course of the nineteenth century, partly through their alliance with Dutch administrators, the Bugis accumulated so much power and prestige that they threatened the old structure formed around the Malay sultan at Lingga. The Bugis 'married' into the *Sejarah Melayu*, that is, Malay genealogy (to borrow a phrase from Vivienne Wee),[4] referring to the marriage of Opu Daeng Marewah, one of the five brothers, to Tengku Mandak, the sultan's sister. Thus, the Bugis forged political alliances by marrying women from the Malay sultan's family, a practice which, from a Malay point of view, was invalid because descent properly followed the male line.[5] Accordingly, Abdul Rahman's accession to the position of sultan in 1885 was considered improper by the Malay faction, because his claim to legitimacy was through his mother, Tengku Fatimah, daughter of the deposed Sultan Mahmud; his father was Raja Muhammad Yusuf, the last viceroy of Riau.[6] This troublesome succession prompted the 'republication' of Raja Ali Haji's treatises on kingship, written after the deposition of Sultan Mahmud in 1857, now issued in printed form by a print shop located at Lingga.[7]

The writer of these treatises, Raja Ali Haji, is considered to be one of the champions of Malay customs, tradition and language, as a custodian of pure Malay culture. However, he was Bugis. This leads to questions revolving around his motivations. As someone who strove to legitimise the presence of Bugis in the Malay world, why did he not turn to his own ethnic background and study Bugis language, culture and tradition? If he really felt himself as belonging to Bugis ethnicity, if he did not consider himself to be a 'true' Malay, why did he place so much emphasis on the creation of a 'pure' Malay culture and language? Of course there was political gain for his family if he was able to define and exemplify the essence of being a 'true' Malay, but it seems hard to imagine that that was the only, or even the primary, motivation.

Politically, Raja Ali Haji had to explain and justify the presence of the Bugis Raja family in the power structure of the Malay kingdom, which he did in various historical writings. His two treatises on kingship from the late 1850s seem also to be politically motivated: by emphasising the Islamic quality of kingship he reduced the 'Malayness' associated with it. Indeed, the Bugis employed the strategy of establishing and enhancing their political role vis-à-vis the Malay sultan's family by presenting themselves as the devout imam through whom the legitimacy of the government of the sultan was established.[8]

However, Raja Ali Haji never openly advocated the Bugis cause against the Malay faction.[9] He seems to have considered the Bugis to be part of the Malay world, an element whose presence and position had to be accounted for but who were at the same time a fully integrated group. In nineteenth-century Riau, therefore, 'Malay' was not limited to people who could trace their ancestors back to Melaka or Bukit Siguntang. Members of the sultan's family seem to have clung to this opinion, but their political position was too weak to enforce it on the others. And that family increasingly felt the presence of 'others' who, as time went on, encroached on their powers by forging alliances and earnestly asked to join in 'playing relatives' with the Malays.[10] The Bugis came to be accepted, and considered themselves to be Malay with Bugis ancestors (Melayu keturunan Bugis), of whom they were proud because these ancestors assisted in shaping the Malay kingdom of Riau-Lingga.

Having given a very rough outline of the background of this chapter, I would like to turn to the vicissitudes of a Bugis who lived in Riau in the nineteenth century. One of his strategies of survival seems to have been not presenting himself as a Bugis or else playing down to the Malays in order to be able to join in the political game that was going on in the polity. This person, Haji Ibrahim by name, occupied a position which seems to have been in between the three parties who were in power in the last century and formed a geographical triangle: the sultan's family at Lingga, the viceregal family at Penyengat and the Dutch at Tanjung Pinang on the island of Bintan.

Much of the information in this article comes from letters Haji Ibrahim wrote to Hermann Von de Wall, a European scholar stationed at Riau in order to collect information and materials for the compilation of a Malay-Dutch dictionary and a Malay grammar. The article focuses on a specific incident that occurred in 1867–68, but before that the life and works of Haji Ibrahim will be properly introduced.

In the *Tuhfat al-Nafis* Ibrahim's name is mentioned for the first time in a passage describing the departure of a flotilla of ships to meet Sultan Abdul Rahman in Trengganu in September 1823. He is referred to as Encik Ibrahim, son of Datuk Syahbandar Abdullah, and is described as one of the elite *Peranakan Bugis*, distinguished from members of the ruling Raja-family and the lower servants, who participated in the voyage.[11] Ibrahim's year of birth is not known, but he was probably in his teens, which would make him very close in age to Raja Ali Haji, who supposedly turned 14 in 1823. The second time Ibrahim appears in the *Tuhfat al-Nafis* is in a depiction of the troubles between Singapore and Riau over the Karimun Islands in 1827, in which he joined his father in a campaign against the forces from Singapore that claimed the islands. Someone even reported to Raja Ahmad, who had returned with his son Raja Ali Haji from a pilgrimage to Mecca, that Ibrahim was killed in battle, but this proved to be untrue.[12] In this passage he still has only the 'title' of *Encik* in front of his name and is mentioned in connection with his father. However, in the latter part of the 1830s, he apparently had been on pilgrimage to Mecca and was referred to as *Haji*, the honorific generally associated with his name.

By this time Haji Ibrahim had become involved in state affairs and eventually took over his father's position as political envoy and negotiator. In this capacity he travelled to Batavia in 1835–36 and again in 1837, in order to soothe Dutch and English anger over the involvement of the ruling family of Riau with piracy. Haji Ibrahim made a favourable impression on the English,[13] as well as the Dutch, who subsequently appointed him 'superintendent' (*oppertoezigter*) of the islands to curb piracy in the region. In one of his letters to Von de Wall, he claims that he was promised in 1834 or 1835 a certain salary of which he only received half.[14] With the help of Von de Wall and Resident Eliza Netscher, the colonial government agreed to Haji Ibrahim's claim, for which he then received a monthly allowance of $f125$.[15]

If Haji Ibrahim really held the position of superintendent of the islands, a post presumably set up as a consequence of the treaty on piracy between the Dutch and the Malays/Bugis, he served two masters at the same time. The ruling family at Penyengat continued to use him as an

envoy to convey letters and messages to the Dutch and he is reported
during the 1850s to have acted as "private secretary to successive *Yang
Dipertuan Mudas*".[16] He was granted the title of *Orang Kaya Muda*,
possibly in return for these services, and he used this title from the late
1850s onwards. Haji Ibrahim even served as the acting commander of the
Malay forces that, in a concerted campaign with Dutch forces, extirpated
the pirates' nest at Reteh in 1858.[17] Perhaps because of this double role,
Dutch Residents who held the post in the 1850s distrusted Haji Ibrahim.
Both Resident F. N. Nieuwenhuijzen and his successor J. H. Tobias reported
that Haji Ibrahim was not to be trusted and that he and Raja Ali Haji
exerted a bad influence on the *Yang Dipertuan Muda*. However, Haji
Ibrahim was also seen as a "very refined, competent and diligent man who
on his voyages to Mecca and Java had learned a great deal and gained a
lot of experience".[18] However, these favourable impressions were given by
men who did not take part in the daily administrative relations between
the Dutch in Tanjung Pinang and the Malay/Bugis in Penyengat. Netscher,
the Resident of Riau in the 1860s, had listed Haji Ibrahim's positive qualities
in an article on Riau published in 1854. As Resident, he reported that he
knew of Haji Ibrahim's bad reputation, but said that this 'schemer' had
improved his conduct.[19]

There is not much information on Haji Ibrahim's position at the
court; he probably inherited his father's title as *Syahbandar*, but the position
was no longer related to harbour master. Ch. van Angelbeek reported that,
after the Dutch established their post at Tanjung Pinang in the early 1820s,
Syahbandar Abdullah was assigned the position of Master of Ceremonies
(*Panglima Dalam*) at the court at Penyengat, but there is no evidence that
Abdullah led or organised any ceremony at court.[20] Haji Ibrahim's family
held a lower position in the hierarchic structure of the state. This inferior
position with lower esteem compared to the more established, and titled,
'Raja' family at the Bugis court of Penyengat is perhaps best exemplified
by an incident that occurred in 1865.[21] In an anxious letter to Von de Wall,
Haji Ibrahim wrote that problems had arisen between his family and that
of Raja Ali Haji. The two men tried to settle the differences but apparently
did not succeed, and blows were exchanged between Haji Ibrahim's son
and one of Raja Ali Haji's grandsons. That same night the viceroy summoned
Haji Ibrahim and two of his sons to appear before him. The father rejected
the summons, fearing he would "say something uncalled for" (*tercampur
mulut*), which would make things only worse.[22] He wrote the letter in
anticipation of things to come, lamenting his situation and the apparent
legal inequality between the two families:

... at half past ten a letter from Raja Marewah came, saying that the viceroy summoned me together with my two sons Abas and Ahmad to appear at court. I answer, if you want to judge my sons, I should not be present. Perhaps I would barge into it. So now I am at home waiting for them (to return) and writing this xxx [sic] letter. I do not know what will become of it, I feel powerless; I feel that if they play it like that, perhaps it is a big case, because the members of the Raja-family are imposing their authority. When the child was hit last Tuesday, as my friend saw for himself, there was no judgement passed, and now that my son has done something, there is going to be punishment.

I have reported by letter and by mouth that I am afraid it would become this way, so, in case my son is judged guilty, I do not know where I would bring my family to; I just feel powerless, there is no one I can turn to ask for help, so I will flee.[23]

In an undated postscript, Haji Ibrahim expressed his hopes that the relationship between the two families would again be as in bygone days. He had always restrained himself, but feared that another clash between the two families would lead to several deaths. The tension between the groups was further complicated with the declaration that he and his family would resist any attack by Raja Bih, one of Raja Ali Haji's sons:

Until now Raja Ali Haji's children several times have done this to me. Once someone even stole my son Ismail's golden kris sheath, but I kept quiet because I really honour Raja Ali Haji. It has not changed, I still hope for Raja Ali Haji. In my feeling, if I was given poison and there was an antidote, I would ask for the antidote, so I hope that there will not be any hurt feelings between us both and that our relationship will be as it used to be. If my son has done wrong, I will bear it, but if he is right but proved wrong, this makes me feel very sad, dispirited. Last night Raja Bih was even rounding up his men to come to my place and kill me and my family, for if someone hits my son, I will surely strike back.[24]

Evidently, Haji Ibrahim's family was inferior to the Raja family in birth and rank.[25] They held a 'middle level' position between the ruling family and ordinary people; in a royal audience they would sit on the ground below the Raja, who would occupy the 'raised dais' together with the sultan family (*tengku*) and the Arabs (*tuan said*).[26] Haji Ibrahim's position at the viceregal court presumably provided an allowance of ƒ130 a month, the same as his father received in the position, but that amount surely was not enough to support his large family. He must have needed additional income, and the arrival of two European officials who were interested in developing Malay dictionaries and grammars and willing to pay for information,[27] must have appeared as a stroke of good fortune: he could read and write and held a respected position that involved travel throughout the islands, and thus had access to much of the written and oral information in the region. Von de Wall must have understood these advantages of employing Haji Ibrahim's services, although he seems to have considered Raja Ali Haji more valuable to his project.

If Haji Ibrahim sought employment with Von de Wall for economic reasons, this was in contrast to Raja Ali Haji, who held a high position at court and shared in the compensation funds the Dutch provided the *Yang Dipertuan Muda*. Raja Ali Haji also received revenue from tin mining operations on Karimun Island. Haji Ibrahim's financial needs and troubles appear time and again in his letters to Von de Wall, sometimes in a very straightforward way and sometimes in stylistically refined Malay.

The first mention of financial problems is from the early stages of their correspondence, when Haji Ibrahim seems to have acted mainly as an envoy between the ruling family at Penyengat and the Dutch in Tanjung Pinang. The letter quoted below makes it clear that the colonial official loaned money to the dignitaries at Penyengat, and also shows the financial difficulties non-elite members of Penyengat society faced.

> I report that your money, which was used by Tengku Nung, the deputy viceroy, in the sum of 200 guilders, is herewith returned, and I ask for a receipt to be handed over to my son who is bringing you this letter. The money I am using is still tied up with Bugis cloth. I am collecting money for the cloth that is sold; when I have enough I will ask someone to hand it over, or bring it over myself.[28]

Haji Ibrahim apparently continued to dabble in the cloth trade to earn income. Two years after this first mention of the Bugis cloth, he wrote to Von de Wall, who was in Batavia at the time, to offer him some cloth from a newly arrived shipment. This example provides a clear indication that Haji Ibrahim could not depend solely on the money he received from the court and possibly from the Dutch government, and was forced to earn money from other sources to survive.

> I am informing you that this morning I received fabric from Lingga to be made into clothes. The usual price for the purple-red cloth is four dollars and three quarters, and for the purple cloth four and a half dollars. It is difficult to obtain this kind of fabrics here, so whichever you like, you can take. I won't order inferior quality cloth to be brought to you, so this is very high quality.[29]

In the beginning of the correspondence, which took place over a period of 15 years from 1858 until 1873, Von de Wall only occasionally asked Haji Ibrahim to do odd jobs in connection with the compilation of the dictionary and the acquisition of manuscripts. With his first letter Haji Ibrahim enclosed documents (*surat*) that he had copied at Von de Wall's request.[30] One-and-a-half months later, he provided a list of the dignitaries travelling with the sultan from Lingga to Riau, as Resident Tobias had requested. Haji Ibrahim asked Von de Wall to help him explain the names to the Resident, because he was not sure the Resident could understand his list in Roman characters.[31] From this example it is clear that Haji Ibrahim did various odd jobs for the Dutch to maintain his position in this expensive region.

In 1867, the year Von de Wall spent in Batavia, Haji Ibrahim became much more involved in work for the colonial authorities. It was in this year, too, that he, along with his son Abdullah and Raja Ali Haji, began copying and amending manuscripts, such as the *Hikayat Kurais* and *Hikayat Golam*. In that same year, Haji Ibrahim not only acted as a 'liaison officer' between Raja Ali Haji and Von de Wall, but also was very busy writing a compilation of conversations, which was partly published in two parts under the title of *Cakap² Rampai²* in 1868 and 1872. The stories and conversations mentioned in the letters are not included in either of the published parts. From time to time Von de Wall would send money as a reward for this work, which also involved compiling lists with names of trees, fish, snakes and snails. In the last few years covered in the letters, Haji Ibrahim seems to have taken up a position in Tengku Nung's office. At that time the reorganisation of the Dutch administration of the residency was taking place, bringing more direct colonial rule to the scattered islands of Riau. This must have increased the size of the indigenous administration, and Haji Ibrahim was a very obvious candidate for employment as he had relevant experience covering a span of 40 years.

However, before he began his 'new' position, Haji Ibrahim dealt with some business involving Sultan Sulaiman and his trip to Batavia in October 1867. A few months before, in May, Haji Ibrahim was suddenly summoned to come to Lingga. He could not refuse because it was a strict order from the sultan, although he seems to have been rather surprised and reluctant to leave the work he was doing on the compilation of conversations for Von de Wall:

> I also inform you that I was writing the conversation about the first ground contact of children in the nobility, when a letter came from Lingga informing me that the sultan summoned me to come to Lingga with great haste. So I will be going to Lingga, maybe in 15 days I will be back in Riau.[32]

Haji Ibrahim was told about the sultan's plans of travelling to Batavia and was ordered to take up his place in the sultan's retinue, which would accompany the ruler on his voyage. At first sight the reasons the sultan would order Haji Ibrahim to accompany him to Batavia seem obvious, since he was one of the senior dignitaries in the kingdom and had made the voyage twice before. Furthermore, Haji Ibrahim was well acquainted with Dutch officials and accustomed to associating with them in formal as well as informal circumstances. However, he was a member of the Penyengat court as well, whose relations with the sultan deteriorated in the course of the 1860s; in 1868 the relationship between the two ruling families seems to have been at its worst.

In the months before their departure, Haji Ibrahim travelled between Lingga and Penyengat as preparations for the voyage proceeded. The party arrived in Batavia on 21 October 1867 on the mailboat *Baron Bentinck*, planning to stay until the beginning of December. They stayed at the house of Pangeran Syarif Abdul Rahman, an Arab who acted as a Protocol Officer for the colonial government. Not much is known of the month the party spent in the capital, except that the sultan had a meeting with the governor general, someone from his party became ill, and they made carriage trips around town.[33] During those excursions the sultan must have stopped at the shop of the exchange officer, J. Speet, where Spanish doubloons, English and Australian golden sovereigns, French Napoleons, American Eagles and Dutch golden 'Willempjes' caught his eye.[34] The sultan apparently pawned two gold belt-buckles with his Arab host to meet his expenses in Batavia. Before returning to Riau, he asked for an advance payment of *f*5,000 on his allowance from the government in order to redeem the servants he apparently had left with Speet to guarantee payment for the gold he had ordered, and to compensate him for the pawned belt-buckles. The transactions were complex, and the discussion involved Haji Ibrahim on the Riau side and Von de Wall as well as Pangeran Abdul Rahman in Batavia.

I am informing my friend about the servants who were left with Mr. Speet. The money I am sending you amounts to two thousand guilders, in a money order addressed to you, as well as one thousand guilders for Pangeran Abdul Rahman, Master of Ceremony. With him there are two golden medallions, so my friend will act as the sultan's representative for paying the Pangeran and collecting the two medallions, as well as for the gold at Mr. Speet's. Enclosed with this letter there is a specification of the shape and the amount of objects, which the sultan expects my friend to bring back with him to Riau.[35]

It would take Haji Ibrahim and Von de Wall until the end of May to sort things out for the sultan, who during this period stayed at Von de Wall's residence in Tanjung Pinang. This, of course, created a very awkward situation, which can be considered emblematic of the relationship between the sultan and the viceroy at that time. The sultan, who had returned from a voyage to Batavia, was expected to live at Penyengat with members of the Raja family. In defiance of all Malay traditions, he chose to stay with the Dutch across the bay, overlooking the small island of Penyengat where his 'subordinates' lived. In his political report in 1868, Resident Netscher wrote that the sultan spent the greater part of that year in Tanjung Pinang while seeking to associate with Europeans. Netscher continued that the relationship between the sultan and the viceroy was not as 'one would wish it to be', mainly because Raja Ali Haji was a zealous advocate of turning Riau into a separate polity from Lingga. The viceroy was too weak to defend himself against the influences exerted by his devious relatives.[36]

Another source contains harsh criticism by the *Yang Dipertuan Muda* (or *Yamtuan*) of the sultan's behaviour. In April 1868, Riau was visited by a group of people from the Johor court, who came to consult specialists at Penyengat concerning the proper title for their ruler and the customs appropriate for a Malay court. The Johor delegation visited Raja Ali Haji at his house, and had a meeting with the viceroy, *Yamtuan* Raja Muhammad Yusuf, who reportedly expressed his unhappiness with the sultan in the following way:

> The viceroy said, "I promised Datuk Tumenggung [of Johor] to come when he would return from Europe, but at this time I can not come yet, because my lord, Sultan Sulaiman, is staying at Tanjung Pinang."
> Then Ungku Haji said, "isn't he coming here?"
> And came the answer, "no, only on holy days. I am also not paying my respects to him, because his stay is not in accordance with traditions; if he would stay at Lingga or Penyengat, we could all pay our respect to him. This is the case with our king, we are worried with a king like that, because he is staying over there without anything to do, and just leaving his homeland."[37]

This is clearly a very biased judgement, blaming everything on the 'other' side, which in itself is very interesting because apparently the 'Malays' from Johor seem to have felt more affiliated with the 'Bugis' at Penyengat than with their 'fellow-Malays' from Lingga.

In the Johor report there is also a description of visits by some of the delegates to the sultan in Tanjung Pinang. The sultan is depicted as a friendly, cuddly, short and stout man with a big moustache who wore his hair in a bun (*berboceng ulunya*)—not a depiction one would expect of a great Malay ruler, descendant of the mythical Iskandar Zulkarnain. It is telling that a description of the sultan's outward appearance was the only passage of that nature in the report. Apparently the people in Johor had never seen the sultan, although there were regular contacts between Riau and Johor. To denigrate the sultan even further, his specious arguments for not staying at Penyengat are quoted in the report. This wonderful example of political writing is quoted in full:

> Encik Wan Abdullah together with Datuk Bentara went to Tanjung Pinang to pay their respect to the lord, Sultan Sulaiman, at Mr. von de Wall's house. When they arrived, they waited in a room where people were received in audience. At that time the lord was in his bedroom writing. Tuan Cik, a local born Arab from Lingga, told him that Abdullah and Bentara had come to pay respect. He ordered, "tell them to sit down a while, I am finishing a letter." After a moment he had still not come out, Abdullah went into the bedroom. Then he came out and sat on the couch, Abdullah sat cross-legged on a chair, and so did Tuan Cik.
>
> As for Sultan Sulaiman, he had a sturdy body, a charming moustache, was not that tall, looked glorious and wore his hair in a bun. At that time he wore a handkerchief, a Javanese muslin jacket and long trousers. He sat there with his kind face, a friendly look in his eyes, alternating his words time and again with laughing, making the people who paid him their respect feeling at ease.
>
> Then he said, "since I have returned from Batavia, I am staying here so I can recover from not feeling too well because of the change in climate with Batavia. Since I am here, I am feeling healthy, I have recovered my strength. I would have stayed at Penyengat, but is too sheltered, there is no wind, and the mud flats smell awful. Furthermore, during the dry season it gets very dry at the island and there is a shortage of water; I have only visited the islands once on a holy day".[38]

Haji Ibrahim was thus placed in an awkward situation when he was ordered to accompany the sultan to Batavia, and he had to deal with the problems that ensued. At the same time, he needed to maintain good relations with his superiors at the court, as well as with the members of the Johor delegation, who visited him twice during their stay in Riau. Haji Ibrahim obviously succeeded in 'playing relatives' with all parties present in Riau, although he must have stretched his wits to the utmost to please everyone and promote the interests of the respective parties. He could only survive by adopting a very opportunistic way of acting, of which the following passage in a letter, sent to Von de Wall while he was in Batavia with the sultan, is emblematic:

I inform you that I have not had the chance yet to come. Please do not feel offended, as the reason why I have come to Batavia outwardly was because I am accompanying the sultan, but inwardly I just want to meet my friend. Please be patient for a little while, so I can finish the job for the sultan.[39]

Surely the story he told the sultan would be diametrically opposed to what he told Von de Wall, and both parties must have realised it. Still, Haji Ibrahim got away with it, and after having dealt with the sultan's problems as a dignitary at the court, he was made the assistant of Tengku Nung, the heir-apparent to the title of *Yang Dipertuan Muda*. In the following years Haji Ibrahim retained his position in the court and travelled throughout the vast Riau Archipelago, at the same time providing Von de Wall with manuscripts, lists with words for his dictionary and medical terms. He also continued selling all manner of objects, from medicinal herbs for a Dutch citizen in Tanjung Pinang to pineapple plants for the Malays in Johor, and occasionally called on Von de Wall for help paying his debts.

The personal letters by Haji Ibrahim and Raja Ali Haji contain no instances in which they presented themselves as being anything other than Malay. As may be expected from the relationship between informants and a Western linguistic scholar, the men give full vent to their knowledge of the language, which was Malay (there is no indication that the two men could speak Bugis). The conversations Haji Ibrahim compiled for the colonial government deal with subjects relevant to the Malay maritime kingdom of Riau-Lingga. The only explicit reference to the Bugis language is in a discussion about the titles used in the Malay state that have a Bugis background, such as *Sulewatang* (the viceregal deputy) and *Kelana* (heir-apparent of the viceroy).

Only in their historical writings, their stories about bygone days, is the role of the Bugis emphasised. They were indeed *Melayu keturunan Bugis*, and this was a source of pride because in the old days the Bugis had defeated Raja Kecik, the 'Minangkabau' pretender to the throne. The legendary Bugis brothers (*Upu*) became rulers in Riau over Bugis and Malays (*sic*), the kingdom prospered, people came to make obeisance to the viceroy from everywhere in the kingdom, and the viceroy entered into an alliance with the Dutch, lest the kingdom fall into the hands of others. As Haji Ibrahim wrote:

because of Upu's magical powers
he became king in Riau
ruling the Bugis and the Malays
the kingdom became populous and prospered

he was given permanent rule over the land
from former times until now
the kingdom is in the hands of native Bugis
who are faithful to the Dutch government
lest what would have become of it
because it would have gone to others[40]

Therefore, as Raja Ali Haji also told his readers, if you are really a descendant of these Bugis rulers, you should follow in their footsteps, for better or for worse. Only then would one be a true descendant of the Bugis noble family:

hear ye, all children and grandchildren
you should remember your forebears
and be aware of their conduct and doings
you should follow whatever you can
whoever is really child or grandchild
you should follow their conduct and doings
as well as their shame and disgrace
or their resolve and loyalty
if you do that
you will be true children and grandchildren
you can be called a descendant of kings
in the land of the Bugis of noble birth[41]

It seems that descendants of Bugis nobility could make perfectly true Malays. In other words, to join in 'playing relatives' one could be proud of one's ethnic background and illustrious forebears, but at the same time, one should adjust to the other relatives of the '*ummat*' (wider Islamic community).[42] If a person married into the surrounding 'family' and presented himself as a pious Muslim, the other family members would eventually accept this self-definition. Neither Raja Ali Haji nor Haji Ibrahim seem to have been trying consciously to divide people into ethnic groups, or to delineate the factions in society. They tried to explain and to legitimise the presence of the Bugis in Riau so that they could fully integrate with people who happened to be Malays.

The political reality in the middle of the nineteenth century was that the Dutch entrusted full power over Riau-Lingga to the Raja family of Penyengat. The Dutch at Tanjung Pinang saw the sultan with his family as a source of trouble and tensions in the society. People like Haji Ibrahim, who were on the fringes between the groups with real power and tried to survive by applying strategies that connected the different groups with each other, maintained a balance of power in the vast polity. Haji Ibrahim and other members of his family were employed by the Raja family in their administration, but at the same time were summoned by the sultan to do certain jobs for him, as well as serving as informants or even as indigenous officials in the colonial administration. It was through these roles in society that Haji Ibrahim was able to negotiate his Malay identity in a quickly changing nineteenth-century society.

A History of an Identity, an Identity of a History: The Idea and Practice of 'Malayness' in Malaysia Reconsidered

SHAMSUL A. B.*

At the outset it may be useful to elucidate my interest in the study of identity in general, and of identity formation in Malaysia in particular, a project that emerged literally 'from the field' about two decades ago, when I was conducting anthropological fieldwork (1979–81) for my doctoral thesis. The findings from that research helped me to gain a better understanding of politics, culture and economic development at the grassroots level in Malaysia.[1] My research also made me realise that a number of fundamental issues relating to Malaysian state and society as well as to Malaysian studies needed to be addressed; the most critical of these were questions of identity contestation and identity formation, in their individual as well as their collective forms.

My earliest response to this question took the form of an attempt to answer a deceptively simple question, namely, "is a Malay anthropologist's knowledge of her/his own people superior to a foreigner's?"[2] In a rejoinder to an article by Judith Nagata on the *dakwah* movement in Malaysia and in my subsequent essays on the same topic, I elaborated on the religious aspect of Malay identity, that is, on the question of how the experience of Islam, since the colonial period an 'ethnic identifier' for the Malays, intensified with *dakwahism*.[3]

My first attempt to examine the theme of 'identity formation in Malaysia', particularly amongst the Malays, in a concrete, if not material way, commenced with a systematic analysis of the concept of *kampung* ('village'), a term that has long been taken for granted by Malaysianists who have too easily treated *kampung* as synonymous with 'Malay' and 'Malayness'.[4]

Kampung has many meanings, and sooner or later we all will come to realise that these meanings are the result of a never-ending contestation between numerous interest groups within 'authority-defined' and 'authority-defining' collectives in Malaysia, both in the past and in the present. I decided to cast my analytical net wider to deal with popular and modern Malay sociopolitical concepts, categories and classifications on a macro level. *Bangsa* (nation), for instance, and *negara* (state), *ketuanan Melayu* (Malay dominance), *gerakan kebangsaan* (nationalist movement or nationalism), *jatidiri bangsa* (national identity) and *bangsa idaman* (nation-of-intent); each has many meanings that ask for further exploration. In a series of essays published between 1996 and 1999, I focused on the 'authority-defined' rather than on the 'authority-defining' perspective.[5]

In analysing these concepts, categories and classifications, I quickly learnt that it was impossible to avoid sensitive issues such as the role of Islam, *dakwah*, the Malay language and Malay royalty. In the most general terms I realised that most knowledge about the Malays has been constructed and elaborated in an Orientalist mould by colonial administrator-scholars and that anthropologists and other specialists in Malay studies subsequently used this knowledge, usually without problematising many of the key terms. These very same concepts, categories and classifications subsequently instituted a host of ideas which politicians, bureaucrats and administrators have been all too happy to use and perpetuate in the form of governmental and official policies up to the present day; references to 'Chinese-ness', 'Indian-ness', 'Kadazan-ness', 'Iban-ness' or 'Asli-ness' have been as difficult to avoid as 'Malayness'.[6] Some Malay and Chinese scholars have tried to distance themselves from these basic Orientalist notions by employing Marxist, functionalist, or postmodernist notions and terms. However, many scholars seem to make use of these novelties in academic journals and publications only to hide their chauvinistic political agenda, while rarely questioning the applicability of these novelties in concrete policies. The old 'addiction' to ethnicised knowledge, a prominent manifestation of Orientalism, is still very strong, so it seems.[7]

This very brief summary of my journey in search of identity at a conceptual level as well as a practical level should serve as the background of this chapter. In the first part I will suggest an interpretation of British-Malay relations that is different from other recent interpretations, such as that developed by Cheah Boon Kheng.[8] Based on an interdisciplinary approach, usually avoided by historians of Malaysia, I will contend that the British colonial conquest was not only a matter of superior weapons, political and diplomatic shrewdness, and economic energy; it was also a cultural invasion in the form of a conquest of the native 'epistemological space'. To formulate this in very simple terms: the British interfered with the local thought system, and by doing this they increasingly disempowered the natives by limiting their ability to define their world; subsequently, the local order of things was replaced by a foreign one, a slow but steady process that has effectively been conducted through a systemic application of a number of so-called 'investigative modalities'.[9] The echoes of these modalities can still be heard. I will then argue that the history of hotly debated concepts such as 'Malay identity' and 'Malayness' is largely based on an Orientalist-colonial construction as reflected in the identity of the history of Malaya and, later, Malaysia. Economically and culturally speaking, the history of what is now Malaysia has been dominated, shaped and 'factualised' by colonial knowledge, and vice versa: the history of colonial knowledge has dominated the economic and cultural history of Malaysia. Hence the title of this essay: "A history of an identity, an identity of a history". Colonial knowledge was produced in the brutal modes of conquest that established colonial authority in the Straits Settlements, later in the Malay States and later still in Sarawak and Sabah; it made possible the effective conquest of British Malaya and the Malays and other natives.

The second part of this chapter takes a brief look at how the three pillars of 'Malayness'—*bahasa, raja dan agama* ('language, ruler and religion')—were instituted during the colonial period within the framework of colonial knowledge, informed by colonial investigative modalities, and inspired by Social Darwinism. Colonial knowledge gave rise to modern ideas of the 'Malay race' and the 'Malay nation' (*bangsa*) as expressed and reflected in the nationalist and anti-colonial movements.[10]

The third and final part of this essay will describe the attempts and struggles of the Malay elite in the postcolonial Malaysian state to redefine the colonial-constructed 'Malayness', first by introducing the term of *bumiputera*, which widened the scope and meaning of 'Malayness' in the framework of the socioeconomic engineering program called the New Economic Policy (NEP) (1971–90), and, second, by dealing with the dilemma that emerged once the NEP threatened to erode the three pillars of 'Malayness'.

Will the emergence of the *Bangsa Malaysia*, or the united Malaysian nation, undermine the three pillars of 'Malayness'? That is the question that will be briefly discussed in the final part of this article.

Colonial Knowledge and the Construction
of a Modern Identity

In Malaysia most historians and other scholars in the humanities accept 'colonial knowledge' as the basis of Malaysian and Malay history. Moreover, they do so in what seems like an almost unproblematised manner, even though politico-academic attempts are being made to 'indigenise' Malaysian history and the 'Malay' viewpoint has been privileged. Such attempts are admirable, and yet it is important to realise that this emphasis on the Malay perspective has been primarily motivated by a 'nationalistic' need to reinterpret history, and not by the urge to question the ways historical knowledge *per se* has been constructed. In Malaysia, historical knowledge, a crucial element in every identity formation, is still based on colonial knowledge; in this connection the question of the good and bad sides of the paternalism which informed this knowledge is not a very relevant one.[11]

This silence about the basis of colonial knowledge and its power in shaping Malay and Malaysian historiography is a cause for intellectual and ideological concern, especially in the context of present-day developments of Malaysian studies.[12] Of course there have been numerous discussions among historians about 'Western elements' and 'colonial influence' in the writing of 'local history', but these discussions generally adopt either a 'foreigner vs. local' or a 'Malay vs. non-Malay' stance rather than problematising the construction and definition of historical knowledge itself. The 'foreigner vs. local' debate is informed, so it seems, by the conflict between 'Eurocentredness' and 'indigenousness'.[13] In the 'Malay vs. non-Malay' debates, the arguments revolve around 'ethnic histories', such as the need to emphasise 'Malay history' as the basis of 'national history' on the one hand, and the contribution of the Chinese and Indians on the other.[14] In short, both have strong 'ethnicised' tendencies.

Malaysian historiography is an ideological struggle involving different interest groups (ethnic, foreign, academic, political and so on), an articulation of the 'unfinished' cultural/ethnic nationalist project in Malaysia. The situation is reminiscent of Ernest Renan's famous essay "What is a Nation?" in which history is placed at the centre of the 'nationalist project': the past requires a careful and selective interpretation, and in this process, Renan argues, "getting history wrong" is the precondition of nationalist history since it requires not only a collective remembering but also a collective forgetting. This forgetting "is a crucial factor in the creation of a nation, which is why progress in historical studies often constitutes a danger for [the principle of] nationality".[15]

Renan's essay points not only to contradictions in the creation of the historical substance of a 'nation' but also to the need to take note of the 'identity' of a particular form of historical knowledge and its construction—the very issues covered in this sketchy essay about the identity of Malaysian historical knowledge. These issues have escaped many scholars and analysts involved in the study of social and ethnic identity in Malaysia.

Following the discourse on Malay identity in Malaysia, one could argue that the colonial methods of accumulating facts and insights and the resultant corpus of knowledge have been critical in providing not only substance but also sustenance to the endeavour of writing about 'Malayness'. The sheer volume of 'facts' that have been accumulated and amassed by the British on, for instance, traditional Malay literature and the modern history of Malaya/Malaysia has established the hegemony of colonial knowledge in Malaysia's intellectual realm, where the discussions about 'Malay identity' are taking place. Anthony Milner has demonstrated in a very convincing manner that even the 'political' discourse (perhaps one might say 'discussions about identity') among pre-war Malay writers-cum-nationalists was mainly informed by or conducted within the framework of colonial knowledge.[16]

Relevant here are the methods of accumulating facts that resulted in the formation and organisation of the corpus of colonial knowledge. The approach anthropologist Bernard Cohn developed to make British rule in India more understandable is extremely useful. The British managed to classify, categorise and connect the vast social world that was India so it could be controlled by way of so-called 'investigative modalities', devices to collect and organise 'facts' which, together with translation works, enabled the British to conquer the 'epistemological space'.[17]

An investigative modality includes the definition of a body of information that is needed and the procedures by which appropriate knowledge is gathered, ordered and classified, and then transformed into usable forms such as published reports, statistical returns, histories, gazetteers, legal codes and encyclopaedias.[18] Some of these investigative modalities, such as historiography and museology, are of a general nature, whereas the survey and census modalities are more precisely defined and closely related to administrative needs. Some of these modalities were transformed into 'sciences' or 'disciplines', such as economics, ethnology, tropical medicine, comparative law and cartography. Their practitioners became professionals. Each modality was tailored to specific elements and needs on the administrative agenda of British rule; each of them became institutionalised and routinised in the day-to-day practice of colonial bureaucracy.

The 'historiographic modality', the most relevant one for my argument, had three important components. First, the production of settlement reports, which were done on a district-by-district basis; they usually consisted of a description of local customs, histories and tenure systems and a detailed account of how revenues were assessed and collected by local, indigenous regimes. Second, the descriptions of indigenous civilisations; these eventually provided the space for the formation of the discourse that legitimised the British civilising mission in the colony. Third, the history of the British presence in the colony; it evoked 'emblematic heroes and villains' and led to the erection of memorials and other 'sacred spaces' in the colony (and in the motherland as well).

The 'survey modality' encompassed a wide range of practices, from mapping areas to collecting botanical specimens, from the recording of architectural and archaeological sites of historic significance to the minute measuring of peasants' fields. When the British came to India, and later to the Malay lands, they sought to describe and classify every aspect of life in terms of zoology, geology, botany, ethnography, economic products, history and sociology by way of systematic surveys; they also created a colony-wide grid in which every site could be located for economic, social and political purposes. Hence, 'surveys' came to cover every systematic and official investigation of the natural and social features of indigenous society through which vast amounts of knowledge were transformed into textual forms such as encyclopaedias and archives.

The 'enumerative modality' enabled the British to categorise the indigenous society for administrative purposes, particularly by way of censuses that were to reflect basic sociological facts such as race, ethnic groups, culture and language. The various forms of enumeration that were developed objectified and stultified social, cultural and linguistic differences among the indigenous peoples and the migrant population, and these differences were of great use for the colonial bureaucracy and its army to explain and control conflicts and tensions.

Control was primarily implemented by way of the 'surveillance modality': detailed information was collected on 'peripheral' or 'minority' groups and categories of people whose activities were perceived as a threat to social order and therefore should be closely observed. For surveillance reasons, methods such as anthropometry and fingerprinting systems were developed in order to be able to describe, classify and identify individuals rather accurately for 'security' and other general purposes.

The 'museological modality' started out from the idea that a colony was a vast museum; its countryside, filled with ruins, was a source of collectibles, curiosities and artifacts that could fill local as well as European museums, botanical gardens and zoos. This modality became an exercise in presenting the indigenous culture, history and society to both a local and European public.

The 'travel modality' complemented the museological one. If the latter provided the colonial administration with concrete representations of the natives, the former helped to create a repertoire of images and typifications, if not stereotypes, that determined what was significant to European eyes; architecture, costumes, cuisine, ritual performances and historical sites were presented in 'romantic', 'exotic' and 'picturesque' terms. These often aesthetic images and typifications were frequently expressed in paintings and prints as well as in novels and short stories, many created by the colonial scholar-administrators, their wives and their friends.

These modalities represented, according to Cohn, a set of "officialising procedures" which the British used to establish and extend their authority in numerous areas:

> control by defining and classifying space, making separations between public and private spheres, by recording transactions such as sale of property, by counting and classifying populations, replacing religious institutions as the registrar of births, marriages, and deaths, and by standardizing languages and scripts.[19]

The colonial state introduced policies and rules that were organised by way of these investigative modalities; thus, the locals' minds and actions were framed in an epistemological and practical grid.

It should be obvious that Cohn's approach could very well be relevant in analysing developments in the Malay lands. The Malay Reservation Enactment 1913, to mention just one example, could serve as a very revealing illustration for this relevance: the Enactment defined, first, who is 'a Malay'; second, it determined the legal category of people who were allowed to grow rice only or rubber only; and third, it was bound to exert a direct influence on the commercial value of the land. This particular Enactment was instituted separately in the state constitutions of each of the eleven *negeri* (state) on the Peninsula, and in each constitution it offered a slightly different definition of who was a 'Malay'. For instance, a person of Arab descent was a Malay in Kedah but not in Johor; a person of Siamese descent was a Malay in Kelantan but not in Negeri Sembilan. It could be argued, then, that 'Malay' and 'Malayness' were created and confirmed by the Malay Reservation Enactment. However, there is more to this: the Act also made 'Malay' and 'Malayness' contested categories.

In different ways, the growth of public education and its rituals
fostered beliefs in how things were and how they ought to be: schools were
(and still are) crucial 'civilising' institutions, seeking to produce good and
productive citizens. By way of schools, many 'facts' amassed through
investigative modalities, and resultant officialising procedures were
channelled to the younger population; in this process governments directed
the people's perception of how social reality was organised. What is more,
with the creation of Chinese, Malay, Tamil and English schools, ethnic
boundaries became real, and ethnic identities became stultified and
essentialised by way of language and cultural practices.

The most powerful and most pervasive by-product of colonial
knowledge on the colonised has been the idea that the modern 'nation-
state' is the natural embodiment of history, territory and society. In other
words, the nation-state has become dependent on colonial knowledge and
its ways of determining, codifying, controlling and representing the past as
well as documenting and standardising the information that has formed
the basis of government. Modern Malaysians have become familiar with
'facts' that appear in reports and statistical data on commerce and trade,
health, demography, crime, transportation, industry and so on; these facts
and their accumulation, conducted in the modalities that were designed to
shape colonial knowledge, lie at the foundation of the modern, postcolonial
nation-state of Malaysia. The citizens of Malaysia rarely question these
facts, fine and often invisible manifestations of the process of Westernisation.

What I have briefly sketched here is the 'identity of a history' since
these 'facts', rooted in European social theories, philosophical ideas and
classificatory schemes, form the basis of Malaysian historiography. It is
within this history that modern identities in Malaysia, such as 'Malay' and
'Malayness' and 'Chinese' and 'Chineseness', have been described and
consolidated.

From Melayu to *Bumiputera*: Officialising Plurality or Accommodating 'Difference'?

In an important essay, loosely framed within Anthony D. Smith's concept
of '*ethnie*', Anthony Reid has sketched the different meanings and
applications of the terms 'Malay' and 'Malayness' in the history of the
Malay Archipelago.[20] Initially, he argues, the terms represented self-referent
categories among the peoples inhabiting the archipelago; then, they became
social labels that were used by the peoples of South Asia and China, who
were mainly traders; and finally, they became social labels that were used

by Europeans, namely, Portuguese, Spanish, Dutch and British, who were travellers, traders and, eventually, colonisers.

In the first and second instances, in non-European contexts that is, by the sixteenth and seventeenth centuries, 'Malay' and 'Malayness' were associated with two major elements, namely: (i) a line of kingship acknowledging descent from Srivijaya and Melaka; and (ii) a commercial diaspora retaining the customs, language and trade practices of Melaka.[21] Kingship (read: *kerajaan* and the royal family) was a prominent pillar of 'Malayness' in the area around the Straits of Melaka; Islam was another pillar because it provided kingship with some of its core values.[22] The commercial diaspora constituted a group of people outside the Straits of Melaka area—Borneo, Makassar and Java—who defined their 'Malayness' primarily in terms of language and customs, two other pillars of 'Malayness'.

Sociologically-speaking, the inhabitants of the archipelago in the pre-European era used the term 'Malay' in both objective and subjective ways. Kingship was used as an objective measure, Islam as both objective and subjective: it was an objective criterion to define the King and his subjects (Muslim and non-Muslims) whereas, subjectively speaking, anyone who claimed to embrace Islam could be counted as 'Malay'. Non-Muslims and non-Malays could be labelled as 'Malays', as long as they spoke and wrote 'Malay' and lived a 'Malay way of life'—meaning that they wore certain clothes, followed certain culinary practices, and became an integral part of the Malay-speaking trading network.

The Portuguese, Spanish and Dutch used the labels 'Malay' and 'Malayness' in much this way. Being merchants first and rulers second, their main concerns were materialistic. They were not active propagators of their national values and ideas but, rather, framed their presence as a 'civilising' force within a vigorously religious orientation, as summarised, for instance, in Norman Davies' *Europe: A History*:

> Europeans sailed overseas ... for reasons of trade, of loot, of conquest, and increasingly of religion. For many, it provided the first meeting with people of different races. To validate their claim over the inhabitants of the conquered lands, the Spanish monarchs, for instance, had to first establish that non-Europeans were human... and their representatives were ordered to read out to all native peoples: "The Lord our God, Living and Eternal, created Heaven and Earth, and one man and woman, of whom you and I, and all the men of the world, were and are descendants". To confirm the point, Pope Paul III decreed in 1537 that "all Indians are truly men, not only capable of understanding the Catholic faith, but... exceedingly desirous to receive it".[23]

In the tradition of merchants and sailors trading across oceans, the preparation of detailed inventory lists of people and things, including cargoes, was a routine exercise for the Portuguese and Dutch merchants and captains. To be able to do this, they had to devise ways of classifying and categorising not only the contents of their ships, but also their crew and their trading partners. That is how Dutch harbourmasters, for example, recognised 'Chinese', 'Javanese', 'Bugis-Makassar', 'Balinese', 'Madurese', 'Arab' and 'Malay' captains, sailors and merchants. They mainly followed local labels, and made no conscious attempt to reconstitute or redefine labels and identities according to some preconceived Western notion. Thus, both the objective and subjective local concepts were embedded in social labels. This pre-colonial process left 'Malay' and 'Malayness' unchanged and unquestioned.

Anthony Reid argues that the subjective aspect of Malay and Malayness, as observed in the sixteenth and seventeenth centuries, allowed a distinct plurality in the subsequent composition of the category of 'Malay' since it was "exceptionally open to new recruits from any background". He concludes that 'Malayness' "can be seen to have evolved towards the idea of *orang Melayu* as a distinct ethnie".[24] The evidence of this plurality, however, allows for alternative constructs; witness, for instance, the fact that the British reconstituted the meaning of 'Malay' and 'Malayness' and almost completely ignored its *'ethnie'* sense.

Rather like the British modes of operation in India described by Cohn, British activities in Singapore and beyond involved a distinct understanding of the local population, in particular of the 'Malays' for whom they fostered special feelings of friendship as early as the days of Raffles. Inspired by the Enlightenment, they operated from the idea that human beings should be classified in a scientific manner. By way of various investigative modalities (such as historiography, surveys, museology, enumeration, travel, surveillance), the British constructed a corpus of knowledge supported by 'facts', and introduced many names, labels and categories that people in Malaysia regard as natural, self-evident and existing since time immemorial.

The activities of the early administrators are illustrative and prominent. Raffles, for instance, renamed a Malay genealogical description of kings and their rituals and ceremonies, originally titled rather simply by its author as *Peraturan Segala Raja-Raja* (Rules for Rulers), as *Sejarah Melayu*, a name that Malays themselves then began to use as well: he gave that text the English name of "Malay Annals", a name that is still used in most scholarly discussions.[25] William Marsden, the author of *History of Sumatra*, declared that the Peninsula was the place of origin of the Malays;

as a result, it was given the name of 'Malay Peninsula', a name that was subsequently translated into Malay as *'Tanah Melayu'* (lit. Malay land), with far-reaching consequences.[26]

Above all, it was Raffles' path-breaking essay, entitled "On the Malayu Nation, with a Translation of its Maritime Institution", in the journal *Asiatic Researches* that set the tone for the subsequent discourse on Malay and Malayness amongst the Europeans—and, later, amongst the Malays themselves. Raffles wrote: "I cannot but consider the Malayu nation as one people, speaking one language, though spread over so wide a space, preserving their character and customs, in all the maritime states lying between Sulu Seas and the Southern Oceans."[27]

After the establishment of the Straits Settlements in 1824, Raffles' concept of 'Malay nation' gradually became 'Malay race', an identity that was accepted by both the colonial power and the Malays themselves, primarily as the result of the growing presence of others whose 'race' was 'European' or 'Chinese'. As early as the 1840s, the writer Abdullah Munshi used the term *bangsa Melayu* ('Malay race' or 'Malay people'), and that term gradually entered the public sphere. The 1891 Colonial Census recognised three racial categories, namely, 'Chinese', 'Tamil' and 'Malay'. With the increased immigration of Chinese and Indian labourers to British Malaya in the early 1900s, a plural society was created in which the concept of Malay as a race became fixed and indelible.[28] When the founders of the first Malay-language newspaper in the Straits Settlement (in 1907) chose the name *Utusan Melayu* ('Malay messenger'), this followed and confirmed colonial knowledge.

English and Chinese schools established at the turn of the century were soon followed by 'Malay' vernacular schools; teaching was in English, Mandarin and 'Malay', respectively. In the textbooks for 'Malay' schools, the British constructed a distinctly 'Malay' historiography and 'Malay' literature in which 'Malay' *hikayats* were used to create and implant a certain sense of historical identity and literary taste. The introduction of the Malay Reservation Enactment in 1913 provided a legal definition of 'Malay', and helped fix the idea of 'Malayness' in the public mind. These activities, supported and sanctioned by the colonial government, gave life to the term and concept of 'Malay', sooner or later accepted by all social actors.

It is not surprising that 'Malay' nationalism, which developed alongside 'Chinese' and 'Indian' nationalism, had a cultural rather than a political character; the discussions that made the 'Malay race' into a 'Malay nation' focused primarily on questions of identity and distinction in terms of customs, religion and language, rather than politics. The debate and conflicts surrounding the transition centred on the question of who could be called the 'real Malay' (*Melayu asli* or *Melayu jati*), and these frictions inevitably led to the emergence of various factions amongst 'Malay nationalists'. Malay nationalism was most strongly articulated when the British tried to impose their own concept of the 'Malayan nation' by way of the so-called Malayan Union, a unitary state project. Strong protests on the part of Malay nationalists forced the British to accept an alternative federalist order, officially known as '*Persekutuan Tanah Melayu*', translated from the English 'Federation of Malaya', incidentally another product of colonial knowledge.

In formulating a Constitution for the independent Federation of Malaya, the 'British', the 'Chinese' and the 'Indians' had to bargain hard with the 'Malays'. The 'Chinese' and the 'Indians' effectively became citizens of the independent state but they had to acknowledge *ketuanan Melayu*, or Malay dominance, which implied that they had to accept 'special Malay privileges' in education and government services, 'Malay' royalty as their rulers, Islam as the official religion and the 'Malay' language as the official language of the new nation-state.

The formation of the Federation of Malaysia in 1963 introduced a new dimension to the understanding and definition of 'Malay' and 'Malayness', arising from the addition of the Muslim groups in Sarawak and Sabah, such as the 'Dusun' and 'Murut' in Sabah and the 'Melanaus' in Sarawak. Unlike the Malays on the Peninsula, these local groups did not constitute a majority in the states, either demographically or politically, for more than 60 per cent of the population consisted of non-Muslim natives and Chinese; in electoral terms, the Muslims could not capture more than 45 per cent of the seats in the local legislative assemblies of Sarawak and Sabah. This posed a major political problem to the Malay-dominated federal government in Kuala Lumpur, which had to cooperate with, and attempt to co-opt, non-Malay Muslims as their political partners. In Sarawak, after the downfall of an Iban chief minister, Stephen Kalong Ninkan, in 1966 Kuala Lumpur managed to install a government led by Melanau Muslims and supported by local Chinese. In Sabah, the Peninsula Malays found a ready partner in Datu Mustapha, who also ruled with the support of the Chinese. The federal government used the term *bumiputera* (son of the soil) to accommodate the Malays and the native Muslims and non-Muslims of Sarawak and Sabah in a single category.

When the New Economic Policy was launched in 1971, *bumiputera* became an important ethnic category: it was officialised and became critical in the distribution of development benefits to poor people and also the entrepreneurial middle class. The *bumiputera*, the 'Malays' and their Muslim counterparts in Sarawak and Sabah, achieved political dominance throughout the country with one exception: in the 1980s the Christian Kadazan in Sabah formed their own opposition party (Parti Bersatu Sabah – PBS) that ruled the state successfully for two electoral terms. During that period, the relationship between Sabah and the federal government could be described, at best, as tense. Sarawak remained under the control of Muslim natives, called 'Malay Melanaus', who confirmed Islam as the single most important pillar of their newly acquired 'Malayness'.

In an attempt to win back Sabah, the leading party in the federal government, UMNO (United Malays National Organisation), made a historic decision in the late 1980s when it opened itself to non-Muslim *bumiputera* so that eventually the UMNO-led Barisan Nasional ('National Front') could regain control over Sabah. These developments show that the need to define the borders and margins of a concept can have far-reaching effects on its central content: 'Malayness' as defined by the Malay nationalist movement in the 1920s and 1930s and implemented and redefined by UMNO, had to be reformulated in Sabah once again, illustrating how flexible the concept or category of 'Malay' is. It also shows that the ongoing discussions about 'Malayness' are at once both important and irrelevant: the concept can easily shift meaning, adapting itself time and again to new situations and making clear-cut statements impossible or incredible.

Conclusion: Identity Contestation in Contemporary Malaysia

What I have tried to demonstrate in a very schematic manner is of how an identity is constituted, in this case 'Malay' and 'Malayness'. The definition of the two terms was (re)created within the framework of colonial knowledge that constructed a 'Malay identity' by way of various investigative modalities. Even the term *bumiputera,* introduced in 1971, does not really refer to something new: it is merely a new term for what in the 1891 census was already officialised as the category of "Malays and other Natives of the Archipelago".

Like most societal phenomena, identity formation takes place within two social realities at once: the 'authority-defined' reality—the reality that is authoritatively defined by people who are part of the dominant power structure—and the 'everyday-defined' reality experienced by the people in their daily life. These two realities exist side by side at any given time. Although intricately linked and constantly shaping each other by way of contestation, they are certainly not identical: 'everyday-defined' social reality is experienced whereas 'authority-defined' social reality is primarily observed and interpreted, and possibly imposed. Both are mediated through the social position of those who observe and interpret social reality and those who experience it.

Woven into the ever-tense relationship between these two social realities is social power, articulated in various forms such as majority—minority discourse and state—society contestation. In concrete terms, social power involves collectives such as nationalist, literary and professional groups, scholar-administrators, academicians, and so on. Their discourses take both oral and written forms; some may be of a literary character, others are simply statistical or factual, but all are equally inspired by ideas about 'social justice' and 'social equality'.

The discussion of 'Malay' and 'Malayness', particularly in the context of colonial knowledge and its investigative modalities, has been driven by an 'authority-defined' perspective. Obviously, that perspective is not homogeneous in nature; it is expressed in various views and positions, some even in opposition to one another.[29] For instance, some British colonial officials were openly paternalistic or benevolent in their attitudes towards the Malays, something especially prevalent amongst educationalists, while others were simply authoritarian or even racist. In other words, contestations existed within colonial knowledge, the result of different emphasIs on the various investigative modalities available. Such contestations were also amply reflected in the competing notions of 'the Malay nation', or the 'nation-of-intent', deployed by Malay nationalists. Some preferred *Melayu raya* as their nation-of-intent, some an Islamic state, and others a united Malay *kerajaan*.[30]

In contemporary Malaysia, the recently introduced concept of *Bangsa Malaysia* is by no means an uncontested one either. As a matter of fact, the very notion of one *Bangsa Malaysia* has generated a vital and healthy debate in authority-defined circles regarding the various possibilities of forging such an entity. Assimilationists prefer a homogeneous *Bangsa Malaysia*; accommodationists prefer a plural one.

It is very relevant to realise that these discussions reflect not only a contestation about the identity of 'Malayness' or *bumiputera*, but also a contestation of the methods or frameworks through which this 'identity' is examined and elaborated. And these methods and frameworks will continue to interfere with one another in very confusing ways.

Reconfiguring Malay and Islam in Contemporary Malaysia

VIRGINIA MATHESON HOOKER*

A plural, multi-religious society is living perpetually on the brink of catastrophe. Relations between Muslims and non-Muslims must be governed by moral and ethical considerations.[1]

Campaigning in the Malaysian general election of November 1999 emphasised once again that in Malaysian politics, Islam is an emotive and powerful topic. The ruling National Front (Barisan Nasional) led by Prime Minister (PM) Dr Mahathir claimed it had a long record of religious tolerance but accused its strongest rival, *Parti Islam SeMalaysia* (PAS), of fanaticism. For the first time at a general election, the National Front faced an opposition coalition which brought together PAS, the Democratic Action Party (DAP) and the National Justice Party (Keadilan), the latter led by Datin Dr Wan Azizah, wife of former Deputy Prime Minister (DPM) Anwar Ibrahim. The opposition coalition called itself the 'Alternative Front' and used the gaoling of Anwar as a prime example of the National Front's corrupt and autocratic behaviour. The Alternative Front campaigned on a platform of social justice for all races and received public support from prominent Chinese and Indian intellectuals and activists, as well as from PAS leaders. In an attempt to subvert the appeal of the Alternative Front to non-Muslim voters (Chinese and Indians), the National Front warned that votes for the opposition would be votes against religious freedom. The Alternative Front was quick to respond with a statement from Anwar (read out by Wan Azizah) accusing the National Front of trying to create a culture of fear. Anwar urged Chinese and Indian voters not to be "easily scared or deceived by the slanders and lies of the National Front" and assured them there would not be riots and Islamic extremism if Dr Mahathir were to be voted out of office.[2]

The politicised references to Islam throughout the campaign drew attention to the fact that racial and ethnic difference (Malay/Chinese/

Indian) in Malaysia has formed the main sub-text for political maneuvering since Independence. The bottom line is now, as it was then, that the Malays (whose religion is Islam) are the numerically and politically dominant race, while economic power lies with the Chinese (whose religion is rarely Islam). Nationalist activity in Malaysia has always been led by the Malays who have ensured that Malay language and religion (Islam) are paramount in the nation-state as stipulated in Article 3 of the Federal Constitution, where Islam is recognised as the official religion of the Federation.

If there were any doubt about the special position of Malays in Malaysia, most analysts would cite the race riots of May 1969 as evidence of Malay sensitivity about their position in 'their own land'. During the riots Malay youths rampaged through Kuala Lumpur in reaction to unexpected gains by Chinese parties in the general election of that year. The government responded to Malay feelings of insecurity by introducing in 1971 the New Economic Policy (NEP). This was a 20-year development plan designed to give Malays a greater share of the country's wealth through special terms for generous loans, positive discrimination in the commercial sector, and a large number of scholarships for tertiary education.[3] When the NEP was reviewed in 1990, it was believed that a better balance had been achieved between race and economic leverage and that the time was ripe for a broader and more nationally oriented ideology and economic programme. It was in this context that Dr Mahathir's Vision 2020 was formulated to achieve greater national unity, increased economic growth and to create a nation-state that was "truly modern and progressive, an industrialised society which is just, moral and rational, with a robust and lively economy as well as its own social and cultural characteristics".[4] The NEP's focus on Malays was replaced by a more embracing vision of 'society' (*masyarakat*)—all the races who are citizens of Malaysia. As an ideology of national unity Vision 2020 makes no specific reference to Islam but calls for the whole of society to be ethical and moral, tolerant, liberal in outlook and compassionate.[5] This is in fact an elaboration of Dr Mahathir's often stated philosophy that modernisation and progress must be based on values such as industry, efficiency, honesty and discipline.

While Vision 2020 was an ideology which addressed all Malaysians, the prime minister remained concerned about what he viewed as conservative interpretations of Islam and the danger this posed for the economic advancement of the Malays. In his book *The Challenge*, written in the mid-1980s, he addressed the link between Islam and modernisation in these terms:

One of the saddest ironies of recent times is that Islam, the faith that once made its followers progressive and powerful, is being invoked to promote retrogression which will bring in its wake weakness and eventual collapse....

Misinterpretation of Islam is only one of the many forms of confusion threatening the Malays today. The challenge is tremendous—the stake survival itself.[6]

To avoid decline, he believed, Malays must choose to adopt and then practice 'good values' and, he stresses, their destiny is theirs to shape.[7] In the context of Islamic beliefs the preservation of spiritual and religious values can be achieved without "abstaining from the mastery and use of modern ways which can safeguard the position and security of Muslims".[8] Thus in 1986 the prime minister made quite clear his belief that Malays needed to adopt a system of 'good values' and these values were to be found in Islam.

Ten years after *The Challenge* was published, DPM Anwar Ibrahim produced his own book entitled *The Asian Renaissance*. Received with acclaim, one of the themes running through the collection of essays is that religious identity is a distinctive feature of Asian cultures ("the Asian Man at heart is *persona religiosa*"). However, Anwar warns, the practice of religion, in its role as the moral bastion of society has not been consistent. He believes that although Asians "take pride in their religiosity" the failure to live out its ethical dimensions has resulted in "the erosion of the social fabric through widespread permissiveness and corruption".[9] Reading Anwar's views with the benefit of hindsight, it is particularly ironic that just two years after the publication of his book he would stand trial for corruption and sexual deviancy. In 1999, despite international criticism of the conduct of his trial, he was found guilty of the former charges and imprisoned for six years. Then in August 2000, after a second trial (the conduct of which aroused even greater international outrage), he received a further nine years' imprisonment for sodomy. Many Malaysians were particularly concerned that Anwar had been assaulted while held in custody by the Inspector General of Police himself. Besides the serious concerns about the state of the Malaysian judiciary, the evidence of police corruption, and the suspicion that Anwar was being imprisoned for political reasons, for many ordinary Malays the charges of sexual misconduct and sodomy against Anwar were considered to be in particularly bad taste and totally deplorable.[10] After all, they remembered him as the first leader of the Malaysian Muslim Youth movement (*Angkatan Belia Islam Malaysia, ABIM*), knew that he was the most prominent government spokesperson on Islamic matters and held positions such as President (Chancellor) of Malaysia's International Islamic University, and that he was regarded as a Muslim intellectual in his own right. They perceived

Dr Mahathir's removal of Anwar as an attack not only on him but on the kind of Islam he had espoused, a kind of Islam which the prime minister had formerly seemed to support.

In the light of Anwar's high profile as a representative of mainstream Islam in Malaysia, it is revealing to return to the period before his expulsion from the United Malays National Organisation (UMNO) and to analyse some of his statements about religion and the Malays. At this time, in 1996, both Anwar and Prime Minister Mahathir had seemed united in their views on the crucial importance of religion as the ethical basis of society. Towards the end of the year and into the early months of 1997, they were both making public statements which were openly critical of the way Malays were failing to implement the principles of Islam in their daily lives. They also repeated their ideas about Islam as a religion which supported modernisation.

The press was quick to pick up these statements and give them front-page status. They were newsworthy items on several counts because they concerned the politically-sensitive areas of religion and the Malays, they had implications for non-Muslims, and they were delivered by the two most powerful figures in the nation. Although the mainstream press in Malaysia regularly carries articles, special features and letters about Islamic matters, the Mahathir and Anwar comments were given special prominence.[11] The leaders' comments focussed on two issues: Malays and social ills, and Islam and development. They were reported in three of Malaysia's most prominent dailies, The Star, The New Straits Times, and Utusan Malaysia. Both The Star and The New Straits Times are widely read English language dailies while Utusan Malaysia is the leading Malay language daily. Each is influential and all are owned by groups close to the ruling coalition (Barisan Nasional). Although this means that anti-Government news is rare, as one observer has noted, the papers often present "different factions and interests within the ruling groups".[12] My purpose in focussing on these reports is to analyse the views of Anwar and Mahathir on the relationship between Islam and the Malays, and to see what messages they were giving Malaysians about the Government's attitude to Islam in the context of the nation-state. We begin with the issue of Malays and what Dr Mahathir referred to as 'social problems'.

Reporting on Malays and Social Ills

The issue was covered for about a week in the English and the Malay language press. It appeared first in The Star on 31 January 1997, in an article describing the prime minister breaking the fast with students at a university near his home town in the north of Peninsular Malaysia. The headline, on the second page of the paper read: "Seek ways to overcome weaknesses, Malays urged". The article continued that Prime Minister Datuk Seri Mahathir Mohammad said today that the Malays should be prepared to admit their weaknesses and shortcomings and should be determined to seek ways to overcome them. He said the Malay community appeared to be facing more social problems than the other races in the country although the environment was the same for all races. Many Malays "were involved in unhealthy activities like corruption, loafing, incest and child abuse". A recent study, he said, revealed that 67 per cent of criminal cases involved Malays. "Development may have brought with it some negative elements. Previously there were not so many nightclubs and men and women did not mingle so freely." In conclusion he said Malays should not be ashamed to admit their weaknesses and shortcomings because "for as long as they fail to do so they could not find the solutions to the social problems they were facing to attain progress".

The following day (Saturday 1 February 1997) a report appeared on the second page of the Malay language daily *Utusan Malaysia* under the headline: "Gagal hayati agama punca gejala social" (Failure to live out religion is at the root of social ills). The article was reporting the comments of DPM Anwar Ibrahim's after the Friday service in a Penang mosque, where he had delivered the *khutbah* (sermon). To paraphrase the report: the DPM said that social problems which are increasingly serious in Malay society are caused by Malays failing to implement, obey and live out the teachings of Islam. Although they are educated and trained in all kinds of religious teachings at home and at school, compared with other religious communities the teachings have no effect because of their own attitude not to fully implement them in their lives. This is strange, he said, because religion is compulsory only for Muslims, but our data suggests that social problems are more connected with the Islamic community. Society should not be blaming its young people, because social problems indicated weaknesses in social institutions including the family, mosque officials, educational institutions, and political and government bodies. The DPM continued by telling Muslims to use Ramadan (the fasting month) to strengthen the discipline of the Muslim community.[13]

The third report on the same topic is again from *The Star*, Thursday 6 February 1997, which carried the large front page headline: "Let's Face It: Find ways to deal with social ills, Dr M tells Malays". The second page of the paper continued the report under the headline: "Non-Malays seem better at facing social ills". On this occasion the context was an official public meeting to discuss social problems among Muslims attended by the PM, the DPM (in his capacity as Chairman of the Cabinet Committee on Social Problems), Muslim cabinet ministers, officials from the Department of Islamic Affairs, senior government officials and principals of institutions of higher education. The front page subheading sets the tone of the report. "Kuala Lumpur: Datuk Seri Dr Mahathir Mohamad told Malays yesterday they must first admit that they are the worst off in terms of social problems compared with other races before remedial steps can be taken". The prime minister said Malays must first face their problems and then find ways of dealing with them. He noted that in a breakdown of Malaysia's population figures Malays constituted 54–55 per cent, Chinese 26 per cent and Indians 10 per cent. He continued, "But when comparing social problems, the Malays involved make up 67 per cent while the Chinese involvement in merely 16 per cent". From statistics, he said, it seems that non-Malays were more able and capable to face social ills than Malays. "We read the newspapers everyday and we can't help see cases of child-abuse—some battered to death—incest, *bohsia*,[14] and the spread of AIDS and HIV. Who are involved? Aren't most of them Malays?" One of the things lacking among Malay youth he said, is the "'inner defence' to stop themselves being influenced". A solution had to be found to the problem, he stressed. Comparing Malays with Chinese, the PM noted that although exposed to the same circumstances as Malays, Chinese had not succumbed to social problems.

Reporting on Islam and Development

We move now to several reports of the leaders' comments on Islam and progress or development. The context of the reports was the occasion of the 39th National Qur'an Recital Competition which was held on 1 November 1996 in the Malaysian state of Perak. *The New Straits Times* presented its report on page seven of the national news section, under the headline "Dr M: Muslims should learn to be self-reliant". In his speech to the participants and audience the prime minister is reported to have said the following: "it is important that Muslims learn to be self-reliant in order that they not be humiliated and oppressed". He is reported as saying that Muslim countries are backward and at the mercy of developed nations. There is a need for Muslims to see that development is important and can be achieved by Muslims, but some of them did not believe in the importance of development in this world. In the age of information technology, Islam can protect against "unhealthy information" which could destroy the people's moral and cultural values.

A report on the same event was also carried on 1 November in *The Star* which ran its article closer to the front of the paper with the headline "Dr M: Religion can see us through". *The Star's* order of presentation of the PM's speech differed from that of *The New Straits Times*. It began with the PM's statement that religion can help shield people from the negative influences of the information explosion and continues with his words that the emergence of a "strong Islamic community could help in overcoming the perception that Islam was an obstacle to development". However, he continued, "there are some Muslims who think that there is no need to pursue progress because, to them, progress for Muslims is not the same as that pursued by non-Muslims. Such thinking enforces the belief of some Muslims that they do not have to progress but also that it is impossible to progress in this world". In his view, it is such thinking which made Islamic countries weak and "forced to seek protection from developed countries". In a section not reported in *The New Straits Times*, *The Star* added the PM's words addressed to all young people: "the country wanted not only a highly educated generation but one which could balance spiritual development with material and physical progress".

Analysis of reportage: the players

The prominence which the press gives to statements by the PM and DPM gives the impression that it is they who are setting the agenda for Islam in Malaysia rather than the traditional leaders of Islam, the Muslim religious scholars. The impression is given that it is the PM and his deputy who decide what kind of Islam is appropriate for Malaysia as it approaches the new millennium. When other opinions about Islam are reported, such as interviews with religious authorities or academics, those opinions are presented as reactions to the statements of the PM and the DPM. The impression that the press conveys is that only these two political leaders take initiatives with regard to the role of Islam in the nation-state.

Analysis of reportage: the contexts

The statements on both issues were delivered in Islamic contexts, that is, at the breaking of the fast in mosques, at a meeting of a committee to examine social ills among Muslims, and at a Qur'anic recitation competition. However, rather than praising Islam, each of the statements was critical of the contemporary practice of Islam both within and outside of Malaysia. As well, because they were reported by the leading dailies, they received almost maximum publicity in Malaysia itself.[15] Theoretically, then, these rather provocative statements about Islam could have reached any literate person in Malaysia and conveyed to them the government's attitude to Islam. The 'ubiquitous' influence of the media on "stimulating, corrupting, influencing, shaping and challenging" the public and in particular its role in informing about Islam has been widely discussed.[16] It is unlikely however, that all newspaper readers in Malaysia would be equally interested in the reports. But several sectors in society keep a watching brief on public statements on religion. Firstly, because the administration of Islam in Malaysia is a matter for each of the individual states (rather than the Federal government), state religious and political leaders pay careful attention to pronouncements coming from the central government to check whether it is overstepping its jurisdiction. The PM would be well aware of their interest. Secondly, a considerable proportion of the newspapers readers (especially of the English language dailies) would be non-Malays and it is likely that the PM and his deputy intended to reassure them that the government was not protecting any anti-social behaviour by Malays, but was addressing and trying to tackle such behaviour.

Analysis of reportage: the issues

The two issues of Malays and social ills, and of Islam and development seem to be very different from each other. In the first, Malays are singled out as being involved in far greater numbers than other races in Malaysia in particularly abhorrent crimes such as child abuse and incest. The implications of the second issue are more complex. Countries whose populations are mainly Muslim, the reports argue, remain under-developed and this is linked to a hostile attitude to material progress. If, however, Muslims were to embrace progress, Islam could be used as a protection against the undesirable effects of development. While these issues appear to be so different, on closer examination, the projected role of Islam is the same. In both contexts, Islam is presented as a source of moral values. In each case, Muslims are described as inferior to non-Muslims but there is an assurance that if Islam were to be implemented as a system of values for individual guidance, then Muslims would be able to participate fully in the modern world.

The sub-text of the Prime Ministerial statements on Islam is critical not of Islam as a religion, but of Islam as it is currently practised both in

Malaysia and beyond. This could be changed, according to the statements as they are reported, if Muslims would adopt and implement the moral and ethical guidance Islamic teachings offer. If this were to be done Malays and all Muslims would be better citizens in the modern world.

Analysis of reportage: the language

If we examine all the reports of both issues (whether in Malay or English), it is striking that both the PM and the DPM speak about Islam and Islamic values without using any Islamic terminology. The only specifically Muslim vocabulary occurs at the most general level with generic references such as 'Islam', 'Islamic' and 'Muslim' (or 'agama Islam' and 'orang Islam'). There seems to be no difference between the rhetoric of both leaders. Each discusses Islam in a non-religious or secular idiom. This is particularly worthy of notice in the light of recent research which highlights the fact that "Islam provides a language for political participation and competition. It also provides a language for debating values in public life and for defining the respective authority of individuals, civil society and the state".[17] Although the Islamic terminology is available for precisely the type of discussion the Malaysian leaders are promoting, they do not draw on it but choose instead the terminology of the secular sphere.

Analysis of reportage: islam and national identity

Dr Mahathir's official agenda for the future of Malaysia is to establish a united and technologised nation by the end of the first quarter of the twenty-first century as defined in his Vision 2020 statement. To achieve this, there is considerable emphasis in contemporary Malaysian government rhetoric on fusing religious identity with national identity, particularly through government moves to bring Islam into the "the heart of all economic and non-economic life".[18] The government's advocacy of 'Islam' is however, focussed specifically on an expression of Islam which will support and complement its political aims of an industrialised and unified nation. Malaysian sociologist, Shamsul A. B., has traced the main expressions and groupings of Islamic modernising and revivalist movements in Malaysia since the race riots in 1969. He is able to show that the views of the 'moderate' Muslim grouping (in contrast to more extremist, that is, more literalist groupings) who emphasise 'the spiritual and moral foundations' required for modernisation, are the views which the government have incorporated into their Vision 2020 framework.[19] It may well be that the statements on Islamic values delivered by the PM and his deputy during Ramadan 1996–97 were framed in terms deliberately chosen to resonate with the views of followers of 'moderate Islam'. But how can religious and national identity be fused in a nation whose citizens do not all follow the same religion?

Since the race riots of 1969, the dominant position of the Malays as the major ethnic group in Peninsular Malaysia has been at the heart of affirmative political and economic policies. A recent study of the concept 'Melayu' expressed the Malay position in these terms:

> The ruling class of the nation state of Malaysia maintains a hegemonic Malay identity based on difference between supposedly indigenous Islamic Malays and 'outsiders', namely Chinese and Indians. This identity is regarded as a natural ethnic base of the state.[20]
>
> The Prime Ministerial statements about Malays and social evils which we examined above, suggest there may be a shift in the attitude of political leaders, if not the 'ruling class'. To publicly criticise Malays as being the worst offenders in crimes of a social nature compared with non-Malays is not maintaining 'a hegemonic Malay identity'. Both the PM and DPM criticised not only Malays for their 'weaknesses' but also Islamic leaders for not making the teachings of Islam more relevant to the lives of Malay, particularly young Malays. In view of these critical comments about Malays let us check the Constitutional definition of this "natural ethnic base of the state".
>
> 'Malay' means a person who professes the religion of Islam, habitually speaks the Malay language, conforms to Malay custom and—was before Merdeka Day born in the Federation or in Singapore or born of parents one of whom was born in the Federation or in Singapore, or is on that day domiciled in the Federation or in Singapore; or is the issue of such a person.[21]

This residence requirement which applies concomitantly with the stipulations concerning Malay religion, language and custom is rarely included in discussions about the constitutional definition of a 'Malay'. It does, however, become very important in the context of Indonesian immigration (legal or illegal) into Malaysia, because although many Indonesians meet the religion, language and custom definitions, they do not meet the residence requirements. Similarly, any other migrant taking up residence in Malaysia after 31 August 1957, unless one or both of their parents were born in Singapore or the Federation of Malaya, even if they meet the other conditions, would not be legally eligible to be regarded as a Malay (although they might be eligible for citizenship).

On the other hand, there are an increasing number of 'Malays' who meet the residence requirements of the Constitution, but are losing their ability to speak the Malay language (as English becomes their working language), and are out of touch with Malay custom. These are educated Malays who as part of the post-1969 affirmative action policies for Malays received a tertiary education (often abroad) and were offered special financial advantages to boost the number in the business sector. This is the group the government refers to as the 'new Malays' (*Melayu baru*) whom it is nurturing to spearhead the implementation of Vision 2020 and to be the future leaders of Malaysia. These 'new Malays' however, with their Westernised outlook and global points of reference, do not habitually speak Malay nor conform with Malay custom. The markers of their ethnicity are their place of birth and their profession of Islam.[22] Of these, Islam is the active constituent in their official identity as Malays. Yet, the PM is openly questioning the degree to which Islam does influence the lives of these 'new Malay' Malays. Here the PM treads a fine line between exhorting Malays to become more Islamic (and thus driving them into what he would consider more extreme expressions of that religion) and motivating them to implement the positive values Islam so that they do not fall prey to 'social ills'. He is in fact exhorting them to be better Muslims so that they can be better citizens of Malaysia. In this way national identity and Islam are interlocked, but in a way which not only promotes civic values but also highlights individual standards of morality.

If we look closely at the comments by the two leaders which urged Malays to implement the teachings of Islam and to live out the values of their religion, we see that they are expressed in language which is more secular than Islamic and we may argue that there are parallels with elements of 'civil religion'. Take for example the description of the way religion (in this case Christianity) has been practised in America since last century. It is characterised as being predominantly activist, moralistic and socially-oriented, rather than being contemplative, theological and innerly spiritual.[23] The Malaysian leaders' calls for Malays to actively apply the teachings of Islam as a solution to social problems are calls for Muslims to use their religion as a moral guide in this world. There are no references to Islam as a means to salvation in the next world—the focus is on what Islam can do for its followers here and now. A strong case can be made for claiming that in their statements Mahathir and Anwar were preparing the way for Islam to become a civil religion in Malaysia.

If the Malaysian leaders were seeking sources of moral values and models of the qualities they considered necessary for 'good citizens' they could also find them in abundance in the traditional customs which are described under the term '*adat Melayu*'. These values were highlighted, for example, in a front page story carried by *The New Straits Times* on 17 March 1997. Under the headline "Villagers help social worker relocate house the old-fashioned way" and with a feature photograph of a group of Malay men lifting a Malay village house to a new location, the report stressed the fact that 200 villagers came together to "shoulder a burden" and work cooperatively for the good of a fellow villager. Somewhat ironically, the photograph of the house relocation shared the front page with a banner headline which read "Reigniting a scientific culture, Anwar: Time for Muslim world to get off sidelines, engage in innovation and ideas". The juxtaposition of the two reports suggested that the traditional Malay values of voluntary cooperative labour were suitable only for rural village life and were now so rare as to be worthy items for front page reporting. In theory, however, the values of group cooperation and support are qualities Dr Mahathir and Anwar might have used in the fight against 'social ills'. But this was not the case. In the press reports during the period under study, Malay traditional values were not chosen by the Malaysian leaders as the cure for Malay social problems. Instead, Islam is highlighted as the vehicle for moral reform.

There are several possible reasons for the federal leaders' attention to Islam. Firstly, as I have already mentioned, it is the most basic and non-negotiable aspect of Malay ethnicity and in that context it can be, and has been, viewed as an impediment to racial harmony within the nation. Islam, in short, could be represented as a threat to national unity. However, by reconfiguring Islam and representing it as a source of 'moral values', and as an ethical code, it can still be acknowledged as the religion of the Malays and at the same time be presented in a manner which non-Malays (non-Muslims) might find more understandable and therefore less threatening.

Secondly, presented as a 'moral code' Islam could serve as the basis for a civil religion which could unite rather than divide Malaysia. It has been noted elsewhere that in modern societies, it is quite common to subordinate the spiritual (religion) to social and civic purposes.[24] In the Malaysian context we can see it operating on two levels. On one level Islam (the spiritual) is being 'used' to control Malay 'social ills' (a social purpose). On another level, it is being presented as a civil religion in an effort to effect national unity (a civic purpose).

Conclusion: Islam, Malay, Malaysian

When Anwar Ibrahim agreed to write an article on Islam in Southeast Asia for *Time* magazine in September 1996, he chose to stress that tolerance is the "hallmark of Southeast Asian Islam". He wrote that because "the seeds of militancy are everywhere" then "each community must ensure that they do not germinate and multiply through discontent and alienation". Tolerance, he argued, cannot be demanded from only one community, but "must be mutual".

The article was reprinted as one of the chapters in Anwar's book *The Asian Renaissance* and frankly acknowledges the fragility of racial and religious coexistence.[25] It is this fragility which seems also to be addressed in the aims of Vision 2020, where it is the fashioning of a *Bangsa Malaysia* which is stressed. This term '*Bangsa Malaysia*' is a critical one for understanding what the prime minister is trying to achieve. Most dictionaries of Malay translate the word '*bangsa*' as 'race' and it is in this sense that it is used to describe the *Bangsa Melayu*, the Malay race. In the phrase *Bangsa Malaysia*, however, there seems to be a new element in the meaning of *bangsa* the adding of a sense of 'nation' to that of 'race'. This fusion could achieve a positive reorientation in focus from a defensive, exclusive attention to the ethno-centric concerns of the individual races, to a more outward and inclusive concern with national unity. The creation of a '*Bangsa Malaysia*' a new race/nation calls for equal commitment and dedication from each of the races who have been resident in Malaysia since Independence or Federation.[26]

In the context of national racial unity, the aims of Vision 2020 are much more ambitious than the older aims of the 1970 Articles of Faith of the State (*Rukunegara*), which declared it was dedicated to "achieving a greater unity of all [Malaysia's] peoples". In Vision 2020 these 'peoples' are actually re-named. No longer Malays, Indians and Chinese, Vision 2020 creates a new race/nation will be "free, steadfast and with spirit; with self-confidence and respected by other races".[27] Vision 2020 shifts the focus from *Rukunegara*'s harmony among the three races in Malaysia, to a new racial unity represented by the '*Bangsa Malaysia*'. In the terms of Vision 2020, the Malays (*bangsa Melayu*) are no longer the pivotal race in Malaysia, the race from whose perspective 'others' are characterised. In the terms of Vision 2020 the Chinese and Indians are no longer the outsiders, the 'other' in Malaysia. Some Malaysian analysts view this new articulation of unity through the fusion of race/nation as the final step in overcoming the divisions inflicted on Malaya by the plural society fostered by British colonial practice.[28]

The rhetoric of Vision 2020 has yet to be proved in practice. It will require an enormous effort to replace the difference-driven discourse of *Melayu* with a new kind of rhetoric which constructs and sustains commonalities so that the concept of the Malaysian race/nation gains credibility and becomes a focus for national loyalty. Until now, most groups representative of Malay interests have been unable to "transform their concept of Malay nationalism (which was used to struggle for independence) into Malaysian nationalism".[29] Dr Mahathir has acknowledged this by admitting that the greatest political challenge facing the nation is the creation of a *Bangsa Malaysia* "in which the different ethnic groups should be able to share a common 'national identity'".[30] This statement was made in 1991 when Malaysia's economic growth was at an all time high (8.7 per cent) to be followed by three years of growth above 8 per cent.[31] Perhaps to capitalise on a time of prosperity for the nation, the prime minister seized the opportunity to launch his *Bangsa Malaysia* vision. The social changes and new attitudes which the policy required of all Malaysia's citizens called for real concessions of status from the Malays, concessions which were most easily given during a period of economic growth. The two leaders' statements on the need for Malays to modernise and at the same time to use Islam as a source of moral values, could be interpreted as presenting Malays to the two other racial groups in Malaysia as closer to them in outlook and ethics.

A crucial part of such a transformation of image is the presentation of Islam as supportive of change. As one scholar of comparative religions has noted: "In the face of actual material and social transformation, an intransigent religion or ideological traditionalism" becomes less and less possible.[32] Both the PM and the DPM in their statements about Islam as a code for Malay behaviour, seemed to be working to establish a public form of religion, a civil religion if you like, whose system of beliefs can form the basis of a shared system for the nation. Closely linked with this representation of Islam as a moral code is the appeal to the nation's legal code as another commonality which can unify all Malaysians. On 2 February 1997, the Sunday edition of the Malay newspaper *Mingguan Malaysia* carried a report about Dr Mahathir's views on the causes of 'social ills' among the Malays. He is quoted as saying: "In Malaysia we can live harmoniously and peacefully not only amongst Muslims but also between Muslims and non-Muslims because we obey laws and regulations."[33]

The statements by Dr Mahathir and Anwar Ibrahim which have been analysed here were delivered only a few months before the onset of the economic crisis which began to affect the Southeast Asian region from mid-1997. The role of religion as an expression of identity in times of stress and disturbance is well known. It remains to be seen whether the foundations which the leaders have laid for Islam to function as a civil religion and as one of the commonalities for a *Bangsa Malaysia* can survive the economic and social pressures which Malaysian society is currently experiencing.

Anwar's challenge "to Muslims and the people of other confessions... to effectively articulate their moral vision and intensify the search for common ethical ground" may be overtaken by the enormity of the economic crisis.[34] If that is the case, economic pressures may widen the racial divides in Malaysia as they did in Indonesia in the late 1990s. The challenge to Malaysian national leaders is to continue seeking and promoting the inter-racial commonalities which underpin Vision 2020.

We should not forget that it is the Federal Government which is setting the national agenda for the role of Islam in national unity, and that the power of the Federal Government does not extend to the conduct of Islamic affairs at the state level. Immediate challenges to this federal policy may come from the constituent states of the Federation, as well as from individual Muslim leaders who may resist the representation of Islam primarily as a code of ethical conduct. There may also be an ethno-nationalist reaction from many Malays to the attempt to reconfigure the nexus between Malay and Islam. If those Malays believe that the Malay sense of identity is threatened by a loosening of the linkage between *Melayu* and Islam, so that some Islamic values could be espoused by non-Malays, then it would be very difficult for Islam to be the basis for a civil religion and serve as a unifying element in the *Bangsa Malaysia*.

The question remains as to whether Dr Mahathir will be able to maintain the representation of Islam as reported in the 1996–97 statements. If the links between Malay and Islam cannot be reconfigured, and Islam is not accepted as the basis for a civil religion, the prime minister may have to turn to secular institutions as strategies for unity. Dr Mahathir has already indicated that recognition of the rule of civil law is an obligation which unites all who live in Malaysia. On the eve of the twenty-first century, however, faced with the severe internal and external pressures on the national cohesion caused by the international monetary crisis, the Government's aim of a united *Bangsa Malaysia* becomes especially critical. Without the rhetoric of a shared revolutionary struggle, which Indonesia's leaders draw on, Malaysian leaders have fewer strategies for national unity.

Attempts to unite the peoples of the region now known as Malaysia are not new. In the lead up to Independence following the Second World War, several political movements tried to forge a united front for all local inhabitants of Malaya. But as one historian has put it, "Mainstream Malays were uneasy about the idea of nationality as it would give citizenship rights and equality to non-Malays. *Bangsa Melayu* was central to their well-being and *tanah Melayu* was claimed as the exclusive property of the Malays".[35] The impediment to an inclusive *bangsa* was that "the Malays in Malaya never conceded to the non-Malays the right to adopt the Malay states as their homeland".[36] Although the Constitution establishes residence as the primary qualification for Malaysia citizenship, in popular understanding the concept of citizenship is not yet intertwined with the concept of *Bangsa Malaysia*. It would appear that if Dr Mahathir's vision of a *bangsa* Malaysia is to be realised the Malays will need to be convinced of at least two points. Firstly that Islam can function both as the religion of 'the Malays' as well as serving as a moral code and the basis of a civil religion; and secondly, that Chinese and Indians who settled in Malaysia before Independence (and in the case of East Malaysia before Federation) are entitled to regard Malaysia as their homeland. If Malaysia's leaders can persuade Malaysian citizens to link national identity with Islam as a civil religion and can persuade Malays to concede that non-Malay citizens have the right to call Malaysia their homeland, then the 'new Malay' as well as Indians and Chinese may indeed give their allegiance to a *Bangsa Malaysia*, and common grounds for real unity may be found. History nudges us here however, to remind us that almost inevitably there will reactions by Muslims and non-Muslims alike to any agenda-setting from the centre of power. It is the process of interaction between these forces which will result in new configurations of Malay and Islam. As one observer of the fluidity of the notion of 'Malayness' has written, "A discursive formation does not necessarily run along the lines a center wants it to run. There is always the challenge, the resistance."[37]

Postscript

The leadership struggle within UMNO in 1998 which resulted in Anwar's dismissal from his ministerial positions, his expulsion from the party and the charges of corruption and sodomy overshadowed the issue of Islam's place in nation-building. The general election of November 1999, however, revived it and statements by both the National Front and the Alternative Front (now the opposition) indicate that the earlier attempts to promote Islam as a civil religion have been side-stepped. The centre may have wanted to reconfigure the Malay-Islam nexus but the Islamic party PAS, strongly supported in the conservative Muslim states of Kelantan and Trengganu, and strengthened by pro-Anwar sentiment, reasserted the links between Islam and Malay. After Anwar's arrest, conviction and sentencing to imprisonment, many Malays who had previously supported the UMNO gave their vote to PAS.

   In the general election, PAS increased its number of federal seats (from 13 to 27) and won a convincing majority of the seats in the less-industrialised states of Kelantan and Trengganu. These are states which have a history of strong allegiance to Islam and fierce pride in Malay ethnicity. Unlike Prime Minister Mahathir, the PAS leaders did not berate Malays for their 'backwardness' nor for being lax in implementing the principles of Islam. Neither was there the constant suggestion of a dichotomy between Western technology and economic development, and 'traditional' (conservative) Islam. In fact, the leading figures in PAS provide examples of a new blend of 'traditional' Islamic values (simplicity, sincerity and piety) with a high use of modern communication technology, including impressive websites. Their behaviour clearly indicates that Dr Mahathir's concept of modernity is not the only one operating in Malaysia. Muslim teachers and leaders in other parts of the world have also been showing that there are a variety of ways of being 'modern' and that "modernity itself is not a single force but rather the temporary conjunction of practices and ideologies that have diverse sources and divergent trajectories".[38]

In the 1999 election, Dr Mahathir did not present Islam as a basis for national unity. Despite his statements in 1997 about Islam as a social ethic and his Vision 2020 philosophy with its emphasis on one *Bangsa Malaysia*, during the campaign he actually cited Islam as a divisive force in Malaysian society. By describing 'radical' or 'extreme' Islam as a threat to Malaysia's unity and progress, he effectively created two Islams. According to Dr Mahathir and the National Front, 'radical Islam' discriminates against non-Muslims, impedes technological development and creates racial discord. And according to the National Front, this is the kind of Islam practised and promoted by its political rival PAS. In contrast to this, Dr Mahathir claims that the 'moderate' Islam espoused by UMNO is tolerant, supportive of change and poses no threat to the rights and status of non-Muslims. The dangers of this claim that there are two forms of Islam are obvious. Firstly it undermines national unity by splitting Muslims into acceptable and non-acceptable groups. Secondly, it continues the discourse of the 'spectre of radical Islam'—rhetoric that is designed to make non-Muslims uneasy about being governed by a Muslim party. Thirdly, it forces Malays to question their allegiances and the expression of their ethnicity. Since the 1999 election, analysts have stated that "it was the non-Malays and non-Muslims who helped the *Barisan Nasional* [National Front] regain two-thirds majority, and not the Malays".[39] The new Deputy Prime Minister Datuk Seri Abdullah Ahmad Badawi, strongly tipped to succeed Dr Mahathir as Prime Minister, admitted that "there is a stronger demand by the Muslims and the younger Muslims that more should be done for Islam".[40] Nevertheless, the DPM Badawi maintained the 'two Islams' dichotomy stressing that "UMNO will not embrace Islamic radicalism to recapture parts of the Malay heartland it lost to PAS".[41]

The election results suggest that while some non-Muslims supported the National Front because they believed that it offered them more security and benefits than the Alternative Front, it is clear that many Malays shifted from UMNO and a large number of them voted for PAS. Among the factors which influenced them must be counted the relationship between Malay ethnicity and Islam, and a concern about the kind of Islam being promoted by the UMNO leaders. DPM Badawi has indicated that UMNO "would need to conduct an intense self-examination".[42] High on the agenda for that 'self-examination' must be UMNO's attitude to the relationship between Islam and Malay. It will also be crucial for the unity of Malaysia to see how Muslims and non-Muslims understand the terms 'Islamic radicalism' and 'religious extremism' and whether those terms will continue to be used in public rhetoric in a manner which is racially as well as politically divisive.

There are signs that the UMNO may be moving into a new phase of re-Islamisation to counter PAS claims that it is the true protector of Islam in Malaysia. In October 2000 draft legislation entitled the "Restoration of Faith Bill" (popularly referred to as the "Apostasy Bill") came before Federal Parliament. Its provisions include periods in 'rehabilitation centres' for Muslims who have renounced their faith.[43] While there has been widespread debate in Malaysia about the pros and cons of such a bill, and its final outcome is not clear at the time of writing, there seems general agreement as to why the bill has been introduced. It is widely believed that UMNO sponsorship of the bill is an attempt to prove to Malays (Muslims) that it can match PAS in its concern for the strength of Islam in Malaysia. The tone of the bill is not consistent with the PM's statements in 1997 and with the National Front's 1999 campaign platform of religious tolerance. It suggests that within the UMNO there is considerable pressure to move away from the Mahathir-Anwar promotion of Islamic values as one of the bases for a united Malaysia. During the comparatively prosperous period of the mid-1990s the PM could afford to discuss Islam in secular terms, and in this he was supported by Anwar Ibrahim, then his deputy. Since the economic downturn and the highly controversial removal of Anwar, the political and social context has altered radically. The PM has lost the credibility among many Muslims which Anwar's support delivered, faces an opposition alliance which for the first time since Independence has shown it has support from Malay voters which can rival that of UMNO, and faces a society which is very anxious about the economy. The appearance of the draft "Restoration of Faith Bill" is one indication that without the credibility of Anwar as an Islamic leader in the National Front new strategies are being developed to prove the UMNO's support for Islam.

As predicted earlier in this paper the individual states of the Federation of Malaysia are not blindly following the Federal Government's policies on Islam. Apart from the obvious examples of the PAS dominated states in the north, Perlis (not a PAS stronghold) has already implemented state legislation "to begin proceedings against Muslims whom they 'suspect' of intending to renounce their faith".[44] Here we have evidence not only of greater state control of religious matters and a more rigid attitude towards Islam, but also of 'the challenge, the resistance' by groups outside the centre to the discursive forms being promoted by the centre.

9

Contesting Straits-Malayness: The Fact of Borneo

JAMES T. COLLINS*

Although Borneo looms large at the geographic centre of the Malay world, and although most specialists agree that Borneo is the prehistoric homeland of the Malay language community,[1] this vast land mass—the world's third largest island—lies at the periphery of Malay studies, as if it were a low-lying coral reef barely visible on the distant horizon. The slight importance ascribed to Borneo in colonial epistemologies may be related to the island's infertile soil, relatively sparse population, transportation obstacles and the comparatively docile ethnic groups. Beyond such economic, demographic and political factors, however, there has been an aesthetic obstacle: the romantic construct of Borneo. Joseph Conrad's frank studies in human frailty and desperation should have taught the world something about the realities of Borneo, but the White Ranee, queen of the head hunters, and Oxford as well as Camel overland expeditions yet hold a stronger grip on imaginings of Borneo than *Lord Jim* or *Almayer's Folly*.

Surely, the time has come to discard Orientalistic geographies of the Malay world. Borneo is not a distant, exotic atoll; rather, it is the central island of the Malay Archipelago and should be a focal point in Malay studies. It is also time to reject Orientalistic views of Malays and Malayness. The Malay world is not a simple dichotomy of Sumatra and the Peninsula— a noetic dualism not coincidentally marked by a colonial boundary line.[2] Borneo and the Malays of Borneo merit attention not simply because of the large number of the latter, nor because of the antiquity of the homeland in Borneo. Borneo offers vantage points from which to view the process of creating and recreating Malayness. To cross over "the perpetually drawn and perpetually blurred boundaries that British imperialism has left behind",[3] it is necessary to reconnoitre beyond the Melaka Straits.

In this preliminary essay, I can only present a few glimpses of the linkages of language and identity in Borneo. Identity, according to Aamer

168

Hussein, is dynamic, multidimensional, composite and continually defining itself.[4] Linguistics can only contribute some insights and pose some questions. In the space allotted here, then, I will limit my discussion first, to a short overview of language and society in western Borneo (Kalimantan Barat, Indonesia) and second, to a linguist's views of three Malay-speaking areas in that region. The conclusion will take up the issue of academic and indigenous classification, and consider the implications of the phenomena studied in Borneo.

Language and Society in Kalimantan Barat

Kalimantan Barat, Indonesia's westernmost province on Borneo, is characterised by a large number of languages and dialects. In addition to the indigenous languages under discussion here, the province has a large Chinese immigrant population, especially centred around the cities of Singkawang and Pontianak. Indeed, province-wide estimates of ethnic Chinese—many of whom still speak Chinese languages as their home language—range between 11 and 12 per cent of the total population of 3.5 million people.[5] Much smaller communities include speakers of Madurese (2 per cent), Javanese (3 per cent) and Bugis (5 per cent); these groups are largely clustered around urban areas.

Still, about 80 per cent of the total population of Kalimantan Barat is 'Malay' or 'Dayak'. Typically, estimates of the province-wide population identify the largest ethnic group as Dayak at around 41 per cent, with Malays comprising the remaining 39 per cent.[6] In this article, the term 'Malay' refers to Muslims who speak a Borneo Malay variant as their home language. Ordinary usage in Kalimantan itself refers to autochthonous people of Borneo who are not Muslims as 'Dayak',[7] although some Muslims also consider themselves Dayak. Most Dayaks in Kalimantan Barat speak Malayic variants—that is, languages that are closely related to Malay or even, in some cases (as we shall see), dialects of Malay.[8] For example, unofficial estimates of the Kendayan, an autochthonous group of Malayic-speakers in the northwestern part of the province,[9] reach a half million. Moreover, Ibanic groups (Iban, Kantu', Mualang, Ketungau and others), a major branch of Malayic, probably approach that total as well, and there are also a number of smaller Malayic groups; for example, about 70,000 Dayaks in the southernmost part of the province, Ketapang regency, speak at least three or four Malayic variants.[10] Thus, the number of first-language speakers of diverse Malayic variants—both Malays and Dayaks—in Kalimantan Barat probably exceeds two million.

This section provides information about the geographical distribution of these Malayic variants as well as other indigenous Austronesian languages spoken in the province, with a focus on Malayic variants spoken within roughly 200 kilometres of the coast because most information available so far has been collected in that long narrow strip. In a 1997 study, I provided a brief description of language distribution further in the interior. For example, non-Malayic, Austronesian subgroups, speakers of Tamanic, Kayan and Ot Danum, can be found in the headwater regions.[11]

In the hilly and montane areas that lie within 100 to 200 kilometres of the coast of the northern part of Kalimantan Barat, there are scattered many small groups speaking a wide range of variants that can be broadly labelled 'Bidayuhic' (following the Sarawak term) or 'Land Dayak'.[12] Bidayuhic-speakers live in hamlets that extend from within westernmost Sarawak in the north all the way to the region north of the Pawan River,[13] but this cluster of Austronesian languages is not very closely related to Malay and, tentatively, has been excluded from the Malayic subgroup.[14] However, some of these variants have attained local importance and some Malayic-speakers have acquired fluency in Bidayuhic variants—a bilingualism that may account for the occurrence of some Bidayuhic words in the basic vocabulary of various Malayic variants.

To the west and south of this tier of hills largely (but not exclusively) inhabited by the Bidayuhic groups, lie the complicated waterways of Kalimantan Barat's three main rivers, namely the Sambas, Kapuas and Pawan Rivers. In these three roughly parallel riverine systems, the deltas, swamps, flood plains and islands stretch north-to-south about 100 kilometres from the coast. It is there that most of the speakers of Malayic variants live. Although some scholars classify large stretches of these riverine systems as 'uninhabited areas',[15] this does not seem to be the case. While some swamps in the Kapuas River delta area may be only sparsely populated, older records indicate that other areas have been populated continuously for a long time,[16] and this view matches the oral traditions of some of the Dayak groups who even now live there, for example Bagan Asam, also in the Kapuas delta.[17]

The antiquity of the occupation of these riverine territories by Malayic-speakers partly accounts for the language diversity in the region. Even if we only consider those Malayic variants spoken by Muslims, that is, 'canonical' Malay dialects, the diversity is remarkable. Recent surveys conducted in Kalimantan Barat identify no fewer than five major canonical Malay dialects spoken in the province (Sambas, Landak, Pontianak, Ketapang and Ulu Kapuas).[18] The tentative classification and rough mapping now available for these dialects already constitute a significant improvement over the somewhat agnostic and most uninformative label "western coastal Malay" offered by Stephen A. Wurm and Shiro Hattori as a cover term for all the kinds of Malay spoken anywhere in the province.[19] Nonetheless, much work still remains to be done.

In addition to these Malay dialects spoken along the western Borneo littoral and the banks of its major rivers, there are numerous other Malayic variants in the lowlands and scattered hills of the region. The villages and hamlets where these non-Malay Malayic variants are spoken are either interspersed with Malay-dialect-speaking communities or occupy distinct territories, sometimes near Malay villages but just as often distant from, or at least non-contiguous to, Malay-dialect-speaking areas. Dozens of names, usually based on a village, valley or clan name, are used to list these variants. Recent studies provide overviews of these Malayic variants, including the Kendayan group in the northwest, the so-called 'Dayak Tebang' group near the delta of the Kapuas River (a region often labelled 'uninhabited' in contemporary linguistic atlases), the Kayung-Pesaguan group in the southern part of the province and the Ulu Jelai group in the southeastern-most part of the province.[20] Other Malayic variants are also spoken in the Ketapang residency, including Gerai, Randau Jeka', Kenyabur and Beginci as well as a cluster of related Malayic variants along the Laur River, a northern branch of the Pawan.

In Borneo, as elsewhere in Southeast Asia,[21] topography plays a significant role in the patterns of language diffusion. To some degree, the tier of foothills and mountains that stretches southward from western Sarawak apparently blocked or at least restricted and funnelled the expansion of Malayic languages to the east.[22] Moreover, communities speaking a non-Malayic language, 'Bidayuhic', in a large number of dialects, inhabited these highlands. This barrier, however, was penetrated and passed by travelling along the broad Kapuas River to the other side of the tier to the expanse of swamps and wetlands in the Kapuas lakes area and to other major 'north-south' tributaries like the Belitang and Ketungau Rivers. As the land flattened before them into alluvial plains and swamps, the Malayic-speakers, represented by today's diverse Ibanic dialect communities, especially speakers of Mualang, Sebruang, Ketungau, Kantu' and Iban, spread out and occupied this familiar environment. Malayic-speakers remaining in the waterways to the west of the Bidayuhic tier similarly dispersed and, as did the Ibanic branch in the Kapuas lakes area, diversified into a large number of closely related but often socially mutually exclusive dialects and languages. The process yielded today's complex distribution of two million Malayic-speakers in Kalimantan Barat.

The second part of this paper considers three Malayic language networks along the Landak, Sekadau and Melawi Rivers—all tributaries of the great Kapuas River. There, patterns of relation and exclusion define identity.

Language and Identity Along Three Kapuas Tributaries

During an early survey of languages in the Ketapang regency (September 1996), I visited several Malay and Dayak villages on the tributaries of the Pesaguan and Pawan Rivers. In one of the Malay villages, Pebihingan, a Muslim hamlet where Ketapang Malay is spoken, respondents often disagreed about the status of some lexical items in their language. One person would volunteer a vocabulary item, but another would state emphatically that that word was not Malay, but Dayak. This process of elicitation and revision occurred frequently during that session. The lexical canon of Malay in Pebihingan did not include all the vocabulary known and used by the respondents. However, in another Malay village, Nanga Tayap, just a few hours by motorcycle from Pebihingan, where Ketapang Malay is also the home language, respondents offered a wide range of vocabulary, including terms specifically rejected in Pebihingan. When queried about those terms, they replied: "Well that's our language; that's how we talk."

Sub-dialects of Malay, of course, often display lexical differences. What interested me was the difference in perception about the status of those words. There was a clear difference in language attitude and social constructs. The lexical repertoire in Pebihingan and Nanga Tayap was the same, but the social features ascribed to some items of the lexicon were different. Respondents in the more rural and isolated village of Pebihingan insisted on a purist canon of Malay vocabulary; the Malays of Nanga Tayap, whose village forms part of a small town, with shops and the administrative offices appropriate to a district (*kecamatan*) capital, rejected such lexical prescriptivism.

Following from this description of an unexpected encounter with two-language 'policies' in the Pawan River area, this section touches on the connections between language and society along three different tributaries of the Kapuas River basin.

The Landak River

The Landak River is a major tributary of the Kapuas debouching in the Kapuas delta in Pontianak city. About 100 kilometres upriver from the mouth of the Landak River, the district capital of Ngabang is sited around the *kraton* of the former Malay sultanate, which traces its genealogy back roughly 600 years. The distribution of communities which speak the dialect of Malay historically associated with this sultanate extends beyond today's district territory; many upriver branches of the Landak River, now assigned to different administrative districts, include villages where Landak Malay is the home language. Yet, the total number of home-language Landak Malay-speakers is not large because they form a minority in a region where most inhabitants speak Kendayan variants as their home language.

In February 1998, I took part in joint research, involving fieldworkers from Universitas Tanjungpura and Universiti Kebangsaan Malaysia, in four upriver villages, Jata', Darit, Betung and Meranti', located on two major tributaries of the Landak River, namely on the Menyuke and Behe Rivers. The results of that survey have not yet been published but some preliminary observations can be reported here.[23]

First, the recordings and wordlists collected in these villages indicate that the kind of Malay spoken along the Menyuke and Behe Rivers must be classified with the Malay spoken in and around the *kraton* of Ngabang, although the distance separating those villages from Ngabang is considerable, and would have been especially so at a time when the rivers were the chief means of transportation. For example, of these four villages, Jata' is the closest to Ngabang, but when travel was still accomplished by poling boats down the Menyuke River, the trip from this, the closest village, would take three nights and four days; with a motorised boat the time could have been reduced by one day. Nonetheless, despite the historical and contemporary isolation of these villages, there is a remarkable uniformity in vocabulary and grammar among all the Landak Malay variants studied thus far.

Second, although the Malays living in Kampung Raja of Ngabang are seldom fluent in the Kendayan language spoken in the villages all around them, many, if not most Malays in the Menyuke and Behe River villages are bilingual in Landak Malay and Kendayan. Local Kendayan-speakers vouch for the fluency claimed by these Malay villagers. For example, Betung, the Malay village furthest up the Menyuke, is a small hamlet of perhaps 20 houses, too small to merit an elementary school, and children walk to the nearest Dayak village to attend classes there. Cash income is chiefly obtained from digging up and collecting sand from the bottom of the Menyuke and selling it by the truckload to contractors. Most of the Betung villages can speak Kendayan (Ahe variant) besides Landak Malay. This fact was not only reported by Malay and Dayak respondents, but also surfaced in the collection of a wordlist. Moreover, the Kendayan-speakers of this area are bilingual in Kendayan and Landak Malay; in fact, some Kendayan-speakers use Malay more often and speak it with more confidence than they do Kendayan. Bilingualism is widespread among both the Malays and Dayaks of the Menyuke and Behe River systems.

Third, this bilingualism has had an impact on the Malay sub-dialects spoken in these river systems but not on the Malays' allegiance to Landak Malay. When participating in a working session to elicit basic vocabulary, the Malay respondents in Betung often mentioned the term *bahasa orang kampung* ('the language of the *kampong* people'). For example, when asked the word for 'neck', a respondent offered [*tege?*] but the chief respondent definitively rejected this; '*bahasa kampung*' was his dismissive assessment. It wasn't Malay. Similarly, the term [*mɔ'tʒadu?*] was also offered for 'to butcher, to cut up' but rejected as *bahasa kampung*. Several other words suggested by various respondents participating in the session, such as [*kita?*] 'you (plural)' and [*supit*] 'ill(?)', were also considered *bahasa kampung*.

In Betung, as in all Malay *kampongs* visited in the Menyuke and Behe River systems, the emblematic language was Landak Malay, although they also spoke Kendayan. Unlike their village language—Malay-Kendayan was (merely?) the language of the other; it was the kampong language. Ideologically, these Malays were not *orang kampung*; indeed, the collocation '*orang kampung*' had already acquired an idiomatic (euphemistic?) strength and simply meant the indigenous non-Malay (non-Muslim) peoples around them.[24] Thus, in the upper tributaries of the Landak River, there are drawn clear ethnic and linguistic lines in a very strong bilingual setting.

The Sekadau River

About 300 kilometres upriver from Pontianak, the Sekadau River meets the Kapuas River in a swampy estuary. The town of Sekadau on the banks of the river is a large and lively market centre with many shops, inns, schools and government and church offices, located on the road that links the far interior of the Kapuas basin with Pontianak. Sekadau was the seat of a Malay princedom that vied with the Sanggau kingdom downriver for regional supremacy. Moreover, the numerous archaeological sites found so far on the Sekadau River or nearby, including a Sanskrit-language memorial tablet, attest to the antiquity of this settlement.[25] Data about this dialect of Malay were collected in 1995 and 1996; a brief survey of Malay and other languages spoken near Sekadau was conducted in April 1996 as well.[26] Unlike the Malay communities on the Menyuke and Behe Rivers, the Malays of Sekadau generally do not speak Dayak languages, such as Mualang, an Ibanic language spoken near Sekadau on the Belitang River or any of the numerous Bidayuhic variants spoken in several hamlets along the Upper Sekadau River and its tributaries. Bilingualism does not appear to be common among the Malays in the bustling cluster of villages that make up Sekadau town.

In Sekadau, the dialect of Malay does not differ greatly from the dialect documented under the sobriquet Ulu Kapuas Malay.[27] As noted above, Ulu Kapuas Malay is one of the 'canonical' dialects of Malay in Kalimantan Barat. A number of innovations distinguish it from other Malay dialects in Borneo. For example, Proto-Malayic *ə in penultimate position shifts to a back round vowel, [O] or [ɔ]; so *betis 'calf' > [botis], *kɔniŋ 'forehead' > [konin]. Also final nasals not preceded by a nasal at the beginning of the syllable undergo consonantal diphthongisation whereby the final nasal is 'stretched' into an occlusive-nasal cluster; so, *makan 'eat' > [makaᵗn], *tulaŋ 'bone' > [tulaᵏŋ], but *kanan 'rightside' > [kanan].

Recently, I compared four variants spoken in this region of the Kapuas, including the variant of Sekadau.[28] The conclusion was that all four variants were closely related, and probably sub-dialects of the same Malay dialect, Ulu Kapuas. Two of the variants, Sekadau and Kalampok, showed some indications of a closer connection, in the form of a few shared lexical innovations. For example, in both variants Proto-Malayic[29] *lihəɣ 'neck' was replaced by [ɣokoŋ] and *mulut 'mouth' by [ˈawa].

On the one hand, this apparent close relationship between the Sekadau and Kalampok variants is not surprising because Kalampok is spoken on the Sekadau River too, about 40 kilometres upriver. Geographic proximity as well as economic and transportation links would lead us to expect such a close connection. On the other hand, the variant in Sekadau is named Malay and spoken by Muslims, whereas the variant in Kalampok is named Dayak and spoken by Catholics. How is it that variants so closely related lexically and grammatically as to be considered by linguists as subdialects of the same Malay dialect can be considered by their speakers to be different languages?

Perhaps the Kalampok-speakers shifted to Malay at some earlier period. Yet Kalampok is not the only Dayak village that speaks this variant as the home language. Recent research conducted in the Ketapang residency (1997–98) resulted in the collection of lexical and textual materials of a Dayak variant spoken in a new hamlet resettled from the Sekadau River a generation ago. This Dayak variant (now spoken by Catholics on the upper reaches of the Keriau River in the Pawan River basin), in Kenyabur village, is very closely related to the Kalampok variant. Moreover, researchers at the Dayakology Institute in Pontianak report that many Dayak villages along the Sekadau River speak this variant, sometimes referred to as 'Taman Sesat'. So the occurrence of a Malay dialect as the home language in Kalampok is not a unique circumstance: a whole cluster of villages spread over a rather wide geographic area speak 'Taman Sesat'.[30]

Just as the variant of Malay spoken in Sekadau is linked closely to a much larger network of Malay variants almost along the whole length of the Kapuas River, the variant of Dayak spoken in Kalampok is linked to a broad network of Dayak variants near the Kapuas. It is unlikely that this large group of Dayaks shifted to Malay, just as it is unlikely that the large group of Ulu Kapuas Malays shifted to Dayak. Rather, we might conclude that both the Sekadau Malays and their congeners as well as the Kalampok Dayaks and their congeners have (by and large) spoken the same language for centuries, probably before they were known as Malays or Dayaks and almost certainly before they became Muslims and Catholics.

In this case, then, in contrast to the rigid lines of language and ethnicity in Betung on the Menyuke River where Malays and Dayaks are bilingual, settlements on the Sekadau River present clear ethnic categories (Malay and Dayak) but blurred linguistic lines—all in a setting with asymmetric multilingualism where most Dayaks are fluent speakers of Ulu Kapuas Malay as well as their own home language and perhaps other Dayak languages (Mualang or a Bidayuhic variant), but the Malays (of Sekadau town, anyway) speak only Ulu Kapuas Malay.

The Melawi River

In the Landak River area, two ethnic groups maintain clear ethnic boundaries while participating in a symmetric bilingual language ecology. They share two different languages but not their identities. In the Sekadau River area, two ethnic groups are distinguished by a whole array of distinct cultural activities yet share the same home language. Despite their very close language affinity—probably sub-dialectal, they maintain separate identities. In both the Landak and Sekadau River basins, then, shared language, whether as a second language or as a first language, does not inevitably lead to shared identity.

But the situation in Kalimantan Barat offers other profiles of language and society that are more problematic. More than ten years ago, Bernard Sellato reported (but did not provide relevant published documentation about) the language situation on the Melawi River, another major tributary of the Kapuas.[31] In the uppermost reaches of the Melawi, the people speak Ot Danum, a non-Malayic Austronesian language related to languages of Central Borneo, but elsewhere along the same river, a variant of Malay is spoken by Malays and non-Malays alike, albeit with some sub-dialectal variation.

In February 1998, Yusriadi, then a graduate student in linguistics at Universiti Kebangsaan Malaysia, carried out a brief survey of language use in and around Nanga Pinoh, more than 400 kilometres from Pontianak in the middle reaches of the Melawi River.[32] Again results are still tentative but merit mention within the present context. Wordlists, narratives and traditional oral art forms were collected and tape-recorded in three villages: Nanga Pinoh, Kebebu and Ponal.

Nanga Pinoh is a district capital, with shops, offices, schools, mosques and churches; the market bristles with satellite receiving dishes. Like Sekadau, it began as a collection of Malay hamlets, Muslim for centuries. Located about 30 kilometres upriver from Nanga Pinoh, Kebebu (also known as Nanga Kabebu) is a small hamlet whose inhabitants converted to Islam and thus became Malay about three generations ago. Less than seven kilometres downriver from Kebebu is the hamlet of Ponal, which only recently (within the last 20–30 years) converted to Catholicism and so remained Dayak. Thus, Malay-Muslim ethnicity includes Malays who have been recognised as Malays for as long as anyone remembers, as well as Malays who acknowledge that their original non-Muslim (animist) grandparents became the first Muslims of the village.

One way to view this Melawi pattern reported by Yusriadi is that there are again two ethnic groups: Malays, both 'old' as well as 'new', and non-Malays, that is Dayaks.[33] But the available language data do not support that classification because all three communities speak Malay as the home language and the Malay dialect that they speak is the same. Moreover, the 'new' Malays speak a subdialect closer to that of the 'new' Catholics than to that of the 'old' Malays. So, linguistic analysis suggests not a bipolar classification of Malays and Dayaks, but rather, a continuum of Malay-speakers. From a linguistic perspective, all these Malay variants are closely related and can be considered sub-dialects of the same Malay dialect.

Apparently there is again conflict between academic, linguistic classification and acknowledged, indigenous social networks. Just as in the Sekadau basin, Malays and Dayaks along the Melawi River speak the same home language, in this case apparently the same sub-dialect. But, there is still the dualistic nomenclature—the 'Malay/Dayak' distinction, now prevalent in Kalimantan Barat, which does not recognise the linkages and continuities discerned by linguists. However, recent developments in the Melawi area indicate that local knowledge does not always conflict with academic analysis. Yusriadi reported that in the past ten years, the Muslims of Kebebu have been active in asserting their identity, not as Malays as their grandparents had, but as members (*warga*) of the Katap Kebahan ethnic group, an identity which encompasses the Muslims of Kebebu and many other Muslim villages (but not Nanga Pinoh) as well as even more non-Muslim villages, many of them Catholic like Ponal.

A 1998 calendar-poster produced and circulated by Muslims of Kebebu reflects these findings. More than half of the space is allocated to a large photograph of the largest mosque in Asia, Mesjid Istiqal in Jakarta, and a schedule of Islamic prayer times, again in Jakarta. However, the largest lettering in the poster, exceeding even the dates of the calendar itself, is the line reading IKATAN WARGA KATAP KEBAHAN (The Association of Katap Kebahan Members—IWKK), followed by a list of 84 villages and hamlets belonging in this network (with a note that there are some villages not yet included in the list). This 84-village list includes both Muslim villages, like No. 27 Nanga Kabebu, and non-Muslim villages, like No. 25 Ponal.

Linguistic research in the Melawi River basin has only begun, so it is impossible to comment on the language classification of these 84 villages, or to provide sociolinguistic information about language attitudes and ethnic allegiance. However, the fact that at least some Malays can affirm an alternative ethnicity that encompasses Malays and non-Muslims alike is of immediate interest to the notion of contesting Malay identity. As in the Sekadau river system, speaking the Malay language as a first, home language is not an automatic marker of Malay identity. Other identities can be chosen and affirmed.

Concluding Remarks

Kalimantan Barat presents a wide range of cultural and sociolinguistic phenomena that are relevant to any discussion of Malay identity. One would expect this to be the case in the very homeland of the Malay language, where for the last 2,000 years Malay-speakers have been in contact with speakers of other closely related languages, and where Malay-speaking Muslim societies interact daily with Malay-speaking non-Muslim societies. In this complex setting, the colonial nomenclature of Malay and Dayak, though widely adopted by the people of Kalimantan, does not adequately represent the intricacy and the fluidity of social relationships and identities. Colonial knowledge matches neither the results of linguistic research nor what the Malays and Dayaks know about themselves, their languages and their identities.[34]

In Kalimantan Barat, it is possible to find groups which are equally fluent in the same two languages but do not share ethnicity, like the Betung Malays and their neighbours, Kendayan-speakers of Ahe, in the upper reaches of the Landak River. There are even groups which speak the same dialect, like the Malays and the ('Taman Sesat') Dayaks of the Sekadau River, yet do not share ethnicity. In contrast to settings of shared languages but distinct identities, there exist other cultural settings where language and dialect are shared but ethnic lines are blurred, or, rather, likely to shift, as they shift even now in the Melawi River basin.

Identity is a matter of choice; it is dynamic, invented and imagined. Language can serve as an emblem of identity, but it cannot serve as a yardstick to establish identity. The nineteenth-century paradigm of nationalism based on a monolingual, monocultural society is not relevant in Borneo, nor in many other parts of the Malay Archipelago.[35]

Scholars must be careful not to exoticise, or ostracise, the situation in Borneo. They should not be hasty in saying that "Well, perhaps, in Borneo this may be so, but not in the Malay heartland, along the Straits of Melaka." In Sumatra, Riau and the Malay Peninsula there exist numerous communities of Malay-speakers who are not Muslims and therefore are not acknowledged as Malay. The Temuan and Jakun groups of the southern part of Malay Peninsula all speak Malay as their home language but display numerous cultural differences with other Malay-speakers in West Malaysia. The Kubu, Lubu, Sakai and other Malay-speaking groups of Sumatra by and large are neither Muslims nor Malay, just as many of the *Orang Laut* groups of the Riau and Lingga Islands have maintained a separate identity despite their allegiance to Malay as their home language. A closer study of these groups may reveal complicated and diverse ways of asserting identity and using language.

Certainly, on the peripheries of the Malay world there have been historical shifts in identity. In Capetown, South Africa, a community originating only in part from Southeast Asia became known as the Cape Malays.[36] But in the mid-twentieth century, in the face of apartheid and thus the need for wider alliances, they renamed themselves South African Muslims, an identity they asserted until quite recently, when they now usually identify themselves again as Cape Malays, although they do not speak Malay as a home language or even as a second or third language, being generally bilingual in Afrikaans and English instead.[37]

In southern Thailand some Muslim Malay-speakers assert their identity as Muslim-Thai or simply Thai, rather than Malay. This is the result of a long history of assimilation policies in Thailand. On the other hand, in central Thailand, tens of thousands of Muslims still consider themselves Malay, though most of them do not speak Malay at all; their home language is Central Thai.[38] However, in northern Malaysia on the island of Langkawi, Paktai, a language closely related to standard Thai, is spoken as the home language in several villages on the north coast of the island; yet these Paktai-speakers are Muslims and unequivocally affirm their Malay identity.

The aspirations and affiliations of Malays and Malay-speakers, whether they live along the remote Melawi River or in the centre of Capetown or Bangkok, reflect Penelope Corfield's assertion that:

> a socially constructed and socially negotiated language implies a linguistic community to construct and use it, and in using it, to develop and re-create it.... Languages are used and articulated within historical contexts, as part of the complex experience of human society. ... [L]anguage cannot evade history.[39]

Only by studying the social history of the social phenomena related to language and society can we expect to reach a deeper, humanistic explanation of the relationship of language and identity.

10

A Literary Mycelium: Some Prolegomena for a Project on Indonesian Literatures in Malay

WILL DERKS*

I

Soon after its inception in 1945, Indonesia became a unitary state, even though it consisted, and still consists, of many distinct ethnic groups and traditions, religious orientations of all kinds, hundreds of languages and dialects, as well as thousands of islands. Initially the almost unanimous enthusiasm among Indonesians for the young, independent state and the efforts to create a national culture inspired by a single standard language tended to silence this enormous potential for difference. By the end of the 1950s, however, armed conflicts ensued between the national government and some more or less culturally or ethnically homogeneous regions in Sumatra and Sulawesi. Although these conflicts probably represented a wish for greater political and economic autonomy rather than a desire to secede, the tension between nation and region has coloured Indonesia's history ever since. Small wonder that the state, especially during the New Order period, has made quite an effort, in a variety of ways, to keep this tension in check by exacting unity while furthering diversity in a uniform way.

Of course, throughout the years the various disciplines within the humanities have dealt with this difference inherent in Indonesia's composite nature from their own specific points of view. This is also the case in the study of what is known as 'modern Indonesian literature'. On the whole, however, these comments and analyses have taken for granted the status quo of the Indonesian unitary state, and any diversity has been interpreted in those terms. In other words, centripetal forces have been highlighted rather than centrifugal ones. No doubt as a sign of the times, this general attitude has changed of late in favour of a stronger focus on ethnic, religious or cultural identities that reach beyond the diversity endorsed by the state.[1] As will be elucidated below, within the study of Indonesian literature specifically, this tendency is reflected by an increasingly palpable shift away from a single Indonesian 'national literature', concretised in the form of a canon, and towards a whole gamut of 'literatures in Malay'. In the following pages, I will propose a project within which this plurality will be of central concern, not least because of the astonishing developments that have recently taken place in Indonesia. Through a focus on current manifestations of this literary plurality, the centrifugal and fragmenting forces that are also characteristic of Indonesia can be captured frame by frame, as it were, and a meaningful contribution can be made to a larger, ongoing debate.

Until fairly recently, the international scholarly discourse on modern Indonesian literature has been characterised by a thoroughly Western view and approach. Among the most profound and far-reaching presuppositions that have moulded the way in which this literature has been studied is the philosophical stand inherited from the European Romanticists, that literature (together with language) constitutes the matrix of a nation and even a civilisation.[2] The assignment of such an elementary role naturally involves the notion that literature consists of a relatively well-defined, stable and tangible collection of texts which, within the typically Western distinction between art and craft, are categorised as belonging to the first part of this dichotomy. In this view, literature is part of the best a particular nation or civilisation is capable of producing, and although it is therefore elitist by definition, literature is thought of as something that should be taught to all who share the standardised language in which it is written.

This powerful Romantic *topos* finds its complement in the equally deeply rooted, unquestioned and often unconsciously upheld premise of the Euro-American ideal of print literacy as the sole basis of any particular discursive formation designated as 'literature', also outside the Western world. Within the study of modern Indonesian literature—with contributions by both Western and Indonesian scholars—preconceptions such as these have led to a set of interconnected, more or less fixed ideas of what this literature is all about, a 'horizon of expectations' that, within the last few decades, has slowly but increasingly been called into question. Needless to say, the same holds true for the often merely implicit value judgements that form a constitutive part of this horizon.

Among the most conspicuous elements belonging to this set of ideas is the central role that is attributed to the printed book, especially in the form of the novel that in Western thought is considered to be the prime genre through which any given literature attains its highest achievements. Where in the West the coming into being of the novel has been totally dependent on the printing press and therefore is absolutely opposed to orality in whatever form, it comes as no surprise that in Indonesian literature, beyond the act of solitary reading, no other means of consumption of literature has ever been considered worthy of attention, or even thought to be possible.[3] The mirror image of this phenomenon is the expectation that literary production comes exclusively in the form of printed matter, indeed as a book, which is as tangible as it is stable and unchanging. Walter Ong has convincingly argued that the association of writing and printing with death, and of printed books with its fixity and immutability, are deeply ingrained habits in the Western mind.[4] Consideration of these formative features of the Western critique of literature has had a direct bearing on the formulation of the research assumptions and methodology for the project proposed here, since in many respects, this project must proceed with an awareness of the limiting role such critiques have played in the past.

It is common in a Western 'literary system' for the printing and allied trades to be concentrated in a single urban centre, which more often than not is also politically and economically dominant.[5] It is also not surprising, therefore, that in the study of modern Indonesian literature almost all energy has been devoted to the literary work of authors published in the capital, Jakarta. Literature originating outside this virtually hegemonic centre has at best been thought of as marginal, if noticed at all. In this connection it is germane to note that George Quinn speaks quite angrily of the 'dismissive tradition' within scholarship on Indonesian literature that has hardly cared about a remarkably vital local and regional literary life detectable throughout the Indonesian Archipelago.[6] Significantly, he suggests that this negative attitude is based on the fact that, generally speaking, Indonesian literature is approached not from an Indonesian point of view but from a set of external criteria.

Naturally, the complex of presuppositions, choices and value judgements suggested here has in the course of the years also functioned as a filter through which a particular group of printed texts has been sanctified as the canon of modern Indonesian literature. This process of selection and rejection has been led and shaped by the agency of Western scholars or Western-educated Indonesian intellectuals—among whom A. Teeuw and H. B. Jassin particularly stand out—who took Batavia/Jakarta as the authoritative centre of literary production. As is always the case when it comes to canon-building, a vital role in the achievement of consensus over the high points of this literature has also been played by the Indonesian educational system (through textbooks as well as curricula), Indonesian publishers and, to a lesser extent, literary criticism in the press. However, it should be emphasised here that, against the background of a relatively strong and constant repression by the state and indirect censorship, the more purely Indonesian contribution to the determination of the canon has been less free and may therefore diverge somewhat from the international consensus. But, by and large, this consensus reflects nevertheless a Western print-literate and Romanticist mode of thought—witness the fact that by far the most prominent author of modern Indonesian literature is the novelist Pramoedya Ananta Toer. This *éminence grise* of Indonesian literature lives, works and is published in the capital, and his widely acclaimed novels have earned him a standing candidacy for the Nobel Prize—the pinnacle of Western literary taste—to a large extent because they are thought to capture the vicissitudes of the Indonesian nation, or civilisation, in the best literary way imaginable.

As a result of these canonising activities, many forms of literary production and consumption in Indonesia have obviously been swept to the margins, sometimes sinking into total oblivion. A case in point is the so-called Sino-Malay literature that blossomed until the early fifties of the twentieth century, as has been convincingly shown by Claudine Salmon.[7] Other scholars who should be mentioned here are Ulrich Kratz, George Quinn, and Farida Soemargono, not only because they too have pointed to absences in the Indonesian literary canon, but also because they all have questioned at least some of the presuppositions and norms discussed above, albeit sometimes merely implicitly and without offering alternatives.[8] The aim of the project proposed here is to develop these preliminary endeavours to change the generally accepted view of modern Indonesian literature in a more systematic way, with the intention of arriving at a genuinely new and innovative approach of the phenomenon at hand, the contours of which may be sketched with the following elements.

Elsewhere, I have shown that the Indonesian literary system is strongly orally oriented.[9] This oral orientation can be explained at least partly by the fact that the printing press arrived in Indonesia only a little over a hundred years ago. However, as soon as its impact came to be felt, other, no less powerful means of communication were introduced, among them telegraph, telephone and radio, and later audio tapes, video, fax, computer and Internet. Therefore, most Indonesians entered the stage of 'secondary orality' (as the result of the influence of these electronic media is sometimes referred to), without first going through a phase of fully fledged print literacy, as was the case in the West. One of the outcomes of this has been that to this very day, specimens of a primary oral tradition still abound in Indonesia, mostly in rural areas.[10] But more significant within the present argument is the fact that one of the most important outlets for modern Indonesian literature is a medium that is unambiguously oral in nature, but that has been neglected in almost all commentaries on modern Indonesian literature, even though it can be experienced everywhere. This phenomenon can be referred to with the Indonesian phrase *pembacaan puisi* or 'poetry reading', a generic term that covers a great variety of popular gatherings, taking place on a regular basis throughout Indonesia, in which short prose and poetry are performed. Verbal art in Indonesia is thus conveyed by word of mouth much more often than by being printed in a book; and it is consumed by listening in the company of others rather than by reading in solitude. Keeping in mind that a performance is an evanescent phenomenon, and given the fact that it is so popular, it can be safely said that modern Indonesian literature is characterised by ephemerality as well as social intimacy, or even congeniality, to an extent unknown in a bookish Western culture.

This typical ephemerality and relative intimacy can also be observed in another medium that is hardly less important. Print is of course a common medium in Indonesia. However, the Western-inspired fixation with the book has tended to obscure the fact that the lion's share of Indonesia's literary artefacts surfacing in print are not novels in book form, but rather poetry, short stories and essays appearing in the pages of the Indonesian press. It is well known that in Indonesia, a literary work published in book form even by a canonised author is considered a bestseller when 5,000 copies are sold, although the number of Indonesian citizens is already more than 200 million. In contrast to this, all local, regional and national newspapers, as well as weeklies and monthlies throughout the archipelago, the great majority written in Malay/Indonesian, regularly publish an enormous amount of poetry and short prose texts, produced by a host of authors who are unknown to most if not all scholars of Indonesian literature—most likely because their literary work will almost never surface in forms beyond such ephemeral publications. This transience, inherent in the products of the press, is strongly reminiscent of orality in general. So, too, is the fact that the newspaper does not cut the reader off from the author or his fellow readers to the extent that the book is capable of doing. Almost as volatile as the spoken word, the newspaper with its daily appearance is a much more social medium that practically leaves intact a closeness between individuals that is characteristic of an orally-determined community rather than of a full-fledged print-literate society.[11] Reading a poem or a short story in a newspaper may well be reading it in the company of others.

Behind such poetry readings and contributions to the literary pages of the press (as well as a great many other orally-oriented, literary activities that will be discussed shortly), are often what may be called 'literary clubs'. However, this term may be misleading in so far as these clubs are not stable or well-defined organisations. On the contrary, they can best be thought of as fluid, informal and extended networks of individuals and groups devoted to verbal art. Although, typically enough, information on this aspect of literary life in Indonesia is also scarce, the evidence available suggests that these transient and fluid associations of kindred spirits are the vital constitutive element in the creation of Indonesian literature. Found in nearly every urban area, sometimes in great numbers, these clubs are often so energetic that a particular city or town may become the literary centre of an entire region for some time. As Soemargono has shown in the only in-depth study of such a centre to date, a myriad of these clubs consisting of 'cultural workers' with quite divergent social backgrounds, can temporarily bring about a highly vibrant local or regional literary life.[12] However, as in the case of Yogyakarta in the 1950s that Soemargono documented, even though such a centre may develop great activity, its impact is often limited and will hardly be felt outside a certain area. This is obvious enough for the poetry readings mentioned earlier: they usually involve participants (performers and audience) who are known to each other, and are often so evanescent that the close of a session brings with it an evaporation, a dispersal whose after-effects are as palpable as they are difficult to measure.

The same holds true for similar activities, frequently organised by the clubs that effloresce in these cities and towns, such as the highly popular declamation and writing contests (*perlombaan*), literary fora *cum* public discussions, literary festivals, or the publication of anthologies of poetry and short prose as well as literary periodicals in typically small editions and with limited orbits. The paradox of print as a transient medium clearly manifests itself in these publications as well, for since they are often only distributed among friends and acquaintances, they evaporate quickly, and in the case of literary periodicals normally after just a few issues. Yet, as T. S. Eliot says of such periodicals in a different context, "their collective importance is out of all proportion to the obscurity in which they struggle".[13]

Thus, such literary periodicals, especially from more remote periods, may be difficult to track down and even great tenacity may lead to the discovery of only a few scattered holdings in various archives. Nevertheless, as the studies of William Roff and Liesbeth Dolk have suggested, these periodicals are a prime source of information through which the common but neglected phenomenon of club life and multi-centredness of literature in the Malay-speaking world can be convincingly assessed.[14] These periodicals that often fold so quickly, and the clubs that produce them, indeed 'write their time', to a large extent because they clearly express the fact that there is always a political aspect involved that functions as an impetus for all kinds of literary life. Roff and Dolk have proposed that the enormous variety of clubs that sprang up during the nationalist period were the forerunners of political organisations—and there is evidence to suggest that this is as true for the literary clubs of today as it was for the clubs during the formative years of Indonesian and Malay nationalism.[15] Moreover, it is also significant here that such historical studies establish a strong and direct connection between clubs and the rash of ephemeral publications they produced on the one hand, and the coming into being of a modern literature on the other. Both were, and still are, inextricably linked; it is a telling fact that this modernity is characterised by a remarkable interpenetration of the spoken and the printed word, as well as of the private and the public sphere.

The project proposed here, then, will endeavour to challenge a view of and approach to modern Indonesian literature that has prevailed until the present day. Generally speaking, it will seek to work with assumptions, criteria and expectations that are not extrinsic to the phenomenon it will comment on. Instead of taking for granted Western print-literate, Romanticist principles, it will make the strong oral orientation of Indonesian literatures in Malay its point of departure. It will focus, therefore, on a complex of interrelated phenomena that all, to a greater or lesser extent, can be classified as 'oral' in nature. Among them are the performance and the press as the predominant media for Indonesian literature. Furthermore, the project will concentrate on poetry and short stories, as these are by far the most important genres that—while frequently surfacing only in the products of the Indonesian periodical press—can be, are meant to be, and frequently are performed.

As suggested above, an endeavour to map the widespread phenomenon of the literary club will certainly also be of crucial importance. This kind of organisation has been responsible for the fact that, at any given time during its history, the Indonesian literary system, rather than having had a single centre as its core (as the conventional wisdom has it), has had many centres. The energies channelled through such clubs, or constellations of such clubs, have in the more remote past made Pulau

Penyengat in the Riau archipelago or Yogyakarta in the post-war period, centres of literary and political activity.[16] As far as present-day Indonesia is concerned, there is much evidence that similar ones are now active in Pekanbaru, Padang, Banda Aceh, Banjarmasin, Ujung Pandang, Denpasar, Ngawi, Solo, as well as other cities and towns.[17] Here it may be germane to note that tentative research, conducted as recently as 1998, shows that even in Greater Jakarta ('*Jabotabek*') more than 50 literary clubs are presently active that are only remotely connected to the capital's literary establishment, pursuing their goals in relative obscurity.[18] In other words, modern Indonesian literature has been, and is, generated by a multitude of active groups, clusters, associations and communities that are spread over a considerable geographical area and develop local and regional variants of a larger tradition. As is the case with related elements within the complex that has been sketched here, the hallmark of these centres seems to be their temporariness and transience: they may rise and decline again within a relatively short period of time, after which their function may be taken over by other places where other clubs are becoming active. It is against this background that the proposed project will postulate a continuum or greater code that makes possible a longitudinal view within which the relatively rapid appearance and disappearance of a particular centre, as well as the fluid networks of individuals with literary and cultural concerns active in them, represent the normal course of events. In order to conceive of such a continuum more easily, as well as to give its intended mapping a more solid base, the mycelium is adopted here.

This metaphor, which figures prominently in the project's title, is taken from mycology, the study of fungi. The mycelium is the main body of the mushroom, which lives underground, consists of a huge network of threadlike strands spread over a very large area, and may live for hundreds of years. As is the case with the Indonesian literary system, which yields many centres at any given point in time, the mycelium is a continuum that produces its fruiting bodies above ground now here, now there, then again elsewhere. The Indonesian literary system is seen as reflecting a mycelium, at any given moment in time bringing forth many separate centres of literary fruition, depending on certain auspicious circumstances in these particular spots—circumstances that will have to be described and analysed as comprehensively as possible, most likely with the help of insights from relevant scholarly disciplines such as urban anthropology, cultural studies and sociology.[19]

The use of the metaphor of the mycelium not only has the advantage of accounting for the multi-centredness of Indonesian literatures in Malay, it also emphasises the conviction that this literature should be seen as a living system: a pulsating, breathing continuum of transience in terms of which literary life may mushroom in various places and by means of a great variety of literary activities that all somehow reflect a strong oral orientation. Given this orientation, it goes without saying that fieldwork is absolutely necessary as a means to study its current manifestations. Moreover, such a view of an Indonesian literary continuum as a living organism strikes at the very roots of the association of literature (in book form) with the immutability of death, which constitutes an important presupposition in Western mainstream scholarship on Indonesian *belles lettres*. Put differently, when it comes to Indonesian literature, it seems much more consistent with reality to think in terms of transience, evanescence and fluidity than in terms of fixity and unchangeability, for because of its strong oral orientation, modern Indonesian literature is always much more in a constant state of flux than any of its Western counterparts.

Of course, the metaphor of the mycelium is reminiscent of the *rhizome* that was introduced by Gilles Deleuze and Felix Guatarri.[20] Both metaphors are taken from the plant world; they are meant as a model for a continuum, and they share a non-hierarchic outlook. But whereas the rhizome seems to constitute a rather general and philosophical endeavour to come to terms with the multiplicity and even chaos of human thinking as a never-ending maelstrom of possibilities, the mycelium is adopted as model to account for a specific set of phenomena in the Malay-Indonesian literary world, which is characterised not so much by centrelessness as by multi-centredness. As a spatial and temporal model, the mycelium helps us to understand why and how modern Indonesian literature constitutes a unique continuum, indeed, one that escapes conventional wisdom and therefore requires an unorthodox approach.

This uniqueness has also been argued in recent contributions to the field that work from a different, post-colonial perspective.[21] Such studies suggest that the language policy of the colonial government in the former Dutch East Indies—the selective spread of the Dutch language among the natives on the one hand and the reinforcement of Malay on the other—has made the literature of the later Indonesian nation-state develop in a quite singular direction. Indonesia is the only former colony in modern history where the coloniser did not impose his language. This choice on the part of the Dutch has had far-reaching consequences that today are not yet fully understood and still await careful analysis. But one thing is certain: because of these factors, Malay and not Dutch became the official language of independent Indonesia.[22] In contrast to other post-colonies, where

European languages (mainly English and French) were given this status, and whose citizens could thus remain in touch with the discourses in these languages and 'write back', the Malay of Indonesia has tended to isolate its speakers and has limited the reception of Western modernity.[23] Thus, another condition was created for Indonesian literature to develop in a way that, seen from a post-colonial perspective, makes it quite unique.

II

"Léve de nieuwe Maleische Letterkunde!"
(C. Hooykaas, *Over Maleische Literatuur*)

A good starting point for presenting a limited case study that will suggest how in a more concrete way the Malay literary mycelium can be approached, may be a workshop on 'endangered languages and literatures' that was held in Leiden, the Netherlands, some years ago. What is 'endangered literature'? The letter inviting scholars from all over the world to participate in the workshop on this theme was not very clear in this respect. By way of elucidation, it said that "[t]his will mainly concern languages and literatures of small minority groups, but the organisers do not want to exclude a discussion of the position of languages and cultures of 'large minorities'". Amongst other things, this presupposes that the literature of a relatively small group of people is more vulnerable than that of a relatively large group and that 'minority literature' will more easily succumb to pressure and eventually, perhaps, become extinct.

One wonders whether this notion, put in such general terms, is a valid basis for an argument about any given literature in danger of 'dying'. A sufficiently large critical mass of individuals who consider a particular literature to be theirs—and therefore collectively participate in canonising activities, endorsing its inclusion in all kinds of school curricula and founding feelings of nationhood upon it—may still fail to warrant this literature's survival. Or, in any case, it may be that profound doubts arise with regard to the chances of a particular literature to survive, despite its being firmly rooted in the minds of the people who constitute the majority in a particular nation-state. For instance, even with regard to a well-established literature such as Dutch, it seems that in recent times, more and more devotees have expressed their worries over what has been termed *ontlezing*. This odd-sounding neologism, for which 'dereading' or 'unreading' might be rather awkward translations, has been devised to refer to the seemingly increasing disinclination of the Dutch—especially of the younger generation—to read, let alone read books or, even less so, literature. What is perceived to be most alarming in this respect is the growing lack of knowledge of high-canonical works. I recall an article in a recently published Dutch newspaper in which a professor of Latin and Greek at the Catholic University of Nijmegen (the Netherlands) gives the example of one of his students who had enthusiastically reported his 'discovery' that Jesus and Christ are one and the same person!

It could be argued, of course, that the Bible is not a part of the Dutch literary canon, but I take it that most people will agree when I say that without some knowledge of Christianity's holy book, a great many works in Dutch literature, and Western literature in general, become incomprehensible. Doesn't such increasing ignorance of the basics constitute the beginning of the end? Maybe it does. However, with regard to Dutch literature it should also be mentioned here that, strangely enough, more literary works than ever have been published over the last few decades. We may assume that in a capitalist economy such as the Dutch one this growing stream of literary publications is only possible when there are enough individuals willing to purchase (and presumably also read) all these books. Moreover, there is a whole machinery working for the benefit of the literature industry, including, for instance, weekly literary sections of national and regional newspapers, autograph sessions with authors in bookshops or regular television broadcasts exclusively focused on new literary works. So one might wonder what is actually happening. Is Dutch literature—the literature of a 'majority', so to speak—slowly going down the drain? Is it 'endangered'? Or is it more vital than it ever was?

Those who are inclined to cultivate their fears often point in this connection to the 'disastrous' influence of television and other modern blessings (video, computer games and Internet), which supposedly have a very negative impact on our reading habits. Some time ago, I witnessed an interesting presentation of this idea when I was reading a boring book in some hotel room while half-watching TV. The station was the music channel MTV. Suddenly my attention was caught by one of this station's typical auto-panegyric advertisements. In it, a curly-haired youngster declared that his parents had scolded him for the fact that he always watched MTV and never read anything. If I am not mistaken, in his 'defence' he argued that MTV provided him with so much information and knowledge so quickly and so sophisticatedly that there was simply no point in trying to acquire the same amount of data and insights through *reading*. Imagine, he went on to argue with a deadpan face, how many newspapers, magazines and books or, God forbid, novels, he would have to read, how much paper would be wasted, how many trees would have to be felled—just to produce an effect that could also be achieved with a simple push on the button of your remote control. Therefore, he concluded, carrying the 'ecological' argument further: "Save a tree, watch MTV."

The makers of this commercial seem to have been well aware of the public debate about the perceived but nevertheless threatening replacement of literacy with 'videocy', as Nobel Prize winner Joseph Brodsky put it.[24] They happily bait and provoke those who fear that we are losing our heritage, particularly our printed, literary heritage, indeed our culture, by amusing ourselves to death in front of a TV screen. "So what?", the commercial seems to ask, not in the least because the curly-haired rascal in it appears to be sitting on a lavatory bowl. "Good question!", I would be inclined to answer, for I feel that the angst this observation, whether valid or not, evokes in us really clouds the issue. As was mentioned earlier, particularly in the Western print-literate psyche, there is a deep-rooted linkage between language and literature on the one hand, and nation and civilisation on the other. Therefore, when we receive the impression that a language is dying out or a literature is vanishing, we automatically conclude that the nation, nay, the civilisation of which this language and literature constitute the matrix, will also become extinct. However, to my mind this Romantic topos as well as the anxiety that seems to go hand-in-hand with it, keep us from dealing with the matter in a sensible or sober-minded way. Why should we be so gloomy anyhow? Why not think in terms of change or transformation rather than in terms of decline? Why not take as our departure point the old wisdom that everything changes continually, that everything is always in a state of becoming? With this *panta rhei* in mind we may decide that a particular language or literature is not so much disappearing as changing —though perhaps in very paradoxical and confusing ways—into something else; something as good, or bad. Why should videocy, say, be unable to function as the matrix of a civilisation?

Incidentally, I watched the commercial I referred to above in a hotel room in Solo, Central Java, Indonesia. The station was MTV-Asia. This suggests, of course, that, in Asia in general and in Indonesia in particular, similar concerns over similar phenomena are being expressed as well. With regard to Indonesia and its literatures, in any case, this does not come as a surprise. Without much exaggeration, it could be said that among its students, there is almost a tradition of lament over literatures in jeopardy or close to extinction. One of the oldest and most famous examples of this is certainly Hans Overbeck's remark that "Malay literature is dead, wasted away, since the glory of the Malay states has faded."[25] No less pessimistic was R. J. Wilkinson, who wrote in 1907: "The destruction of the old Malay literary instinct—even more than the loss of so much of the literature itself—is a painful feature of the change that has come over Malay letters since they have been entrusted to European guidance."[26] Much later, I myself joined the wailers when I stated, referring to the Sumatran-Malay oral tradition that I had studied in the Indonesian province of Riau, that its prospects were "not very optimistic".[27] Even with regard to modern Indonesian literature, it has been suggested recently that it is as good as dead.[28]

As for my own pessimism, I began to have doubts when I revisited one of the professional Malay storytellers I had worked with in 1988–89, during fieldwork for my dissertation, in which he figures prominently. During this period, it appeared that Pak Taslim, as he is called, had only one story in his repertoire that could take him three long nights to perform. So when I met him again a year or so after I had worked with him and we started chatting, I was glad to hear that he was doing well in every respect. In this connection he told me, with barely concealed pride, that he recently had been able to purchase a black-and-white television set. "So much for storytelling", I said to myself in a first, spontaneous response in which, it seems, that fixed turn of thought we have inherited from our Romantic predecessors surfaced again. However, it transpired that Taslim had added another story to his repertoire and was invited to perform more than ever. This made me wonder: Are the forces of modernity always as strong as we think they are? Is an oral tradition such as the Sumatran-Malay one so inherently weak or vulnerable that it begins to deteriorate the instant it is confronted with them? How resilient is an oral tradition and how far is it able to adapt to what is inevitably coming anyhow? Had I been thinking in too simplistic a manner about these things?

Such questions became even more acute when, some time ago, I was asked to proofread a first draft of a forthcoming book that strives to contain a survey of the names, the whereabouts and the repertoires of *all* Malay oral specialists in the province of Riau. In 1988, I found it quite an effort to locate just two men who were acknowledged by their respective communities as professional storytellers (one of them being the aforementioned Pak Taslim). However, this survey, industriously compiled by the men and women of the Pusat Pengajian Melayu (Centre for Malay Studies) of the Universitas Islam Riau in Pekanbaru, shows that to this very day more than a hundred individuals are still active as oral professionals.[29] Of course, we do not know how many storytellers there were in Riau one, two or more generations ago; how and when they performed; and for what types of audiences. There simply are no data on these questions and the transient character of orality in general guarantees that they are gone forever. But the fact that more than a hundred Malay singers of tales are still performing in that region today suggests that Malay oral tradition there—Malay literature, if you will—is still very much alive, despite constant contact of the people even in the remotest corners of this sparsely populated area with the many-headed monster of modernity.

Naturally, as unknown as this tradition's past is its future. However, against the backdrop of the discussion so far we could well assume that its prospects are bright. Why not? After all, Malay storytelling has survived in a presumably 'pure' form, although the Malays of Riau are a minority in Indonesia and an oppressed one at that.[30] But even if this would prove to be too optimistic a view, there are, I think, other ways and means through which this tradition may succeed in carrying over its basic traits into a new era. Here it may be relevant to remind ourselves of Overbeck's statement again. His observation that Malay literature was dead may, in retrospect, be understandable but it was also premature, for something called 'Malay literature' is still undeniably present. Apart from other changes it has just changed its medium. For Overbeck 'Malay literature' was to be found exclusively in manuscripts and at the time he made his pessimistic statement, the so-called chirographic tradition was indeed coming to a close in the Malay lands. But with this development was Malay literature gone as well? Depending on how one looks at it, one could say that almost as soon as it died it re-emerged again, for instance in the form of what is called *sastra liar* or 'wild literature', a popular form of literary production in print of the early twentieth century. Thus, this phoenix rose from its ashes and next to the typical genres of what came to be known as 'classical' Malay literature—the *syair* and the *hikayat*—other types of literary composition came to be practised and Malay literature simply survived. For it changed, it adapted to changing circumstances, it became 'modern'.

It has been suggested that this change was quite radical; that there occurred a 'break', for the essential characteristics of the all-powerful print capitalism that emerged around the beginning of this century were totally incompatible with orally conveyed stories as well as with manuscripts, which, incidentally, are understood today as belonging to a radically oral manuscript literature rather than to the Euro-American ideal of print literacy. The chirographic heritage was considered dead; the oral tradition was, at best, thought of as dying. As for the latter, we have seen that it is still alive and kicking, and there are signs that the Malay manuscript tradition also is making itself felt until this very day. Limiting myself again here to the Indonesian province of Riau, I can, by way of example, point to the island of Penyengat, opposite Tanjung Pinang in the Riau archipelago where, until the beginning of this century, a remarkable group of literati were active in producing a great many works in manuscript form. Most famous amongst them is, and was, Raja Ali Haji, whose works and deeds are an object of study to this day.[31] Of course, scholarly attention alone is not good enough to keep a tradition alive; it sometimes even seems that such attention, conversely, sounds the death knell of the tradition concerned. A much more decisive factor for its survival would be the degree to which subsequent generations are willing to re-use, rearrange, reconstruct, re-shape or reinterpret—in short, 'translate'—the tradition they have inherited in such a way that it remains meaningful to them.

What this might entail can be seen in the literary periodical *Menyimak* that began to appear in Pekanbaru in 1992. Aside from publishing poems and short stories by Malay literati living and working in Riau today, as well as translations of works from a host of international authors from Japan to Somalia and from Sweden to Mexico, this periodical has right from the start presented itself as the heir to the Malay chirografic tradition in general, and 'Penyengat' in particular. This is expressed in various ways. Sometimes just extracts from famous 'classical' Malay works are printed without comment. For instance, in the first and fourth issues we find passages from the *Hikayat Hang Tuah* and the *Sejarah Melayu*.[32] At other times, we come across articles in which certain Malay authors who were directly or indirectly involved in the group of literati in late nineteenth-century Penyengat, known as the *Rushdiah Klab*, are put in the limelight.[33] However, perhaps more interesting are those instances in which parts from the chirographic tradition are manipulated, changed, adapted or hammered into shapes that suit contemporary needs. One of the main literary genres in modern Malay-Indonesian literature is, no doubt, the short story. Therefore it may not be surprising that in the third issue of *Menyimak* we come across an extract from Raja Ali Haji's *Syair Kitab Nikah* that is presented as a short story (*cerpen Raja Ali Haji*), entitled *Penyair dan Tuan Puteri* (The Poet and the Princess). Typically, in an additional comment this anachronism is neither explained away nor obscured. Rather it is emphasised that the poetry of the *syair* genre was deliberately turned into prose (*sengaja diantar dalam bentuk prosa*). Moreover, the anonymous *pengelola* (the one who did the adaptation) confesses that he replaced certain unidentified Malay words that today are virtually unknown (*yang sudah sangat kurang dikenal*), as well as Arabic words with more current Indonesian ones. Then he goes on to note: "Of course, these changes do not meet the demands of philology, yet they were made with the consideration to present a work from the past as a reading for today."[34]

This is survival in a nutshell. A work from the past, belonging to a literature that was declared 'dead' long ago, is changed into something that can be appreciated and enjoyed today. If this requires extreme modification, for instance a transmutation of the text from the original genre (the *syair*) to a different set of literary conventions (the short story), so be it. For renewal is vital, it bespeaks a literature's vitality. In this connection there is some irony in the fact that the *pengelola* thinks he has to cover himself against the demands of philology. At first glance, his manipulations of Raja Ali Haji's text indeed look like a philologist's nightmare. However, on second thought, it might be argued that he did precisely what the scribes in the Malay manuscript tradition used to do. They had no absolute respect for the text they were copying. If necessary, they just changed it and adapted it to current needs—for which reason they became the philologist's *raison d'être*. Seen in this way, Raja Ali Haji's 'short story' is a continuation of the tradition rather than a deviation from it.

These contributions to *Menyimak* still keep relatively close to the texts from the chirographic tradition and it may be significant also that—as was the custom when this tradition still reigned supreme—they are all anonymous. However, in a last example taken from this literary quarterly, this anonymity is typically abandoned. With '*Tanamlah Aku Seperti...*' ('Bury me like...'), Hasan Junus wrote a *cerpen* or short story that is imbued with references and allusions to 'Penyengat' while at the same time, as a literary composition, it exudes a very modern or even postmodern spirit. Take for instance its beginning, which runs as follows:

> from right to left. And after every time he has read one string of letters on the musty yellow paper, his fingers press the keys of the keyboard and he looks at the result on the screen.
>
> He reads: *ta-alif-nun-mim-lam-ha alif-kaf sin-pa-ra-ta-ya mim-nun-alif-nun-mim sin-hamzah-waw-ra-nga*, and writes: *tanamlah aku seperti menanam seorang...* [bury me like you bury a...]
>
> Click! Suddenly there is a power failure, and all the letters disappear into the dark.[35]

Musty old paper, *Jawi* script, a computer and a power failure: this telling mix of old and new ingredients constitutes the overture to an almost plotless and fragmentary story that hovers ambiguously between fact and fiction and, as far as textual genres go, between narrative, essay, biography and brochure. The text that is being transliterated in the opening passage constitutes a part from the *surat wasiat* (last will and testament) of Marhum Mursyid, one of the *yamtuan muda* (viceroys) of Riau-Lingga kingdom, who lived on Penyengat. Both his testament and that of his older brother and predecessor as viceroy, Marhum Kantor, contain an admonition not to bury them as monarchs but as *fakir* (poor person, mendicant), hence the story's title. These similar phrases in the last will of these two prominent figures from nineteenth-century Penyengat form the framework of Hasan Junus' story in which the narrator, who is transliterating these dying exhortations, reflects on his own life and death and mirrors these reflections with a fictionalisation of Marhum Mursyid's last days. This gives him the opportunity to have Raja Ali Haji himself play a part in the story, as well as his friend the Dutch colonial officer von de Wall, his relative Haji Ibrahim and the latter's *Hikayat Raja Damsyik*. In passing, as it were, we are also given an account of the controversy over *talkin* in the Malay world in that period, in which reformist Muslims (the *Kaum Muda*) and their conservative co-religionists (the *Kaum Tua*) were diametrically opposed to each other.[36] Finally an extract from the diary (*catatan sehari-hari*) of Encik Abdul Karim is woven into the story's fabric that deals with an orally transmitted testamentary admonition of a certain Wak Jali (who was a *fakir* but wanted to be buried as king).[37]

However tempting it would be here to have a closer look at the literariness of this remarkable short story, it is in the present context probably more relevant to emphasise that apparently 'Penyengat' and the rich literary heritage it produced are still a source of inspiration for present-day Malay authors. Their 'literary instinct' does not seem to be affected in the least by modern times; on the contrary, it makes them return to the works of their forebears in such a way that it saves these works from fossilisation. They are used and re-used, reconsidered, reinterpreted again, as are the less well-known ones. They do not need literary history or a street name as a last refuge. In other words, although once the odds seemed to be against it, the chirographic tradition—or rather, what was transmitted in that tradition—can after a long period of time still looks quite viable and there is no real tension between a nineteenth-century manuscript and a twentieth-century computer.

It should not go unnoticed here that this tradition is kept alive not only through the medium of print but also through the voice. In this connection it is relevant to point out that the Malay verb "*menyimak*" means both 'to gather' and 'to listen attentively'. It may seem strange that a literary periodical, a printed matter, adorns itself with such a name.

However, with this verb the founders of this quarterly refer quite rightly, and presumably quite self-consciously as well, to the fact that in modern Malay-Indonesian literature a work of verbal art is preferably read aloud and performed before a gathering of listeners, rather than read alone in seclusion.[38] Moreover, this holds true not only for the poems and short stories that are produced today by modern authors, but also for the works of the Malay manuscript tradition. Also, in this respect this literature is certainly not something that is dead and buried; it still exists next to or alongside what is considered to be modern. The first time I became aware of this was in 1988, when I heard R. Abdurrachman recite the *Syair Burung Nuri* on Penyengat. Some time after that, I was present when he performed part of perhaps the most famous Malay classical text, the *Hikayat Hang Tuah*; and quite recently I saw him perform again, this time reciting a part of Raja Ali Haji's *Tuhfat al-Nafis* before a large audience.[39] Significantly, the occasion for this latter performance was a poetry night during a festival held to commemorate Raja Ali Haji and his works as well as those of the members of the *Rushdiah Klab*.[40] Therefore it is perhaps not surprising that another, no less famous work by this author, the poem *Gurindam Duabelas*, was also recited on that same night even twice. In both cases, the performance was done by a whole group of people of which the first took turns in reciting a few quatrains of this poem while the second group staged a kind of *Gesamtkunstwerk* consisting of song, dance and musical accompaniment.

Typically, these performances of Malay poetry and prose alternated with those in which modern Malay authors read their poetry.[41] Thus, although the festival in general and this poetry night in particular were dedicated to an author of classical Malay literature, it was apparently not considered strange or anomalous to have modern authors perform their work as well. This proximity of tradition and modernity, which suggests a continuum rather than a pair of two distinct phenomena with clear-cut boundaries, came to the fore most clearly that night during the performance of the Pekanbaru-based poet Idrus Tintin. This *doyen* of modern Malay poetry from Riau not only performed parts of his own work, but also recited the *Syair Nasib Melayu* ('An Epic Poem of the Malay's Fate') in a way that made the audience regularly interrupt his performance with cheers and applause. A philologist will search the catalogues in vain for this title, for it is not a text from the nineteenth century or so; it was composed recently by Tenas Effendy, another man of Malay letters and a walking encyclopaedia of all things Malay, also living and working in Pekanbaru today. The fact that this is not the only *syair* he composed in recent years intimates yet again that when we think of a literature as 'endangered' or even 'dead' we may be jumping to conclusions.[42] In this connection it seems to me to be no less significant that, also recently, a young man from Pekanbaru called Zuarman gave a performance there in the manner of Sumatran-Malay oral professionals such as Pak Taslim, who chant their texts for hours on end while sitting down on the ground and beating a little drum (the *gendang* or *rebana*). The telling difference with someone such as Taslim was, however, that he did not perform a traditional story. Rather, he chanted his (extended) version of another *cerpen* by Hasan Junus, entitled "Pengantin Boneka" (The Puppet Bride), a short story that appeared in print in an Indonesian literary journal a few years ago and later was translated into English and published in Malaysia.[43]

Against this background I might emphasise again that, as I suggested earlier, it seems to be more fruitful, more productive, to think in terms of change or transformation instead of decline, for 'change' leaves open the possibility of seeing manifestations of the old in the new and, inversely, germs of the new in the old; or seeing the old still exist alongside of the new, for instance through oral transmission; or seeing what was once considered to be dead re-emerge again, although never in precisely the same form, for instance, a new *syair* that is not written by hand but typed on a computer and then distributed through photocopies. Put differently, when less heavily burdened with partly or wholly groundless pessimism, we may be able to take a more longitudinal view in which the emphasis is indeed laid on a possible continuum, a greater code in terms of which this change was and is coming about.

The case study I have presented here consists of very recent data. Starting from 'Penyengat', however, one could also point to other literary centres where transformations of Penyengat's 'endangered' or even 'dead' literature took place. Historically speaking it would, for instance, have been more obvious to refer to Singapore, which is relatively close to Penyengat. When literary life was on the decline on the small island in the Riau-Lingga kingdom in the beginning of this century, it began to take shape in Singapore in a way that was still highly reminiscent of its neighbour. As William Roff has shown, Singapore not only produced an impressive number of religious treatises, as did Penyengat, it also brought forth

an increasing spate of other material in Malay, ranging from old and new translations of classical romances and legends of Arabic and Persian origin and Islamic flavor, traditional folktales, and poetry to the modern autobiographical cronicles of Abdullah b. Abdul Kadir Munshi's *Hikayat Abdullah* and its successors, and reams of topical *shaer* (verse) on recent and current events.[44]

It is certainly no coincidence that a major role in Singapore's literary life was played by Sayid Shayk b. Ahmad Al-Hadi, who had lived on Penyengat since he was fourteen years old and who had taken part in the *Rushdiah Klab* there, just as he took part in similar 'study and recreation clubs' that sprang up everywhere in Singapore a few decades later on.[45] When, again later, Singapore's role as a literary centre was taken over by Penang, Sayid Al-Hadi was prominently present once more to produce

> a remarkable stream of romantic novels and thrillers (adapted from Egyptian and Turkish originals), a variety of homilectic literature, and two periodicals. He also established a printery, the Juletong Press, from which most of the publications emanated. These efforts changed the whole face of Malay literary life.[46]

This is not the place to go into details about the role of Singapore and Penang as literary centres, but the obvious link between these two in that capacity may serve to suggest the way I would conceive of the continuum I proposed earlier, namely a greater whole that is multi-centred: a mycelium. Roff may be right when he says that particularly in Penang in the 1920s and 1930s "the whole face of Malay literary life" was changed, but this change, it seems to me, had come about naturally and some crucial characteristics had remained the same. What links Penyengat, Singapore and Penang as centres of Malay literature is, for instance, the temporary nature of their status as centres. Malay literature seems to move around and sap energies now here, then there, then somewhere else again. This temporary character is mirrored by the ephemerality of the literary clubs and societies that appear and disappear again, although they are sometimes present in a certain place in such crucial numbers or emanating such force there that Malay literature may decide to move on again, so to speak, while changing and transforming itself on its way.

Moreover, with regard to the temporary centres discussed so far (including Pekanbaru), a political aspect is clearly involved that functions as an impulse for all kinds of literary life: the literati of Penyengat resisted (in vain) the machinations of the Dutch colonial government to abolish the Riau-Lingga kingdom; those of Singapore and Penang constituted the origins of Malay nationalism; their colleagues in present-day Pekanbaru make various efforts to construct their Malay identity in the face of appalling economic neglect as well as Indonesian national culture forced on them by the state.[47] Furthermore, a last common characteristic I can point to here may be the inclination in Malay literary life to convey literary artefacts orally, be it in the form of a *syair* recitation, or by having someone read aloud from 'vernacular papers' (or the indeed often 'ephemeral periodicals') before a group of eager listeners, or a performance of a modern poet during a poetry reading.[48]

Against this background, we may widen our scope again from 'Malay literature' to 'literature in Malay', for from the beginning of the twentieth century up until the present day, authors from outside the Malay lands, particularly from the Indonesian Archipelago, who did not and do not have Malay as their first language, have contributed considerably to Malay literary life. These contributions, I would argue, were also made in terms of the continuum whose contours I have tried to outline by means of a few essential characteristics above. As I suggested earlier, to some extent such an argument may suffer from the fact that the study of modern Indonesian literature—a literature in Malay—has almost always been focused on a single centre of authority, for which reason we do not have a clear view of what has happened and still happens outside this monolithic centre.[49] Fortunately, however, there are a few exceptions to this rule. One of them is Farida Soemargono's in-depth study of what she called the 'Yogya Group', a phrase with which she referred to a whole conglomerate of often short-lived study and discussion groups of poets, journalists, actors and painters in Yogyakarta, most of them, if not all, communicating in Malay through ephemeral publications and oral performances in which they often took sides with the oppressed and the voiceless proletariat.[50]

Similarly reminiscent of Penyengat, Singapore and Penang—centres of Malay literature rather than literature in Malay—is the literary scene in central Java in a later phase, as described by Rosslyn Marie von der Borch. Interestingly, she suggests that during the period covered by her study (roughly the late 1970s and early 1980s) the function of the temporary centre shifted from Yogya to Solo although, again, some essential traits remained the same. She emphasised, for instance, not only the importance of 'oral recitation,' but also the vital role played by a larger whole of diverse clubs and societies. What these groups held in common, she observed, is of greater consequence than the differences between them. Together these groups were

> links in an informal and fluid network of people with social concern and people on society's fringe, which encompass artists, cultural activists, student activists, young street-dwellers, villagers and *kampung* people ... Their aim is not to 'do good' but to describe the situation of people on society's margins, and, sometimes, to empower through example and the imparting of new skills and knowledge. They are both artist and activist.[51]

Studies such as these are scarce and it is not easy to be sure of where other possible centres may be located. However, there are signs that in the last few years energies are building up as well in such places as Magelang, Denpasar, Banjarmasin and Palembang. As in the case of Pekanbaru, about which I am better informed, these signs come in the form of, again, ephemeral publications that have local orbits and are hard to come by. Among them are, for instance, literary periodicals such as *Kolong* (Magelang), *Cak* (Denpasar), or *Diksi* (Palembang), or a voluminous 'literary history' in typescript from Banjarmasin that appeared in two editions of 30 and 20 copies, respectively.[52] In combination with the data I have presented above, these signs of vital literary life in various spots throughout the archipelago serve to suggest yet again that Malay literature may best be thought of as a continuum in terms of which, through time and spread over a large area, constant renewal, re-adaptation and reinterpretation is taking place.

If we speak, about 'endangered' literatures that may 'become extinct' or even 'die', as was done in the workshop mentioned above, we perhaps unwittingly have recourse to a particular category of metaphors that belong to the realm of living organisms. Therefore, also in this respect it may be less far-fetched than it seems that I here propose a particular biological species— the mycelium—as a metaphor that might be 'good to think with' when trying to conceive of the continuum I am advocating in this article. While the comparison cannot be pressed too far, it is interesting to note that, as seems to be true for Malay literature as well, the greatest magic of the mycelium, the fairy ring, is always brought forth at its periphery. Thus, when such a magic ring within Malay literature 'dies', as, for instance, did 'Penyengat', we should not panic but wait and see what happens over time. A similar one may mushroom a century later, hundreds of miles to the west, in Pekanbaru, where someone starts writing and reciting new *syair* again; where someone else in the most natural way of the world performs a printed short story in the manner of Malay oral professionals; or where yet another devotee of Malay literature publishes a collection of *cerpen* in November of the year 1996 with the title *Sandiwara Hang Tuah*,[53] which not only bespeaks his indebtedness to a tradition that was considered dead long ago, but also revives it and makes it present again.

11

An Epic Poem of the Malay's Fate

TENAS EFFENDY

translated by
*Timothy P. Barnard and Rohayati Paseng Barnard**

With 'Bismillah' as the opening words   1
Composing this poem in the middle of the dark night
Letting the heart say words
Releasing whatever feeling is being felt

The fate of the Malays is the title of this work   2
It's about the Malays in the past up until today
Although much has been reflected upon
There is nothing wrong in repeating it

Toward Malays there are many different perceptions   3
There is praise, there are insults
There are people who praise excessively
There are people who insult with ridicule

There are many opinions about the Malays   4
Good and bad go side by side
Seasons change, eras pass
The fate of the Malays is still uncertain

It has been recorded in history   5
The Malays were powerful people
Many kingdoms with much wealth
Their sovereignty strong, their dignity growing

203

The Malays once were very famous 6
Their seas extensive, their lands spacious
Their forests dense, their farms expansive
Their earth filled with precious metals

Malay lands were renowned for their beauty 7
Where the people were well mannered and friendly
It was easy to interact with them
Towards outsiders they held out open arms

From Bintan the Malays started 8
Toward Temasik spreading their wings
In Melaka their fame grew
Supporting its rule were many Malays

The Melaka era were golden years for the Malays 9
It was a great kingdom treated with respect
The culture was advanced, the economy was developed
The people were peaceful, life was tranquil

But, like the saying goes 10
Customs change all the time
In the morning they stand, in the afternoon they fall flat
When the happiness is over, difficulties arise

Because the Malays were known to be rich 11
Many visitors came from many different nations
Seizing wealth and authority
Playing the people against one another

Melaka then fell into Portuguese hands 12
The great Malays started to weaken
Their sovereignty reduced, their power thinning
The golden era slowly dissipated

Thanks to the All Mighty God 13
Melaka fell, Johor emerged
Like a tree in the middle of a field
There is where the Malays settled

Johor rose to great power   14
Becoming the heir to Melaka's throne
The Malays then breathed a sigh of relief
They became a united people

The glory of Johor did not last long   15
Many disasters came along
Internally and externally disputes started
Eventually Johor weakened

Although Johor continued to decline   16
Many new kingdoms started to grow
Some were near, some were far
Each trying to become stronger

There was a kingdom in Riau Lingga   17
Controlling the islands in the Straits of Melaka
There was also the kingdom of Siak Sri Indrapura
Its lands were spread along the Sumatran coast

In Kampar appeared clearly Pelalawan   18
Standing as tall as Mount Sahilan
Lifting the dignity of the Malays with care
Bearing the responsibility whether heavy or light

In Kuantan there was the kingdom of Indragiri   19
Since Melaka's rise to power
It knew good times and bad
While gradually strengthening itself

In Rokan there also were many kingdoms   20
Upstream and downstream they sat side by side
All emerged gradually
Raising the Malays who were wallowing in mud

Similar things happened on the Peninsula   21
Many kingdoms could be praised
It is also there that Malays moved to dwell
Propping up their fate in a secure place

But this was the fate of the Malays   22
Many kingdoms, none united
Easily divided, easily conquered
Coaxed into becoming enemies

There were battles among themselves   23
Fathers and sons fought over the thrones
There was hatred due to greed
Feuding subjects, declining kingdoms

Seeing the Malays weaken   24
Warmed the hearts of the colonisers
The English and the Dutch divided the lands
The vast Malay region shattered into pieces

One by one the kingdoms fell   25
Under the coloniser's feet they were ready to obey
Sovereignty lost, glory shattered
They fell into decadence

Although the kingdoms still existed   26
They lost all meaning
Sovereignty was not in their hands
Thoroughly ruled by the coloniser

The Malay kings became puppets   27
Before the conqueror they bowed
Most of the population faced difficulties
Because they were being colonised

Hundreds of years they were oppressed   28
Crawling like a gecko
Sitting they were pressed down, standing they were kicked
Power and glory had disappeared

While the Malays were colonised   29
Learning was scant, knowledge was scarce
Among themselves they were scattered
Divided and ruled by the coloniser

People suffered, life was difficult   30
Feet were shackled, hands were cuffed
If one talked back, the tongue was cut
If one opposed, the throat was cut

The fate of the Malays worsened   31
Crawling under other people's feet
Kept like animals in a pen
One mistake, crushed by the millstone

But as the elders say   32
Even the ant can fight back
Malays then raised their heads
To oppose the coloniser with all their hearts

Many Malay men fought   33
Attacking the coloniser until they were dead and gone
Some were killed, some were lost
Some were caged like animals

Because the Malays were not united   34
The resistance fell apart piece-by-piece
The colonisers remained strong
The Malays remained powerless

Thanks to Almighty God   35
The Second World War broke out
The English and the Dutch were at the end of their power
Attacked by Japan they were completely destroyed

When the Japanese arrived   36
They were welcomed on the oceans and on the land
The older brother had come as a savior
Because they drove away the damn colonisers

But this was the fate of the Malays   37
Escaping a corpse you meet a ghost
The Japanese did not come to help
Instead they colonised like a drunken ghost

The Japanese colonisation was very ferocious   38
The people suffered, life was miserable
Whoever rebelled their throat was slit
Whoever protested, they were skinned

The Japanese colonisation was very violent   39
Many people were beaten to death
Wealth was stolen, people were punished
Forced labour day and night

The Japanese colonised using trickery   40
Food was stolen, the people starved
Everywhere corpses lay on the ground
Like chicken dying from the plague

Thank God the Japanese did not stay long   41
Defeated by the Allies' atomic bomb
The Malays again lifted their heads (faces)
Liberating themselves to become independent

But before all could be liberated   42
The English and the Dutch returned
Intending to continue their colonisation
Ruling the Malays as before

But the Malays put their fear to the side   43
Rather than be colonised, they were willing to die
They then arose bravely
The English and the Dutch were opposed

War broke out everywhere   44
Opposing the English or the Dutch
Fighting while sacrificing their lives
So they may secure independence

The struggle was not in vain   45
The coloniser left, the Malays were free
The nation rose, the people to be reckoned with
There was a president and kings

The Malay people stood erect again   46
To rebuild a country that had been destroyed
Obstacles were huge, hindrances were many
But hope never faded

Slowly the Malays rose   47
Developing their country little by little
Searching for medicine to cure their illness
Strengthening sovereignty despite the difficulties

Decades after independence   48
Seasons change, eras pass
Yet the Malays remained on the bottom
Their fate was not yet one of prosperity

Why are the Malays haunted by misfortune   49
From the past until today
Living miserably day and night
Poverty and destitution always present

It is here that there are many perceptions   50
People studied the causes and effects
Some are wrong, some are right
Some are in-depth, some are superficial

If we want to be frank   51
Speaking honestly about all sides
Definitely shows that which is wrong and deficient
Causing the Malays to remain backward

The main cause the Malays have been left behind [is]   52
Due to a lack of knowledge
Modern developments they do not follow
With modern people they cannot compete

Many Malays have a poor education   53
They cannot take their knowledge to the front
Competing in knowledge they surely lose
Investing in it there is no profit

Malays' education is not yet sufficient   54
From the past until the present
Because their heads are empty
If competing they surely fade

It is even more so today   55
Many people compete for a chance
Whoever is stupid will not win
Whoever is weak will be cast away

The Malay world develops quickly   56
In the sea as well as the land
Many opportunities are within reach
Many businesses can be built

But, since knowledge is absent   57
Opportunities simply are wasted
Filled by others, we just watch
Eventually sitting, feeling disappointed

In the Malay world there are many opportunities   58
Which can be used as a source of income
Since the body is empty of knowledge
Other people use them

Now knowledge is the measuring stick   59
For getting a job
Regardless whether they are Malays or not
Whoever has the credentials gets the privilege

This is where the Malays fall   60
Because there are many who remain stupid
Possible opportunities grow farther away
The sad fate and misfortune continues

Certainly not all Malays are stupid   61
There are also smart and strong ones
If they really try
Certainly they are able to live properly

Another weakness of the Malays   62
They live in the past
Times change, they do not want to
Eventually living stupidly like imbeciles

The modern era is little investigated   63
Changing seasons go unnoticed
Striving for knowledge is but a dream
Eventually their fate worsens

Some Malays are spoiled   64
Their lives depend on their inheritance
On individual efforts they do not trust
Eventually their fate continues to be one of torment

Some Malays are arrogant   65
They are too satisfied to do hard work
To become a coolie they do not like
Eventually their fate floats like driftwood

Some Malays are choosy about jobs   66
If it is tough they move
If competing certainly they are pushed aside
Eventually life is heavy with pain

Some Malays don't want to exert themselves   67
Only searching for easy jobs
If competing of course they lose
Eventually their lives are goalless

Some Malays have no clear goals   68
One minute to the left, the next minute to the right
Like a ship without a compass
Eventually they live in the shadows

Some Malays are not thorough   69
Looking for opportunities, they are not incapable
Waiting all their lives
Eventually dreaming night and day

Some Malays depend on others   70
They are afraid to try themselves
Very little self-confidence
In the long run they are cast away

Some Malays are very shy   71
It is taboo to ask for help
Waiting so long mould develops
Rather than asking for help anywhere

Some Malays lack enthusiasm   72
While working they drag themselves around
Searching for work they are at the end of their rope
Eventually they continue to be poor

Some Malays are unsure what to do   73
They always doubt and are uncertain
To face challenges they are afraid
Eventually they are left with the bones

Some Malays have heavy hearts   74
In addition the have little knowledge
If they compete they must fall behind
Eventually they live in regret

Some Malays pout quickly   75
Short sighted, narrow-minded
If competing their heads are down
Eventually they live in a dark corner

Some Malays are not decisive   76
Not to mention their low education
Competing for chances they of course lose
Eventually they complain and sigh

Some Malays are not intelligent   77
They possess wealth but are unable to manage it
They do not prepare for their future
Eventually they are excessive and exhausted

Some Malays certainly seek to build castles in the air   78
Everywhere they go they just talk bullshit
Knowledge is absent working without ethics
Eventually they are just gasping for breath

Some Malays simply are apathetic   79
They do not keep up with developments
They pass the times, waste the days
Eventually they live in debt

Some Malays are easy going   80
Waiting at the door of opportunity
No effort, not even an attempt
Eventually they are haunted by misfortune

Some Malays don't want to exert themselves   81
Many excuses not to work hard
When competing of course they lose
Eventually living in a cesspool

Some Malays are not self-conscious   82
The refuse to take account of their weaknesses
Others live in abundance, Malays in envy
Eventually shame hits them

Some Malays are narrow-minded   83
Facing the future, they don't think ahead
Forgetting their needs for the present life and after
Eventually they regret when it is too late

Some Malays enjoy putting on airs   84
Bragging about themselves, they swell up
They allow their villages to decline
Eventually they end up eating crumbs

There are Malays that form groups   85
One group against the others
Insults and curses piled on each other
Eventually they pull each other down

Some Malays fight over inheritance 86
Brothers are suspicious of one another
Compassion disappears, disaster arrives
Life then is hellish

Some Malays fight for position 87
Brothers insult each other
One rises, he is held down by ten
Eventually all end up with nothing

Some Malays are cowards 88
Afraid to stand up for the right things
They sit sulking on the side
Eventually life disappears in the fog

Some Malays bite their tongue 89
Because they follow an oath
Losing their minds, manners disappear
Eventually life without glory

Some Malays worship the material world 90
Desiring position, hunting wealth
Religion declines, faith is empty
Eventually living in humiliation

Some others have brown noses 91
Sucking up, kissing ass
Glory disappears, prestige lost
Eventually life is insulting and degrading

Some crazily sell their wealth 92
Forest and land, all is sold
Oceans and rivers are also included
Children and grandchildren become poor and destitute

Some crazily demean others 93
Spreading slander day and night
Creating jealousy toward the outsiders
The once peaceful harmony begins to loosen

Some then crazily stir things up   94
Playing one against the other, looking for followers
The peaceful life becomes chaotic
Among brothers, they put each other down

Some crazily flatter   95
So they can obtain a profitable position
With their siblings they fight like animals
Eventually life is shattered

Other changes also occur   96
Living only to worship wealth
Many Malays become insane
Competing for wealth

Because wealth has been worshipped   97
People fight for the profit
Loosing the sense of helping one another
Brothers undercut each other

Because wealth has become the standard   98
Manners are disregarded more and more
Tradition and institutions are forgotten
Eventually consumed by greed

In the Malay world there are many outsiders   99
Fighting for prosperity, sharing opportunities
Since the Malays lack knowledge
In their own house, they moan

Every day more outsiders arrive   100
Yards are filled, homes overflow
Forests are chopped, bushes are cleared
Malays are pushed aside, loosing their lands

The outsiders are creative thinkers   101
Forest and bushes are turned into fields
Malays are stupid, they just watch
Wealth lessens, riches disappear

Although the Malays have vast lands   102
They are neglected due to laziness
Used by others, they are disturbed
Slowly they lose everything

Malays with position act differently   103
Grabbing opportunities for their relatives
Stupid or ignorant, it doesn't matter
So that others become the victims

Some Malays already have position   104
Their hometowns are forgotten
Living isolated, far from the masses
Afraid to share what they have achieved

Due to the presence of many outsiders   105
Malay culture becomes shakier
Oppressed by other people's cultures
They seep in it to their bones

From the beginning Malays were receptive   106
Outsiders were welcomed with open arms
Lands were taken without opposition
Eventually living in poverty and destitution

Malays are afraid to fight back   107
They don't want to appear rude
Wealth is taken, it is allowed
Eventually suffering from hunger

The Malays are softhearted   108
To do bad things they are mostly afraid
Fighting over wealth is regarded as improper
Eventually they live eating moss

So this is the fate of the Malays   109
The trunk is big, the shoot is limp
Others are content, they are sluggish
Living in poverty for all time

Already their fate has been full of mishaps 110
In their own home they are ordered around
Life is difficult without enough to eat
The bones are showing

Some Malays are not satisfied 111
Their plantations gone, their lands stolen
They want to complain, but are afraid of being destroyed
Eventually limping along breathless

Some Malays feel oppressed 112
In their own home they starve
Every opportunity is seized in competition
There is no way out

Some Malays feel evicted 113
Pushed by the outsiders upstream and downstream
They come like a flood
Taking opportunities until the end

Some Malays are disappointed 114
Lands taken, no compensation
Wishing to claim, they are powerless
Wishing to take it up in court is more expensive

Some Malays have given up hope 115
Pouting they leave their villages
Farms sold, nothing left
Eventually life is continual suffering

Some Malays are worried 116
Facing problems that continue to grow
Sitting the chair is too small, standing you bump your head
Opportunities hoped for, everything is gone

Some Malays are confused 117
Because changes are occurring too rapidly
Life is hard, prices rise
No work, life floats away

Some Malays become poorer   118
Forest and land are slashed
Wishing to farm they are unable
Wishing to earn a wage competition is keen

Some Malays are powerless   119
In their villages they cannot find jobs
Since now the ones with power
Control all down to the village

Some Malays are jealous   120
Watching others who develop further
In Malay villages they gather
Any opportunities are swept away

Some Malays are confused   121
In their own villages they don't get any opportunities
All chances filled by others
Wishing to compete, they lack knowledge

Some Malays just complain   122
Because they can't make a living
Forests are gone, bushes are cleared
Sea and rivers polluted with waste

Some Malays sit groaning   123
Their heritage controlled by others
Powerless to forbid it
Dark is the time that is coming

Some Malays continually suffer   124
Because they cannot find jobs
Wishing to compete, they have no education
Wishing to establish businesses, they have no capital

Some Malays are fooled by others   125
Seduced and deceived, wealth disappears
Farms are sold, lands are auctioned
Life is miserable, living in debt

Some Malays feel deceived 126
Because they were given false promises
Wealth is gone, debt waits
Wishing to complain, no one helps

Some Malays live a sad life 127
In they own village they are oppressed
Wishing to fight they are unable
Wishing to complain they are slaughtered

Some feel they are not yet free 128
Justice and prosperity haven't been distributed equally
Life is always in suffering
Pleasure is reserved only for certain groups

Some feel they are still colonised 129
Because they can not speak freely
The slightest said, the head is smashed
The slightest complaint, they are whipped

Some feel life has been wasted 130
Because they have been treated arbitrarily
Wherever they complain no one responds
Furthermore the masses never win

Some feel life is unjust 131
Laws only apply to common people
For the rulers laws are shaky
For the rich laws are not applicable

Some feel humiliated 132
Because they have been treated arbitrarily
Wealth is stolen with power
Or taken through manipulation

Some feel the world is growing smaller 133
Because making a living is getting more difficult
Income small, prices skyrocket
They can hardly buy food, entangled in debts

Some feel increasingly neglected   134
Getting a job is difficult, setting up a business hard
The gorge of poverty grows wider
Many have already gone bankrupt

Some feel the world is depressing   135
Due to joblessness day and night
Empty stomachs, dark minds
Eventually forgetting what is forbidden or not

Some try to survive   136
Guarding their possessions with all effort
But because there are many pressures
He has to let go of everything

Some also try to compete   137
Enter the ring without fangs
Once kicked, fall rolling around
Wishing to stand up, they are run over

Some try to open businesses   138
Some are small, some are medium
But due to stupidity and weakness
Businesses fail, debt increases

Although many Malays are unfortunate   139
Some Malays are prosperous
Because they manage to snatch away opportunities
Much wealth, position, prestige

Some Malays sit in the government   140
Some are high, some are low
Life is good, wealth is abundant
Their descendants will never suffer

Some Malays become high officials   141
Their position is good, their rank high
But most are narrow-minded
Since they only think of their own relatives

Some have high positions   142
In their field they hold the controls
Unfortunately the don't care about the people
Only relatives are taken care of

Some Malays lead respected lives   143
High positions, and not lacking wealth
But unfortunately they are not tolerant
Their own village they do not remember

Some also become leaders   144
Glorious position, livelihood guaranteed
Unfortunately they stand with the others
With their own people they have no sympathy

So this is the fate of the Malays   145
Changing continuously
Little enjoyment, much sorrow
Only God knows the future

But not all is bad   146
There are also Malays who are nice
Working to the point of excess
Although life is poor

There are also Malays who are resilient   147
Facing life bravely and heroically
They will face any challenge
Raising honor, guarding dignity

There are also Malays who are tenacious   148
Working hard, never complaining
Willing to work, wet with sweat
In order to pursue a prosperous life

There are also Malays who are wise   149
Facing challenges, their heart is set
Saving for a rainy day
So that there are no regrets in the future

There are also Malays who are well-mannered   150
Doing good deeds with a content heart
Defending their brothers, willing to suffer (a financial loss)
With their people they share their prosperity

There are also Malays who are chosen   151
Becoming leaders, there are role models
Pure hearts, strong faith
Helping without favouring friends

There are also Malays who are well-known   152
Strong in traditions as well as religion
Well-mannered, noble character
Honoured by old and young alike

There are also Malays who are brave   153
Facing enemies, they never flee
Defending what's right, willing to die
Bravely standing up for the truth

There are also Malays who are loving   154
Willing to sacrifice for others
Helping hands, accepting hearts
They honestly do good things

There are also Malays who are knowledgeable   155
Smart and intelligent, they should be imitated
Guiding and teaching, they are never bored
To raise the dignity of the Malays

Most Malays are very open   156
Receiving guests with open arms
Toward others they assume the best
Whoever comes they accept

Most Malays like to help   157
Doing good things, without wanting praise
If something is broken, they fix it
If someone is in trouble, they protect him

Most Malays are friendly 158
Whoever comes, they are invited in
Drinking, eating and sitting in the same house
High or low it doesn't matter

Most Malays are tolerant 159
Knowing how to understand other's feelings
Before acting they always consider
So they don't mistreat others

Most Malays like to have friends 160
Living, eating and drinking as brothers
More and less they forgive
Bitter and sweet they accept

Most Malays are not confrontational 161
Rather than argue they just give in
Losing a little is not a problem
As long as it doesn't reduce dignity

Most Malays prefer peace 162
Living in harmony, abstaining from splits
Prosperity enjoyed together
Rice in fields they harvest together

Most Malays are generous 163
Helping each other without compensation
Always giving, presenting alms to the poor
Although their lives are also difficult

Most Malays are relaxed 164
Although life is difficult they appear calm
They never want to burden others
Begging is strongly forbidden

Most Malays are humble 165
Rarely is there one who brags about himself
Speaking with a soft voice
Addressing others with good manners

Most Malays are softhearted   166
Coax them and they will follow
Doing cruel things they are afraid
Speaking coarsely is not appropriate

Most Malays are modest   167
Searching for just enough wealth
As long as they can eat and drink
So that their household is safe

Most Malays know how to behave   168
They avoid kissing each other's butt
Flattering is forbidden
Although it means that they live on the margins

Most Malays appreciate knowledge   169
Sitting they read, standing they study
In order to speak their tongue is not stiff
Facing life they won't be ashamed

Most Malays abhor treason   170
Toward the government as well as parents
Remaining patient as long as they can
Until they reach the limit of their patience

Most Malays are not vengeful   171
Once the anger passes, the hate disappears
Animosity doesn't survive the night
A feud doesn't bring despair

Most Malays don't complain much   172
More and less is not a problem
Although life is difficult
Rather than argue they give in

Most Malays follow orders   173
Keeping promises, maintaining oaths
Rather than break a promise, they would perish
Rather than betray, they would rather be broken

But as the saying goes   174
In good there is also bad
In bad there is also good
It all depends on the heart's desires

Malay characteristics are mostly beautiful   175
But there are also many ugly ones
Sometimes they are mixed
Like rice inside the pot

If we can be honest   176
About the fate of Malays today
There is more sadness than happiness
Because they are caught between a rock and a hard place

In the past Malay woodlands were extensive   177
They were free to utilise its produce
For plantations there was no limit
For farms just slash [the forest]

Nowadays land is argued over   178
The price skyrockets as if buying diamonds
And it is there that many crimes occur
Robbing and deceiving is what people do

The price of land continues to rise   179
Due to the extensive development
Some Malays are beginning to be pushed aside
The ignorant are trampled to death

Since land has become more valuable   180
The stupid Malays are busy selling
The lands of the forefathers are all sold
Eventually they are washed away with everything they own

The life of the Malays becomes harder   181
Of the extensive lands little is left
Wishing to survive is difficult
Eventually it is lost little-by-little

Everywhere people are building   182
Creating industry as well as plantations
The stupid Malay sits gazing
Eventually they suffer all year long

The Malays' fate is increasingly painful   183
In the city, in the village, they are pushed aside
Land ownership has shifted
Any effort, they are stepped on

On the seas, on the land, the Malays are moved aside   184
Life is rough and effort destroyed
Prestige and glory are fading more and more
The competitive spirit lessens

Although there are Malays who are brave   185
Standing strongly to defend themselves
Unfortunately their heads are empty
If they litigate they are weak

Some Malays try to fight on   186
Defending their traditional village lands
Because they are pressured from left and right
All slips out of their hands

If Malays do not have lands   187
Vanished is their prestige, lost is their glory
Their future unquestionably is difficult
The descendents have nothing to go to

These signs are becoming more apparent   188
Of once extensive lands, only a field remains
Everywhere they are pushed aside
Wishing to hold on, too many weaknesses

Why is the fate of the Malays like this   189
Because they Malays don't know the right ways
Living carelessly forgetting the days
Eras changed they were not aware

It is now that Malays begin to remember   190
Unfortunately their consciousness is too late
Others control the ocean and the land
Searching for opportunities, competition is tough

But as the saying goes   191
It is better to die than give up
Malays then try to take first steps
Changing fate, searching for prestige

Many Malays try to rise up   192
Fighting for their chance, although it is hard
Defending their rights, although it is painful
Raising in dignity, although oppressed

The young generation slowly becomes conscious   193
Seasons change, eras pass
Without knowledge life is hard
Therefore many study hard

Many have college degrees   194
Various knowledge fills the body
But opportunities are hardly available
To study is of little use

Although many types of knowledge are searched for   195
It doesn't mean much
Because they are unable to support themselves
Their only goal is to become government employees

Becoming a civil servant is not easy   196
Due to the abundance of candidates
There is where the problems emerge
In addition the work is wrong

People compete to become civil servants   197
Gathering together like ants
Most fail, their desires unfulfilled
Eventually life is uncertain

Since they want to become civil servants   198
Other jobs are neglected
Knowledge obtained, never used
In the end the Malays are show offs

If a Malay wants to make an effort   199
Certainly there are many job opportunities
But because they just wait
In the end the knowledge is useless

There have been many young Malays   200
Having titles, possessing knowledge
But sadly they do not make an effort
In the end life is uncertain

So this is the fate of the Malays today   201
Well educated, lacking in effort
The available opportunities taken by others
In their own homes they moan

Not to mention living in this era   202
Changes occur all day long
If Malays are not careful
They will go hungry in their own homes

In the modern era people compete   203
Looking for jobs on the land and on the ocean
Whoever is careless will fall behind
Whoever is stupid of course will drift away

In the modern era the competition is keen   204
Looking for a job the requirements are high
Whoever is careless will not succeed
Whoever is weak will be disregarded

In the modern era there is no favoritism   205
Whoever is strong will advance
Whoever is weak is rendered totally powerless
It doesn't matter if you are Malay

The modern era is a technological era   206
Developing knowledge moves fast
Whoever is idiotic will be pushed aside
Whoever is competent becomes successful

The modern era is a competitive era   207
Native or foreigner regardless
Whoever is not prepared will be crushed
Whoever is careless is defeated

In the modern era competition is open   208
There are soft and hard ones
There are tricksters interfering with each other
There are mean ones who fight everyone

In the modern era everything is competitive   209
Looking for opportunities in a hurry
Slightly careless, prosperity is lost
When waiting the stomach is hungry

The modern era is individualistic   210
Among brothers, they do not care
They prey on each other
Just so they can be prosperous

The modern era is crazy   211
Wealth and position are the goals
Feelings of friendship disappear
Forgetting brothers, people are not ashamed

In the modern era much is demolished   212
Manners disappear, attitudes collapse
Immorality expands, crime spreads
Prestige disappears, power thrown away

In the modern era everything is sophisticated   213
Competing for knowledge to obtain more
Whoever is on top oppresses more and more
Whoever is on the bottom increasingly gets hurt

In the modern era faith lessens   214
Local culture is fading away
The material world is what people chase
Thus there is much immorality and trickery

The modern era is an era of globalisation   215
Changes occur everywhere
People competing for position
Few win, most loose

The modern era is an upside down time   216
Immoral behaviour is considered fine
The honest ones are strangled
The sincere ones' heads are pulverized

The modern era is a time when everything is wrong   217
Those in control eat the weak
Those who are rich become greedier
Those with knowledge divide people

The modern era is a time for evil   218
Deceiving, robbing without shame
Manipulating people as much as possible
The people are oppressed, land is sold

In the modern era many are crazy   219
Some are crazy chasing wealth
Some are crazy chasing power
Some are crazy due to oppression

In the modern era many people fall   220
Some fall due to stupidity
Some fall because they are caned
Some fall because they are ordered

In the modern era there are many entrepreneurs   221
Buying and selling a variety of goods
Some sell other people's land
Some selling other's families

The modern era is a business era   222
Because authority is in his hands
His pointing index finger is law without him watching
Whatever he says, people listen

The modern era is an industrial era   223
Factories built here and there
Capital flows in everywhere from abroad
The moronic Malays are pushed further aside

Since industry continues to develop   224
Land for farming becomes scarce
Natives are pushed aside, hopes lost
Their lives increasingly uncertain

Large plantations are also opened   225
Stretching into the millions of hectares
Burned to the ground are forests and bushes
Many local residents are left with nothing

Months change into years   226
The fate of the Malays rises and falls
Losing their minds they sit gazing
Eventually they rot like cucumbers

Many seasons have passed   227
The fate of the Malays is still uncertain
Their lives are still doubtful and uncertain
Wealth disappears little by little

Although now many are aware   228
That the Malays often are neglected
Wishing to rise, many oppose them
Wishing to speak out, the tongue trembles

Many Malays are trying to stand up   229
Lifting their heads, opening their wings
Since they live divided
Eventually they fall with a thumping sound

Some Malays raise their voices   230
Speaking of the fate of their miserable lives
Unfortunately they are not speaking as one
Their tongues become stiff without result

Many Malays also criticise   231
Through essays long and short
But they are not too bright
Eventually life remains oppressive

Many Malays also hold seminars   232
Gathering experts and specialists
[But] because it is controlled by outsiders
The Malays keep on drifting

There are also Malays who are brave   233
Conveying criticism everywhere
But because they walk alone
Eventually they end up in a box

There are also Malays who are reckless   234
Fighting the power that becomes stronger against the current
Anywhere they go they are whipped
Their own brothers curse them

There are Malays who speak out   235
At forums they are respected
But when questioned by people
They then keep silent and turn away

There are Malays who represent their people   236
Cleaver in speaking with beautiful speeches
But unfortunately they don't pay attention to the masses
Many mandates and oaths they forget

There are Malays known as experts   237
Spending their times at seminars
Unfortunately their speeches are not heard
Returning home to a starving family

Actually many Malays are well-known 238
Titles lined up, their knowledge trustworthy
But because they are afraid of being arrested
They take care of themselves, the people are sacrificed

There are also many Malays who are obedient 239
Trying to stand to defend their people
Unfortunately they themselves live miserably
On their first steps they are already in agony

Many Malays feel sorry 240
Seeing their community in trouble
Wishing to help they are hungry
Wishing to act they have no strength

Many Malays feel compassionate 241
Witnessing the fate of the masses
Wishing to help they are impoverished
Wishing to act they have no power

Many Malays whisper 242
Telling the fate of the Malays today
Speaking out they do not dare
Afraid of being cast aside or handcuffed

There are Malays living in prosperity 243
Because they are two-faced
Over here they praise, over there they praise
Their community is miserable, they don't care

There are Malays who live comfortably 244
Because they live under someone's armpit
Their community is in trouble, they don't care
Their dignity is gone

There are high ranking Malays 245
Because they diligently praise their superiors
The fate of their subordinates, they don't notice
Whether they live or die

There are also proper Malays   246
Defending their people patiently
But unfortunately their position is low
Facing their superiors they bite their tongues

There are already many problems striking down   247
The shoulders of the desperately poor Malays
Therefore their lives remain uncertain
Changing their fate, nobody knows when

Problems come one after the other   248
Striking down the Malays very harshly
Burdens accumulate every day
Who knows when they can rise up

If you really think about it   249
The Malays' pride is fading away
In the Malays' home others enjoy themselves
They are pushed aside, their lives are thrown away

If you consider carefully   250
Many Malays are basically cowards
Stepping into the arena they do not dare
They choose to live in isolation

If you look closely   251
The fate of the Malays today
Many are miserable, few are happy
In their own homes they are like strangers

If you visit the villages   252
Malays appear increasingly confused
Their forests and land are divided
Taken by people without compensation

In the villages people are weeping   253
Disasters come one after another
If they have land, it is taken away
If they have fields, they run out of seeds

That is the fate of the Malays   254
Like a tree that is withering
Their glory remains in the past
The future is not yet known

The fate of the Malays is becoming more uncertain   255
Struck by disasters from all sides
In their own villages they are strangers
Scratching like a chicken for food day and night

The fate of the Malays is uncertain   256
Shaken to the left and right
We say that development is digressing, but it appears to progress
Heirlooms perish one by one

If you glance at it momentarily   257
In the Malay lands development progresses
Factories everywhere, plantations spread out
But all belong to other people

If you glance at it briefly   258
The Malay nation is really prosperous
Development progressing swiftly downstream and upstream
Although not much benefits the Malays

So this is the Poem of the Malays' fate   259
True or false only God knows
Written to release my heart's desires
Informing people who do not yet know

Toward God we surrender   260
Hoping Malays live properly
Standing and sitting in glory
Future generations may be blessed

Toward God we plead   261
The Malay race may be successful
That which is ripped is together folded again
That which is broken is together built up again

To the young generation we hope   262
Strengthen your spirit, correct your attitude
Strengthen your faith, improve your manners
So that Malays stand strongly

To the young generation we leave an appeal   263
Destroy lazy and over-respectful attitudes
Enrich yourselves with knowledge
So that the Malays will not be left behind

To the young generation we leave instructions   264
Grab opportunities, don't be careless
In competition hope to be patient
So that Malays can live in dignity

To the young generation we advise   265
Distance yourself from butt kissing attitudes
Avoid doing immoral deeds
So that Malays may live safely

To the young generation we recommend   266
Avoid living in division
Helping each other in good times and bad
So that Malays will be blessed by God

To the young generation we appeal   267
Admit your weaknesses, don't be ashamed
While taking action, don't hesitate
So that Malay glory rises

To the young generation we speak   268
Make a definite decision, straighten your heart
In competition be brave
So that you can be lord in your own home

To the young generation we have one last wish   269
Develop culture, strengthen tradition
Know how to count, be wise in spending
So that prosperity reigns in life and afterlife

My fellow Malays we remind   270
Don't be blinded by riches
Balance wealth and faith
So that you will be safe in the future

Together as a nation we leave an appeal   271
Don't eat your friends
Greed and avarice we avoid
So that brotherhood can last forever

Live together as a nation   272
Be mutually considerate, feeling for each other
If in power don't force each other
The rich don't sell your race

Our race is a well-mannered race   273
Upon good deeds they stand
Satisfaction is not enjoyed individually
Opportunity and prosperity is shared together

Toward the outsiders we remind   274
Searching for subsistence, don't destroy everything
Consider the fate of the local people
In order to avoid animosity

Each outsider should remember   275
The Malay people carry their traditions
Don't teach them hatred and immoral deeds
So that everyone can live in safety

Each outsider has to understand   276
The Malay people have a good character
Because they are nice don't underestimate them
Malays also will bravely face their death

Each outsider shouldn't be bombastic   277
Acting anyway they please
Deceiving and robbing the property of others
The Malays also can fight the sword

Each outsider should know　　　　　　　　　　278
Respect Malay traditions and culture
Don't come to make trouble
Avoid becoming enemies

Each outsider should be aware　　　　　　　　279
That Malays forbid being taunted
Avoid unjust and tricky attitudes
So that Malays won't lose their patience

Each outsider should understand　　　　　　　280
That most Malays are Muslims
Don't practice forbidden behaviour
So that Malays don't bear malice

Each outsider shouldn't show off　　　　　　　281
Presenting much power and riches
You cannot touch a Malay on the head
Once they fight, much is destroyed

This Malay proverb may serve as a warning　　　282
The worst thing for a fish is no water
The worst thing for a man is to make him feel ashamed
The worst thing for a Malay is to be insulted

If outsiders disobey these taboos　　　　　　　283
Treating the Malays as they wish
That is where the Malays become angry
One is lost, two will arise

Although Malays like to compromise　　　　　　284
A little more or less is not a problem
But don't slap their heads
They will run amok with blood everywhere

Although Malays are soft-hearted　　　　　　　285
Toward new comers they talk sweetly
But don't take away their rights
Malays are willing to face death

Although the Malays are open hearted   286
Toward others they like to compromise
But don't restrain their lives
It is there they lose their patience

Although the Malays like to make peace   287
Living together in harmony
But don't make it hot for them
Killing others, the Malays know how

Although Malays are forbidden to commit treason   288
Toward the leaders they are loyal
But don't oppress them
Malays also are brave enough to put their lives on the line

Although the Malays live simply   289
Making do with their livelihood as it is
But don't insult them
Malays also know how to keep their dignity

Although most Malays are poor   290
Living poorly, eating little
But don't trap them
Malays also are brave to defend their status

Although the Malays life is difficult   291
On the ocean and on the land they search for subsistence
But don't whip them
Whoever whips them, their heads will be broken

Although many Malays are stupid   292
But don't treat them like idiots
Or treat them improperly
They are also able to kill

Although the Malays faith is strong   293
They are known for being religious
But don't betray them
Malays also are able to act recklessly

Although Malays like to have friends   294
Living as friends forever
But don't trick them
They also are able to become adversaries

Although the Malays like to help   295
Helping others indiscriminately
But it's forbidden for them to be tricked
If tricked they become foes

At this point the poem ends   296
The truths and the mistakes may be seen
Hopefully it could become a reminder
In the future it can be useful

This is the end of An Epic Poem of the Malays' Fate   297
The content of my heart has been expressed
The pure intention is to raise the Malays
Not to make them feel disgraced and embarrassed

The Poem is already finished being written   298
Hoping to produce something useful
The Malays stand upright living in dignity
The fate betters, their glory grows

With Alhamdulillah as the closing words   299
Praise only to the one God
Hoping to avoid all bad deeds
Malays live happily and tranquilly

12

Afterword: A History of Malay Ethnicity

ANTHONY MILNER*

Reviewing the essays in this volume—a collection, it must be said, that demonstrates the current liveliness of the field of Malay studies—a series of analytic issues emerges.[1] In some cases they emerge in a way that is almost disorienting. The essays, of course, do not provide the last word on any of these issues; but more importantly, they do deepen our understanding of Malay ethnicity and even help to establish an agenda for future research. They advance the history of Malay ethnicity— a project that is a new departure in Southeast Asian studies and, in addition, provides a focus of broad intellectual interest at a time when historians are seeking ways to subvert the 'nation state' as the primary object of historical enquiry.

Issues

The first issue these essays highlight is 'just who are the Malays'? In 1913, as Shamsul A. B. explains in his contribution, a person of Arab descent was defined as Malay in Kedah, but not in Johor; someone of Siamese descent was considered Malay in Kelantan but not in Negeri Sembilan. Looking back at earlier centuries, key texts in Malay literature give the impression that the 'Malays' were primarily people associated with Melaka and its successor state, Johor;[2] for Dutch officials in seventeenth-century Makassar in eastern Indonesia, however, the 'Malays' included people from Minangkabau, Kalimantan and Java as well as Johor. The early eighteenth-century Dutch scholar, Francois Valentijn, as Amin Sweeney has observed, sometimes used the term 'Malay' so broadly that it seems to have been an equivalent of 'Moor' or 'Mohammedan'.[3]

In the twentieth century, some 'Malays' continued to use the term broadly. The writer and politician Ibrahim Yaacob, who was in close sympathy with Indonesian nationalism, referred to the people living throughout the Archipelago as 'Melayu'. As he put it in 1941, 'Melayu' did not simply mean the two and a half million Peninsular Malays but also the 65 million across Indonesia.[4] In opposition to this, the first Prime Minister of Malaya and Malaysia, Tunku Abdul Rahman, took a narrower, peninsular viewpoint; and when he proposed an expanded state with the name 'Malaysia' (which was sometimes translated as 'Melayu Raya' or 'Greater Malaydom') he was thinking only of an expansion into north Borneo.[5]

Just what was involved in being Malay? Leonard Andaya stresses the idea of identification with a Malay homeland, but where was it located? In developing the idea of a Malaysian state in the 1960s, the term 'homeland' was used with reference to the Malay Peninsula—for instance, when Tunku Abdul Rahman observed that the people of Brunei saw Malaya as 'almost their homeland'.[6] Andaya, however, suggests that "historical and linguistic evidence for a Melayu homeland in southeast Sumatra is overwhelming". James Collins' essay takes yet another position, drawing attention to the linguistic and cultural role of western Borneo. It is in this region, he suggests, that we find the "prehistoric homeland of the Malay language community".[7]

Collins is focussing on Malay language usage, and we might go on to ask what relationship exists between language usage and ethnicity. The national constitution of Malaysia is quite explicit on this matter; it defines 'Malays' as people who not only profess Islam, and conform to Malay custom, but also "habitually speak the Malay language".[8] Anthony Reid's essay in this volume refers to 'Malayness' as a "cultural complex centred in the language called Melayu", but Collins' examination of "Malayic language networks" makes a clear distinction between language and ethnicity. He identifies groups which are equally fluent in the same language, and even speak the same dialect, but "do not share ethnicity". He reminds us as well that Temuan and Jakun groups on the Malay Peninsula speak Malay "as their home language", while in southern Africa Cape Malays do not speak Malay "as a home language or even as a second or third language". Similarly, in Thailand there are also groups which do not speak Malay but call themselves Malay. Even in Malaysia, as Virginia Hooker explains, an "increasing number of 'Malays'" who meet the residence requirements of the Constitution are nevertheless "losing their ability to speak the Malay language (as English becomes their working language)".

William Marsden referred to a related issue two centuries ago when he discussed the extent to which the language was actually referred to as 'Malay', explaining Jawi or 'Bahasa Jawi' was often used instead.[9] In the early eighteenth century, the Dutch scholar, George Hendrik Werndly, wrote of "*bahasa di bawah angin*' (the language of below the wind)", and expressed the view that it was actually 'born' in the "Island of Sumatra".[10]

What about the other key element in the official Malaysian definition of 'Malay': Islam? Time and again the link between the two is made. We are often reminded that to convert to Islam can be described as '*masuk Melayu*', to 'enter Malayness'. In this volume, Collins uses the term 'Malay' to refer to 'Muslims who speak a Borneo Malay variant'. Writing on the eighteenth-century Melaka Straits region, however, Timothy Barnard insists that the Malay identity being adopted in Siak and elsewhere during this period "was not associated with Islam". Religion, he says, "did play a part", but Malayness was based primarily on a "common trading culture" along the Melaka Straits and South China Sea. Further afield, in parts of eastern Indonesia, according to James Fox (quoted here by Reid), there is a real dissociation between 'Malayness' and 'Islam'. In fact, in certain situations to '*masuk Melayu*' can actually mean to become a Christian.

The authors of this volume have not systematically pursued the third element in the official Malaysian definition of 'Malay': the extent to which a person "conforms to Malay custom".[11] Indeed, the dramatic social change that has occurred in Malay societies makes it difficult to identify an essential core of custom to which a person must adhere in order to be considered 'Malay'. In Malaysia, as Virginia Hooker has discussed, the concept of the 'new Malay' (developed in the last decade) implies a revolutionising of Malay world views—a deliberate overturning of many customs, and of long-standing feudalistic and fatalistic behaviour. It suggests the acquisition of a new, aggressive, entrepreneurial and managerial approach, which is quite the reverse of the social manner often associated with Malays in the past.[12] Seeking a continuing core of custom is also difficult because such vital elements in the Malay political heritage as the sultanate (or *kerajaan*) have been radically transformed over a century—redefined in fundamental ways to meet the challenge of modern concepts of government and society.[13]

Turning to Malay literature as a possible component of core culture, the first problem is that it is not the exclusive domain of ethnic Malays. As Sweeney has noted, the Malays of the Peninsula and their British administrators encouraged the "notion of the Malays' possessing sole proprietary rights to all that was written in Malay".[14] In fact, however, this was akin to suggesting that Latin was the "sole prerogative of ethnic Romans".[15] It might even be asked whether what we would today refer to as classical or traditional Malay literature was known as 'Malay' literature at the time it was written. Reid reminds us in this volume that the renowned work the 'Malay Annals' was not in fact called by this name until Thomas Stamford Raffles gave the text its new title. The original name stated in the text itself is the 'Genealogy of the Rajas', and it is certainly a book about *rajas* or *kerajaan*—about kingship—rather than Malay ethnicity. Only in later years was it redefined as the great text of the 'Malay people'.[16]

Whatever name might have been given to traditional Malay literature in contemporary times, it must be asked whether elements of that literature can be employed today in defining Malayness. Some scholars have argued that a 'break' runs so deeply through Malay writing that its current relevance is open to question. The break is at least partly the result of a shift from an oral to a written culture, and has aroused the anxiety (expressed by Muhammad Haji Salleh and Harun Mat Piah in 1983) that there "may soon arise a Malaysian generation that not only is no longer well-acquainted with its traditional literature but that also will continue to reject these works as products of a benighted past that has become useless for them".[17]

In this volume Will Derks presents a counter view of Malay literary development, playing down the idea of a radical discontinuity. In the Riau province of Indonesia he finds that the "oral tradition" is still "alive and kicking" and that the Malay manuscript tradition continues to make "itself felt until this very day". In the provincial capital, Pekanbaru, a modern literary periodical has published passages from such texts as the *Hikayat Hang Tuah* and the Malay Annals, and a mid-nineteenth century poem presented as a short story in prose, with the language updated to reflect modern usage. Derks describes this as "survival in a nutshell", whereby a "work from the past", as he puts it, "is changed into something that can be appreciated and enjoyed today". It is a "continuation of the tradition rather than a deviation from it".

Another instance of the persistence of tradition Derks cites is the manner in which modern Malay poetry—such as the *Syair Nasib Melayu* reproduced in this volume—is performed today. It is recited as poems were recited in the past, and the performance is frequently interrupted by the audience as it would have been long ago. For Derks, "re-adaptation and reinterpretation" in the development of Malay literature in various locations in the Archipelago "may best be thought of as a continuum". Derks's argument, then, suggests that at least for specific Malay communities a particular Malay heritage can give substance to Malay identity.

The Power of *Melayu*

Reviewing the debates about homeland, religion, language and literature can cause frustration in an attempt to pin down Malay ethnicity. Adrian Vickers argues that 'Malay', like 'Javanese', has no essence—particularly a 'national essence'. Some commentators (myself among them) have suggested that Malay ethnicity is a time-bound, socially-constructed phenomenon—a product primarily of the colonial period, when 'race' was introduced as a fundamental, 'scientific' classifactory unit for human-kind. It adds to the liveliness of this volume, however, that this view is challenged here, particularly by Leonard Andaya, who defends the idea of an '"essential" core' that defines the Malay grouping. He argues that a 'Melayu ethnicity was being developed along the Straits of Melaka beginning perhaps as early as the seventh century'.

In Andaya's view, 'Melayu identity' was a powerful concept, and something to be claimed or appropriated. Fifteenth-century Melaka, as he sees it, promoted itself 'as the new centre of the Melayu'. In the seventeenth century, the Malay Annals—which Andaya calls "the story of the Melayu" and a "document that makes Melaka the measure of all things Melayu"— were written to reaffirm the "central position in Melayu" of Johor, the successor state to Melaka. On the other hand, Aceh in north Sumatra announced 'its own claims to Melayu leadership' in the *Hikayat Aceh* (The Story of Aceh); while the Minangkabau "reasserted their claims to Melayu".[18] 'Melayu civilisation' or 'Melayu identity' was in Andaya's analysis clearly something worth fighting over.

Timothy Barnard's essay in this collection also insists on the potency of the concept of Malayness. Following the murder of Sultan Mahmud of Johor in 1699, Barnard suggests that "competing groups strove for ... the right to assume the Malay identity associated with power in the region". Barnard interprets the *Hikayat Siak* as seeking to portray the "ideal of Malay courage and masculinity", and explaining to its listeners/readers "how to become an eighteenth century Malay".[19] Considering Barnard's and Andaya's perspectives, however, it might continue to be asked whether so much emphasis can be placed on Malay identity or Malay civilisation as a driving force, a driving aspiration, in the pre-nineteenth century Archipelago?

With respect to Barnard's observation about the Siak text's educational role, some years ago I suggested that a text from east Sumatra, the *Hikayat Deli*, had the purpose of teaching people (in this case members of the Batak community) how to become Malays. I remain convinced that the text was used as a tool in a process of what we would call cultural or civilisational change, but I am less certain that the new culture would have been described in terms of a specifically Malay ethnicity. The danger of reading modern concerns about ethnicity into an eighteenth and nineteenth century context troubles me. What we can more safely conclude from the evidence, I would now say, is that the Bataks were being inducted into a particular *raja*-centred polity and culture.[20]

In this respect, Jan van der Putten's essay makes an interesting observation about the Bugis, noting that Malay rivalry is often portrayed as a dominant theme in nineteenth-century Riau. This rivalry is said to have had a formative influence on the development of Malay ethnicity, but van der Putten argues that the tension between the two groups did not "seem to have been caused by ethnic distinctions". The real consideration was the "'political incorrectness' of the Bugis pedigree": the Bugis could not "trace their ancestors back to Bukit Siguntang" (that is to say through the Melaka royal line). Such genealogical connections were a "prerequisite to holding a high position in a Malay polity". But again, if the tension itself is not conceptualised in ethnic terms, one might now proceed to ask whether the word 'Malay' deserves to be given such emphasis here. Is it the royal category or 'Melayu' that should be privileged?[21]

Can we then assume that Malayness or Malay identity was such a force in earlier periods, as Andaya and Barnard suggest? Did Johor, Aceh and Minangkabau struggle over 'Melayu' leadership? Did Melaka in its time (the fifteenth century) seek to be 'the measure of all things Melayu'? These are difficult questions to answer. It happens that we have very little contemporary Malay evidence—at least in the sense that the Malay writings which would be critical in providing an answer, whatever their date of composition, mostly survive in nineteenth-century manuscripts. Furthermore, even the texts often seen to be central to the Melaka-Malay tradition (and thought to have been originally composed well before the nineteenth century) cannot be said to be preoccupied with the issue of Malayness. In this respect, recall again that the Malay Annals (nineteenth-century manuscripts, of what is most likely a seventeenth-century text) had no such title before Raffles intervened to try to make it the 'Story of a People',[22] rather than a text about rajas. The contents of the text are by no means the story of a people, or of a specifically Malay civilisation. It should also be noted that the *Hikayat Hang Tuah*, the other Malay language text often presented as encapsulating Melaka-Malay heritage, stresses royalty (and loyalty) rather than Malayness. Its opening sentence announces that it is the "account of Hang Tuah, who was extremely loyal to his lord, and gave devoted service for his lord". The text then proceeds to describe the operations of a "heavenly kingdom".[23] Certainly the *Hikayat Hang Tuah* and the Malay Annals often use the term 'Melayu'—they speak of Malay rajas, Malay people, Malay custom, Malay dress—but this is not to say that Malayness is itself the central or major theme of the texts. In fact, they do not even contain an unambiguous formulation of Malay ethnicity as a phenomenon extending beyond the specific Melaka or Johor sultanate.

Forming a Malay Diaspora?

The absence or presence of Malay ethnicity in these texts deserves attention in the context of the present volume because of the suggestion in Reid's essay that a specifically Malay diaspora began to emerge from the sixteenth century. In contrast to Andaya, Reid insists that in the seventh to thirteenth centuries, although there was mention of a polity called 'Melayu', "Melayu did not establish itself as the name for a people." In Melaka times 'Melayu' had a special association with that state's ruling dynasty, which claimed to have come to the Peninsula from Sumatra. This association is reflected in the early sixteenth century Malay word list in Antonio Pigafetta's account of the Magellan expedition, which only travelled in the eastern Archipelago. In the list 'Cara Melayu' is defined simply as the 'ways of Melaka'.[24]

Reid suggests that after the Portugese conquest of the city in 1511 the "heritage of Melaka went in two directions". The first related to the royal dynasty and its court; the second involved the spread of merchants from Melaka across the Archipelago. These merchants, Reid observes, constituted a "community of wonderfully mixed ethnic origins"—Javanese, Chinese, Gujerati, south Indian and so forth. When dispersed around the Archipelago, Reid proposes they "became simply Malays"—people who would later be conceptualised as a distinct 'race' or 'nation' or 'people', with the help of Raffles and other Europeans.

The tracing of a Malay diaspora back to the traders who left Melaka after the conquest is a provocative thesis possessing wide implications, and will send other historians back to the source materials. As noted earlier in this essay with respect to Makassar, Dutch records certainly use 'Malay' in a very general fashion in the seventeenth and eighteenth centuries, and recent research has made available much new evidence of such usage.[25] But one question that will be asked is to what extent European usage reflected the way 'Malay' was employed among the people of the Archipelago themselves. The European evidence will need to be carefully examined, but it is here that we must also return to Malay writings, such as the *Hikayat Hang Tuah* and the Malay Annals.

With respect to European writings of the period, the National University of Singapore historian, Peter Borschberg, urges caution in interpreting their frequent use of 'Malay'. These European writings are problematic in ways that might be quite critical in the history of Malay ethnicity. To give just one example, a distinction must be made between relatively formal and relatively informal Portuguese and Dutch documents. In more formal documents—relating, for instance, to treaties, legal disputes and hostage taking—great care would have been taken about language, particularly about the precise terminology that was preferred by the 'Malay' principals concerned, and in these formal documents the word 'Malay' was not used. The emphasis was on individual rulers.[26]

Further investigation is required into this topic, but Borschberg's observations do suggest that the generalised European usage of 'Malay' as a convenient code word for those concerned with trade, diplomacy and administration in the region is likely to have gone well beyond the categoratisations used by the people themselves. When Reid observes in the present volume that by the eighteenth century the "category (of 'Malay') had expanded in meaning to embrace all the Malay-speaking Muslims who came to Batavia from Sumatra, Borneo and the Peninsula", the question needs to be asked with even greater urgency: just who employed this category, the Dutch officials in Batavia or the people themselves? Was the Malay commercial diaspora in the Archipelago self-defined, or is it the result of a coding employed for the convenience of busy European administrators?[27] William Marsden's *The History of Sumatra* seems to reflect the latter view, noting that the name 'Malay' was "bestowed by Europeans upon all who resembled them in features and complexion".[28] In another work, Marsden strengthens the impression of European agency when he comments on the rarity of the use of 'Malay' among the people themselves. In all the correspondence he read from 'Malay' states when working in Sumatra at the end of the eighteenth century, he found the writers "very rarely" called themselves 'Malay'.[29]

Turning now to look more closely at Malay literature for evidence of Malay ethnicity in this period, it requires stressing that the number of texts is not large, and particularly that there are very few actual manuscripts dating from before the nineteenth century. Preliminary investigations, however, give little indication of a Malayness detached from the Melaka royal family. Thus Virginia Hooker has noted that in the Malay Annals 'Malay' tends to be used with reference to those people who were "descended from Sumatran-Palembang forebears, and thus were close to the Si Guntang-Melayu Dynasty"[30]—that is the dynasty of the Melaka rulers and of their successors based in Johor. The *Hikayat Hang Tuah* (an eighteenth-century manuscript of a text likely to date from the seventeenth century) certainly uses 'Melayu' frequently but nevertheless stresses that 'all' the *negeri* ('settlements' or 'states') in *Tanah Melayu* (the 'Malay lands') were associated with the Melaka court, at least in the sense of sending tribute to the Melaka rulers.[31] Moving away from Melaka-oriented texts, the *Hikayat Patani* (probably composed in the early eighteenth century) only uses 'Melayu' once, with reference to Johor.[32] The seventeenth-century *Hikayat Aceh* (from north Sumatra) uses 'Melayu' more frequently, but not in reference to Aceh itself or to Deli in east Sumatra, which would certainly have been called 'Malay' in the twentieth century. Exactly which rulers are considered to be 'Malay' in the text is not clear, but there is a suggestion that they tended to be associated with Johor, perhaps at least being located on the west coast of the Peninsula or nearby islands.[33] These texts, then, offer little evidence of the endogenous use of 'Melayu' to describe a people, or a diaspora, spread across the Archipelago. Such a solidarity may well have been coming into being but it was by no means an accomplished fact.

Pre-Ethnicity

Based on these observations, I wonder how useful the concept of Malay ethnicity (or ethnicity itself) is when speaking about the period before the nineteenth century. The term 'ethnicity' clearly troubles a number of authors in this volume, at least to the extent that they seek to qualify their statements about ethnic identity. Thus, when Reid writes of a 'Malay diaspora' in pre-colonial times he states that it was "exceptionally open to new recruits"; van der Putten suggests "Malay society in general, and local communities in particular, seem to have been much more accommodating toward other ethnic groups than common views on identity would allow"; Heather Sutherland explains that in seventeenth- and eighteenth-century Makassar ethnicity was "adjustable" and writes of "problematic" and "blurred" category boundaries. Leonard Andaya has written of 'Melayu' being an "expansive" ethnicity, "because in the past it has tended to absorb many different ethnic groups within its fold".[34] In this volume Adrian Vickers refers to "interactions and types of identity", "shifting identities", "patterns of cultural overlapping" and "alternative models of ethnicity". And, in a recent essay on multiculturalism in Indonesia, Malaysia and Singapore, Robert Hefner describes ethnic solidarities of the pre-modern period as "permeable" or "flexible".[35] Surveying all these observations, however, the question one might ask is whether it is misleading to assume the presence in the region in pre-modern times even of a qualified ethnicity.

What type of solidarities and identities, then, did operate in the region at this time, and how did Malay ethnicity develop? Regarding the first question, William Marsden—who had remarked that 'Malay' letter writers seldom called themselves 'Malay' in the late eighteenth century—observed that Malays did "familiarly employ the phrase of *orang debawah angin* 'the people beneath the wind'".[36] He suggests, however, that this phrase referred to Javanese, Acehnese, Bugis and many other groups as well as Malays (or the people who would eventually adopt the name 'Malay').

Religious patterns are also evident. Malay literary texts demonstrate a degree of familiarity with the Middle East and Central Asia—particularly in the frequent references to Rum or the Ottoman Empire. Popular Arab literary works, as is well known, were also adapted into Malay, and the Southeast Asian rulers appropriated titles from the Persian and Arab worlds.[37] Membership of a more restricted Islamic community was represented by the term 'Jawi'. In this volume, Reid mentions that João de Barros employed the word in the sixteenth century to refer to people living on the coast of Sumatra (who were likely later to have been called 'Malay'); the *Hikayat Patani* writes of a certain Haji Yunus as a 'Jawi from Patani' (although the translation of the text gives the meaning as 'a Malay from Patani').[38] Like 'people beneath the wind', however, 'Jawi' possesses a semantic range that geographically extends well beyond the community that would later be distinguished as 'Malay'. In the late eighteenth century, C. Snouck Hurgronje, after visiting Mekka where the term was often employed, said that under the name 'Jawah' were "all the people of the Malay race in the fullest meaning of the term ... the geographical boundary is perhaps from Siam and Melaka to New Guinea". It even included non-Muslims from the region, but he reported these were "all slaves".[39]

Malay writings that appear to derive from the pre-nineteenth century are suggestive about the types of community that operated at that time in the Archipelago. With the help of Ian Proudfoot's Malay Concordance Project (based at the Australian National University),[40] we can see that people were identified, for instance, as *orang Johor*, *orang Patani* or *orang Sarapat*—all references to toponyms but, as the last one indicates, not all of these toponyms were places of substance or the location of a raja.[41] Nor is it clear that each toponym was a *negeri*, defined as "settlement; city-state" and sometimes "used loosely of any settlement, town or land".[42] '*Negeri*' is a word often encountered, but does not necessarily imply a distinct, separate community. It was possible for a *negeri* to be quite small (for instance, *negeri Tioman*),[43] or to be subordinate to or contained within another *negeri*. It is not clear that every *negeri* had a raja; and some rajas seem to have had many *negeri*. One thing that does appear certain about '*negeri*' is that they had to have people; the expression '*isi negeri*' (the 'contents of the *negeri*') refers to the people living in it. I have seen no suggestion, however, that in pre-modern times the *negeri* was expected to be a focus of allegiance or loyalty for these people. *Negeri* seems not to have been an emotive word; it was rather a more prosaic, matter-of-fact description of a settlement of people. Loyal declarations of allegiance in this period tend to have been made to a raja.

The community or solidarity, in fact, that I have given most attention in my own writing on the pre-modern Archipelago is the kingdom or the sultanate—the *kerajaan*.[44] "I am the subject of the Raja of Lingga"[45] was the answer given when British officials interviewed certain 'Malays' regarding piracy in the early nineteenth century, and in this answer we see a reflection of the term '*rakyat*', used so often in the Malay Annals and other Malay texts. '*Rakyat*' were 'subjects'. Often they are explicitly described as subjects of a particular raja or sultan, and my impression is that until modern times it is always implied that to be a 'subject' was necessarily to be the subject of a particular ruler. With the development of the territorially-defined, bureaucratic state in the nineteenth and twentieth centuries, there was a shift in loyalty from ruler to state, and then we do have the notion of the 'subject' of a state rather than a raja.[46]

Another reason I would propose for seeing the institution of monarchy as pivotal in the social architecture of the pre-modern archipelago is the degree of structural definition it offered. The hierarchical relationships of the *kerajaan* are enunciated in Malay writing, and both Malay and European sources indicate that they were enforced in detail by sumptuary laws, and by what today might be seen as a religiously based understanding of the relationship between ruler and subject.[47] The structure of ranks and titles in the *kerajaan* polity, together with the hierarchy of privileges and duties, are a reminder of the need to beware of characterising the Archipelago in terms of shifting, mobile, blurred community identification. There may not have been strongly defined ethnicities giving structure to social relations, or the type of distinct territorial borders that mark out the nation states of the region today, but the *kerajaan* nevertheless provided the definition for a community—comprised of royal subjects.

A History of Malayness

Although it is not the purpose of this volume to attempt a reconstruction of pre-ethnicity social architecture in the Archipelago—to do so would certainly require in addition an analysis of kin and what Barbara Andaya has termed "imagined kin relations"[48]—some of the essays have raised questions about the pattern of solidarities that would have operated in the absence of the structure of ethnicities of the type we encounter today. It is within this context, of course, that Malay ethnicity developed in the region. Exactly how it emerged and took shape is a question that often comes to mind when reading these essays. In thinking about the agenda for a history of Malay ethnicity, a preliminary issue is just what were the conditions of possibility for this development? The conditions commence, one might assume, with the spread of Malay-language use in the Archipelago (noting Collins's insistence on a Borneo starting point), and go on to include a successful, prestigious, Sumatran-based empire associated with the name 'Melayu'. Andaya points to the location of Melayu in the Jambi region in Sumatra, and E. Edwards McKinnon has called the Muara Jambi region "the most extensive and probably the most important archaeological site in Sumatra".[49] As is well known, the Malay Annals link the dynasty that came to rule in Melaka (and later, Johor) with another Melayu river, located near Palembang—a region where inscriptions have been found in the Old Malay language, suggesting the presence of a kingdom in the seventh century. Was it perhaps the case that the earliest *orang* Melayu were called '*orang* Melayu' because of their association with a Melayu River settlement, just as people in other areas were called '*orang* Patani' or '*orang* Sarapat'?

If the Palembang and Jambi polities were in fact focused on the ruler and dynasty, and not on a territorially-defined state, this must have helped to make possible the concept of a mobile political entity, one able to transcend specific geographic locations. At a relatively early period this polity also appears to have developed a culture capable of being transported, or transferred. Malay writings certainly suggest (as we have already noted) the presence of a specifically 'Malay' civilisation (Malay custom, Malay dress, Malay music) in the supposed successor state of Melaka. The direction and manner in which the civilisation spread is suggested by the fact that in the early sixteenth century Portuguese observation continued to associate the word 'Malay' with Palembang, Jambi and other nearby areas in east Sumatra, as well as with Melaka.[50] Does this reflect the memory or trace of a Malay civilisation left behind in east Sumatra? In later years the east Sumatran association tended not to be mentioned—though, as we have seen, 'Malay' eventually began to be applied to people all over the archipelago including in east Sumatra.

What promoted the later diffusion of Malay civilisation and, eventually, Malayness? Just how far was Malayness encouraged by the way

Europeans (and Chinese) increasingly used the term 'Melayu' to refer to people right across the Archipelago? We have noted Marsden's comment that Europeans "bestowed" the name on many people, and he also observed that the word 'Malay' had begun to be used more widely by the people themselves. In the first edition of his *History of Sumatra*, which was originally published in 1783, Marsden stated that although 'Malay' had 'originally and strictly' been used with reference to the inhabitants of the Peninsula, it was "now understood to mean a Mussulman, speaking the Malay language and belonging by descent at least to the kingdom of Menangkabau or to that part of the coast bordering on it".[51] Any analysis of the spread of 'Melayu' must take account of the agency of the 'Malay' people. The diffusion of 'Malayness' certainly required de-linking the concept of Malay civilisation from the Melaka/Johor monarchy, and this, one imagines, entailed challenging long-established thinking. The way Malays in Melaka/Johor might have pondered the change is suggested in an anecdote in the *Hikayat Hang Tuah*, referred to in this book by Timothy Barnard. When the warrior, Hang Tuah, goes to Inderapura (in Sumatra) he is told that the people of the place are only 'hybrid' (*kacukan*) and not 'real' (*sungguh*) Malays, and that the 'real Malays' were in Melaka. He replies that the Melaka people are themselves 'hybrid Malays', because they are 'mixed with the Javanese of Majapahit'. Later, one of the leadership group of Inderapura refers to "playing relatives" with Hang Tuah.[52] The suggestion of a Malayness that is not 'real' (even in Melaka), and a relationship that is not kin-based, but "playing" at being kin-based, hints at a level of tentativeness regarding the developing concept of 'Malay'—the sort of uncertainty that is likely to occur in a period of transition. In discussing the detaching of 'Malayness' from the Melaka context, it also points to the way Malayness was being conceptualised to make it a civilisation (and eventually an ethnicity).

Apart from experiments in conceptualising Malayness, another condition of possibility for Malay ethnicity is suggested in the evidence, at least from the western Archipelago, of the actual development of a degree of cultural homogeneity among the polities of the region. We see similarities between a number of separate monarchies before we find evidence of the use of 'Malay' or any other name to describe such a civilisation. Thus, Ma Huan's account of the region, arising from the early fifteenth-century Zheng He (Cheng Ho) expedition, is revealing in the way it notes the similarity (in speech, writing, marriages, funerals and dress) between Melaka, Aru and Semudra (the latter two being in Sumatra), and observes also the differences between these communities and Siam and Champa. He sees

Java as 'somewhat' similar to Melaka; the "speech of the people in (Melaka) and their writings, and marriage rites are somewhat the same as (Java)".[53] The fact that Aru and Semudra (neither of which were subordinate to Melaka) are identified as sharing cultural features with Melaka—features that are not shared across all the 'lands beneath the winds'—demands recognition in a history of Malayness. In later periods this type of cultural similarity was often noted: "the dresses of all Malays are so much alike in almost all countries",[54] said a British official in the early nineteenth century; and another of the same period noted that 'a description of the town and its inhabitants' in the east Peninsular state of Trengganu could "answer equally well for all the independent Malay states on the Peninsula".[55] By the nineteenth century, however, all these situations tended to be termed 'Malay'; in the fifteenth century the existence of the commonalities of customs and dress merely seems to us today, and perhaps seemed also to contemporary European (and Chinese) observers, to have announced the need for a new classifactory term.

A decisive step in the constituting of Malay ethnicity seems to have taken place at the opening of the nineteenth century, as the European colonial powers were beginning to consolidate their rule in the 'Malay' regions. It is at this time, as noted above, that Governor Raffles was changing the name of the Malay Annals to highlight the Malay people rather than a royal genealogy; and it was the period also in which Europeans, influenced by the scientific thinking about race as a key classification in the analysis of humankind, began to speak and write of the 'Malay people' and the 'Malay race'. The extraordinary writer/translator and teacher, Munshi Abdullah, was much influenced by this new European thinking and went on himself to write about the Malay race (*bangsa Melayu*), and focus his works on its plight and its future rather than the successes and struggles of rajas.[56] In the same tradition, Tenas Effendy's 'rhymed chronicle', published here in English translation, records what it describes as the 'fate of the Malays', commencing even before the Melaka period and focusing on the challenges that 'the Malays' face today.

In the present volume Shamsul in particular stresses the relative modernity and colonial context of Malay ethnicity. He highlights the significance of what he calls 'colonial knowledge', including the colonial development of the field of 'Malay studies'. He notes as well the colonial legislation known as the Malay Reservation Enactment, introduced in 1913. This Enactment, he explains, defined who was a 'Malay', and then 'determined the legal category of people who were allowed to grow rice only or rubber only'. The colonial education system was a further area,

Shamsul explains, in which the colonial government "directed the people's perception of how social reality was organised". With the creation of Malay, Chinese and other schools "ethnic boundaries became real". Such a stress on the nineteenth-and twentieth-century colonial context has been a feature of my own work on the Malays, and I have been especially indebted to Charles Hirschman's analysis of the way race was used by the British in population censuses, and how this importation of a western racial category by the British helped to create the "racial ideology (which) continues to haunt contemporary Malaysia".[57]

In the Dutch East Indies, as Henk Maier has explained, a similar process was underway: "through authoritative words and actions, ethnic or racial diversions were gradually substituted for caste distinctions, and the heterogeneous Dutch Indies society turned into a society organised along lines of race."[58] In the case of the Malays, both Malay custom (*adat*) and language were standardised as never before—standardised on the basis of what was considered the Malay heartland around the Straits of Melaka.[59]

An Agenda

The development of Malay ethnicity would by no means stop with the introduction by the colonial regimes of the concept of 'race'. A history of the subject would make use of the available analysis, located in this volume and elsewhere, to examine the local ideological work and local ideological contests that took place after the concept of *bangsa Melayu* had been appropriated. The topics that would need to be covered in such a history include the following:

- How the Malay *bangsa* or 'race' was invested with emotive power.
- What changes occurred in its relation to the *kerajaan* as a focus of loyalty (the character of the competition between the two and, later, the way in which some proponents of the *bangsa* drew upon ideological elements from the *kerajaan*). The changing relationship with Islam (including the continuing contest over whether the *Bangsa Melayu* would have priority over the *umat* Islam or vice versa).[60]
- How Dutch and British formulations of 'Malay' differed, and how those differences influenced post-colonial practice.
- Following the latter, what variations exist in the geographic scope of Malayness? In particular, would 'Melayu' incorporate people from right across the Archipelago—as some European (especially Dutch) colonial writers had proposed—or merely the Malays of the

Malay Peninsula and certain regions in Kalimantan, Sumatra and
the Riau Archipelago (as the British tended to urge from the
nineteenth century).

- How 'Malays' were given certain racial characteristics by European
  writers: Frank Swettenham, for instance, in a widely read book
  referred to 'Real Malays' as loyal, disinclined to work, sensitive,
  conservative, and companionable;[61] Dutch administrators attempted,
  as already noted, to make the Malay language and customs of Johor
  and Riau the standard.
- The way Dutch and British colonial regimes created an ideological
  as well as geographic divide in the Archipelago (for instance, in their
  different treatment of the local rulers and to some extent of Islam).
- The reach of 'Melayu' in terms of descent—for instance, whether,
  when, and in what circumstances people of largely Indian, Arab,
  Chinese or Thai descent were considered 'Melayu'.[62]
- The differing impact of the independent states—Malaysia (West and
  East), Indonesia, Brunei, Thailand and others (on the development
  of Malay ethnicity). In Indonesia, as Sukarno once explained at
  Medan airport (in one of Indonesia's historic 'Malay' regions), "there
  is only one nation, Indonesia, and one *bangsa* Indonesia".[63] Groups
  such as the Malays are demoted to being '*suku bangsa*' ('ethnic'
  groups). In Malaysia there has also been a challenge to the idea of
  bangsa as 'race'. Over the last decade or so, as Virginia Hooker
  explains above, the use of the phrase '*Bangsa* Malaysia' by the
  Mahathir government suggests '*bangsa*' is assuming the meaning of
  'nation' rather than 'race'. Is this a recognition of the comparative
  potency of '*bangsa*' as a concept (and the lack of potency of *negara*,
  'state' or 'country')? More important for the research topic I am
  discussing here, what impact will the new use of '*bangsa* Malaysia'
  have on the conceptualising of the *bangsa* Melayu?[64] In Malaysia,
  for instance, the Government promoted seemingly feudal values in
  developing Malay ethnic consciousness,[65] and then fostered
  entrepreneurial anti-feudal values in the making of what was termed
  the 'new Malay' (mentioned above).
- The issues that have arisen in promoting an international Malay
  diaspora, reaching across to Sri Lanka and South Africa—an
  endeavour fostered by the Malaysian leadership and yet entailing
  a definition of 'Melayu' that extends enormously the more common
  understandings (including official understanding) in Malaysia
  itself.[66]

These are the types of questions around which a history of Malay ethnicity might be structured. Many of them arise from analysis in this book, and it is an achievement that these essays not only enrich our knowledge of Malay community and identity but also help to establish the case and the agenda for future research.

Notes

Preface

* Timothy P. Barnard is an Assistant Professor of History at the National University of Singapore. His research focuses on the history and culture of the Melaka Straits region. E-mail correspondence can be directed to histpb@nus.edu.sg.
  Hendrik M.J. Maier is a Professor of Southeast Asian Studies at the University of California, Riverside. His main area of research is Malay literature and the influence of British and Dutch colonialism on our understandings of Malay society. E–mail correspondence can be directed to hmjmaier@hotmail.com.
1. *Review of Indonesian and Malaysian Affairs*, 34, 2 (2000): 1–27.
2. Tenas Effendy, *Tunjuk ajar Melayu (butir-butir budaya Melayu Riau)* (Pekanbaru: Dewan Kesenian Riau, 1994).

Chapter 1

* Anthony Reid is the Director of the Asia Research Institute at the National University of Singapore. He is currently completing a number of projects on the pre-colonial history of Southeast Asia, notably a broad economic history of the region. His interests concern the shaping of identities in modern Indonesia and Malaysia, and the way these have interacted historically with nationalism. E-mail correspondence can be directed to aridir@nus.edu.sg.
1. The first version of this paper was presented at the 15th Conference of the International Association of Historians of Asia, held in Jakarta in August 1998. It is an evolving think-piece, and the author would welcome comments.
2. Benedict Anderson, *Imagined Communities: Reflections on the Origin and Spread of Nationalism* (London: Verso 1983; new edition 1991); John A. Armstrong, *Nations Before Nationalism* (Chapel Hill: University of North Carolina Press, 1982); Ernest Gellner, *Nations and Nationalism* (Oxford: Blackwell, 1983); Anthony D. Smith, *The Ethnic Origins of Nations* (Oxford: Blackwell, 1986); Liah

Greenfeld, *Nationalism. Five Roads to Modernity* (Cambridge: Harvard University Press, 1992).

3. Hans Kohn, *The Idea of Nationalism: A Study in Its Origin and Background* (New York: Macmillan, 1944), pp. 572–73.

4. Smith, *Ethnic Origins of Nations*, pp. 134–40.

5. Greenfeld, *Nationalism*, p. 11.

6. Smith, *The Ethnic Origins of Nations*, p. 212.

7. For more information on the origins of *Melayu*, see Leonard Andaya's article in this volume.

8. Henry Yule and A. C. Burnell, *Hobson-Jobson* (New Delhi: Munshiram Manoharlal, 1979), pp. 545–46.

9. Pigeaud translates "Malayu" of Canto 13 of the *Nagarakertagama* as "country of Malayu" or Sumatra; and Robson as "the Malay Lands"; Th.G. Th. Pigeaud, *Java in the Fourteenth Century* (The Hague: 1960–62), III: 16; Stuart Robson, trans., *Desawarnana (Nagarakrtagama)* (Leiden: KITLV Press, 1995), p. 33.

10. *The Junk Trade from Southeast Asia: Translations from the Tosen Fusetsu-gaki, 1674–1723*, ed. Yoneo Ishii (Singapore: ISEAS/ ECHOSEA, 1998), e.g. pp. 63, 103, 118, 119, 121, 123, 124, 133, 146, 255, 259–61.

11. Wang Gungwu, "The Melayu in *Hai-kuo wen-chien lu*", in *Community and Nation*, ed. Wang Gungwu (Singapore: Heinemann for ASAA), pp. 108–17.

12. Virginia Matheson, "Concepts of Malay Ethos in Indigenous Writing", *Journal of Southeast Asian Studies*, 10, 2 (1979): 351–71.

13. R. O. Winstedt, "The Malay Annals or Sejarah Melayu", *Journal of the Malayan Branch of the Royal Asiatic Society*, 16, 3 (1938): 108, 117–18.

14. Ibid., p. 192.

15. *Hikayat Hang Tuah*, ed. Kassim Ahmad (Kuala Lumpur: Dewan Bahasa dan Pustaka, 1971), p. 175.

16. *The Travels of Ludovico di Varthema in Egypt, Syria, Arabai Deserta and Arabia Felix, A.D. 1503 to 1508*, trans. J. W. Jones (London: Hakluyt Society, 1863), p. 226. Also Anthony Reid, *Charting the Shape of Early Modern Southeast Asia* (Chiang Mai: Silkworm, 1999), pp. 73–76.

17. *The Suma Oriental of Tomé Pires*, trans. Armando Cortesão (London: Hakluyt Society, 1944), p. 265.

18. "*Hamzah Sharnawi zahirnya Jawi; Batinnya cahaya Ahmad yang safi*"—"Hamzah of Shahrnawi [Ayutthaya], outwardly Jawi [or perhaps, of Jawi birth]; inwardly the pure light of Ahmad", in *The Poems of Hamzah Fansuri*, ed. G. W. J. Drewes and L. F. Brakel (Dordrecht: Foris, 1986), p. 7.

19. João de Barros, *Da Asia* (Lisbon: Regia Officina, 1777; reprinted Lisbon, 1973), II, 9, p. 352. Though Raffles appeared unaware of Barros' interpretation of *Jawi*, he also understood it as "the Malay term for anything mixed or crossed; as when the language of one country is written in the character of another, it is termed b'hasa jahui [*bahasa jawi*] , or mixed language; or when a child is born of a Kiling father and Malay mother, it is called 'anah jahui' [*anak jawi*], a child of mixed race". Raffles' view at this early stage (1809) was that the Malays emerged from the encounter with Islam, like the Mapillas of Malabar or the Chulias of Coromandel. Like them the Malays were "gradually formed as nations, and separated from their original stock by the admixture of Arabian blood, and the introduction of the Arabic language and Moslem religion" (Sophia Raffles, *Memoir of the Life and Public Services of Sir Thomas Stamford Raffles: Particularly in the Government of Java, 1811–1816, Bencoolen and its Dependencies, 1817–1824* [London: Duncan, 1835], I, pp. 40–41). George Henrik Werndly described *bahasa jawi* in the eighteenth century as the high literary Malay written in Arabic script, and R. Roolvink, *Bahasa Jawi: De Taal van Sumatra* (Leiden: Universitaire Pers, 1975), as the common name for Sumatra-derived Malay. On Werndly see Amin Sweeney, *A Full Hearing: Orality and Literacy in the Malay World* (Berkeley: University of California Press, 1987), pp. 50–59.

20. J. N. Miksic, "Archeology, Trade and Society in Northeast Sumatra" (Ph.D. diss., Cornell University, 1979).

21. *Ming Shi-lu*, as cited in Geoffrey Wade, "The *Ming Shi–lu* (Veritable Record of the Ming Dynasty) as a Source for Southeast Asian History: Fourteenth to Seventeenth Centuries" (Ph.D. diss., University of Hong Kong, 1994), vol. II, pp. 247–48.

22. Anthony Reid, "Introduction", *Sojourners and Settlers: Histories of Southeast Asia and the Chinese*, ed. Anthony Reid (Sydney: Allen and Unwin, 1996), pp. 21–37; Reid, *Charting the Shape*, pp. 72–76.

23. *First Voyage Round the World*, trans. J. A. Robertson (Manila: Filipiniana Book Guild, 1969), p. 88.

24. Anthony Reid, in *Southeast Asia in the Age of Commerce, c. 1450–1680, II: Expansion and Crisis* (New Haven: Yale University Press, 1993), p. 128.

25. Bima chronicle cited in Helius Syamsuddin, "The Coming of Islam and the Role of Malays as Middlemen on Bima", in *Papers of the Dutch-Indonesian Historical Conference*, ed. G. J. Schutte and Heather Sutherland (Leiden: Bureau of Indonesian Studies, 1982), pp. 296–97.

26. C. Skinner, *Sja'ir Perang Mengkasar (The Rhymed Chronicle of the Macassar War) by Entji' Amin* (The Hague: Martinus Nijhoff, 1963), pp. 19–20.

27. Remco Raben, "Batavia and Colombo. The Ethnic and Spatial Order of Two Colonial Cities, 1600–1800" (Ph.D. diss., Leiden University, 1996), pp. 207–10.

28. Ibid., Appendix.

29. Ibid., p. 97.

30. Gerrit Knaap and Luc Nagtegal, "A Forgotten Trade: Salt in Southeast Asia, 1670–1813", in *Emporia, Commodities and Entrepreneurs in Asian Maritime Trade, c.1400–1750*, ed. Roderich Ptak and Dietmar Rothermund (Stuttgart: Franz Steiner, 1991), p. 140.

31. Gerrit Knaap, *Shallow Waters, Rising Tide. Shipping and Trade in Java around 1775* (Leiden: KITLV Press, 1996), pp. 66–77.

32. Anthony Reid and Radin Fernando, "Shipping on Melaka and Singapore as an Index of Growth, 1760–1840", *South Asian Studies*, 19 (1996): 64–75.

33. Ibid., pp. 70–72.

34. William Marsden, *The History of Sumatra* (Kuala Lumpur: Oxford University Press, 1966), p.40. The taxonomy of Marsden and other Enlightenment writers has been well made by Mary Quilty, *Textual Empires: A Reading of Early British Histories of Southeast Asia* (Clayton: Monash Asia Institute, Monash University, 1998).

35. Marsden, *The History of Sumatra*, pp. 40–41.

36. William Marsden, *A Dictionary and Grammar of the Malayan Language* (London: Longman, 1812), vol. II, p. ix.

37. Thomas Raffles, "On the Maláyu Nation, with a Translation of its Maritime Institutions", *Asiatic Researches*, 12 (1818): 103. The early version of the introduction to this paper is reproduced in Sophia Raffles, *Memoir of the Life,* vol. I, pp. 28–49, where it is placed in its 1809 context, when first submitted to the Asiatic Society by a young man of 27.

38. An extraordinary vision of a British-guided Javanese people spreading out to colonise much of eastern Asia and Australia, is offered in Raffles' *History of Java* (London: John Murray, 1817), vol. I, pp. 71–72.

39. Sophia Raffles, *Memoir of the Life*, vol. I, pp. 426, 433.

40. Winstedt, "The Malay Annals or Sejarah Melayu", p. 42.

41. *Malay Annals: translated from the Malay Language by the Late Dr John Leyden*. with an introduction by Sir Thomas Stamford Raffles, FRS (London: Longman, 1821), p. v.

42. Marsden, *History of Sumatra*, p. 326.

43. Alexander Hamilton, *A New Account of the East Indies*, ed. William Foster (London: Argonaut Press, 1930), vol. II, p. 41. François Valentijn, writing at a similar period, also referred to the west coast of the peninsula as the 'Malay coast', and appeared to see this as the heartland of 'true Malays' (Sweeney, *A Full Hearing*, p. 59).

44. P. J. Begbie, *The Malayan Peninsula* (Madras: Vepery Mission Press, 1834; reprinted Kuala Lumpur: Oxford University Press, 1967).

45. Matheson, "Concepts of Malay Ethos in Indigenous Writing", p.361.

46. Marsden, *History of Sumatra*, p. 327; John Crawfurd, *History of the Indian Archipelago* (Edinburgh: Archibald, 1820), vol. II, pp. 371–73.

47. Ibid., p. 376.

48. Raja Ali Haji, *The Precious Gift: Tuhfat al-Nafis*, trans. Virginia Matheson and Barbara Watson Andaya (Kuala Lumpur: Oxford University Press); compare, e.g., pp. 12–17 with pp. 101–3.

49. Anthony Milner, *The Invention of Politics in Colonial Malaya: Contesting Nationalism and the Expansion of the Public Sphere* (Cambridge: Cambridge University Press, 1995), p. 51.

50. In this it followed by a half-century the *Selompret Melajoe* of Semarang (1860), which sustained the third of my nineteenth-century meanings of Malayness, below—see Ahmat Adam, *The Vernacular Press and the Emergence of Modern Indonesian Consciousness (1855–1913)* (Ithaca: Cornell University Southeast Asia Program, 1995), pp. 23–57.

51. I owe this information to James Fox, who was referring particularly to Roti and other islands of contemporary Nusa Tenggara Tengah (eastern Indonesia).

52. Hugh Clifford, *Saleh, a Prince of Malaya* (New York: Harper and Brothers, 1926).

53. Quoted in Ariffin Omar, *Bangsa Melayu: Aspects of Democracy and Community among the Malays* (Kuala Lumpur: Oxford University Press, 1993), p. 5.

54. Malayan Federal Council 1920, quoted in William Roff, *The Origins of Malay Nationalism* (Kuala Lumpur: University of Malaya Press, 1967), pp. 138–39; see also Shamsul A.B.'s essay in this volume.

55. Ibid., pp. 121–25.

56. High commissioner for FMS in Federal Council 1919, quoted in ibid., p. 138.

57. Wilkinson was mainly responsible for founding in 1900 the Malay College in Melaka to train teachers for the vernacular government primary schools, and was later inspector of Malay Schools (1903–06). He personally encouraged the study of Malay literature by the students. Khoo Kay Kim, "Local Historians and the Writing of Malaysian History in the Twentieth Century", in *Perceptions of the Past in Southeast Asia*, ed. Anthony Reid and David Marr (Singapore: Heinemann, 1979), p. 302. Roff, *Origins of Malay Nationalism*, pp. 28n. and 135, notes that teaching in the Malay schools was often done almost entirely from *Sejarah Melayu*, *Hikayat Abdullah* and the newspaper *Utusan Melayu*.

58. R.J. Wilkinson, *Malay Literature, Part I: Romance, History, Poetry* (Kuala Lumpur: Government of Federated Malay States, 1907), quoted in Hendrik M.J. Maier, *In the Center of Authority* (Ithaca: Cornell University Southeast Asia Program, 1988), p. 119.

59. Ibid., p. 119.

60. R.O. Winstedt and Daing Abdul Hamid bin Tengku Muhammad Salleh, *Kitab Tawarikh Melayu* (Singapore, 1918). This was followed by a more ambitious three-volume book along similar lines: Abdul Hadi bin Haji Hasan, *Sejarah Alam Melayu* (Singapore: Education Department, 1925–30). This early development of a 'national' history of the ethnie contrasts markedly with Indonesia, where no national history in the national language appeared until 1938. Anthony Reid, "The Nationalist Quest for an Indonesian Past", in *Perceptions of the Past*, ed. Reid and Marr, p. 281.

61. Charles Hirschman, "The Meaning and Measurement of Ethnicity in Malaysia", *Journal of Asian Studies*, 46, 3 (1987): 561.

62. C.A. Vlieland, *British Malaya: A Report on the 1931 Census and Certain Problems of Vital Statistics* (London: Crown Agents for the Colonies, 1932), quoted in ibid., p. 565.

63. Milner, *Invention of Politics*, p. 269.

64. Ariffin, *Bangsa Melayu*, p. 18.

65. Ibid., pp. 16–18; Roff, *Origins of Malay Nationalism*, pp. 244–45; Judith Nagata, "In Defence of Ethnic Boundaries: The Changing Myths and Charters of Malay Identity", in *Ethnic Change*, ed. Charles Keyes (Seattle: University of Washington Press, 1981), pp. 87–116.

66. Ariffin, *Bangsa Melayu*, pp. 198–99.

67. Quoted in ibid., p. 107.

68. Cited in ibid., p. 109.

69. Mahathir bin Mohamad, *The Malay Dilemma* (Singapore: Donald Moore, 1970), p. 122.

70. Ibid., pp. 122–26.

71. Raben, "Batavia and Colombo", pp. 242–43.

72. Ahmat Adam, *The Vernacular Press*.

73. Deliar Noer, "Yamin and Hamka: Two routes to an Indonesian Identity", in *Perceptions of the Past*, pp. 249–53; Reid, "Nationalist Quest for an Indonesian Past", ed. Reid and Marr, pp. 286–87.

74. Quoted in Ariffin, *Bangsa Melayu*, p. 209.

75. Negeri Brunei, *Laporan Banchi Pendudok Brunei 1971* (Bandar Seri Begawan: Star Press, 1972), p. 82.

76. Ibid., p. 34.

77. Ibid., p. 5.

78. Pehin Orang Kaya Laila Wijaya Dato Haji Abdul Aziz Umar, "Melayu Islam Beraja Sebagai Falsafah Negara Brunei Darussalam", in *Sumbangsih*, ed. Dato Seri Laila Jasa Awang Haji Abu Bakar bin

Haji Apong (Gadong: Akademi Pengajian Brunei, 1992), p. 10 (my translation).

79. Haji Hashim Abd. Hamid, "Konsep Melayu Islam Beraja: Antar Ideologi dan Pembinaan Bangsa", in ibid., p. 27 (my translation).

Chapter 2

Author's Note: I would like to thank Mark Hobart for his comments on this paper. Mark, as well as Peter Carey, Henk Maier, Clive Kessler, and Gijs Koster, have also provided various ideas, sources, and comments that I have appropriated in different ways over the years.

*   Adrian Vickers is an Associate Professor in the History and Politics Program at the University of Wollongong. His research interests are Balinese history and culture with special reference to pre-colonial cultural history, the role of modernity in present-day culture, and the history of tourism. E-mail correspondence can be directed to Adrian_Vickers@uow.edu.au.

1.   Amin Sweeney, *Reputations Live On. An Early Malay Autobiography* (Berkeley: University of California Press, 1980), p. 52.

2.   Ibid.

3.   Ronald Inden, *Imagining India* (Malden, MA: Blackwell Publishers, 1990; reprinted London: C. Hurst, and Bloomington: University of Indiana, 2000), p. 20.

4.   R. J. C. Young, *Colonial Desire: Hybridity in Theory, Culture and Race* (London: Routledge, 1995).

5.   Clive Kessler, "Archaism and Modernity: Contemporary Malay Political Culture", in *Fragmented Vision. Culture and Politics in Contemporary Malaysia*, ed. Joel S. Kahn and F. Loh Kok Wah, Asian Studies Association of Australia Southeast Asia Publications 22 (Sydney: Allen and Unwin, 1992), pp. 133–57.

6.   Francis Loh Kok Wah, "Modernisation, Cultural Revival and Counter Hegemony: The Kadazans of Sabah in the 1980s", in *Fragmented Vision: Culture and Politics in Contemporary Malaysia*, ed. Kahn and Loh, pp. 225–53.

7.   Heather Sutherland, *The Making of a Bureaucratic Elite* (Singapore: Heinemann Educational Books (Asia), 1979).

8.   Onghokham, "The Inscrutable and the Paranoid: An Investigation into the Sources of the Brotodiningrat Affair", in *Southeast Asian Transitions: Approaches through Social History*, ed. Ruth T. McVey (New Haven: Yale University Press, 1978), pp. 112–57.

9.   Donald M. Nonini, *British Colonial Rule and the Resistance of the Malay Peasantry 1900–1957* (New Haven: Yale University Southeast Asia Studies, Yale Center for International and Area Studies, 1992).

10. Eric Hobsbawm and Terrence Ranger, eds. *The Invention of Tradition*. Cambridge: Cambridge University Press, 1983. See also Kessler, "Archaism and Modernity".

11. Benedict Anderson, *Imagined Communities: Reflections on the Origins and Spread of Nationalism* (London: Verso, 1983).

12. John Pemberton, *On the Subject of "Java"* (Ithaca: Cornell University Press, 1994).

13. Jennifer Lindsay, *Klasik, Kitsch Kontemporer Sebuah Studi tentang Seni Pertunjukan Jawa* (Yogyakarta: Gajah Mada University Press, 1991).

14. S. Supomo, "The Image of Majapahit in Later Javanese and Indonesian Writing", in *Perceptions of the Past in South Fast Asia*, ed. Anthony Reid and David Marr (Singapore: Heinemann Educational Books Asia, 1979), pp. 171–85.

15. Pemberton, *On the Subject of Java*, pp. 152–160.

16. Merle C. Ricklefs, *War, Culture and Economy in Java, 1677–1726: Asian and European Imperialism in the Early Kartasura Period*. Asian Studies Association of Australia Southeast Asia Publications 24 (Sydney: Allen and Unwin, 1993), p. 225.

17. P. Norindr, *Phantasmatic Indochina: French Colonial Ideology in Architecture, Film, and Literature* (Durham and London: Duke University Press, 1996); Thongchai Winichakul, *Siam Mapped: A History of the Geo-Body of a Nation* (Honolulu: University of Hawaii Press, 1994).

18. D. Chakrabarty, "The Difference-Deferral of a Colonial Modernity: Public Debates on Domesticity in British Bengal", in *Tensions of Empire: Colonial Cultures in a Bourgeois World,* ed. F. Cooper and A. L. Stoler (Berkeley: University of California Press, 1997), pp. 373–405.

19. Ibid., p. 400.

20. See Ann L. Stoler, "Sexual Affronts and Racial Frontiers: European Identities and the Cultural Politics of Exclusion in Colonial Southeast Asia", in *Tensions of Empire*, ed. Cooper and Stoler, pp. 198–237.

21. See *Tensions of Empire*, ed. Cooper and Stoler.

22. Chakrabarty, "The Difference-Deferral of a Colonial Modernity", p. 400.

23. The most astonishing exemplification of the micro-techniques of power in the Indies is Onghokham's study of the Brotodiningrat Affair.

24. Sumarsam. *Gamelan. Cultural Interaction and Musical Development in Central Java* (Chicago and London: University of Chicago Press, 1995), p. 100.

25. Anthony Milner, *The Invention of Politics in Colonial Malaya: Contesting Nationalism and the Expansion of the Public Sphere* (Cambridge: Cambridge University Press, 1995).

26. H. M. J. Maier, *In the Center of Authority: The Malay Hikayat Merong Mahawangsa*. (Ithaca: Southeast Asia Program, Cornell University, 1988). See also Maier, "The Laughter of Kemala al-Arifin; the Tale of the Bearded Civet Cat", in *Variation, Transformation and Meaning: Studies in Indonesian Literatures in Honour of A Teeuw*, ed. J. J Ras and S. O. Robson (Leiden: KITLV Press, 1991), pp. 53–73; Maier, "From Heteroglossia to Polyglossia: The Creation of Malay and Dutch in the Indies", *Indonesia*: 56, 37–65; Maier and G. L. Koster, "A Fishy Story: Exercises in Reading the Syair Ikan Terubuk", in *Cultural Contact and Textural Interpretation*, ed. C. D. Grijns and S. O. Robson (Dordrecht: Foris, 1986), pp. 204–18, Koster and Maier, "A Medicine of Sweetmeats: On the Power of Malay Narrative", *Bijdragen tot de Taaln, Landen Volkenkunde* (hereafter *BKI*), 141 (1985): 441–60, and Koster, "The Soothing Works of the Seducer and their Dubious Fruits: Interpreting the Syair Buah-Buahan", in *A Man of Indonesian Letters: Essays in Honour of Professor A Teeuw*, ed. C. M. S. Hellwig and S. O. Robson (Dordrecht: Foris, 1986), pp. 73–99.

27. Jane Drakard, *A Malay Frontier Unity and Duality in a Sumatran Kingdom* (Ithaca: Southeast Asia Program, Cornell University, 1990), and Drakard, ed. *Sejarah Raja-Raja Barus*. Naskah dan Dokumen Nusantara 7 (Jakarta: Angkasa and Ecole Française d'Extrême-Orient, 1988).

28. Amin Sweeney, *A Full Hearing. Orality and Literacy in the Malay World* (Berkeley: University of California Press, 1987).

29. Maier, *In the Center of Authority*, p. 65.

30. Cyril Skinner, *The Battle for junk Ceylon. The Syair Sultan Maulana. Text, Translation and Notes*. Bibliotheca Indonesica 25 (Dordrecht: Foris, 1985), *contra* G. L. Koster, "The Kerajaan at War: On the Genre 'Heroic-Historical Syair'", paper presented at the 4th Indonesian-Dutch History Conference, Yogyakarta, 1983.

31. Ahmad, A. Samad. *Hikayat Amir Hamzah* (Kuala Lumpur: Dewan Bahasa dan Pustaka, 1987).

32. Rattiya Saleh, *Panji Thai dalam Perbandingan dengan Cerita-Cerita Panji Melayu* (Kuala Lumpur: Dewan Bahasa dan Pustaka, Kementerian Pendidikan Malaysia, 1988); Adbul Rahman Kaeh, *Panji Narawangsa* (Kuala Lumpur: Dewan Bahasa dan Pustaka, Kementerian Pendidikan Malaysia, 1989).

33. Siti Chamamah Soeratno, *Hikayat Iskandar Zulkarnain. Analisis Resepsi*. Seri ILDER (Jakarta: Balai Pustaka, 1991).

34. Monique Zaini-Lajoubourt, *Abdullah bin Muhammad al-Misri*. Naskah dan Dokumen Nusantara 6. (Bandung: Angkasa and Ecole Française d'Extrême-Orient, 1987).

35. V. I. Braginsky, *The System of Classical Malay Literature* (Leiden: KITLV Press, 1993).

36. Inden, *Imagining India*, pp. 23–25.

37. Ibid., p. 25; see also M. Hobart, "The Patience of Plants: A Note on Agency in Bali", *Review of Indonesian and Malaysian Affairs*, 24, 2 (1990): 90–136.

38. G. Deleuze and F. Guattari, *A Thousand Plateaus. Capitalism and Schizophrenia*, transl. Brian Massumi (London: Athlone, 1988).

39. Appearing too late for mention by Maier was a study by Mustafa Mohd Isa on the structure of Malay story telling in the Kedah tradition. See his *Awang Belanga* (Kuala Lumpur: Dewan Bahasa dan Pustaka, 1987).

40. Maier, *In the Center of Authority*, p. 129.

41. Milner, *The Invention of Politics*.

42. B. A. Hussainmiya, *Orang Rejimen: The Malays of the Ceylon Rifle Regiment* (Bangi: Universiti Kebangsaan Malaysia, 1990).

43. Ibid., pp. 57–58, 64–67.

44. Ibid., p. 29 n. 1.

45. V. J. H. Houben, H. M. J. Maier and W. van der Molen, eds. *Looking in Odd Mirrors: The Java Sea.* SEMAIAN 5 (Leiden: Vakgroep Talen en Culturen van Zuidoost-Azie en Oceanic, Rijksuniversiteit te Leiden, 1992).

46. W. van der Molen, ed. *Indonesiana. Cultuurkunde van Indonesie.* SEMAIAN 1 (Leiden: Vakgroep Talen en Culturen van Zuidoost-Azie en Oceanie, Rijksuniversiteit te Leiden, 1989).

47. J. J. Ras, "The Shadow of the Ivory Tree. Language, Literature and History in Nusantara", in *Looking in Odd Mirrors*, p. 161.

48. Supomo, "The Image of Majapahit".

49. Maier, "The Malays, the Waves and the Java Sea", in *Looking in Odd Mirrors*, pp. 24, 26.

50. Kessler, "Archaism and Modernity".

51. Virginia Matheson, "Concepts of Malay Ethos in Indigenous Malay Writings", in *Journal of Southeast Asian Studies*, 10 (1979): 351–71.

52. Anthony Milner, "'Malayness': Confrontation, Innovation and Discourse", in *Looking in Odd Mirrors*, pp. 51–52.

53. Ras, "The Shadow of the Ivory Tree", pp. 146–62.

54. J. J. Ras, *The Shadow of the Ivory Tree. Language, Literature and History in Nusantara* (Leiden: Vakgroep Talen en Culturen van Zuidoost-Azie en Oceanie, Rijksuniversiteit te Leiden, 1992).

55. Ibid., p. 242.

56. James A. Boon, *Affinities and Extremes: Crisscrossing the Bittersweet Ethnology of East Indies History, Hindu-Balinese Culture, and Indo-European Allure* (Chicago: University of Chicago Press, 1990).

57. J. Fisch, *Hollands Ruhm in Asien. Francois Valentyns Vision des Niederlandischen Imperiums im 18 Jahrhundert* (Stuttgart, 1986);

W. Eisler, ed. *Terra Australis. The Furthest Shore* (Sydney: NSA Art Gallery, 1988).

58. John Gascoigne, personal communication (with reference to a forthcoming part of his multi-volume study of Banks) informs me that Banks regularly corresponded with Marsden and made great use of his materials on Sumatra and the Malay language.

59. Boon, *Affinities and Extremes*, pp. 30–32.

60. Paul M. Taylor, and Lorraine V. Aragon, *Beyond the Java Sea: Art of Indonesia's Outer Islands* (New York: Abrams, 1991). Originally curated by Paul Taylor and shown in three venues in the U.S.A. 1991–92, with the National Museum of Natural History, Smithsonian Institution, as its home venue, before being exhibited in the Rijksmuseum for Ethnography, Leiden, the Netherlands, 1992, then in a greatly modified form at the Museum Nasional Jakarta, 1993, curated by Suhardini Chalid, and in a different form at the Australian Museum, Sydney, 1993, with myself as curatorial advisor.

61. Information from the research of Ian Black on the history of Borneo (personal communication).

62. See *Shade of the Ivory Tree.*

63. Most of these points are well illustrated in H. Ibbitson Jessup, *Court Arts of Indonesia* (New York: Abrams, 1990), figs 53, 89, 92, 100, 106, 173, 175.

64. Adrian Vickers, "Hinduism and Islam in Indonesia: Bali and the Pasisir World", *Indonesia*, 44 (1987): 30–58; Vickers, "From Bali to Lampung by way of the Pasisir", *Archipel*, 45, 5 (1993): 5–76.

65. G. W. J. Drewes and L. F. Brakel, *The Poems of Hamzah Fansuri.* Bibliotheca Indonesica 26 (Dordrecht: Foris, 1986).

66. John R. Bowen, *Sumatran Politics and Poetics: Gayo History, 1900–1989* (New Haven: Yale University Press, 1991).

67. Ibid., p. 41. Figure 1.

68. Meier, "From Heteroglossia to Polyglossia", see also C. D. Grijns, "Van der Tuuk and the Study of Malay", *BKI*, 52, 3 (1996): 353–81.

69. J. Fabian, *Language and Colonial Power. The Appropriation of Swahili in the Former Belgian Congo 1880–1938* (Berkeley: University of California Press, 1986).

70. Milner, "'Malayness'".

71. Sweeney, *A Full Hearing*, ch. 2 and esp. p. 29.

72. Cited in Boon, *Affinities and Extremes*, pp. 8–12.

73. Ibid., p. 10.

74. Ibid.

75. Sweeney, *A Full Hearing*, pp. 54, 59.

76. Grijns, "Van der Tuuk and the Study of Malay".

77. Maier, "From Heteroglossia to Polyglossia".
78. Sweeney, *A Full Hearing*, ch. 2.
79. Ibid., pp. 56–57.
80. P. B. R. Carey, "Core and Periphery, 1600–1830: The Pasisir Origins of Central Javanese 'High Court' Culture", in *Regions and Regional Developments in the Malay-Indonesian World*, ed. Bernhard Dahm (Wiesbaden: Otto Harrassowitz, 1992), pp. 91–105.
81. Boon, *Affinities and Extremes*, ch. 3.
82. See C. Pelras, "Religion, Tradition and the Dynamics of Islamization in South Sulawesi", *Archipel*, 29 (1985): 107–35, and M. N. Pearson, "Conversions in Southeast Asia: Evidence from the Portuguese Record", *Portuguese Studies*, 6 (1990): 53–70.

Chapter 3

* Leonard Y. Andaya is a Professor of History at the University of Hawaii at Manoa, where he specialises in the early modern history of island Southeast Asia. E–mail correspondence can be directed to andaya@hawaii.edu.

1. A.C. Milner, *Kerajaan: Malay Political Culture on the Eve of Colonial Rule* (Tucson: University of Arizona Press, 1982); A.C. Milner *Invention of Politics in Colonial Malaya: Contesting Nationalism and the Expansion of the Public Sphere* (New York: Cambridge University Press, 1995); Anthony Milner, "Ideological Work in Constructing the Malay Majority"; and Shamsul A. B., "Bureaucratic Management of Identity in a Modern State", in *Making Majorities: Constituting the Nation in Japan, Korea, China, Malaysia, Fiji, Turkey, and the United States*, ed. Dru Gladney (Stanford: Stanford University Press, 1998), pp. 135–50, 151–69; Jane Drakard, *A Kingdom of Words: Language and Power in Sumatra* (Kuala Lumpur: Oxford University Press, 1999); *Idem., A Malay Frontier: Unity and Duality in a Sumatran Kingdom* (Ithaca: Southeast Asia Program, 1990); Hendrik M.J. Maier, *In the Center of Authority: The Malay Hikayat Merong Mahawangsa* (Ithaca: Cornell Southeast Asia Program, 1988); Adrian Vickers, "'Malay Identity': Modernity, Invented Tradition, and Forms of Knowledge", *Review of Indonesian and Malaysian Affairs*, 31, 1 (June 1997): 173–211.

2. There is a large amount of literature on ethnicity an identity, written principally by anthropologists. The debate has swung between two poles, with one arguing the existence of 'primordial' values that identify a group, and the other emphasising instead the 'situational' circumstances that determine who a group is at any particular time and place. There is also an intermediate position that suggests that

there is an dialectic at play, in which the primordial values change in response to circumstances with reinterpretations becoming transformed and reified as a primordial sentiment. Ethnicity and identity are thus not fixed but continually moving between primordialism and situationalism and evolving in a spiral fashion. See especially Stephen Cornell and Douglas Hartmann, *Ethnicity and Race: Making Identities in a Changing World* (Thousand Oaks: Pine Forge Press, 1998). The working of such an dialectic has important implications for the interpretation of Southeast Asian history.

3. This is the approach that I am taking in my latest project to examine the process of ethnic formation in the Straits of Melaka in the early modern period (c.1500–1800).

4. Maier, *In the Center of Authority.*

5. Georges Coedès and O. W. Wolters were among the most influential scholars who sought to document the existence of Srivijaya. See Georges Coedès, *The Indianized States of Southeast Asia* (Honolulu: East–West Centre Press, 1968); O. W. Wolters, *Early Indonesian Commerce: A Study of the Origins of Srivijaya* (Ithaca: Cornell University Press, 1967), and *The Fall of Srivijaya in Malay History* (Ithaca: Cornell University Press, 1970).

6. As Bruce Kapferer so aptly put it: "No tradition is constructed or invented and discontinuous with history." See his *Legends of People, Myths of State: Violence, Intolerance, and Political Culture in Sri Lanka and Australia* (Washington, DC: Smithsonian Institution Press, 1988), p. 211.

7. The complexity of the term 'Malay' or 'Melayu' is captured nicely in Philip Yampolsky's introduction to his CD on Melayu music in Sumatra and the Riau Islands. See "Introduction" to *Melayu Music of Sumatra and the Riau Islands,* Compact Disc recording, *The Music of Indonesia Series* (Washington: Smithsonian Institution, 1994), pp. 3–6. It is premature to distinguish a 'primary' from an 'extended' Melayu cultural area based on rule by a Melayu raja or sultan. Research is still needed to determine what Melayu meant in specific periods in the past.

8. Peter Bellwood, *Prehistory of the Indo-Malaysian Archipelago* (Honolulu: University of Hawaii Press, 1997), p. 118.

9. Peter Bellwood, "Hierarchy, Founder Ideology and Austronesian Expansion", in *Origins, Ancestry, and Alliance: Explorations in Austronesian Ethnography,* ed. James J. Fox and Clifford Sather (Canberra: Department of Anthropology, the Research School of Pacific and Asian Studies, 1996), pp. 18–40.

10. Peter Bellwood, "Austronesian Prehistory in Southeast Asia: Homeland, Expansion and Transformation", in *The Austronesians:*

Historical and Comparative Perspectives, ed. Peter Bellwood *et al.* (Canberra: Department of Anthropology, The Research School of Pacific and Asian Studies, 1995), p. 103.

11. Bellwood, *Prehistory*, p. 242.
12. K. Alexander Adelaar, "Borneo as a Cross-Roads for Comparative Austronesian Linguistics", in *The Austronesians*, ed. Bellwood *et al.*, p. 84; personal communication with Bob Blust, 15 May 2001.
13. See Collins' article in this volume. Personal communication with Alexander Adelaar, 10 May 2001.
14. James T. Collins, *Malay, World Language: A Short History* (Kuala Lumpur: Dewan Bahasa dan Pustaka, 1998), p. 5.
15. K. Alexander Adelaar, "Borneo as the Homeland of the Malay Language: Fifteen Years down the Road", paper presented to the conference on "Borneo as the Malay Homeland", Institute of Malay World and Civilisation (ATMA), Universiti Kebangsaan, Bangi, Malaysia, April 2000, p. 2.
16. Bellwood, *Prehistory*, pp. 224, 227, 245.
17. Collins, *Malay*, pp. 3–5; Bernd Nothofer, "Migrasi orang Melayu purba: Kajian awal", paper presented to the Fourth Biennial Conference of the Borneo Research Council, Bandar Seri Begawan, 10–15 June 1996.
18. As Bellwood points out, the use of such terms is for heuristic purposes, and the reality is the intergrading of both. *Prehistory*, p. 70.
19. This is not to say, however, that the Neolithic culture found in the Peninsula was due entirely to the migration of the southern Mongoloid population. It has been argued that in the later Neolithic in the second half of the first millennium BCE, stone and glass beads found in cist-graves in the Bernam valley and in sites in Kuala Selinsing, Perak indicate trade links of the inhabitants with India, Sri Lanka, the Mediterranean and possibly Africa. See Nik Hassan Shuhaimi bin Nik Abd. Rahman, "Tracing the Origins of the Malays and Orang Asli: From Archaeological Perspective", *Jurnal Arkeologi Malaysia*, 10 (1997): 102.
20. Bellwood, *Prehistory*, pp. 265–66.
21. Geoffrey Benjamin, "Issues in the Ethnohistory of Pahang", in *Pembangunan Arkeologi Pelancongan Negeri Pahang*, ed. Nik Hassan Shuhaimi bin Nik Abd. Rahman *et al.* (Pahang: Lembaga Muzium Negeri Pahang, 1997), pp. 92–93.
22. Personal communication, Dr Uri Tadmor. See also Geoffrey Benjamin, "Ethnohistorical Perspectives on Kelantan's Prehistory", in *Kelantan Zaman Awal: Kajian Arkeologi dan Sejarah di Malaysia*, ed. Nik Hassan Shuhaimi bin Nik Abd. Rahman (Kota Bharu: Muzium Negeri Kelantan, 1987), pp. 123–30.

23. Anthony Milner, E. Edwards McKinnon and Tengku Luckman Sinar, "A Note on Aru and Kota Cina", *Indonesia*, 26 (1978): 26–27.

24. Barbara Watson Andaya, *To Live as Brothers: Southeast Sumatra in the Seventeenth and Eighteenth Centuries* (Honolulu: University of Hawaii Press, 1993), pp. 15–16.

25. I-Tsing, *A Record of the Buddhist Religion*, trans. J. Takakusu (Oxford: Clarendon Press, 1896), pp. xxx, xxxiv, xxxvi, xl.

26. The Boom Baru inscription is the most recent find and is now housed in the Palembang Provincial Museum. It is written in Pallava script. Based on paleography, scholars believe the inscription dates from the seventh century. It contains eleven lines and appears to be an oath originating from a Srivijayan authority. It was placed at a port of entry to the city of Palembang.

27. J.G. de Casparis, "Some Notes on the Epigraphic Heritage of Srivijaya", *SPAFA Digest*, 3, 2 (1982): 29.

28. Coedès, *Indianized States*, pp. 82–83.

29. Georges Coedès, "Les incriptions malaises de Çrivijaya", *Bulletin de l'École Française d'Extrême-Orient* [hereafter *BEFEO*], 30 (1930): 34, 35, 37, 53, 58.

30. Louis-Charles Damais, "Bibliographie Indonésienne: V. Publications du Service archéologique de l'Indonésie", *BEFEO*, 51, 2 (1963): 555.

31. Rouffaer argues that 'Malaiyu' derives from the Tamil word, *malai*, 'hill', and *uur*, 'city', hence 'Malaiyur' or 'Hill City'. He provides no reference to support his claim that the Tamils and Malays claim Jambi as a motherland. G. P. Rouffaer, "Was Malaka Emporium vóór 1400 AD Genaamd Malajoer", *Bijdragen tot de Taal-, Land-, and Volkenkunde van Nederlandsch-Indie* [hereafter *BKI*], 77 (1921): 16–18.

32. Wolters, *Fall of Srivijaya*, pp. 45, 194, fn. 9; Friedrich Hirth and W. W. Rockhill (trans. and ann.), *Chau Ju-kua: His Work on the Chinese and Arab Trade in the Twelfth and Thirteenth Centuries Entitled Chu-fan-chi* (New York: Paragon, 1966), p. 66, fn. 18.

33. De Casparis, "Some Notes", p. 34.

34. F. D. K. Bosch, "Een Maleische inscriptie in het Buitenzorgsche", *BKI*, 100 (1941): 49–50.

35. Anton Postma, "The Laguna Copper-Plate Inscription: Text and Commentary", *Philippine Studies*, 40, 2 (1992): 185, 187, 190, 195, 197.

36. De Casparis, "Some Notes", pp. 29, 34.

37. Boechari, "Preliminary Report on the Discovery of an Old-Malay Inscription at Sodjomerto", *Madjalah Ilmu-Ilmu Sastra Indonesia*, 3, ii and iii (Oct. 1966): 242–43, 245–56. Although Boechari dates this inscription to the beginning of the seventh century, most believe it to be of a later period.

38. Coedès, *Indianized States*, pp. 108–9.
39. Ferrand writes 'Jawaga', but according to a French Arabist, J. Sauvaget, the old Arabic system of transcription would have written 'b' for the 'v' and 'z' for the 'j'. Thus 'Jawaga' becomes 'Zabag', and 'Sribuza' becomes 'Srivija(ya)'. See Coedès, *Indianized States*, pp. 130–31, 320 (fn. 173).
40. Gabriel Ferrand, *Relations des voyages et textes géographiques Arabes, Persans et Turks relatifs a l'Extrême-Orient du VIII au XVIII siécles* (Paris: Ernest Leroux, 1913), pp. 82–84.
41. Ibid., pp. 91–94, 99–100; Coedès, *Indianized States*, pp. 242–43.
42. Ferrand, *Relations*, p. 175.
43. Hirth and Rockhill, *Chau Ju-kua*, p. 66, fn. 18.
44. F. M. Schnitger, *The Archaeology of Hindoo Sumatra* (Leiden: E. J. Brill, 1937), p. 8.
45. N. J. Krom, *Hindoe-Javaansche Geschiedenis* ('s-Gravenhage: Martinus Nijhoff, 1931), pp. 335–36.
46. Andaya, *To Live as Brothers*, ch. 3.
47. Krom, *Hindoe-Javaansche*, pp. 393–94.
48. Coedès, *Indianized States*, p. 232.
49. Krom, *Hindoe-Javaansche*, pp. 393–94.
50. Wolters, *Fall of Srivijaya*, pp. 57–58, 75.
51. Rouffaer, "Was Malaka", p. 51.
52. *Desawarnana (Nagarakrtagama) by Mpu Prapanca*, ed. Stuart Robson (Leiden: KITLV Press, 1995), p. 33.
53. *The Suma Oriental of Tome Pires*, vol. I, ed. Armando Cortesão (New Delhi/Madras: Asian Educational Services, 1990), p. 158.
54. *Desawarnana*, pp. 33–34.
55. For a useful overview of earlier and more recent debates on archaeological sites on the Peninsula, see Leong Sau Heng, "Collecting Centres, Feeder Points and Entrepôts in the Malay Peninsula, 1000 BC-AD 1400", in *The Southeast Asian Port and Polity*, ed. J. Kathirithamby-Wells and John Villiers (Singapore: Singapore University Press, 1990), pp. 17–38.
56. Benjamin, "Issues in the Ethnohistory of Pahang", p.87.
57. John Miksic, "From Prehistory to Protohistory", and "Wider Contacts in Protohistoric Times", in *The Encyclopedia of Malaysia*, vol. IV (*Early History*) (Singapore: Archipelago Press, 1998), pp. 64, 75.
58. John Miksic, "Entrepôts along the Melaka Strait", in *Encyclopedia of Malaysia*, vol. IV, p. 117.
59. John Miksic, "Trade Routes and Trade Centres", in *Encyclopedia of Malaysia*, vol. IV, p. 78.
60. Nik Hassan Shuhaimi Nik Abdul Rahman, "The Bujang Valley", in *Encyclopedia of Malaysia*, vol. IV, pp. 106–107.
61. Leong, "Collecting Centres", p. 29.

62. Alastair Lamb, "Miscellaneous Papers", *Federation Museums Journal*, 6 (1961): 21, 33, 34, 81–82; John Miksic, "Expansion of Trade", in *Encyclopedia of Malaysia*, vol. IV, p. 77; Miksic, "Entrepôts along the Melaka Strait", p. 117.

63. Ibid., p. 117.

64. Leong, "Collecting Centres", p. 28; Alastair Lamb, "Takuapa: The Probable Site of a Pre-Malaccan Entrepôt in the Malay Peninsula", in *Malayan and Indonesian Studies*, ed. John Bastin and R. Roolvink (Oxford: Clarendon Press, 1964), pp. 83–84.

65. Lamb, "Takuapa", pp. 76, 80–83.

66. Paul Wheatley, *The Golden Khersonese: Studies in the Historical Geography of the Malay Peninsula before A.D. 1500* (Kuala Lumpur: University of Malaya Press, 1961), pp. 17, 28, 36, 42, 49, 51, 55, 194, 290; Nik Hassan Shuhaimi Nik Abdul Rahman, "Chi tu: An Inland Kingdom", in *Encyclopedia of Malaysia*, vol. IV, pp. 68–69.

67. Benjamin, "Issues in the Ethnohistory of Pahang", p. 86.

68. Nik Hassan Shuhaimi bin Nik Abdul Rahman, "Arkeologi di Kelantan: Satu Tinjauan Sejarah, Prasejarah dan Proto-Sejarah", in *Kelantan Dalam Perspektif Arkeologi: Satu Kumpulan Esei* (Kota Bharu: Perbadanan Muzium Negeri Kelantan, 1986), p. 3.

69. Wheatley, *The Golden Khersonese*, pp. xxvi–xxvii.

70. Miksic, "Trade Routes and Trade Centres", p. 79.

71. Benjamin, "Issues in the Ethnohistory of Pahang", p. 93.

72. This is known as the Winstedt version, named for the man who published it in printed Jawi in 1938. C. C. Brown published a romanised version in 1952. See R. O. Winstedt, "Sejarah Melayu: The Malay Annals, Raffles MS No. 18", *Journal of the Malayan Branch of the Royal Asiatic Society* [hereafter *JMBRAS*], 16, 3 (1938): 1–226; C. C. Brown, "Sejarah Melayu or 'Malay Annals', A Translation of Raffles MS 18", *JMBRAS*, 25, 1–2 (1952).

73. *De Hikajat Atjeh*, ed. Teuku Iskandar ('s–Gravenhage: M. Nijhoff, 1958).

74. Drakard, *A Kingdom of Words*, pp. 238–43.

75. *Hikayat Siak*, ed. Muhammad Yusoff Hashim (Kuala Lumpur: Dewan Bahasa dan Pustaka, 1992); Leonard Y. Andaya, *The Kingdom of Johor 1641–1728* (Kuala Lumpur: Oxford University Press, 1975), ch. 9.

76. Sión Jones, *The Archaeology of Ethnicity: Constructing Identities in the Past and Present* (London: Routledge, 1997), pp. 1–10.

77. J. G. de Casparis, *Selected Inscriptions from the 7th to the 9th Century AD* (Bandung: Masa Baru, 1956), pp. 15–20.

78. O. W. Wolters, *History, Culture, and Region in Southeast Asian Perspective* (Ithaca: Cornell Southeast Asia Program, 1999), p. 131.

79. Pierre-Yves Manguin, "Palembang and Srivijaya: An Early Malay Harbour-City Rediscovered", *JMBRAS*, 66, 1 (1993): 33.

80. Oki Akira has used the nineteenth-century sources to show the intricate way that the major rivers of east Sumatra were strategically linked through tributaries, land routes and *pangkalan*. Oki Akira, "The River Trade in Central and South Sumatra in the 19th Century", in *Environment, Agriculture and Society in the Malay World*, ed. Tsuyoshi Kato *et al.* (Kyoto: Centre for Southeast Asian Studies, 1986), pp. 3–48.

81. De Casparis, *Selected Inscriptions*, p. 31.

82. Schnitger, *Archaeology*, pp. 1, 4.

83. See Leonard Y. Andaya, "Aceh's Contributions to Standards of Malayness", *Archipel*, 61 (2001): 29–68.

84. In 1987 the then minister of education, Anwar Ibrahim, called for a strengthening of Malay values as symbolised by the kingdom of Melaka.

Chapter 4

Author's note: This paper would not have been possible without the help of the staff of the Arsip Nasional, Jakarta, and the Algemeen Rijksarchief (ARA), The Hague, or the assistance of Ankie de Jonge and Deborah Fernandez-Voortman. I owe a special debt of gratitude to the members of the Kerukunan Keluarga Indonesia Keturunan Melayu (KKIKM), the association for people of Malay descent in Makassar, particularly H. Ince Nurcahaya Dg. Ngai, Ince Abdullah, H. Ince Munir Razak, Drs. Ince Mansyur Yacub and Drs. Ince Amir Jahja.

*   Heather Sutherland is Professor of History at the Vrije Universiteit in Amsteram, the Netherlands. Her recent research has focused on the history of the trade and political situation of Makassar, 1600–1950. E-mail correspondence can be directed to hsutherland@compuserve.com.

1. O.W. Wolters, *The Fall of Srivijaya in Malay History* (Oxford: Oxford University Press, 1970).

2. Barbara W. Andaya and Leonard Y. Andaya, *A History of Malaysia* (London: Macmillan, 1982); L. F. F. R. Thomaz, "The Malay Sultanate of Melaka", in *Southeast Asia in the Early Modern Era: Trade, Power and Belief*, ed. Anthony Reid (Ithaca, NY: Cornell University Press, 1993), pp. 69–90.

3. J. Noorduyn, "De Handelsrelaties van het Makassaarse Rijk Volgens de 'Notitie' van Cornelis Speelman uit 1670", *Nederlandse Historische Bronnen*, 3 (The Hague: Martinus Nijhoff, 1983),

pp. 96–123. Anthony Reid, "The Rise of Makassar", *Review of Indonesian and Malaysian Affairs* [hereafter *RIMA*], 17 (1983): 117–60; Reid, *Southeast Asia in the Age of Commerce 1450–1680: Volume Two: Expansion and Crisis* (New Haven: Yale University Press, 1993); John Villiers, "Makassar: The Rise and Fall of an East Indonesian Maritime Trading State, 1512–1669", in *The Southeast Asian Port and Polity: Rise and Demise*, ed. J. Kathirithamby-Wells and J. Villiers (Singapore: Singapore University Press, 1990), pp. 143–59; J. Noorduyn, "De Islamisering van Makassar", *Bijdragen tot de Taal-, Land- en Volkenkunde* (hereafter *BKI*), 112 (1956): 247–66.

4. Anthony Reid, "Pluralism and Progress in Seventeenth-Century Makassar", in *Authority and Enterprise among the Peoples of South Sulawesi*, ed. R. Tol, K. v. Dijk and G. Acciaioli (Leiden: KITLV Press, 2000), p. 61.

5. W. Cummings, "The Melaka Malay Diaspora in Makassar, c.1500–1669", *Journal of the Malaysian Branch of the Royal Asiatic Society* (hereafter *JMBRAS*), 71, 1 (1998): 107–21; Reid, *Age of Commerce*, vol. II, ch. 3.

6. VOC 1127 ff. 576–577. References in this format designate documents from the VOC archive in the National Archives in The Hague, and give inventory number and folio (page). The VOC officials in Batavia summarised much of Kerckerinck's report in their report to the Netherlands in December 1638, in *Generale Missiven van Gouverneurs-Generaal en Raden aan Heren XVII der Verenigde Oostindische Compagnie* (hereafter *Generale Missiven*), *Deel I* ('s-Gravenhage: Martinus Nijhoff, 1960), pp. 668–70, also *Deel II* (1964), p.12. The volumes of the *Missiven* have had various editors and published, and cover (so far) the period 1614–1750 (although 1737–43 has yet to appear).

7. Noorduyn, "De Handelsrelaties".

8. VOC 1217 f. 247.

9. VOC 1224 f. 433.

10. Abdurrahim, "Kedatangan Orang Melaju di Makassar", in *Kenallah Sulawesi Selatan*, ed. H. D. Mangemba (Jakarta: Timun Mas, 1956), pp. 143–46; G.J. Wolhoff and Abdurrahim, *Sedjarah Goa* (Makassar: Jajasan Kebudajaan Sulawesi Selatan & Tenggara, 1960); Cummings, "Melaka Malay Diaspora"; Reid, "Pluralism and Progress", p. 66; "De Kapitein Melajoe te Makassar", *Adatrechtbundels XXXI: Selebes* (The Hague: 1929), pp. 110–12; Kerukunan Keluarga Indonesia Keturunan Melayu (KKIKM), *Sejarah Keturunan Indonesia Melayu*, (Makassar?: unpublished photocopy, c. 1987), p. 3.

11. Noorduyn, "Islamisering van Makassar"; KKIKM, *Sejarah*, p. 3; Cummings, "Melaka Malay Diaspora", p. 111.

12. "De Kapitein Melajoe"; KKIKM, *Sejarah*; Cummings, "Melaka Malay Diaspora"; while Datuk Maharaja Lela is described as coming from Patani, it is worth noting that the Dutch Admiral Speelman, who knew him personally, described Ince Muda, a Minangkabau, as "coming from the same village as Radja Lella" (Speelman "Notitie", Aanwinsten eerste Afdeling, ARA, 1928, nrs.10 and 11, f. 744). This is a manuscript copy of the encyclopaedic memorandum submitted to the VOC by Admiral Cornelis Speelman after the conquest of Goa; see Noorduyn, "Handelsrelaties" for more details.

13. C. Skinner, *Sja'ir Perang Mengkasar (The Rhymed Chronicle of the Macassar War) by Entji' Amin* (The Hague: Martinus Nijhoff, 1963); on Ince Amin, see p. 91. The prefix variously spelled 'Ince', 'Intje', 'Encik', 'Enchik', 'Entji', etc. was used to designate Malays (and sometimes *Peranakan* Chinese).

14. Skinner, *Sja'ir*, pp. 147, 168, 144 (Skinner's translations).

15. Speelman "Notitie", f. 744. This is in marked contrast to the image of the Malays in Mattulada's *Menyusuri Jejak Kehadiran Makassar dalam Sejarah (1510–1700)* (Ujung Pandang: Hassanuddin University Press, 1991), pp.55, 74, 97–98. Mattulada presents the Malays as being inherently pro–Dutch, and only briefly, under the influence of Datuk Maharaja Lela, allying themselves with the Makassarese; his sources are not clear, and Speelman himself is unequivocal in seeing the Malays as his enemies.

16. L.Y. Andaya, *The Heritage of Arung Palakka: A history of South Sulawesi (Celebes) in the seventeenth century* (The Hague: Martinus Nijhoff, 1981), pp. 125, 126, 128. Skinner, *Sja'ir*; Ince Amin describes how the Malays, together with the Makassarese, had the task of protecting the sultan and how, when the battle turned against them, they refused to obey the command to withdraw until forced by Datuk Maharaja Lela (pp. 209, 217).

17. Speelman "Notitie", f. 744. The case of Soppeng illustrates the time's complexities. The young king was a VOC ally. His Malay wife was anti-Dutch and stayed in Goa during the fighting; she only joined her husband after the war. Nonetheless, she was his favourite. Goa held his father, the ex-king, hostage, but Soppeng troops also fought for Makassar. They only defected in October 1667, when defeat was inevitable; F.W. Stapel, *Het Bonggais Verdrag* (Ph.D. dissertation, University of Leiden, 1922), pp.98, 115, 158, 166.

18. Ibid. on Kaicili' Kalimata see Skinner, *Sja'ir*, pp.159, 274, and Andaya, *Heritage of Arung Palakka*, p. 50.

19. Ibid., p.130.

20. KKIKM, *Sejarah*, p. 4.

21. Leonard Andaya, "The Bugis-Makassar Diasporas", *JMBRAS*, 68, 1 (1995): 119–38. The sensitivities that still surround these events

are reflected in the different accounts. The KKIKM *Sejarah*, p. 4, notes that *Karaeng* Karunrung asks the Malays to leave suddenly as they were not needed in the negotiations. The anonymous Indonesian typescript (Chabot Collection, KITLV Hisdoc OR432 no. 29), collected c. 1951, says that Karaeng Karunrung drove the Malays out, for unknown reasons, and despite their previous support; perhaps because it was feared they might ally themselves with the Dutch. Mattulada (p.74) has no doubts: the Malays had always been treacherous. Andaya *Arung Palakka* p. 130 describes the Malays as fleeing a lost war; this seems likely, and is similar to the Soppeng troops' reaction. Speelman graphically describes the departure of the main contingent: "The Malays (having been the enemy's bravest warriors) withdrew with wives and children along the river at Garassi (HS the Djeneberang south of Makassar). Despite the fact that this was closely blockaded by our ships and sloops, on the night of the 25th, they slipped out through the fleet in about a hundred small and large vessels. Although (the VOC fleet) reacted alertly, with grape-shot, and hit home, they escaped, some to Mandar, some to Bima and Sumbawa and other places. Given the modest manpower of our ships and sloops we did not consider it wise to pursue them in their flight". Quoted in *Generale Missiven Deel III*, p.680.

22. Andaya, *Heritage of Arung Palakka*, ch. VIII.
23. Speelman "Notitie", f. 744ff.
24. VOC 1276 f. 926.
25. Skinner, *Sja'ir*, p. 125; see also pp. 89, 160.
26. Speelman "Notitie", f. 707. Refugee Malays later left Jepara for a more hospitable home in Banten, *Generale Missiven Deel III* p. 842, while famine in Pasir in 1685 forced 150 Malay fighting men, with their families (about 500 people all told), to leave Kalimantan and return to Makassar, *Deel IV* (1971), p. 798.
27. KKIKM, *Sejarah*, p. 4; J. Noorduyn, "The Wajorese Merchants' Community in Makassar", in *Authority and Enterprise, ed.* Tol *et al.*
28. Speelman "Notitie", f. 707ff.
29. VOC 1347 f. 386.
30. VOC 1400 f. 6; *Generale Missiven Deel IV*, p. 656.
31. VOC 1438 f. 235.
32. VOC 1426 f. 348, 1438 f. 243.
33. VOC 1438 f. 305, 290.
34. VOC 1438 f. 333.
35. VOC 1775 ff. 53–60; Andaya, "The Bugis-Makassar Diasporas". Andaya, "The Bugis-Makassar Diasporas". Traders from Makassar, however, could still have connected with Johorese in areas they both

frequented, such as Riau, the Kalimantan pepper ports and Nusa Tenggara, including Manggarai in west Flores and the Alas Straits between Sumbawa and Lombok; *Generale Missiven Deel VI* (1976) pp.674, 682; *Deel VII* (1979), pp. 133, 135, 220, 278, 340, 278, 488.

36.   VOC1775 f. 53.
37.   See Gerrit Knaap and Heather Sutherland, *Monsoon Traders: captains, commodities and shipping in eighteenth century Makassar* (Leiden:KITLV Press, forthcoming).
38.   Andaya and Andaya, *History of Malaysia*, ch. 3; see also Wolters, *The Fall of Srivijaya*.
39.   Noorduyn, "The Wajorese Merchants' Community"; Knaap and Sutherland, *Monsoon Traders*.
40.   "Kapitein Melajoe" states that it was Datuk Maharaja Lela who made this request to Speelman, but—as noted above—Speelman writes in his "Notitie" that the Malay leader died in Mandar. KKIKM, *Sejarah* attributes the petition to 'Datuk Tumenggung', which could refer to Datuk Maharaja Lela or another Malay leader. Some Malays benefited from these turbulent times: Mandar, where many dissidents had fled, became a major slave market for stolen people, much frequented by Malay and Javanese traders, *Generale Missiven Deel III*, pp.752–55.
41.   VOC 1320 f. 274–75.
42.   VOC 1365 f. 394.
43.   *Kampung* ethnic names do not necessarily mean that all or even most inhabitants came from a given group. While this was often the case initially, populations soon shifted and blended; in other cases a *kampung* housed few people from the eponymous area. Kampung Buton, for example, was very much a mixed settlement; the name may have been derived from its proximity to a landing place for boats from that island, rather than any settlement by Butonese.
44.   VOC 1426 f. 504.
45.   VOC 1595 f. 320.
46.   VOC 1979 f. 96–7.
47.   VOC 1358 f. 295, 1403 f. 254.
48.   VOC 1365 f. 449. These disasters seem to have caused Ince Buang major financial problems: in 1680 he borrowed 6,500 *rijksdaalders* from the Makassar VOC, at one per cent per month; Speelman was one of his guarantors. He was, however, unable to pay this back for some time, and was detained by the Company. *Generale Missiven Deel IV*, pp.717, 800. Eventually (in 1689) Speelman's estate was told to refund him 496 rds. *Deel V*, p.348.
49.   Five compounds were along the beach to the west of Vlaardingen's wall; four of these belonged to Malays and one to a Chinese. Of the 16 compounds stretching from the sea along Vlaardingen's northern

wall seven were owned by Malays, two by Chinese, two by Makassarese aristocrats, one by a prominent *mestizo* family, and four by other Sulawesians. Two of the seventeen remaining '*kampung*' belonged to the *Kapitan Melayu*, nine were held by other Malays, and the rest by other Sulawesians. Two of the seventeen remaining '*kampung*' belonged to the *Kapitan Melayu*, nine were held by other Malays, and the rest by other Sulawesians.

50. ARNAS Mak. 289/2. References in this format refer to documents from the Makassar collection, in the Arsip Nasional, Jakarta.
51. VOC 3939 f. 80.
52. ARNAS Mak. 289/2.
53. VOC 1992 f. 49, VOC 3700 f. 46.
54. See Speelman "Notitie", f. 744, and Skinner, *Sja'ir*, pp. 159, 274.
55. Remco Raben, "Batavia and Colombo: The Ethical and Spatial Order of Two Colonial Cities, 1600–1800" (Ph.D. diss., University of Leiden, 1996) describes the early Malay *Kapitans* in Batavia, where Malays of Patani birth or descent held the position from at least 1644 to 1732 (pp. 208–10).
56. Noorduyn, "The Wajorese Merchants' Community", p.103.
57. VOC 1711 f. 201.
58. KKIKM, *Sejarah*, p. 5.
59. A diary of the *Kapitan Melayu* between 1781 and 1818 exists; unfortunately I was unable to consult it while preparing this article. See Helen Cerpokovic, "The Diary of the Kapitan Melayu", in *Living Through Histories: Culture, History and Social Life in South Sulawesi*, ed. K. Robinson and M. Paeni (Canberra: Department of Anthropology, ANU, 1998), pp. 55–66.
60. ARNAS Mak.313/1.
61. For another example of the translator's position, see Noorduyn, "The Wajorese Merchants' Community" on their legal role, VOC 3150 ff. 163–68.
62. ARNAS Mak.313/1.
63. Noorduyn, "The Wajorese Merchants' Community"; this expansionist trend by Bone continued through to the later nineteenth century (Heather Sutherland, "Power and Politics in South Sulawesi: 1860–1880", *RIMA*, 17 [Winter/Summer 1983]: 161–207).
64. ARNAS Mak.313/1. He was dismissed in 1728 and sent to Batavia for punishment, because of his "faithless disposition". *Generale Missiven Deel VIII*, p.134 notes his "ontrouw humeur".
65. ARNAS Mak.163 f. 121. "Ince Somma" had previously been "Lieutenant der Maleiers", *Generale Missiven Deel VIII*, p.134, he was appointed in Makassar in 1727, confirmed in 1728.
66. Noorduyn, "The Wajorese Merchants' Community".
67. VOC 3273 ff. 1–2.

68. Noorduyn, "The Wajorese Merchants' Community". Over enthusiastic exploitation of the profitable possibilities of such a position could be fatal: Kapitan Melayu Ince Jamaluddin was dismissed in 1747 for 'inhaligheid', greed or covetousness; *Generale Missiven Deel XI* (1997), p. 516.

69. VOC 3273 ff. 53–54.

70. Noorduyn, 'The Wajorese Merchants' Community', p. 107.

71. Heather Sutherland, "*Mestizos* as Middlemen? Ethnicity and Access in Colonial Macassar", in *Papers from the Dutch-Indonesian Historical Conference, Lage Vuursche, June 1980* (Leiden: Bureau of Indonesian Studies, 1980), pp. 250–77; Gerrit Knaap, "A City of Migrants: Kota Ambon at the End of the Seventeenth Century", *Indonesia*, 51 (1991): 105–28; H.E. Niemeyer, "Calvinisme en koloniale stadscultuur. Batavia 1619–1725" (Ph.D. diss., Free University of Amsterdam, 1996); Raben, "Batavia and Colombo". On shifting boundaries, see Lombard and Salmon, "Islam and Chineseness", *Indonesia*, 57 (April 1994): 118–19.

72. One page of almost illegible carbon typescript in the possession of H. Ince Munir Razak, Makassar. Denys Lombard and Claudine Salmon, "Islam and Chineseness" give an extract from this story, drawn from a Romanised Malay manuscript 'Sedjarah Melajoe di Makassar' held pre-1985 by the Yayasan Sulawesi, Makassar. This manuscript can no longer be found in the collection, currently administered by the Makassar Archives. However, it is probably the same as the carbon typescript 'Sedjarah Melaju di Makassar' in the Chabot collection of the KITLV in Leiden, OR532 (30); see p. 18 of the latter. This text was a major source for the KKIKM *Sejarah*, on which the rest of this paragraph is based.

73. KKIKM, *Sejarah*; Lombard and Salmon, "Islam and Chineseness", pp. 188–89.

74. Interviews, Makassar, December 1999, May 2000, April–May 2001, including with the present Imam of the Mesjid Mubarrak, H. Muhammed Saleh Tahir. Claudine Salmon, "Ancestral Halls, Funeral Associations and Attempts at Resinicization in Nineteenth Century Netherlands India", in *Sojourners and Settlers. History of Southeast Asia and the Chinese*, ed. Anthony Reid (St. Leonards: Allen and Unwin, 1996), pp. 199–200, notes that the first Imam was Ince Taha (1814–37), while the last in the list she was given was Mohd. Jafar (1924–45). She describes the founder of the mosque as a convert, which may underestimate his Islamic roots. Haji Ince Munir Razak and Ince Anas b. Hassan (interviews, Makassar May 2000, July 2002, see note 96) suggest the peranakan Imams were also Malays, that Ince Taha's brother Ince Abdul Razak Datuk Kadhi, who helped establish the Buton mosque and its associated

wakaf, had been Imam of the Malay mosque, and that Ince abidin b. Abdul Muttalib, the last Imam of the line, lasted into the early 1970s. From the late 1950s the Department of Religion gradually replaced hereditary Imam families with elected and state approved officials.

75. Interviews, Makassar, with members of the KKIKM, Dec. 1999.

76. VOC 2780 f. 85. If the wife in question was the indomitable Daeng Talele, then she was from the Soppeng royal family, which had close ties with the Malays; *Generale Missiven Deel IV*, pp. 434, 751.

77. VOC 2780 ff. 85–93. In the 1740s the VOC, in the interests of harmony, decided to appoint a separate Lieutenant for the *Peranakan* Chinese, this arrangement lasted for four years; VOC 2837 f. 97. However in 1765 one Ince Tengarie was appointed to the same rank, as the *Peranakan* refused to accept the authority of *Kapitan* Limhamseeng, VOC 3210 f. 22. During the 1980s PITI (*Persatuan Indonesia Tionghoa Islam*, the official Indonesian Association of Muslim Chinese) invited Makassar's prominent Sino-Malay Muslims to join. They, however, refused. They did not consider themselves Chinese, but were Malays of Chinese descent.

78. Noorduyn, "The Wajorese Merchants' Community", pp. 109–10. This would suggest that mere household location was not enough to determine who was subject to whom; in the case of the *Peranakan* cited above, residence was only decisive when combined with ambiguous ethnicity

79. VOC 2780 ff. 85–86.

80. Heather Sutherland, "Trepang and Wangkang: The China Trade of Eighteenth Century Makassar", in R. Tol *et al.* ed., *Authority and Enterprise*, pp. 73–94; see also Knaap and Sutherland, *Monsoon Traders*. Ince Ali Asdullah's grave, the most important place of pilgrimage among Makassar's Malays today, is located on the Spermonde island of Barrang Lompo about 22 km. off-shore. Datuk Pabean is said to have used the islands as a base for his own trading ventures and as an outpost for controlling shipping. Barrang Lompo's inhabitants today include assimilated Bajo, and it is still a centre of trepang fishery (interviews, Makassar and Barrang Lompo, May 2001). Ince Ali Asdullah's father is buried on the family's home island of Sabutung; his grave is widely regarded as spiritually potent by the people of the Spermonde archipelago. Datuk Pabean is said to have used the islands as a base for his own trading ventures and as an outpost for controlling shipping.

81. KKIKM, *Sejarah*.

82. The above account is based on ibid.

83. John Butcher and Howard Dick, *The Rise and Fall of Revenue Farming* (London: St. Martins Press, 1993).

84. VOC 1910 ff. 105–09.
85. Knaap and Sutherland, *Monsoon Traders.*
86. Ibid.
87. VOC 3181 ff. 30–1, Resoluties (Decisions) ff. 12,13, 97–99.
88. VOC 3598 ff. 141–42, 153–56; Knaap and Sutherland, *Modern Traders.*
89. VOC 3181, ff. 89–90.
90. Els M. Jacobs, *Koopman in Azie. De handel van de Verenigde Oost-Indische Compagnie tijdens de 18de eeuw* (Zutphen: Walburg Press, 2000).
91. VOC 3465 f. 17, 3552 ff. 38–39, 3700 ff. 29–35.
92. Noorduyn, "The Wajorese Merchants' Community", p. 114.
93. KKIKM, *Rangkuman Riwayat Singkat Kedatangan Orang–Orang Melayu di Indonesia Khususnya di Sulawesi selatan Hingga Terbentuknya Organisasi Kerukunan Keluarga Indonesia Keturunan Melayu (KKIKM)* (Makassar: unpublished document, 1996), p. 5. As noted above, the earlier *Kapitan* Ince Cukka also built a mosque in 1705 (1117 A.H.).
94. KKIKM, *Sejarah*, p. 5; the list of Imam of the Malay mosque (pp. 18–19) begins with Ince Budiman in 1740 (see p. 106 in this book).
95. Ibid., p. 20. This implies a correlation between descent and marriage practice, i.e. that only Malay women could be primary wives, non-Malay women being restricted to *gundik* or secondary status. The *wakaf* grounds were registered with the Dutch administration in 1845.
96. Interview with two half-brothers, descendants of Ince Ali Asdullah, the head of the *yayasan* (foundation) Dato' ri Bandang (which administers the Mesjid Makmur Melayu) Ince Anas b. Hassan, and the Imam of the Mesjid Makmur Melayu, H. Ince Unais b. Hassan (Makassar, Apr. 2001). Their acknowledgement of Sino-Malay ancestry may reflect either a deviation from the rule or the impossibility of establishing inter-group boundaries.
97. J. Rush, *Opium to Java: Revenue Farming and Chinese Enterprise in Colonial Indonesia, 1860–1910* (Ithaca, NY: Cornell University Press, 1990); Carl Trocki, *Opium and Empire: Chinese Society in Colonial Singapore, 1800–1910* (Ithaca, NY: Cornell University Press, 1991).
98. Knaap and Sutherland, *Monsoon Traders.*
99. Ibid, Ch.V.
100. G.J. Knaap, "Manning the Fleet", paper presented at the Conference on Indonesian Social History, Universitas Indonesia, Dec. 1999, Table 2.
101. VOC 1882 f. 2.
102. For example, VOC 2192 f. 1017, 2628 f. 140g.

103. VOC 3441 f.168.
104. VOC 3905 f. 56, Comite Oost Indische Handel 94, f. 102. If Ince Ali Asdullah was still alive then, he must have reached a good age as he was marriageable in 1733.
105. For example, VOC 2192 ff. 697–8, 2933 ff. 43–51; see Knaap and Sutherland, *Monsoon Traders*, for information on trade routes and commodities.
106. Heather Sutherland, "Money in Makassar: credit and debt in an eighteenth century VOC settlement", paper presented at the Conference on "The Indonesian Town Revisited", Leiden, Dec. 2000.
107. VOC 2569 ff. 327–30.
108. ARNAS Mak. 342/1.
109. In 1765 jurisdiction over criminal cases, particularly those involving possible corporal or capital punishment, was removed from the Malay *Kapitans*, after a particularly violent incident. They retained the right to hear civil cases involving Malays or other Asians in a meeting with other community heads and the VOC's chief translator; VOC 3150 ff. 163–68. A publication on the courts of Makassar is in preparation.
110. KKIKM, *Sejarah*, p. 4.
111. Wolters, *The Fall of Srivijaya*, pp. 173–74.
112. However, they retained a composite identity as "*Moor Mardijker*" ship-owners into the 1720s (VOC 1995 ff. 96–97).
113. As Mona Lohanda reminds us, until the nineteenth century 'Peranakan Chinese' meant Muslim Chinese (Mona Lohanda, *The Kapitan China of Batavia 1837–1942* [Jakarta: Djambatan, 1996], p. 6). The later notion that *Peranakan* means locally born of mixed descent can not be applied automatically. Specific information Ince Amin gives on at least one of his protagonists suggests the need for further nuance: Datuk Sri Amar di Raja was a Cham from Cambodia (Skinner, *Sja'ir*, p. 147).
114. James C. Scott, *State Simplifications: some applications to Southeast Asia* (Amsterdam: Centre for Asian Studies Amsterdam, 1995) describes how modern states need to manage, subordinate and tax; this was also characteristic of earlier polities, although their managerial skills were more limited.

Chapter 5

* Timothy P. Barnard is an Assistant Professor of History at the National University of Singapore. His research focuses on the history and culture of the Melaka Straits region. E-mail correspondence can be directed to histpb@nus.edu.sg.

1. A. C. Milner, *Kerajaan: Malay Political Culture on the Eve of Colonial Rule* (Tucson: University of Arizona Press, 1982); Milner, *Invention of Politics in Colonial Malaya: Contesting Nationalism and the Expansion of the Public Sphere* (New York: Cambridge University Press, 1995); Milner, "Ideological Work in Constructing the Malay Majority", and Shamsul A. B., "Bureaucratic Management of Identity in a Modern State", in *Making Majorities: Constituting the Nation in Japan, Korea, China, Malaysia, Fiji, Turkey, and the United States*, ed. Dru Gladney (Stanford: Stanford University Press, 1998), pp. 151–69, 135–50; William R. Roff, *The Origins of Malay Nationalism* (Singapore: University of Malaya Press, 1967).

2. Among the best studies on this subject is Virginia Matheson's "Concepts of Malay Ethos in Indigenous Malay Writings", *Journal of Southeast Asian Studies*, 10, 2 (1979): 351–71.

3. Milner, *Kerajaan*.

4. *Hikayat Hang Tuah*, ed. Kassim Ahmad (Kuala Lumpur: Dewan Bahasa dan Pustaka, 1994), pp. 213–14; Henk Maier, "'We Are Playing Relatives'—Riau: The Cradle of Reality and Hybridity", *Bijdragen tot de Taal-, Land-, en Volkenkunde* [hereafter *BKI*], 153, 4 (1997): 672–75; R. J. Wilkinson, *A Malay-English Dictionary (Romanised)*, vol. I (New York: St. Martin's Press, 1959), p. 490.

5. *Peringatan Sejarah Negeri Johor, Eine Malaiische Quelle zur Geschichte Johors im 18. Jahrhundert*, ed. Ernst Ulrich Kratz (Wiesbaden: O. Harrassowitz, 1973), p. 44.

6. Leonard Y. Andaya, *The Kingdom of Johor, 1641–1718* (Kuala Lumpur: Oxford University Press, 1975), p. 189.

7. VOC 1911 (Part II): Malacca to Batavia, 28 Sept. 1718, f. 99. For other examples of people in eastern Sumatra protesting their treatment as 'slaves' or their perception of Malays as despotic, see VOC 2700: Malacca to Batavia, 29 Mar. 1747, f. 424; and Lene Ostergaard, "Between Minang and Malay: Intimations of Identity in Central Sumatra", *Kabar Seberang*, 22 (1991): 36.

8. *Hikayat Siak*, ed. Muhammad Yusoff Hashim (Kuala Lumpur: Dewan Bahasa dan Pustaka, 1992), pp. 111–12; Andaya, *Kingdom of Johor*, pp. 258–59.

9. For example, the most famous denigration of Siak, and the source of much popular understanding of the polity, is the celebrated *Tuhfat al-Nafis*. See Raja Ali Haji ibn Ahmad, *The Precious Gift (Tuhfat al-Nafis)*, trans. and ann. Virginia Matheson and Barbara Watson Andaya (Kuala Lumpur: Oxford University Press, 1982). The attempt by Raja Kecik to claim a Malay identity was not apocryphal. Many contemporary sources, particularly the Dutch archives, record his claims to Malay heritage, although Raja Kecik abandoned this claim after a few years. For example, see VOC 1895: Malacca to Batavia,

20 Aug. 1717, ff. 97–98 and VOC 1911 (3rd Part): Malacca to Batavia, 22 Jan. 1719, ff. 33–35. See also Timothy P. Barnard, *Raja Kecil dan Mitos Pengabsahannya* (Pekanbaru: Pusat Pengajian Melayu, 1994).

10. Milner, *Kerajaan*, p. 89. During times of upheaval in a society, such as the eighteenth and nineteenth centuries in the Melaka Straits, literature was often a method not only of spreading the basic tenets of a society, but also of reinforcing sovereignty and identity. This was also true in other areas of Southeast Asia during this time. See Helen Creese, "New Kingdoms, Old Concerns: Balinese Identities in the Eighteenth and Nineteenth Centuries", in *The Last Stand of Asian Autonomies: Responses to Modernity in the Diverse States of Southeast Asia and Korea, 1750–1900*, ed. Anthony Reid (New York: St. Martin's Press, 1997), pp. 345–66.

11. Milner, *Kerajaan*.

12. For convenience in citations I will use the published version, edited by Muhammad Yusoff Hashim in 1992, of the *Hikayat Siak*. The Cod. Or. 7304 version of the *Hikayat Siak* is 647 folio pages, the first 400 being a version of the *Sejarah Melayu*. R. O. Roolvink, "The Variant Versions of the Malay Annals", *BKI*, 123 (1967): 301–24; *Hikayat Siak*. For a discussion of the pre-eminent place that the *Sejarah Melayu* has achieved in the study of the Malay literature and history, see Hendrik M. J. Maier, *In the Center of Authority: The Malay Hikayat Merong Mahawangsa* (Ithaca: Cornell Southeast Asia Program, 1988), pp. 29–30, 42.

13. *Sejarah Melayu or Malay Annals*, ed. C. C. Brown (Singapore: Oxford University Press, 1970), p. 110.

14. Ibid., p. 176.

15. *Hikayat Siak*, pp. 131, 156.

16. Vivienne Wee, "Material Dependence and Symbolic Independence: Constructions of Melayu Ethnicity in Island Riau, Indonesia", in *Ethnic Diversity and the Control of Natural Resources in Southeast Asia*, ed. A. Terry Rambo, Kathleen Gilloghy and Karl L. Hutterer (Ann Arbor: Michigan Papers on South and Southeast Asia, No. 32, 1988), pp. 210–13.

17. *Hikayat Siak*, p. 158.

18. *Peringatan Sejarah Negeri Johor*, p. 48.

19. Ibid., p. 73.

20. Ali Haji, *Tuhfat al-Nafis*, p. 210; Matheson, "Concepts of Malay Ethos", p. 369.

21. *Hikayat Siak*, p. 207.

22. "*Kita ini anak Raja Siak, bukan Raja Palembang, sudah kami ini biasa bermain gelombang, anak laut, bukannya anak ulu*" (*Hikayat Siak*, p. 247).

23. The role of the ocean in Malay identity is discussed in H.M.J. Maier, "The Malays and the Sea, the Waves and the Java Sea", in *Looking in Odd Mirrors: The Java* Sea, ed. V.J.H. Houben, H.M.J. Maier and W. van der Molen (Leiden: Vakgroep Talen en Culturen van Zuidoost-Azie en Oceanie, Rijksuniversiteit Leiden, 1992), pp. 1–26.

24. *Hikayat Siak*, p. 156.

25. According to the *Syair Perang Siak*, another Malay text commissioned during Raja Ismail's lifetime, after an uncle proposed that Raja Ismail be married into the Trengganu royal family, a young advisor remarked, "if Your Majesty wishes to take a wife, we too shall find a niche again". See *Syair Perang Siak: A Court Poem Presenting the State Policy of a Minangkabau/Malay Family in Exile*, ed. Donald J. Goudie (Kuala Lumpur: Malaysian Branch of the Royal Asiatic Society, 1989), p. 219. Marriage also provided an opportunity for the authors of texts such as the *Hikayat Siak* to begin an encyclopaedic account of the culture of a society, in this case that of Malays of Siak and their *adat*. See Tony Day and Will Derks, "Narrating Knowledge: Reflections on the Encyclopedic Impulse in Literary Texts from Indonesian and Malay Worlds", in *BKI*, 155, 3 (1999): 318–20.

26. *Hikayat Siak*, pp. 173–74.

27. Ibid., pp. 174–75.

28. For another example of this same phenomenon in another part of the archipelago, see Esther J. Velthoen, "'Wanderers, Robbers, and Bad Folk': The Politics of Violence, Protection and Trade in Eastern Sulawesi 1750–1850", in *The Last Stand of Asian Autonomies*, ed. Reid, pp. 367–88.

29. *Hikayat Siak*, p. 177.

30. For a contemporary description of Raja Ismail as 'one of the greatest pirates' in the sea, see J. C. M. Radermacher, "Beschryving van het Eiland van Sumatra, in zo verre het zelve, tot nu toe, bekend is", *Verhandelingen van het Bataviaasch Genootschap van Kunstenen Wetenschappen*, 3 (1781): 89.

31. VOC 3245 (Second Part): Malacca Secret Resolutions, 16 Nov. 1767.

32. VOC 3245 (Second Part): Incoming Letters from Outer Areas: Letter from Sultan Abdul Jalil, King of Siak, to Governor and Council in Malacca (received 29 June 1767); Letter from Younger Brother (Raja Ismail) to Older Brother (Raja Muhammad Ali) (received in Malacca, 29 July 1767).

33. *Hikayat Siak*, pp. 157–63.

34. VOC 3245 (Second Part): Malacca Secret Resolutions, 16 Nov. 1767; *Hikayat Siak*, p. 166.

35. Ibid. In Nov. 1767, the VOC reported that the Palembang sultan had paid Raja Ismail 3,000 Spanish *reals*. See VOC 3245 (Second Part): Malacca Secret Resolutions, 16 Nov. 1767.

36. *Hikayat Siak*, p. 167; *Carita Bangka: Het Verhaal van Bangka*, ed. E.P. Wieringa (Leiden: Vakgroep Talen en Culturen van Zuidoost–Azie en Oceanie, Rijksuniversiteit Leiden, 1990), p. 89; Barbara Watson Andaya, *To Live as Brothers: Southeast Sumatra in the Seventeenth and Eighteenth Centuries* (Honolulu: University of Hawaii Press, 1993), pp. 223–24.
37. Ali Haji, *Tuhfat al-Nafis*, pp. 140–41.
38. In addition to basic food items, the gifts included a *laksa* of *reals*, a *kris*, state spears, scores of lacquered boxes and hundreds of sweetcakes. *Hikayat Siak*, pp. 170–72.
39. Ibid., p. 166.
40. Ibid., pp. 179–80, 186.
41. Ibid., p. 182.
42. Ibid., pp. 189–90.
43. Milner, *Kerajaan*, pp. 19–20.
44. Maier, "'We Are Playing Relatives'"; Wee, "Material Dependence and Symbolic Independence".

Chapter 6

* Jan van der Putten is an Assistant Professor in the Malay Studies Department at the National University of Singapore. His research interests focus on nineteenth century Malay literature, with particular focus on Raja Ali Haji and Munshi Abdullah. E-mail correspondence can be directed to j.putten@quicknet.nl.
1. There are numerous sources for this history. The most easily accessible are Barbara Watson Andaya, "From Rum to Tokyo: The Search for Anti–Colonial Allies by the Rulers of Riau, 1899–1914", *Indonesia*, 24 (1977): 123–42; Timothy P. Barnard, "*Taman Penghiburan*: Entertainment and the Riau Elite in the Late 19th Century", *Journal of the Malaysian Branch of the Royal Asiatic Society*, 67, 2 (1994): 17–46.
2. There have been numerous printings of these works. Two recent ones are: Raja Ali Haji, *The Precious Gift (Tuhfat al-Nafis)*, trans. and ann. by Virginia Matheson and Barbara Watson Andaya (Kuala Lumpur: Oxford University Press, 1982); Raja Ali Haji, *Salasilah Melayu dan Bugis* (Petaling Jaya: Fajar Bakti, 1984).
3. As the Malays at Lingga were so desperately seeking to do: see Virginia Matheson's "Strategies of Survival: The Malay Royal Lineage of Lingga-Riau", *Journal of Southeast Asian Studies*, 17, 1 (1986): 5–38.
4. Vivienne Wee, "Melayu: Hierarchies of Being in Riau" (Ph.D. diss. Australian National University, 1985), p. 68.

5. However, tracing descent through the female line is acceptable in traditional Southeast Asian cognatic kinship systems. See O.W. Wolters, *History, Culture and Religion in Southeast Asian Perspectives* (Ithaca: Cornell University Southeast Asia Program, 1999), pp. 17–18.

6. Matheson, "Strategies of Survival", pp. 10–11.

7. Jan van der Putten, "Printing in Riau, Two Steps Toward Modernity", *Bijdragen tot de Taal-, Land- en Volkenkunde*, 153,4 (1997): 728–29.

8. Matheson, "Strategies of Survival", p. 166.

9. Having said this, I realise that Dutch Resident Eliza Netscher actually reported that Raja Ali Haji was trying to separate the kingdom into two parts, but I am at the same time very suspicious about Netscher's reports because he seems to have had a personal dislike of Raja Ali Haji. See Jan van der Putten and Al Azhar, *Di dalam berkekalan persahabatan. In everlasting friendship. Letters from Raja Ali Haji* (Leiden: Vakgroep Talen en Culturen van Zuidoost-Azie en Oceanie, Rijksuniversiteit Leiden, 1995), p. 17.

10. Henk Maier, "'We Are Playing Relatives': Riau, the Cradle of Reality and Hybridity", *Bijdragen tot de Taal-, Land- en Volkenkunde* 153, 4 (1997): 676.

11. Raja Ali Haji, *Tuhfat al-Nafis*, p. 239.

12. Ibid., pp. 252–55.

13. See the reaction of Governor Bonham, who sailed on the British warship *Andromache* on an expedition against pirates in Riau, when Haji Ibrahim demanded a reply to the letter he had brought to the governor: "His Excellency Governor Bonham, smiled and clapped him on the back, saying, 'Spoken like a true envoy'" (ibid., p. 270).

14. Letter from Haji Ibrahim, 5 June 1870 (letters from several Malay dignitaries to Von de Wall, 1856–73, ML 174 & 175, Perpustakaan Nasional Jakarta; and Cod. Or. 3388, Leiden University Library).

15. *Indisch Besluit* , 20 July 1870, no. 8.

16. Raja Ali Haji, *Tuhfat al-Nafis*, p. 397.

17. ARA: Verbaal 16 Oct. 1858, no. 39: letter from Resident Tobias to Batavia, 30 July 1858.

18. van der Putten and Al Azhar, *Di dalam berkekalan persahabatan*, p. 62.

19. E. Netscher, *Memorie van Overgave van de Resident E. Netscher*, 20 May 1870. KITLV, Hs. 420.

20. *Rapport door Ch. van Angelbeek, omtrent zijn zending naar Riau,* 1825, KITLV Hs. 494.

21. van der Putten and Al Azhar, *Di dalam berkekalan persahabatan*, pp. 66–67.

22. Unfortunately this passage of the letter is partly missing: the entire paper was used for writing the letter, and this passage is at the very top, where the letter was cut to fit it into the bundle of letters.

23. Letter from Haji Ibrahim, 25 Aug. 1865 (ML 174 Perpustakaan Nasional Jakarta).

24. Undated postscript by Haji Ibrahim (ML 174 Perpustakaan Nasional Jakarta).

25. Haji Ibrahim's lower position is also indicated in a letter he sent to Raja Ali Haji, in which he refers to himself as *hamba engku* (literally: Prince's slave), a very humble term for the first person singular.

26. Wee, "Melayu: Hierarchies of Being", pp. 168–72.

27. Von de Wall arrived in 1857 and H. C. Klinkert, who was commissioned to make a new translation of the Bible, was sent to Riau to improve his knowledge of 'pure' Malay, arriving at Tanjung Pinang in 1864.

28. Letter from Haji Ibrahim, 19 Jan. 1860 (ML 174 Perpustakaan Nasional Jakarta).

29. Letter from Haji Ibrahim, 29 May 1862 (ML 174 Perpustakaan Nasional Jakarta).

30. Letter from Haji Ibrahim, 6 Aug. 1858 (ML 174 Perpustakaan Nasional Jakarta).

31. Letter from Haji Ibrahim, 28 Sept. 1858 (ML 174 Perpustakaan Nasional Jakarta).

32. Letter from Haji Ibrahim, 26 May 1867 (ML 174 Perpustakaan Nasional Jakarta).

33. Pangeran Abdul Rahman submitted a large expense account of ƒ1603.50 for the hire of carriages for the sultan's party (*Indisch Besluit*, 22 Jan. 1868, no. 2) and the government agreed to pay bills submitted by the doctor and pharmacist for the sultan's medical care which amounted to ƒ471 (*Indisch Besluit*, 20 Jan. 1868, no. 2).

34. See advertisements in the *Java-Bode* of 16 Nov. 1867 and 20 May 1868, in which Speet published lists of golden coins that had recently arrived and could be purchased at his office. The full name of the firm was: J. Speet, Verwisselings-kantoor, Handel in Gouden en Zilveren speciën en edele metalen (J. Speet, Exchange Office, Trading Gold and Silver Coins and Other Precious Metals).

35. Letter from Haji Ibrahim, 28 Jan. 1868 (ML 174 Perpustakaan Nasional Jakarta).

36. Netscher, Political Report of 1868, KITLV.

37. Quoted from the *Kisah Pelayaran ke Riau* with a few minor adjustments in comparison to the published version in M. A. Fawzi Basri, *Warisan Sejarah Johor* (Kuala Lumpur: Persatuan Sejarah Malaysia, 1983), p. 25. The *Kisah* relates the visit of this delegation from Johor and includes a note on titles and responsibilities of dignitaries in the Malay realm by Raja Ali Haji, with information on the flags they should to fly on their boats provided by Haji Ibrahim. The 'Ungku Haji' mentioned in this passage does not refer

to Raja Ali Haji, as regularly is the case in Haji Ibrahim's letters to Von de Wall, but to a member of the Johor delegation.

38. Fawzi Basri, *Warisan Sejarah Johor*, pp. 28–29.

39. Letter from Haji Ibrahim, 26 Oct. 1867 (ML 174 Perpustakaan Nasional Jakarta).

40. This is a part of a so-called *pantun berkait* (connected verse) written by Haji Ibrahim who sent it to his son Abdullah in order to copy it and show it to Von de Wall (enclosed with a letter from Haji Ibrahim to Abdullah in Batavia, Oct. 1869). Part of the published piece was in a collection of *pantun* assembled by Haji Ibrahim and published by the Dutch government in 1877. Hadji Ibrahim, *Pantoen₂ Malajoe*, edited and published by H. Von de Wall (Betawi: Bruining, 1877), p. 140.

41. Part of the concluding *syair of the Silsilah Melayu dan Bugis*, quoted from Hasan Junus *et al., Raja Ali Haji dan karya-karyanya* (Pekanbaru: Pusat Pengajian Bahasa dan Kebudayaan Melayu, UNRI, Badan Perencanaan Pembangunan Daerah 1995/96), p. 137.

42. Virginia Matheson, "Pulau Penyengat: Nineteenth Century Islamic Centre of Riau", *Archipel*, 37 (1989): 168.

Chapter 7

* Shamsul A. B. is a Professor of Social Anthropology and, currently, Director of the Institute of the Malay World and Civilization (ATMA) at the Universiti Kebangsaan Malaysia. His research focuses on the development of Malay identity. E-mail correspondence can be directed to pghatma@ukm.my.

1. Shamsul A. B., *From British to Bumiputera Rule: Local Politics and Rural Development in Peninsular Malaysia* (Singapore: Institute of Southeast Asian Studies, 1986).

2. Shamsul A. B., "The Superiority of Indigenous Scholars? Some Facts and Fallacies with Special Reference to Malay Anthropologists and Sociologists in Fieldwork", *Manusia dan Masyarakat* (New Series), 3 (1983): 23–33.

3. Judith Nagata, "Islamic Revival and the Problem of Legitimacy among Rural Religious Elites in Malaysia", *Man: The Journal of the Royal Anthropological Institute* (N.S.), 17, 1 (1982): 42–57; Shamsul A. B., "A Revival in the Study of Islam in Malaysia", *Man* (N.S.), 18, 2 (1983): 399–404; Shamsul A. B., "Religion and Ethnic Politics in Malaysia: The Significance of the Islamic Resurgence Phenomenon", in *Asian Visions of Authority: Religion and the Modern States of East and Southeast Asia*, ed. Charles F. Keyes *et al.* (Honolulu: University of Hawaii Press, 1994), pp. 99–116; Shamsul A. B., "Inventing Certainties: The Dakwah Persona in

Malaysia", in *The Pursuit of Certainty: Religious and Cultural Reformulations*, ed. Wendy James (London: Routledge, 1995), pp. 112–33; Shamsul A. B., "A Question of Identity: A Case Study of Islamic Revivalism and the Non-Muslim Response", in *Nation-State, Identity and Religion in Southeast Asia*, ed. Tsueno Ayabe (Singapore: Singapore Society for Asian Studies, 1998), pp. 55–80.

4. See, *inter alia*, Shamsul A. B., *Formal Organisations in a 'Malay Administrative Village': An Ethnographic Portrait* (Kent: Occasional Paper No. 15, Centre of Southeast Asian Studies, University of Kent at Canterbury, 1990).

5. See, *inter alia*, Shamsul A. B., "Debating about Identity in Malaysia: A Discourse Analysis", *Tonan Ajia Kenkyu*, 34, 3 (1996): 566–600; Shamsul A. B., "The Making of a Plural Society in Malaysia: A Brief Survey", in *Emerging Pluralism in Asia and the Pacific*, ed. David Wu, H. McQueen and Y. Yamamoto (Hong Kong: Institute of Pacific Studies, 1997), pp. 67–83; and Shamsul A. B., "Nationalism: Nationsbyggande och kolonial kunskap: Fallet Malaysia", *Orientaliska Studier*, 96–7 (1998): 25–35.

6. Shamsul, "Debating about Identity in Malaysia" and "Nationalism: Nationsbyggande och kolonial kunskap".

7. Ibid.

8. Cheah Boon Kheng, "Writing Indigenous History in Malaysia: A Survey on Approaches and Problems", *Crossroads: An Interdisciplinary Journal of Southeast Asian Studies*, 10, 2 (1997): 33–81.

9. Bernard Cohn, *Colonialism and Its Forms of Knowledge: The British Rule in India* (Princeton: Princeton University Press, 1996), p. 4.

10. William R. Roff, *Origins of Malay Nationalism* (Kuala Lumpur: University of Malaya Press, 1967); Ariffin Omar, *Bangsa Melayu: Malay Concepts of Democracy and Community 1945–1950* (Kuala Lumpur: Oxford University Press, 1993); Anthony Milner, *Invention of Politics in Colonial Malaya* (Melbourne: Cambridge University Press, 1996).

11. Cheah, "Writing Indigenous History in Malaysia"; Charles Hirschman, "The Making of Race in Colonial Malaya: Political Economy and Racial Category", *Sociological Forum*, 1 (Spring 1986): 330–61.

12. A. J. Stockwell, "The Historiography of Malaysia: Recent Writings in English on the History of the Area since 1874", *The Journal of Imperial and Commonwealth History*, 5 (1986): 82–110; Khoo Kay Kim, "Local Historians and the Writing of Malaysian History in the Twentieth Century", in *Perceptions of the Past in Southeast Asia*, ed. Anthony Reid and David Marr (Singapore: Heinemann, 1979), pp. 299–311; Khoo Kay Kim, "Recent Malaysian Historiography", *Journal of Southeast Asian Studies*, 13, 2 (1979): 28–39; Khoo Kay Kim, "Malaysian Historiography: A Further Look", *Kajian Malaysia*, 19, 1 (1992): 37–62.

13. D. P. Singhal, "Some Comments on the Western Element in Modern Southeast Asian History", *Journal of Southeast Asian History*, 2, 2 (1960): 72–102; Khoo, "Local Historians and the Writing of Malaysian History"; Anthony Milner, "Colonial Records History: British Malaya", *Kajian Malaysia*, 4, 2 (1986): 1–18; Yeoh Kim Wah, "The Milner Version of British Malayan History: A Rejoinder", *Kajian Malaysia*, 5, 1 (1987): 1–28.

14. Kassim Ahmad, "Satu Konsep Sejarah Kebangsaan Malaysia", *Dewan Masyarakat*, 19 (Nov. 1981): 47–54; Lim Say Hup, "The Need for a Reinterpretation of Malayan History", *Malaya in History*, 5, 2 (1990): 41–43; Malik Munip, *Tuntutan Melayu* (Kuala Lumpur: Sarjana Enterprise, 1975); Kua Kia Soong, *Malaysian Cultural Policy and Democracy* (Kuala Lumpur: The Resource and Research Center, Selangor Chinese Assembly Hall, 1990).

15. Ernest Renan, "What is a Nation?", in *Nation and Narration*, ed. Homi Bhabha (London: Routledge, 1990), p. 11.

16. Milner, *Invention of Politics in Colonial Malaya*. Mohd. Taib Osman addressed this same issue in his inaugural lecture on 'Malay Studies', which was published as *Pengajian Melayu Sebagai Bidang Ilmu di Universiti. Inaugural Lecture for the Chair of Malay Studies* (Kuala Lumpur: Universiti of Malaya Press, 1991).

17. Cohn, *Colonialism and Its Forms of Knowledge*.

18. Ibid., p. 5.

19. Ibid., p. 1.

20. See Anthony Reid's contribution to this volume.

21. See Leonard Andaya's contribution to this volume.

22. A. C. Milner, *Kerajaan: Malay Political Culture on the Eve of Colonial Rule* (Tucson: University of Arizona Press, 1982); Rita Smith Kipp, *Disassociated Identities: Ethnicity, Religion, and Class in an Indonesian Society* (Ann Arbor: University of Michigan Press, 1996), pp. 20–38.

23. Norman Davies, *Europe: A History* (London: Pimlico, 1997), pp. 510–11.

24. Anthony Reid, "Malayness and the Forging of National Cultures in Southeast Asia", a paper for an international seminar on "External Challenge and Local Response: Modern Southeast Asia in Historical Perspectives", 20–22 Sept. 1997, Universiti Brunei Darussalam, Brunei, p. 8.

25. Ibid., p. 11.

26. William Marsden, *The History of Sumatra* (Singapore: Oxford University Press, 1986), pp. 40–42.

27. Thomas Stamford Raffles, "On the Malayu Nation", *Asiatic Researches*, 12 (1816): 103.

28. Charles Hirschman, "The Making of Race in Colonial Malaya", and "The Meaning and Measurement of Ethnicity in Malaysia: An

Analysis of Census Classification", *Journal of Asian Studies*, 46, 3 (1987): 555–82.

29. H. R. Cheeseman, *Bibliography of Malaya, being a Classified List of Books Wholly or Partly in English Relating to the Federation of Malaya and Singapore* (London: Longmans Green, 1959); Tan Chee Beng, *Bibliography on Ethnicity and Race Relations in Malaysia* (Kuala Lumpur: Institut Pengajian Tinggi, Universiti Malaya, 1992).

30. Ariffin Omar, *Bangsa Melayu*; Shamsul A. B., *Malaysia in 2020: One State Many Nations? Observing Malaysia from Australia*. The Seventh James Jackson Memorial Lecture, Malaysia Society, Australia (Bangi: Dept. of Anthropology and Sociology, Universiti Kebangsaan Malaysia, 1992); Shamsul A. B., "Nations-of-Intent in Malaysia", in *Asian Forms of the Nation*, ed. Stein Tønnesson and Hans Antlöv (London: Curzon and Nordic Institute of Asian Studies, 1996), pp. 323–47.

Chapter 8

Author's Note: This essay was originally presented at the Contesting Malayness Conference held in Leiden, the Netherlands in April 1997, and appeared in the *Review of Indonesian and Malaysian Affairs* 34, 2 (2000): 1–27. It is a pleasure to acknowledge the generosity of the Harry S. Truman Research Institute for the Advancement of Peace, Hebrew University Jerusalem, which supported me as a Research Fellow early in 1998, and where I did much of the work for this paper. I would also like to thank Will Derks whose careful reading of an earlier version and provocative comments stimulated me to re-work some parts of the original version. Thanks are due to a RIMA reviewer for suggestions concerning contemporary Malaysian responses to some of the issues raised in the paper, and to RIMA for allowing me to reprint the essay as part of the present collection.

* Virginia Hooker is Professor of Indonesian and Malay in the Faculty of Asian Studies, The Australian National University. She has recently published *A Short History of Malaysia* and a study of the personal experience of Islam in contemporary Indonesia. She can be contacted at Virginia.Hooker@anu.edu.au.

1. Anwar Ibrahim, *The Asian Renaissance* (Singapore/Kuala Lumpur:Times Books International, 1996), p. 123.

2. *The Jakarta Post*, 27 November 1999, p. 12.

3. Harold Crouch, *Government and Society in Malaysia* (St. Leonards, NSW: Allen and Unwin, 1996), pp. 25–27.

4. "Terbentuknya sebuah negara-bangsa Malaysia yang benar-benar moden dan maju, sebuah masyarakat industri yang adil, bermoral

dan rasional, teguh dan tangkas ekonominya, selain mempunyai keperibadian sosial dan budayanya sendiri." Rustam A. Sani, *Melayu Baru dan Bangsa Malaysia: Tradisi Cendekia dan Krisis Budaya* (Kuala Lumpur: Utusan Publications, 1993), p. 45.

5.   Anonymous, *Penjelasan mengenai Wawasan 2020 oleh YAB Perdana Menteri di Seremban pada 26 Mei 1991* (location unknown: Kementerian Penerangan, Jabatan Percetakan Negara, 1991), p. 3.

6.   Mahathir Mohamad, *The Challenge* (Petaling Jaya: Pelanduk Publications, 1986), Introduction.

7.   Ibid.

8.   Mahathir, *The Challenge*, p. 81.

9.   Anwar Ibrahim, *The Asian Renaissance*, p. 19, 27.

10. For example, see Maznah Mohamad, "15 Years of solitude for Anwar ... And for Malaysia?" *Aliran*, 20, 6 (2000): 2–6

11. An indication of the range of articles on Islamic topics carried by the press can be gauged from the following list which I assembled after scanning Malaysian newspapers between November 1996 and February 1997: Islam and values; Islam and social problems; Islam and modernity; Islamic courts; polygamy; reports about activities during Ramadan (the month of daylight fasting). In addition, the papers carried regular features by Islamic scholars to inform readers about specific issues such as Islamic banking, insurance policies for Muslims, or to explain religious obligations such as the pilgrimage to Mecca.

12. Crouch, *Government and Society in Malaysia*, p. 87.

13. "Masalah sosial yang semakin serius di kalangan masyarakat Melayu disebabkan mereka gagal mengamal, mematuhi dan menghayati ajaran agama Islam, kata Timbalan Perdana Menteri Datuk Seri Anwar Ibrahim. Katanya, walaupun mereka didedah dan dididik dengan pelbagai ajaran agama di rumah dan di sekolah berbanding masyarakat agama lain, ajaran itu tidak memberikan kesan kerana sikap mereka sendiri yang kurang menghayatinya. 'Ini perkara yang aneh, kerana pendidikan agama di sekolah hanya diwajibkan kepada pelajar Islam, tetapi dari data yang kita perolehi menunjukkan pelbagai masalah sosial lebih menjurus kepada masalah masyarakat Islam...Masyarakat tidak seharusnya menyalahkan golongan muda... kerana masalah itu melambangkan kelemahan institusi masyarakat termasuk keluarga, anggota jawatankuasa kariah masjid, institusi pendidikan, badan politik dan jabatan kerajaan".

14. A term used to describe the behaviour of teenage girls who wait around public places hoping to be picked up by men.

15. It is likely that television reporting may reach a wider audience than newspapers but the impact of television, because of its restricted duration and ephemeral form, may be less.

16. Akbar S. Ahmed, *Postmodernism and Islam: Predicament and Promise* (London and New York: Routledge, 1992), p. vii; Robert W. Hefner, "Introduction", in *Islam in an Era of Nation-States: Politics and Religious Renewal in Muslim Southeast Asia*, ed. R. Hefner and P. Horvatich (Honolulu: University of Hawaii Press), p. 6.

17. Barbara D. Metcalf, "Islam in Contemporary Southeast Asia: History, Continuity, Morality", in *Islam in an Era of Nation-States*, pp. 318–19.

18. Shamsul A. B., "Identity Construction, Nation Formation, and Islamic Revivalism in Malaysia", in *Islam in an Era of Nation-States*, p. 210.

19. Shamsul A. B., "Identity Construction", p. 224.

20. Adrian Vickers, "'Malay Identity': Modernity, Invented Tradition, and Forms of Knowledge", *Review of Indonesian and Malaysian Affairs*, 31, 1 (1997): 175.

21. *Laws of Malaysia: Federal Constitution*, Article 160 (Kuala Lumpur: Percetakan Nasional Malaysia, 1997), p. 152.

22. Shamsul A. B., "Identity Construction", p. 210.

23. Robert N. Bellah, *Beyond Belief: Essays on Religion in a Post-Traditional World* (New York: Harper and Row, 1970), p. 180.

24. Ruth McVey, *Redesigning the Cosmos: Belief Systems and State Power in Indonesia* (Copenhagen: Nordic Institute of Asian Studies, 1995), p. 35, fn. 39.

25. Anwar Ibrahim, *The Asian Renaissance*, p. 123.

26. *Laws of Malaysia*, Part III, pp. 23–26.

27. "membentuk sebuah bangsa Malaysia yang bebas, teguh dan terbentuk jiwanya, yakin akan diri sendiri dan dihormati oleh semua bangsa lain". Anonymous, *Penjelasan mengenai Wawasan 2020*, 3.

28. Rustam, *Melayu Baru dan Bangsa Malaysia*, pp. 49–50.

29. "...mentransformasikan fahaman nasionalisme Melayunya (yang telah memperjuangkan kemerdekaan negara ini) menjadi nasionalisme Malaysia". Rustam, *Melayu Baru dan Bangsa Malaysia*, p. 50.

30. Shamsul A. B., "The Construction and Transformation of a Social Identity: Malayness and Bumiputeraness re-examined", *Journal of Asian and African Studies*, 52: 16.

31. Shamsul A. B., "The Construction and Transformation of a Social Identity", p. 15.

32. Bellah, *Beyond Belief*, p. 69.

33. "Di Malaysia, kita boleh hidup rukun dan damai bukan saja di kalangan orang Islam tetapi juga antara orang Islam dan bukan Islam kerana kita mematuhi peraturan dan undang-undang".

34. Anwar Ibrahim, *The Asian Renaissance*, 124.

35. Ariffin Omar, *Bangsa Melayu: Malay Concepts of Democracy and Community, 1945–1950* (Kuala Lumpur: Oxford University Press, 1993), p. 213.

36.   Ariffin Omar, *Bangsa Melayu*, p. 214.
37.   Henk Maier, '"We Are Playing Relatives"—Riau: The Cradle of Reality and Hybridity', *Bijdragen tot de Taal-, Land-, en Volkenkunde*, 153, 4 (1997): 695.
38.   Katherine Pratt Ewing, *Arguing Sainthood: Modernity, Psychoanalysis, and Islam* (Durham: Duke University Press, 1997), p. 4; John Bowen, "Modern Intentions: Reshaping Subjectivities in an Indonesian Muslim Society", in *Islam in an Era of Nation-States.*
39.   *The Straits Times*, 1 Dec. 1999.
40.   Ibid., p. 39.
41.   Ibid., p. 1.
42.   Ibid.
43.   *The Australian*, 4 Oct 2000.
44.   Ibid., p. 6.

Chapter 9

Author's Note: I am grateful to Bernd Nothofer, Amin Sweeney and Shamsul A. B. for discussions about some of the topics in this essay. Their insights and suggestions were most helpful, however the errors and generalisations remain with me.

*   James T. Collins is a professor at the Institute of the Malay World and Civilization, Universiti Kebangsaan Malaysia, where he specialises in research on the Malay language. He may be contacted at pshatma@pkrisc.cc.ukm.my.
1.   In the last decade, numerous Austronesian linguists have argued in favour of this homeland hypothesis. For the most important works, see R. A. Blust, "Malay Historical Linguistics: A Progress Report", in *Rekonstruksi dan Cabang-Cabang Induk Bahasa Melayu Induk*, ed. Mohd. Thani Ahmad and Zaini Mohamed Zain (Kuala Lumpur: Dewan Bahasa dan Pustaka, 1988), pp. 1–33; K. A. Adelaar, "Proto-Malayic: The Reconstruction of its Phonology and Parts of its Lexicon and Morphology", *Pacific Linguistics* C-119 (Canberra: Australian National University, 1992); Bernd Nothofer, "Migrasi Orang Melay Purba Kajian Awal", *Sari*, 14 (1996): 33–52; and James T. Collins, "The Malays and non-Malays of Kalimantan Barat: Evidence from the Study of Language", paper presented at Conference on Tribal Communities in the Malay World, Institute of Southeast Asian Studies (Singapore), 24–27 March 1997. Peter Bellwood, *Prehistory of the Indo–Malaysian Archipelago*, rev. edn. (Honolulu: University of Hawaii Press, 1997) provides an archaeological framework that accommodates this linguistic hypothesis, a hypothesis that rests on

well-established principles of comparative historical linguistics (see Nothofer's abovementioned work for an overview of the methodology). On 10–11 April 2001, the Institute of the Malay World and Civilisation (ATMA), in cooperation with Dewan Bahasa dan Pustaka, organised a Colloquium on "Borneo as the Homeland of Malay: Implications for Research". The papers Blust, Nothofer, Adelaar and Bellwood presented shed new light on this hypothesis and laid the groundwork for ATMA's current research project focused on testing the hypothesis. The essay presented here, however, is not concerned with the validity of this homeland hypothesis. Rather, it offers a preliminary description of language affiliation and ethnic identity based on the analysis of contemporary language use and language attitudes among some speech communities in Kalimantan Barat.

2. James T. Collins, "Malay Dialect Research in Malaysia: The Issue of Perspective", *Bijdragen tot de Taal-, Land- en Volkenkunde* [hereafter *BKI*],145, 2 (1989): 235–64.

3. Michael Gorra, as cited in in Peter Kemp, "Hymns to the Hybrid", *The Times Literary Supplement*, 4921 (1997): 21.

4. Aamer was writing about Pakistani identity, which he insisted was not monolithic. Although 'Malay' is an older identity than 'Pakistani', the idea of a dynamic, redefining identity is relevant to the communities discussed in this essay. Aamer Hussein, "Indus Man's Resistance", *The Times Literary Supplement*, 4923 (1997): 11; see also Anthony Reid's contribution to this volume.

5. Collins, "The Malays and non-Malays of Kalimantan Barat".

6. Sudarsono *et al.*, "Ketika kerusuhan mengguncang bumi khatulistiwa", *Forum Keadilan*, 5, 24 (1997): 12–16.

7. Kenneth Sillander, "Local Identity and Regional Variation: Notes on the Lack of Significance of Ethnicity Among the Luangan and the Bentian", *Borneo Research Bulletin*, 26 (1995): 69–95.

8. In this essay, the term 'Malayic' refers to all the Malay dialects spoken in the Malay world, but also to a large number of languages that are closely related to Malay, for example Iban and Kendayan (the latter includes Selako), and other variants spoken by non-Malays and non-Muslims as their home languages. So the term 'Malayic'-speakers includes Malays, who speak Malay dialects, and non-Malays, some of whom speak separate languages such as Iban and some of whom who speak variants which appear to be Malay dialects. This naming praxis parallels other language nomenclature. For example, 'Germanic' refers to separate languages, such as English and German, but also to variants that are apparently mutually intelligible, such as Swedish and Norwegian. For a discussion of Malayic and its members, see Adelaar, *Proto-Malayic*.

9.   Studies of the Kendayan language can be found in the following
      sources: Donatus Dunselman, "Bijdrage tot de kennis van de taal en
      adat der Kendajan Dajaks van west-Borneo", *BKI*, 105 (1949): 59–
      105, 147–218; Donatus Dunselman, "Bijdrage tot de kennis van de
      taal en adat der Kendajan Dajaks van west-Borneo. II", *BKI*, 106
      (1950): 321–73; Dunselman, "Adat-gebruiken van Kendajan-Dajak's
      van west–Borneo in acht te nemen na een brand", *BKI*, 108 (1952):
      62–68; Yoseph Thomas *et al.*, *Sistem perulangan dalam bahasa Dayak
      Kendayan* (Jakarta: Departemen Pendidikan dan Kebudayaan, 1991).
10.   Anonymous, *Kabupaten Ketapang dalam angka* (Ketapang: Bagian
      Hubungan Masyarakat Setwilda Tingkat II Ketapang, 1995); James
      T. Collins, "Klasifikasi Varian Melayik di Ketapang: Kepelbagaian
      Bahasa di Kalimantan Barat", *Dewan Bahasa*, 42 (1998): 233–60;
      Bernd Nothofer, "Klasifikasi varian-varian Melayik di antara Sungai
      Semandang dan Sungai Pawan/Sungai Keriau (Gerai, Tanjung
      Beringin, Randau Jeka')", paper presented at Seminar Internasional
      Bahasa dan Budaya di Dunia Melayu (Asia Tenggara), Universitas
      Mataram, 21–23 July 1997.
11.   Collins, "The Malays and non-Malays of Kalimantan Barat"; K.A.
      Adelaar, "The Classification of the Tamanic Languages", in
      Language Contact and Change in the Austronesian World, ed. T.
      Dutton and D. Tryon (Berlin, New York: Mouton de Gruyter,
      1994), pp. 1–41; *Language Atlas of the Pacific Area. Part II, Japan
      Area, Philippines and Formosa, Mainland and Insular South-east
      Asia*, ed. Stephen A. Wurm and Shiro Hattori (Canberra: The
      Australian Academy of the Humanities in collaboration with the
      Japan Academy, 1983), Sheet 42.
12.   'Bidayuh' is the term widely used in Malaysia to refer to those
      communities of western Sarawak that speak closely related languages,
      for example Jagoi, Biatah and others. *Bidayuh* is derived from *bi*
      (person) and *dayuh* (interior), but here the term is used to refer
      narrowly to the language group that Hudson, following colonial
      nomenclature, called 'Land Dayak'. 'Land Dayak' was chosen as an
      exonym that contrasted with 'Sea Dayak', the colonial term for the
      Iban group of Sarawak. Because 'Sea Dayak' is no longer used as an
      exonym referring to Iban groups, the usefulness of its contrastive
      dyad, 'Land Dayak', seems questionable. In view of the growing use
      of terms like 'Malayic', 'Ibanic' and 'Tamanic' to refer to clusters of
      languages and dialects in Borneo, I propose using 'Bidayuhic' to
      refer to the widespread and diverse group of languages formerly
      known as 'Land Dayak'. Collins, "Klasifikasi Varian Melayik di
      Ketapang"; A. B. Hudson, "A Note on Selako: Malayic Dayak and
      Land Dayak languages in Western Borneo", *Sarawak Museum
      Journal*, 18 (1970): 301–18.

13. In fact, in the upper reaches of the Laur River, a north-side tributary of the Pawan River itself, there are more than 500 speakers of a Bidayuhic variant in the village of Selangkut (Aleksandra, personal communication, 17 Sept. 1998).

14. R. A. Blust, "The Reconstruction of Proto-Malayo-Javanic: An Appreciation", *BKI*, 134 (1981): 456–69.

15. *Language Atlas of the Pacific Area*, ed. Wurm and Hattori, Sheet 42.

16. See, for example, P.J. Veth, *Borneo's wester-afdeeling. Geographisch, statistisch, historisch* (Zaltbommel: Joh. Noman en Zoon, 1854).

17. Collins, "The Malays and non-Malays of Kalimantan Barat".

18. Ibid., and Nothofer, "Klasifikasi varian-varian Melayik".

19. *Language Atlas of the Pacific Area*, ed. Wurm and Hattori.

20. Collins, "The Malays and non-Malays of Kalimantan Barat" and "Klasifikasi Varian Melayik di Ketapang".

21. James T. Collins, "Malay Dialect Research in Malaysia: The Issue Of Perspective", *BKI*, 145 (1989): 235–64.

22. Collins, "The Malays and non-Malays of Kalimantan Barat".

23. I am grateful to Professor Mahmud Akil, S. H., then Rector of Universitas Tanjungpura, who designated Dr Chairil Effendi as my research counterpart. Dr Chairil Effendi has proven a particularly resilient and insightful colleague, whose participation in the fieldwork of February 1998 greatly enhanced our ability to record reliable data. It was a pleasure to work with him in Kalimantan in February and to join him on the same conference panel in Leiden the following April.

24. In each village visited, Malay informants volunteered very positive observations about their Kendayan neighbours. In Jata', for example, Malay informants repeatedly acknowledged that they themselves were related by blood to people of the nearby Kendayan villages. These positive expressions should be re-examined in an in-depth study of interethnic relations, with language and language competence forming a component of the study.

25. G. P. Rouaffer, "Zijn er nog Hindoe-Oudheden in Midden-Borneo aan de Boven-Sekadau", *Tijdschrift voor Indische Taal-, Land- en Volkenkunde*, 51 (1909): 456–69.

26. Since July 2000 the Institute of the Malay World and Civilisation (ATMA), with funding from the Southeast Asian Studies Regional Exchange Program (Tokyo), has undertaken an extensive study of language variants spoken in the Sekadau River basin. Although the data collected through this project are more diverse and extensive than the preliminary data used in this essay, the broad outlines of the sociolinguistic setting appear to match the situation reported here.

27. W. A. L. Stokhof (ed.), "Holle lists: Vocabularies in languages of Indonesia, Vol. 8, Kalimantan (Borneo)" (Materials in languages of

Indonesia no. 31), in cooperation with Alma E. Almanar, *Pacific Linguistics* D69 (Canberra: Australian National University, 1986). Kats included a dialogue and Azaharie *et al.* a description of this variant as it is spoken in Sanggau; see J. Kats, *Spraakkunst en taaleigen van het Maleisch. Deel 2 (Met medewerking van Marah Soetan)* (Weltevreden: N.V. Boekhandel Visser, 1921); Azharie Arief *et al., Morfologi dan sintaksis bahasa Melayu Sanggau* (Jakarta: Departemen Pendidikan dan Kebudayaan, 1989).

28.   Collins, "The Malays and non-Malays of Kalimantan Barat".

29.   As delimited in the reconstructed vocabulary of Adelaar, *Proto-Malayic.*

30.   Indeed, the fieldwork conducted by ATMA in the Sekadau River basin (July 2000 until now) has demonstrated the existence of a large cluster of settlements along the Taman River, a tributary of the Sekadau, in which this Malayic variant, locally known as Taman Sesat, is spoken as the home language. Fieldwork conducted in the Pawan River basin in September 1998 indicated that in addition to the migration of Sekadau Dayaks to the Keriau tributary (Kenyabur village), there are numerous migrants who speak the Sekadau Dayak variant of Malay in villages along the Laur River. However, these migrants are apparently shifting to the language spoken by indigenous Laur Dayaks (Fidelis, personal communication, 17 Sept. 1998). A brief description of one of these Laur variants, Sepotong, was presented in James T. Collins, "Malayic variants in southwestern Borneo: Gerai and Sepotong", paper presented at The Eighth Annual Meeting of the Southeast Asian Linguistic Society, Kuala Lumpur, 20–22 July 1998.

31.   Bernard J.L. Sellato, "An Ethnic Sketch of the Melawi area West Kalimantan", *Borneo Research Bulletin*, 18, 1 (1986): 46–58.

32.   Yusriadi, born about 700 kilometres upriver from the Kapuas delta, is himself a speaker of a variant of Ulu Kapuas Malay closely related to the kind of Malay spoken in the Melawi River basin. I am grateful for his strong contribution to the UKM–Untan cooperative project, in particular for the data collected during his Melawi field trip.

33.   Personal communication, Yusriadi, 28 February 1998.

34.   For more information, see Shamsul's contribution in this volume.

35.   In a survey of multilingualism, identity and changing notions of nationalism in Europe, Eric Hobsbawm observes that Balkanisation of language and identity has emerged as a political alternative to plurilingualism. Eric Hobsbawm, "Language, Culture and National Identity," *Social Research*, 63 (1996): 1065–80. I would like to thank my colleague at Goethe-Universität in Frankfurt, Klaus Schreiner, who first directed my attention to Hobsbawm's essay.

36. Christo van Rensburg, "When the Slaves Came: Malay and Cape Afrikaans", and S. Koolhof and R. Ross, "Upas, September and the Bugis at the Cape of Good Hope: The Context of a Slave's Letter"; both are unpublished manuscripts.
37. M. Rakiep, personal communication, 3 Feb. 1998.
38. Uri Tadmor, "Language Contact and Systemic Restructuring: The Malay Dialect of Nonthaburi, Central Thailand" (Ph.D. diss., University of Hawai'i, 1995).
39. Penelope J. Corfield, "Introduction: Historians and Language", in *Language, History and Class*, ed. P.J. Corfield (Oxford: Basil Blackwell, 1991), pp. 28–29.

Chapter 10

*   Will Derks is an independent scholar living the Netherlands. His research interest focuses on oral literature in Indonesia, with particular interest in new methods of producing traditional literature in areas outside the centre (Jakarta). E-mail correspondence can be directed to willderks@planet.nl.
1. See, for example, Pascal Boniface, "The Proliferation of States", *The Washington Quarterly*, 213 (1998): 111–27.
2. Kwame Anthony Appiah, *In My Father's House* (London: Methuen, 1993), p. 79.
3. Walter Benjamin, "The Storyteller", in *Illuminations*, ed. Hannah Arendt (New York: Schocken Books, 1969), pp. 83–109.
4. Walter Ong, *Interfaces of the Word: Studies in the Evolution of Consciousness and Culture* (Ithaca: Cornell University Press, 1977), pp. 231–71.
5. 'Literary system' is based on Itamar Even-Zohar, "Polysystem Theory", *Poetics Today*, 11, 1 (1990): 7–94; and Franco Moretti, "Conjectures on World Literature", *New Left Review*, 1 (Jan–Feb. 2000): 54–68.
6. George Quinn, *The Novel in Javanese* (Leiden: KITLV Press, 1992), p. 95.
7. Claudine Salmon, *Literature in Malay by the Chinese of Indonesia* (Paris: Édition de la Maison des Sciences de l'Homme, 1981).
8. Ernst Ulrich Kratz, *A Bibliography of Indonesian Literature in Journals* (Yogyakarta: Gadjah Mada University Press, 1988); George Quinn, "The Case of the Invisible Literature: Power, Scholarship, and Contemporary Javanese Writing", *Indonesia*, 35 (1983): 1–36, and *The Novel in Javanese*; Farida Soemargono, *Le 'Groupe de Yogya' 1945–1960: Les voies javanaises d'une littérature indonesiénne* (Paris: Association Archipel, 1979).

9. Will Derks, "'If Not to Anything Else': Some Reflections on Modern Indonesian Literature", *Bijdragen tot de Taal-, Land- en Volkenkunde*, 152, 3 (1996): 341–52.

10. Will Derks, *The Feast of Storytelling: On Malay Oral Tradition* (Jakarta/Leiden: RUL, 1994).

11. Amin Sweeney, *Authors and Audiences in Traditional Malay Literature* (Berkeley: Center for South and Southeast Asian Studies, 1980), p. 26.

12. Soemargono, *Le 'Groupe de Yogya'*.

13. T. S. Eliot, *On Poetry and Poets* (New York: Farrar, Strauss and Cudahy, 1957), p. 40.

14. William R. Roff, *Bibliography of Malay and Arabic Periodicals Published in the Straits Settlements and Peninsular Malay States* (London: Oxford University Press, 1972); Roff, *The Origins of Malay Nationalism* (Kuala Lumpur: Oxford University Press, 1994); Liesbeth Dolk, *Twee Zielen, Twee Gedachten: Tijdschriften en Intellectuelen op Java* (1900–1957) (Leiden: KITLV Press, 1993).

15. Will Derks, "Malay Identity Work", *Bijdragen tot de Taal-, Land- en Volkenkunde*, 153, 4 (1997): 699–716, and "'Because I am a Malay': Taufik Ikram Jamil between Nation and Region", in *New Developments in Asian Studies*, ed. Paul van de Velde and Alex McKay (London/New York: Kegan Paul, 1998), pp. 234–51.

16. Barbara Watson Andaya, "From Rum to Tokyo: The Search for Anticolonial Allies by the Rulers of Riau, 1888–1914", *Indonesia*, 24 (1977): 123–56.

17. *Seulawah: Antologi Sastra Aceh Sekilas Pintas*, ed. L. K. Ara, Taufiq Ismail and Hasyim KS (Jakarta: Yayasan Nusantara/Pemerintah Daerah Khusus Istemewa Aceh, 1995); Darma Putra, "Kebangkitan Puisi Indonesia Modern di Bali", *Basis* (Oct. 1994): 384–96; Will Derks, "Poets and Power in Pekanbaru: On Burgeoning Malay Consciousness in Indonesia", in *IIAS Yearbook 1994*, ed. Paul van der Velde (Leiden: International Institute for Asian Studies, 1995), pp. 60–72; Derks, "*Sastra Perjuangan*: Literary Activism in Present-Day Indonesia", in *IIAS Yearbook 1995*, ed. Paul van der Velde (Leiden: International Institute for Asian Studies, 1996), pp. 42–52; Thomas M. Hunter, "Figures in the Carpet: A Selection of Modern Indonesian Poetry of Bali", *Review of Indonesian and Malay Affairs*, 32, 1 (1998): 1–23.

18. Melani Budianta et al., *Pemetaan Komunitas Sastra di Jakarta, Bogor, Tangerang dan Bekasi* (Jakarta: Komunitas Sastra Indonesia, 1998).

19. Ulf Hannerz, *Exploring the City: Inquiries Toward an Urban Anthropology* (New York: Columbia University Press, 1980); Hannerz, *Cultural Complexity; Studies in the Social Organization*

of Meaning (New York: Columbia University Press, 1992); Fred Inglis, *Cultural Studies* (Oxford: Blackwell, 1993); Manuel Castells, *The Rise of the Network Society* (Cambridge, MA: Blackwell, 1996).

20.   Gilles Deleuze and Felix Guatarri, *Rhizome: Introduction* (Paris: Editions de Minuit, 1976).

21.   Keith Foulcher, "In Search of the Postcolonial in Indonesian Literature", *Sojourn*, 10, 2 (1995): 147–71; Henk Maier, "From Heteroglossia to Polyglossia: The Creation of Malay and Dutch in the Indies", *Indonesia*, 56 (1993): 37–65.

22.   Kees Groeneboer, *Weg tot het Westen. Het Nederlands voor Indië 1600–1950* (Leiden: KITLV Press, 1993).

23.   Bill Ashcroft, Gareth Griffith and Helen Tiffin, *The Empire Writes Back: Theory and Practice in Post–Colonial Literatures* (London: Routledge, 1989).

24.   Joseph Brodsky, *On Grief and Reason* (New York: Farrar Straus Giroux, 1995), p. 203.

25.   Hans Overbeck, *Malaiische Geschichten* (Düsseldorf: Eugen Diederichs, 1975), p. 3.

26.   R. J. Wilkinson, *Papers on Malay Subjects, Part I, Malay Literature* (Kuala Lumpur: Oxford University Press, 1907), p. 61.

27.   Derks, *Feast of Storytelling*, p. 20.

28.   Henk Maier, "Moderne Indonesische Poëzie", in *Traditionele en Moderne Poëzie van Indonesië*, ed. Bernhard Arps, Sirtjo Koolhof and Henk Maier (Leiden: Instituut Indonesische Cursussen, 1994), p. 61. Not all scholars have been so pessimistic. In the motto for this second part of my paper I quote Hooykaas with fervour: "Long live the new Malay literature!" Interestingly, in the larger context of this quotation Hooykaas refers also to Overbeck's famous statement. The original Dutch reads: "*Een vijftiental jaren geleden begon Overbeck, kenner der Maleische letteren als weinig anderen, een van zijn boeken over Maleische literatuur met de woorden: De Maleische Literatuur is dood. De klassieke letterkunde ís het, maar de moderne is springlevend, en evenals bij de bekendmaking van den dood van een Fransch [sic] koning moge nu terstond volgen: Léve de nieuwe Maleische letterkunde!*" C. Hooykaas, *Over Maleische Literatuur* (Leiden: E.J. Brill, 1937), p. 193.

29.   The preliminary title of this book, which is based on collective fieldwork carried out by a team of students and university teachers at the Centre for Malay Studies, is *Bibliografi Kajian Melayu dan Peta Sastra (Tradisi) Lisan Melayu di Riau* (Supriadi, forthcoming). It may be relevant to note here that the draft of this book that I saw still did not cover all the *kabupaten* (districts) of the province of Riau. It is likely that the planned inclusion in this survey of the

Kabupaten Kepulauan (the Riau Archipelago), which consists of more than 3,000 islands, will add significantly to the number of oral professionals that have been tracked down on the Riau mainland so far. Incidentally, it is telling that this work has not been published as a book and is still only available in the form of a photocopy.

30. In an earlier paper I have tried to show how this oppression takes shape in the context of the central government's policies concerning a national Indonesian culture as well as how these policies are resisted, particularly through literary activism in present-day Pekanbaru, the capital of Riau. In a subsequent paper I took up the same theme, though this time focusing on other means of resistance there. Derks, "Poets and Power in Pekanbaru" and "Malay Identity Work".

31. See, for instance, Andaya, "From Rum to Tokyo"; Virginia Matheson, "Strategies of Survival: The Malay Royal Lineage of Lingga-Riau", *Journal of Southeast Asian Studies*, 17, 1 (1986): 5–38; Hasan Junus, *Raja Ali Haji; Budayawan di Gerbang Abad XX* (Pekanbaru: Universitas Islam Riau Press, 1988); Jan van der Putten and Al Azhar, *Di Dalam Berkekalan Persahabatan; In Everlasting Friendship. Letters from Raja Ali Haji* (Leiden: Department of Languages and Cultures of Southeast Asia and Oceania, 1995); and Timothy P. Barnard, "*Taman Penghiburan*: Entertainment and the Riau Elite in the Late 19th Century", *Journal of the Malaysian Branch of the Royal Asiatic Society*, 67, 2 (1994): 17–46.

32. The first issue explains how the Malay culture hero Hang Tuah managed to learn twelve languages (*Menyimak* , 1 [28 Oct. 1992–28 Jan. 1993]: 47), while in the fourth issue we are presented with the story of King Suran who explored the ocean with a submarine (*Menyimak*, 4 [28 July–28 Oct. 1993]: 46). Of course, these extracts were not chosen at random, but with the aim of emphasising Malay greatness. Incidentally, the latter of the two passages was especially transliterated for the occasion.

33. In the sixth issue of *Menyimak*, for instance, Sayid Al–Hadi is honoured as the "the first Malay author who produced a novel as a form of literary work". The work meant here is his *Hikayat Faridah Hanum* (see *Menyimak*, 6 [28 Jan.–28 Apr. 1995]: 43–44). Another example would be the discussion of the life and times of Abu Muhamad Adnan, the pen name of Raja Haji Abdullah bin Hasan who was a grandson of Raja Ali Haji. Although he too is praised as an early novelist in the literature that was produced in Riau (*novelis awal dalam kesusa-straan yang dihasilkan di Riau*), only a part of one of his *syair* is given as an example of his *oeuvre* (*Menyimak*, 7 [28 Apr–28 July 1994]: 43–46).

34. See *Menyimak*, 3 [28 Apr–28 July 1993]: 30–32. The original Indonesian reads: "*Tentulah penguba-han ini tidak serasi dengan kehendak filologi, namun hal itu dilakukan dengan pertimbangan untuk menyu-guhkan suatu karya dari masa lampau untuk bacaan masa kini.*"

35. Ibid. The original Indonesian reads: "*dari kanan ke kiri. Dan setelah setiap satu rangkaian huruf-huruf dibacanya pada kertas kuning apak itu, jarinya menekan tombol-tombol di keyboard dan melihat hasilnya di layar.*
   Ia membaca: *ta-alif-nun-mim-lam-ha alif-kaf sin-pa-ra-ta-ya mim-nun-alif-nun-mim sin-hamzah-waw-ra-nga, dan menulis: tanamlah aku seperti menanam seorang...*
   Klik! Tiba-tiba listrik padam, dan semua huruf lesap dalam gelap.*"

36. On the *talkin* controversy, see Roff *Origins of Malay Nationalism*, p. 78. Roff defines *talkin* as follows: "a short address recited over the grave at the close of the funeral service consisting of advice to the dead man on how to reply to the questions of the Interrogators of Dead".

37. Hasan Junus suggests that both these figures lived on Penyengat and that the diary of Encik Abdul Karim is still kept at the yellow mosque in Penyengat in the form of a 'crumpled' (*kumal*) manuscript. I have not been able to verify this as yet. Incidentally, the *surat wasiat* of Marhum Kantor and Marhum Mursyid are extant manuscripts. It is probably no coincidence that they were published recently. See Hasan Junus *et al.*, *Raja Ali Haji dan Karya-karyanya* (Pekanbaru: Pusat Pengajian Bahasa dan Kebudajaan Melayu, 1996), pp. 306–11.

38. It may be germane to note here that, after *Menyimak* folded, its successor was named *Suara*, 'Voice'.

39. R. Abdurrachman lives on Penyengat and is well known for his talent, although he is certainly not the only gifted reciter on this charming island. All performances I mention here were recorded on tape.

40. The festival called *Hari Raja Ali Haji* took place on Penyengat from 1–31 Oct. 1996.

41. These poets were Ediruslan Pe Amanriza, Idrus Tintin, Sutarji Calzoum Bachri and Taufiq Ismail from Indonesia, Suratman Markasan from Singapore and A. Samad Said from Malaysia.

42. I know of two others, the *Syair Kera* [Poem of the Monkey] and the *Syair Lebah* [Poem of the Bee]. None of the three has been published. They circulate in the form of photocopies—a form of distribution that is certainly not uncommon in present-day Indonesia.

43. As far as I know, this was Zuarman's first performance as a 'traditional' storyteller. In Pekanbaru he is better known as a musician and as an interpreter of traditional Malay music. His performance took place on 15 Oct. 1996 in the Dang Merdu building in Pekanbaru. For Indonesian and English versions of the short story, see Hasan

Junus, "Pengantin Boneka", *Horison*, 25, 2 (1991): 58–67, and "The Puppet Bride", in *Diverse Lives*, trans. Jeanette Lingard (Kuala Lumpur: Oxford University Press, 1995), pp. 108–17.

44. Roff, *Origins of Malay Nationalism*, pp. 45–46.

45. Ibid., pp. 53, 62–63; Barnard, "*Taman Penghiburan*", pp. 29–32.

46. Roff, *Origins of Malay Nationalism*, p. 82.

47. Ibid.; Andaya, "From Rum to Tokyo"; Derks, "Poets and Power in Pekanbaru".

48. References to the reading aloud of newspapers and periodicals can be found in Roff, *Origins of Malay Nationalism*, pp. 167, 177.

49. For a discussion of some of the reasons for this fixation on a single centre of authority in the study of modern Indonesian literature, see Derks, "*Sastra Perjuangan*".

50. It may be relevant to note here that Soemargono was well aware of the centralising view that was and still is dominant in the study of modern Indonesian literature when she said about her own approach: "*[N]otre perspective prend à rebours la vision centralisatrice telle qu'elle a toujours été pratiqueé par les analyses venant de Jakarta ou de l'extérieur. Mais elle nous paraît mieux correspondre à la variété des réalités indonésiennes.*" Soemargono, Le '*Groupe de Yogya*' 1945–1960, p. 47.

51. Rosslyn Marie von der Borch, "Art and Activism; Some Examples from Contemporary Java" (BA Honours Thesis, School of Social Sciences, Flinders University of South Australia, 1987), p. 28.

52. The 'literary history' of Banjarmasin I refer to is Tajuddin Noor Ganie's *Sejarah Lokal Kesusastraan Indonesia di Kalimantan Selatan 1930–1995* (Banjarmasin: Pusat Pengkajian Masalah Sastra Kalimantan Selatan, 1995). The already astonishing evidence in this publication is even surpassed by a kind of "Who's Who" in contemporary literary life in Banjarmasin, written by the same author; see Tajuddin Noor Ganie, *Apa dan Siapa Sastrawan Kalsel* (Banjarmasin: PUSKAJIMASTRA, 1996).

53. Taufik Ikram Jamil, *Sandiwara Hang Tuah* (Jakarta: Grasindo, 1996).

Chapter 11

Translators' note: This work originally appeared in 1995 as a typed manuscript entitled *Syair Nasib Melayu*. The author, whose original name is Tengku Nasyaruddin, is a scholar living in Pekanbaru, Indonesia. He spent his youth in the *kerajaan* of Kampar, and currently works as an advisor to the provincial government on a variety of cultural projects. His numerous works, including original poems, *pantuns*, and collections of other sayings, reflect his commitment to the preservation of Malay traditions and literature. A copy of the original Malay *syair* is available through Ian Proudfoot's Malay Concordance Project at Australian National University.

*   Tenas Effendy is the head of the Yayasan Setanggi, a Malay cultural organization located in Pekanbaru, Riau, Indonesia. E–mail correspondence can be directed to histpb@nus.edu.sg.
       Rohayati Paseng Barnard is the head of the Southeast Asia collection in the Hamilton Library at the University of Hawaii at Manoa. Her research interests focus on collection development of Southeast Asian materials in the United States and the Bugis in Sumatra. E–mail correspondence can be directed to rohayati@hawaii.edu.

Chapter 12

Author's Note: For assistance in writing this essay I am grateful to Timothy Barnard, Peter Borschberg, Diana Carroll, Claire Milner, Ian Proudfoot and Sharon Siddique.

*   Anthony Milner is a Professor of Asian Studies at the Australian National University. His research has focused on Malay understandings of society, colonialism and leadership. E–mail correspondence can be directed to Anthony.Milner@anu.edu.au.
1.   Any quotes that are not cited are from the contributions in this collection.
2.   Virginia Matheson (Hooker), "Concepts of Malay Ethos in Indigenous Malay Writings", *Journal of Southeast Asian Studies*, 10, 2 (1979): 360.
3.   Amin Sweeney, *A Full Hearing: Orality and Literacy in the Malay World* (Berkeley: University of California Press, 1987), p. 59.
4.   Ibrahim Yaacob, *Melihat Tanah Air* (Kota Bharu, 1941), p. 12.
5.   See Anthony Milner, "'Malayness': Confrontation, Innovation and Discourse", in V.J.H. Houben, H.M.J. Maier and W. Van der Molen (eds), *Looking in Odd Mirrors: The Java Sea* (Leiden: Rijksuniversiteit, 1992), pp. 43–59.
6.   Ibid., p. 46.
7.   See also James T. Collins, *Malay, World Language: A Short History* (Kuala Lumpur: Dewan Bahasa dan Pustaka 1998), p. 15.
8.   L.A. Sheridan, *Federation of Malaya Constitution* (Singapore: University of Malaya Law Review, 1961), p. 145.
9.   W. Marsden, *A Grammar of the Malayan Language* (Tokio: Mitake Torie, 1930; orig. pub. 1812), pp. xiii–xiv.
10.   Sweeney, *A Full Hearing*, p. 50.
11.   Sheridan, *Federation of Malaya Constitution*, p. 145.

12. See, for instance, Shamsul A. B., "From Orang Kaya Baru to Melayu Baru", *Culture and Privilege in Capitalist Asia*, ed. M. Pinches (London and New York: Routledge, 1998), pp. 86–110. See also, T.N. Harper, "New Malays, New Malaysians: Nationalism, Society and History", *Southeast Asian Affairs 1996* (Singapore: Institute of Southeast Asian Studies, 1997), p. 242.

13. See, for instance, Anthony Milner, *The Invention of Politics in Colonial Malaya: Contesting Nationalism and Expansion of the Public Sphere* (Cambridge: Cambridge University Press, 2002). Compare the view of Tenas Effendy from Riau in Indonesia, that "so long as Malay moral, social and cultural values continue to exist then so does the *alam Melayu*" (Malay world); Ashley Turner, "Cultural Survival, Identity and the Performing Arts of Kampar's Suku Petalangan", *Bijdragen tot de Taal-, Land-, en Volkenkunde*, 153, 4 (1997): 658.

14. Sweeney, *A Full Hearing*, p. 53.

15. Ibid., p. 46.

16. Hendrik M.J. Maier, *In the Center of Authority: The Malay Hikayat Merong Mahawangsa* (Ithaca: Cornell University Southeast Asia Program, 1988), pp. 29–30. See also Reid's chapter in this volume.

17. Ibid., p. 155. See also chapters 5 and 6 of this book for discussion of 'the break'.

18. See also Andaya's "The seventeenth-century Acehnese Model of Malay Society", *Reading Asia. New Research in Asian Studies*, ed. F. Husken and Dick van der Meij (Richmond: Curzon Press, 2001), pp. 83–109.

19. Also see Timothy P. Barnard, *Multiple Centres of Authority: Society and Environment in Siak and Eastern Sumatra, 1674–1827* (Leiden: KITLV, 2003).

20. A. C. Milner, *Kerajaan: Malay Political Culture on the Eve of Colonial Rule* (Tucson: University of Arizona Press for the Association of Asian Studies, 1982).

21. Having issued this warning, there is still good reason to believe that Malayness may have had a growing potency in the society of the nineteenth century Riau Archipelago. As Virginia Hooker has observed, the presence of a large and influential Bugis community would have "stimulated a feeling of ethnic identity among the Malays". The nineteenth-century text, the *Tuhfat al-Nafis*, for instance, could be seen to engage in such provocation when it frequently refers to a "Malay faction, or Malay group" (*kaum Melayu, pihak Melayu*) and often blames this group for stirring up anti-Bugis feeling; Matheson, "Concepts of Malay Ethos", p. 362.

22. See Anthony Reid's contribution to this volume.

23. Kassim Ahmad, ed., *Hikayat Hang Tuah* (Kuala Lumpur: Dewan Bahasa dan Pustaka, 1968), p. 1.

24. Anthony Reid, *Chinese and Malay Identities in Southeast Asia* (Taipei: PROSEA, Academia Sinica, 2000), p. 16.

25. See Heather Sutherland's and Reid's contributions to this volume.

26. Personal communication

27. Sweeney, *A Full Hearing*, p. 53 (and many others) refer to '*masuk Melayu*' as 'the traditional way of referring to conversion to Islam'. At what stage, one might ask, did it gain this meaning for people living outside the Melaka/Johor sphere? Similarly, when Valentijn in the early eighteenth century says that only Melaka people are called 'Malay'—others in the region are called 'Melayu-Johor', 'Melayu-Patani' and so forth—when did this terminology begin to be used by the people themselves? Ibid, p. 59; F. Valentijn, *Oud en Nieuw Oost Indien* (Dordrecht, Amsterdam: Johannes van Braam and G. onder de Linden, 1724), Vol. 7, pp. 317–18.

28. William Marsden, *The History of Sumatra* (London: Marsden, 1811), 325. When the British took over the administration of Ceylon in the late eighteenth-century, they chose the term 'Malay' for the varied community of people with origins in the Malay Archipelago; the community was so diverse that 'Javanese' did not seem appropriate; B. A. Hussainmiya, *Lost Cousins: The Malays of Sri Lanka* (Bangi, Selangor: Institut Bahasa, Kesusasteraan dan Kebudayaan, Universiti Kebangsaan Malaysia, Universiti Kebangsaan Malaysia , 1987), p. 58. Note, however, that the Tamils of the island called the community 'people from Java', B. D. K. Saldin, *The Sri Lankan Malays and their Language* (Dehiwala: Sridevi, 1996), p. 6.

29. Marsden, *A Grammar of the Malayan Language*, p. ix.

30. Matheson, "Concepts of Malay Ethos", p. 360.

31. Ibid., p. 361.

32. Note also that Brunei was not considered to be a Malay land. Ibid., 369.

33. Teuku Iskandar, ed., *De Hikajat Atjeh* ('s-Gravenhage: Martinus Nijhoff, 1958), p. 153.

34. Leonard Y. Andaya, "Orang Asli and the Melayu in the history of the Malay Peninsula", *Journal of the Malaysian Branch of the Royal Asiatic Society*, 75, 1 (2002): 39. Andaya gives examples of '*orang asli* "becoming Malay", and vice versa', pp. 40–42. For Bataks "becoming 'Malay'", see Milner, *Kerajaan*, ch. 5.

35. Robert W. Hefner, "Introduction" *The Politics of Multiculturalism: Pluralism and Citizenship in Malaysia, Singapore and Indonesia*, ed. Robert W. Hefner (Honolulu: University of Hawaii Press, 2001), pp. 12–15.

36. Marsden, *A Grammar of the Malayan Language*, p. ix.

37. See, for instance, B. Shrieke, *Indonesian Sociological Studies. Part 2: Ruler and Realm in Early Java* (The Hague and Bandung: Van Hoeve, 1957), pp. 230–67; Anthony Milner, "Islam and Malay Kingship", *Journal of the Royal Asiatic Society of Great Britain and Ireland*, 1 (1981): 46–70.

38. The phrase is '*Jawi Patani asalnya*'. See A. Teeuw and D.K. Wyatt (eds.), *Hikayat Patani. The Story of Patani* (The Hague: Martinus Nijhoff, 1970), pp. 131, 200.

39. C. Snouck Hurgronje, *Mekka in the Latter Part of the 19th century*. (Leiden: Brill, 1970), p. 215; on the use of 'Jawi', see also Michael Laffan, *Islamic Nationhood and Colonial Indonesia* (London: Routledge Curzon, 2003), pp. 13–14.

40. <http://www.anu.edu.au/asianstudies/ahcen/proudfoot/MCP>.

41. Sarapat is near Bandjarmarsin; J.J. Ras (ed.), *Hikajat Bandjar* (The Hague: Martinus Nijhoff, 1968), pp. 382, 408.

42. R.J. Wilkinson, *A Malay-English Dictionary (Romanised)* (London: Macmillan, 1959), p. 802. Marsden defines '*negeri*' as 'city, town; a country; province, district". *A Dictionary of the Malayan Language* (London: Marsden, 1812), p. 350.

43. Tioman is an island off the east coast of the Malay Peninsula.

44. Milner, *Kerajaan*.

45. Cited in ibid., p. 2; see also p. 118.

46. See the discussion of this shift in Milner, *The Invention of Politics in Colonial Malaya*, ch. 8.

47. The religious understanding of allegiance is expressed in such vocabulary as '*bhakti*' (the devoted service a subject might offer a raja)—a word that we associate with the Devotionalist Hindus (bhaktis) of India; Milner, *Kerajaan*, ch. 6 and Conclusion. For Islamic-influenced understandings of rulership in the Malay world, see my "Islam and Malay Kingship".

48. Barbara Andaya has drawn attention to the kin-infused understanding of relations with a raja. The king, she says, was the 'father' of his people, and his genealogy and marriage connections "helped personify a network of kinship relationships...." She stresses "imagined family" relationships as well as actual ones; *To Live as Brothers: Southeast Sumatra in the Seventeenth and Eighteenth Centuries* (Honolulu: University of Hawaii Press, 1993), p. 7. See also p. 248.

49. E. Edwards McKinnon, "Early Polities in Southern Sumatra: Some Preliminary Observations Made on Archaeological Evidence", *Indonesia*, 40 (1985): 28. See also J.G. de Casparis, "Srivijaya and Melayu", *Final Report. Consultative Workshop on Archaeological and Environmental Studies on Srivijaya* (Padang: SEAMEO Project, 1985), pp. 245–53.

50. A. Cortesao (ed.), *The Suma Oriental of Tome Pires* (New Delhi: Asian Educational Services, 1999), pp. 154, 260, 261.

51. William Marsden, *A History of Sumatra* (London: Marsden, 1783), p. 36. I am grateful to Diana Carroll for drawing my attention to this statement.

52. See also the discussion of this episode in Henk Maier, "'We Are Playing Relatives': Riau, the Cradle of Reality and Hybridity", *Bijdragen tot de Taal-, Land-en Volkenkunde*, 153, 4, (1997): 673.

53. J.V. Mills (ed.), *Ma Huan Ying-yai Sheng-lan. The Overall Survey of the Ocean's Shores* (1433) (Cambridge: Cambridge University Press for the Hakluyt Society, 1970), pp. 77–85, 102–6, 111.

54. Cited in Milner, *Kerajaan*, p. 2.

55. Ibid.

56. See Milner, *Invention of Politics in Colonial Malaya*, ch. 4.

57. Charles Hirschman, "The Making of Race in Colonial Malaya: Political Economy and Racial Category", *Sociological Forum* (Spring 1986): 330–61; Cited in Milner, *Invention of Politics in Colonial Malaya*, p. 108.

58. H. M. J. Maier, "From Heteroglossia to Polyglossia: the Creation of Malay and Dutch in the Indies", *Indonesia*, 56 (1993): 42.

59. Ibid., pp. 54, 62.

60. See, for example, Milner, "Ideological Work", pp. 167–68.

61. Frank Swettenham, *British Melaya: An Account of the Origin and Progress of British Influence in Malaya* (London: Bodley Head, 1907), p. 134.

62. See also Tan Liok Ee, *The Rhetoric of Bangsa and Minzu: Community and Nation In Tension, the Malay Peninsula 1900–1955* (Clayton: Monash University, Center of Southeast Asian Studies, 1988), pp. 10–11; Anthony Milner, "Ideological Work in Constructing the Malay Majority", in *Making Majorities. Constituting the Nation in Japan, Korea, China, Malaysia, Fiji, Turkey and the United States*, ed. Dru C. Gladney (Stanford: Stanford University Press, 1988), p. 161.

63. Quoted in Ariffin Omar, *Bangsa Melayu. Malay Concepts of Democracy and Community, 1945–1950* (Kuala Lumpur: Oxford University Press, 1993), p. 215.

64. Nevertheless, in modern Indonesia the Malays have moved up from the ninth (in 1930) to the third largest ethnic group. Is this due to a high birth rate or, as Sharon Siddique has suggested, to "the problematic definition of 'Malay' as an ethnic category"? These views are based on her assessment of Leo Suryadinata, Evi Nurvidya Arifin and Aris Ananta, *Indonesia's Population: Ethnicity and Religion in a Changing Political Landscape* (Singapore: Institute of Southeast Asian Studies, 2003) in *The Straits Times*, 5 May 2003.

65. Joel Kahn, "Constructing Malaysian Ethnicity: A View from Australia", *Ilmu Masyarakat*, xiv, (1988–89): 6–8.
66. See, for example, the speeches and papers from the second International Conference on Malay Civilisation, 1989; Ismail Hussein, A. Aziz Deraman and Abd. Rahman Al-Ahmadi, eds., *Tamadun Melayu* (Kuala Lumpur: Dewan Bahasa dan Pustaka, 1995).

Index